PRODUCTION FOR GRAPHIC DESIGNERS

PRODUCTION *for* GRAPHIC DESIGNERS

ALAN PIPES

Prentice Hall, Englewood Cliffs, NJ 07632

1993 North and South American editions
published by Prentice Hall, Inc.
A Division of Simon & Schuster
Englewood Cliffs, New Jersey 07632

10 9 8 7 6 5 4 3 2 1

1992 British edition published by Laurence King

ISBN 0–13–739285–0

This book was designed and produced by
CALMANN & KING LTD
71 Great Russell Street, London WC1B 3BN

Designed by Richard Foenander
Typeset by Bookworm Typesetting, Manchester
Originated, printed, and bound in Singapore by Toppan Pte Ltd

Type: Clearface ITC, News Gothic Bold, Alternate Gothic No. 1
Typeset on: Linotronic 300
Screen rulings: 175 lines
Paper: 100 gm^2 Snow White Korean Matte Art
Cover: 320 gm^2 artboard and oriented polypropylene lamination
Binding: sewn in sections of 16 pages with cover four-scored
with 6 mm hinge on either side of the spine

Cover:

The cover takes as its theme the process inks used for printing in full color – yellow, magenta, and cyan – but subtly avoids the obvious by replacing black with dark navy.

Pasting-up – cutting graphic elements to size and pasting them down to produce a mechanical.

Cylinders at the press of R. R. Donnelley in Chicago. Engraving gravure cylinders is very expensive, and thus the process is only economical for long runs.

The computer has transformed the landscape of the graphic designer's studio, supplementing the traditional drawing board and drawing instruments.

Contents

0.1 The author at work.

0.2 Editing the text.

Contents

2. Text and Type

0.4 Correcting the galley proofs.

0.3 Keying in the copy.

0.5 Loading the photosetting cartridge.

0.6 Outputting bromide.

Contents

3. Illustration

0.9 Drawing the line art on a Mac.

Contents

4. Prepress

0.10 Preparing the layouts.

0.11 Making up the text mechanicals.

0.12 Making up the film.

0.13 Correcting the color proofs.

0.14 Retouching the films.

Contents

5. On Press

0.15 Checking ink densities.

0.16 Platemaking.

0.17 On press.

Contents

6. Computers

Preface

This book has grown from a need to provide a comprehensive and detailed account of all the print production processes that today's graphic designer is likely to encounter in the course of his or her career. It aims to teach and update students and practicing designers alike, through the use of "what you will need" equipment lists, clear photographs and diagrams, and an extensive glossary of terms and acronyms. Each chapter is rounded off with a concise summary of what has been learnt and, throughout, you will find "self-referential" examples, which illustrate how the book you are now reading was put together.

Books on the various aspects of print production can be discovered on the shelves of bookstores and libraries in three distinct locations: in the art section, there are books on graphic design for designers; in the technical section, you find books on printing for printers; and, more recently, in the computing area there are books on "do-it-yourself" desktop publishing, targeted mainly at lay people with neither a graphic design nor a printing background. This book provides a professional one-stop shopping approach, bringing together all three aspects – everything you need to know – in one volume.

The graphic design profession has seen a revolution take place in recent years. The proliferation of affordable desktop computers and the software we know as dtp has changed everything. And that's no understatement. True, printing was revolutionized once before – back in the 1960s – with the adoption of offset litho as *the* print process, along with the widespread availability of almost any display face you might want in the form of rub-down lettering from suppliers such as Letraset. What you could put on a piece of paper or board, you could print. The combination of offset and Letraset sparked off an explosion of print and gave a huge boost to the design profession.

But this time, it is different. There really is a revolution going on. Not just inside the graphic design industry, but everywhere. Anyone who can buy a computer can now get access to all the tools (and some of the knowledge) that typesetters and printers have been keeping to themselves for the past 500 years. There are more fonts to choose from, and many imaginative ways to use them.

The whole graphic design business has been turned on its head. Many of the things you could only request politely that a typesetter or printer should do in the past, you have now been enabled to do yourself – and see that it is done to your specifications – right in front of your eyes, on the computer screen.

But along with this freedom comes responsibility, for the quality of the finished product. No more passing the buck, blaming bad communication when you get something different than how you imagined it would look! It has become ever more vital to have a thorough understanding of the whole design-to-print process. And that is how this book came about. Its aim is to help demystify and explain not only all the parts of the print production cycle that usually happen somewhere else – at the typesetters, the repro house, and the printers – but also to say something about the enabling technology itself, the ubiquitous computer, and to place it in context, within the continuing evolution of print production.

The book is intended not only for those students starting out in the profession of graphic design, but also for those adventurous old hands willing to embrace the new technology and all the potential benefits it has to give to them. It will be useful to those compositors and printers eager to expand their range of services; to everyone involved in book and magazine production: print buyers, art directors, production managers, writers, illustrators, and photographers; and finally to those courageous members of the general public who want to make better use of their computer systems and perhaps try a little simple graphic design and desktop publishing from their own homes. A greater awareness of the principles of typography and an understanding of what graphic designers do can only help advance the profession.

I should like to thank the friends and colleagues who helped in the production of this book, particularly my editor Ursula Sadie at Calmann & King, picture researcher Elizabeth Loving, designer Richard Foenander, Chris Myers at Bookworm Typesetting, and Rosemary Bradley, who commissioned me to write it. Grateful thanks are also offered (alphabetically) to: Aldus UK for a copy of FreeHand with which to produce the line drawings; Joty Barker of Face to Face; the staff of Brighton Polytechnic Library; Jane Brotchie for access to her DeskWriter; Roger Burg of Monotype Typography; John Christopher of Strong Silent Type; Ellie Curtis at the Royal College of Art, London; Karen Donnelly for the text of "Sketching can be fun," which was first published in the Brighton Illustrators Group Newsletter; Bob and Sue Harrington of RH Design; Nikki Morton and Ruth Jindal for their help in locating and retrieving books; Stan Noble of Towers Noble Design; William Owen; Kanwal Sharma of Lewis Sharma Design; Martin Shovel for the use of his StyleWriter; Vic Short and Maurice Poissenot for my new studio; and Elvis the goldfish for his or her calming influence.

A. P.

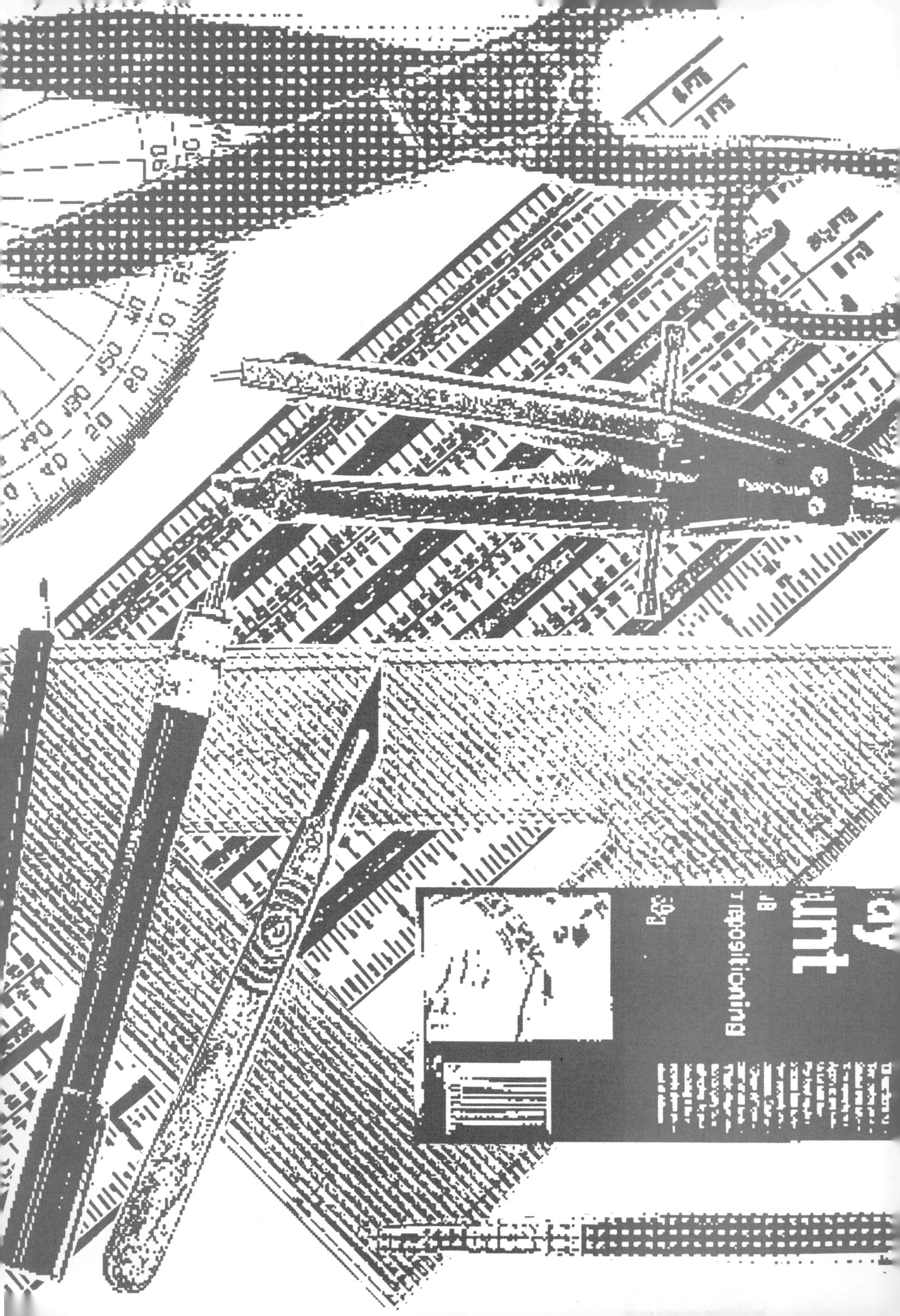
repositioning

1. Introduction

Words and pictures. Paper and ink. These are the raw materials of the graphic designer. They are about to meet, go on a journey, and undergo several transformations, before ending up in a printed and finished publication that you designed. Something that will communicate ideas and images to large numbers of people.

But how do words and pictures get onto the printed page? Printing has always been a mysterious craft. And until quite recently, graphic designers were excluded from its secrets. The purpose of this book is to demystify and help you understand some of those arcane processes.

There is a long-standing misconception that to learn the craft part of any profession can be a chore. The temptation is to jump right in there and get on with the creative stuff. Print production, in particular, with its many different stages and processes, can seem dull, the very sound of words like "mechanical" conjuring up visions of production lines of automatons cutting and pasting like galley slaves. On the other hand, there are some designers, and many typographers, who are so in love with the process that they forget the purpose of the job they are doing. What use is a beautiful piece of design or typography, without meaning or content? The graphic designer's role, first and foremost, is that of communicator. But if you can communicate cost-effectively with wit, economy, and elegance, then you are a very good graphic designer indeed.

In graphic design, free expression cannot exist apart from the process. Walter Gropius, the founder of the Bauhaus – a German art school that has become the model for most of our present schools of art and design – suggested in his manifesto of 1919 that art cannot be taught, but that craft can. "A foundation in handicraft is essential for every artist," he said. "It is there that the primary source of creativity lies."

The playwright Tom Stoppard has, perhaps with tongue in cheek, put it another way: "Skill without imagination is craftsmanship . . . imagination without skill gives us Modern Art." Gropius says, without any desire to offend, that: "The artist is an exalted craftsman."

Graphic designers are both artists and craftspeople. This book does not major on how to be an artist, but it will tell you much that you need to know about the craft of printing. And when you have learnt all about print production, the creativity will be able to come shining through. A sound understanding of all stages of the print production process will at the very least prevent your designs from failing for technical reasons.

The chapters are arranged to follow the tracks of both the design process and the print process – from the choosing of type and the preparation of illustrations and photographs, through their arrangement on the mechanical or inside the electronic page make-up program, to the printing and finishing of the publication. The design process may follow a linear path, but many of the design decisions up front are affected by processes downstream. Every stage of the print production process will exert some influence on your design.

The choice of paper and print technology, for example, will affect the kind of typefaces you can use and the way in which halftones are treated. In turn, the size of print run determines the print technology. You may be asked to design a range of product labels, for example – some to be printed on paper stock using high-quality litho presses, while others will be printed directly onto plastic yogurt pots using flexography or screenprinting. Your design will have to work well on both.

Part 1: some history

When you open the parcel from the printer, and you look at the finished copy of your design, it is as well to pause and appreciate that this printed product is a tribute to every advance in printing technology since the first wooden block was inked and pressed against a sheet of paper.

The history of printing began in the East: in China, Korea, and Japan. Paper was invented in China – its invention was officially announced to the Emperor by Ts'ai Lun in AD 105 – and printing using wooden blocks had become a flourishing fine art by the tenth century. The oldest known printed book, the *Diamond Sutra*, is dated at AD 868, though books were almost certainly being printed a century before. Words and pictures were carved together onto the same wooden blocks, and a fresh set of blocks had to be cut for each new book. Printing presses with type cast from individual pieces of clay that could be used time and time again were in use in China by AD 1041, and Korean printers were casting metal type before AD 1400. But because the languages of the East use symbols for whole words – some tens of thousands of them – rather than putting together words from relatively few characters in an alphabet, the

1.1 Benjamin Franklin (1706–90) is perhaps America's most famous printer. This wood engraving shows him at the London print shop of Cox & Sons in 1785; note the wooden screw press.

THE PRINTING-OFFICE OF MESSRS. COX BROTHERS, GREAT QUEEN-STREET, LINCOLN'S-INN-FIELDS.

THE HOUSE IN WHICH FRANKLIN RESIDED WHEN AGENT FOR PENNSYLVANIA; NO. 7, CRAVEN-STREET, STRAND.

development of so-called "movable" type was not so significant there as it later was in Europe.

Textiles have been printed in Europe since at least the sixth century, and playing cards were certainly being printed, using wooden blocks similar to those of the Chinese printers, by the 14th century. But it is Johannes Gutenberg (1398–1468) who is credited with the invention of printing in the West, sometime before 1440.

Gutenberg was a goldsmith by trade, living in Mainz, in what is now Germany. All the technology necessary for the invention of printing was in place at the time – it was just waiting for the right mind to put all the pieces together. He knew how to cast objects in metal, there were presses already available (for wine making), he had ink and paper. And he saw a market opportunity for mass-produced books, to stock the libraries of all the universities being founded at that time.

Before that, in the Middle Ages, all books were created by hand. Scribes and artists worked together to create one-off books, often copying from existing texts. They were beautiful objects, mostly "illuminated" with ornamental letters, paintings, decorative borders, and gold blocking. There was even a form of mass-production in operation. In scriptoria, a chief scribe would dictate aloud the text to be copied by a team of under-scribes. Nevertheless, it was a slow process, and their books could be possessed only by the very rich.

Gutenberg's invention was the process of letterpress: the concept of casting individual letters which could be assembled into words, printed, then cleaned and put away, and used over again. First he cut a steel punch for each character and punctuation mark. This punch was then struck into a softer metal to form the matrix in which the type was cast. Finally lead, with the addition of some antimony for hardness and tin for toughness, was poured into the mold and the type cast. The most original part of Gutenberg's process was a mold of adjustable width, used to hold the different sizes of matrix. (See Chapter 2 for a fuller description of the process of hot-metal typesetting.)

Gutenberg's original idea was to imitate in type the handwritten books of the scribes (but without the graphic embellishments). To do that he had to create a set of over 300 characters, including all the variations of letterforms and joined letters that a scribe might use. In comparison, a modern printer's alphabet might contain only 50 or so characters.

The invention of printing spread across Europe. The first book in English was printed by William Caxton, who learnt his craft in Cologne, Germany, and set up a press in London in 1476, using Flemish equipment. Printing was brought to America by Joseph Glover, who imported a press and three printers from Cambridge, England to Cambridge, Massachusetts. Sadly, Glover died on the voyage, but the press was installed by Stephen Daye and his two sons in 1638, and operated under the auspices of Harvard College (Fig. 1.2).

Progress in the technology of printing was slow until the Industrial Revolution. Wooden wine-type presses with huge screws (Fig. 1.1) were gradually replaced by iron presses operated by a simpler lever mechanism. The first was developed by Earl Stanhope in 1804, and this was followed by the more ornate Columbian and Albion presses. By 1812, there were presses in operation powered by steam, and huge rotary machines followed soon after.

Printing became a more industrialized process with the invention of automatic typesetting machines, first from Linotype in 1886, and from Monotype in 1887. Until the beginning of this century, however, it was very difficult to combine type and pictures on the same printed page.

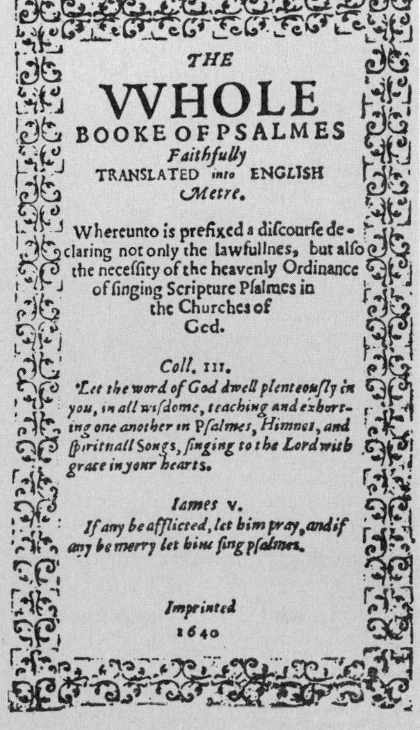

THE

VVHOLE

BOOKE OF PSALMES

Faithfully

TRANSLATED *into* ENGLISH

Metre.

Whereunto is prefixed a diſcourſe declaring not only the lawfullnes, but alſo the neceſſity of the heavenly Ordinance of ſinging Scripture Pſalmes in the Churches of Gcd.

Coll. III.

Let the word of God dwell plenteouſly in you, in all wiſdome, teaching and exhorting one another in Pſalmes, Himnes, and ſpirituall Songs, ſinging to the Lord with grace in your hearts.

Iames V.

If any be afflicted, let him pray, and if any be merry let him ſing pſalmes.

Imprinted

1640

1.2 Title page from *The Whole Booke of Psalmes* (1640), the first book to be published in North America, by Stephen Daye of Cambridge, Massachusetts.

1.3 Until the end of the 18th century, the only way to print type and illustrations combined on the same page was by using woodcuts. These have period charm but lacked the capacity for fine detail, as is obvious from this depiction of the 1456 visit of Halley's comet, from Conrad Lycosthenes' *Prodigiorum ac ostentorum chronicon*, 1557.

Printing pictures

Letterpress is a relief method of printing, in which a raised surface is inked and pressed against the paper. However, throughout the early history of printing almost every method of reproducing images used the intaglio process. The only exception was the woodcut – a relief process that predates printing – which could be used for decorative initials and simple illustrative work (Fig. 1.3). Woodcuts are made with a knife on the long grain of the wood. The result is a rather rough image, but one that can be printed with the type.

For fine illustrative work, the only alternative was the intaglio process. Intaglio is the opposite to relief. Here it is the incised lines that print. A plate is inked, wiped almost clean, and the ink that remains in the grooves is drawn out, under pressure, to form the image on the dampened paper. Both engraving and etching are intaglio methods of printing (Fig. 1.4).

1.4 Because etching is an intaglio process, illustrations had to be printed separately from the text and were "tipped in" when the book was bound. This baker's shop, 1635, comes from a series of 22 etchings on the arts and crafts by Jan Joris van der Vliet.

1.5 Etchings and engravings were originally made on copper plates, which quickly wear out. In the 19th century, the problem was overcome by coating them with steel. This steel engraving of emigrants to America crossing the Plains was first published in New York in 1869.

So, before the Industrial Revolution, letterpress was used for printing text, in large print runs. Intaglio was used for refined work, where the print run was relatively small and the expense not so crucial. Artists had been making engravings on copper plates since the Renaissance. By the 18th century, the process was used commercially for printing invitation cards, banknotes, and stamps. The engravers used a sharp instrument called a burin to incise lines onto copper plates. And because any lettering had to be drawn by hand, it was often very elaborate. Hence the term "copperplate" is now used for a particular kind of formal handwriting. In the late 19th century, methods were developed for engraving on steel plates (Fig. 1.5), which are more durable than copper.

A later development was etching, in which marks are made with a needle or any other sharp instrument to scratch off an acid-resistant coating on the surface of a copper plate. This is then placed into a bath of acid, and the drawing is etched chemically into the surface of the plate. The image on an etched plate was usually tidied up and detail added by hand, by engraving directly into the plate with a burin.

Another intaglio process was mezzotint, in which a burnisher is used to smooth the rough texture on the surface of the plate, created previously by the action of an abrasive "rocker" (the smooth areas would be white on the finished printed material). Aquatint is a type of etching that builds up tones using resin and stopping-out varnish. **Resist** is applied to the plate to prevent the non-printing areas from etching. Both these latter processes were used mainly to reproduce watercolor paintings. All of these methods are still used today by artists to produce limited edition prints, but are no longer used by commercial printers.

4 HISTORY OF QUADRUPEDS.

THE ARABIAN HORSE.

THERE is ſcarcely an Arabian, how poor ſoever in other reſpects, but is poſſeſſed of his Horſe, which he conſiders as an invaluable treaſure. Having no other dwelling but a tent, the Arabian and his Horſe live upon the moſt equal terms: His wife and family, his mare and her foal, generally lie indiſcriminately together; whilſt the little children frequently climb without fear upon the body of the inoffenſive animal, which permits them to play with and careſs it without injury. The Arabs never beat their Horſes; they ſpeak to, and ſeem to hold friendly intercourſe with them; they never whip them; and ſeldom, but in caſes of neceſſity, make uſe of the ſpur. Their agility in leaping is wonderful; and if the rider happen to fall, they are ſo tractable as to ſtand ſtill in the midſt of the moſt rapid career.—The Arabian Horſes, in general leſs than the Race-Horſes of this country, are eaſy and graceful in their motions, and rather inclined to leanneſs.—It is worthy of remark, that, inſtead of

1.6 An arabian horse from Thomas Bewick's *General History of Quadrupeds*, 1790. Bewick had the bright idea of cutting boxwood on the end grain, and thus invented wood engraving. Despite its name, this is a relief method, which is capable of a dazzling tonal range and delicacy of line.

From Gutenberg's time until the Industrial Revolution, it was common for images in books to be printed separately from the text using an intaglio process. They were tipped-in (inserted among the text pages) during the binding process.

Things improved, however, when Thomas Bewick (1753–1828) developed the art of wood engraving (Fig. 1.6). At last publishers had at their disposal the means to print fine line work and areas of rich black, in among the text.

Wood engraving is a relief process, despite the similarity of its name to copper engraving, which is an intaglio process. Wood engravings are made with tools similar to those of the engravers, on the end grain of boxwood (Fig. 1.7). Scratchboard, or scraperboard, is a contemporary method of illustration that simulates the appearance of a wood engraving.

By the middle of the 19th century, wood engraving had become an industry, and engravers such as Joseph Swain and the Dalziel brothers were as famous as the illustrators whose work they interpreted. Magazines such as the *Illustrated London News* used a system of separating large blocks into more manageable pieces, sending them out to a team of engravers, then reassembling them – an overseer had the job of disguising the joins. Journalistic accuracy came second to visual impact, with the same blocks used over and over, whenever there was a public hanging or a shipwreck.

1.7 The tradition of Bewick is carried on today by contemporary wood engravers such as Nick Day, who are more likely to be seen cutting vinyl floor tiles than boxwood.

Enter lithography and photography

In fact, there was a process that could quite easily combine type and pictures on the same page, and it had been around since the end of the 18th century.

It was lithography (Fig. 1.8), invented in Prague by Alois Senefelder around 1796–9. Neither a relief nor an intaglio process, it is better described as a planographic process. It is based on the principle that oil and water do not mix (much more in Chapter 5), and in effect everything happens on a flat surface.

Ironically, it was the versatility of the process that prevented it from being taken up more universally. Almost any greasy mark made on the lithographic stone, or, from the end of the 19th century, on a prepared metal plate, will print. Illustrators could at last work directly and spontaneously. By the end of the 19th century, greetings cards, postcards, decorative "scraps", maps, sheet music, and posters were all being mass-produced by lithography.

Offset lithography – in which the image is transferred from the stone or plate to a rubber roller, and then to the **substrate** – entered the scene surreptitiously. The process was first used in around 1875 for printing ornamental decorations onto tinplate, for applications in packaging.

Type produced by letterpress could be transferred onto the stone using special transfer paper, but this was not a totally satisfactory process. One more ingredient was necessary before lithography could take over from letterpress as the most versatile of all the printing processes: the invention of photography in the late 1830s.

Photography is the basis for every print production process in use today. The first application of photography to the reproduction of illustrations was quite modest, however. It was used to sensitize the surface of the boxwood used for wood engravings. These still had to be cut by hand, but the illustrator's original drawing could be preserved and, furthermore, the method could be used to reproduce photographs.

Early photographers were eager to reproduce their work in large numbers. They were an extremely experimental group of individuals, and much of the pioneering developments in print production were made by

1.8 The process of lithography revolutionized print production, but it was a long time coming. Early lithographic illustrations, like engravings, had to be printed separately from the text, but were used extensively for color work. This express train was first published in 1870 by Currier & Ives in New York as a color lithograph. Note that here it has to be reproduced as a halftone from a photograph of the original.

1.9 It was the experimental photographers of the late 19th century who pushed forward the technology of print production, inventing better methods of reproducing continuous-tone artwork and the technique of producing color separations. This picture of Joseph Bazalgette, the architect of London's sewerage system, was first reproduced by Woodburytype – a form of collotype patented by Walter Bentley Woodbury in 1866 – a process said to produce hard and brilliant prints.

them. Collotype (Fig. 1.9) was the first method used for reproducing photographs, and this slow and expensive process was soon followed by photogravure.

Collotype – the name comes from the Greek word for glue – uses a plate coated with photographically sensitive gelatin which hardens in proportion to the amount of light falling onto it. A negative is exposed in contact with the plate, which is then moistened and absorbs more water where there was less light. Impressions are taken using greasy ink, as in lithography. Collotype gives an almost facsimile reproduction of pencil, pastel, and crayon. To date it is the only commercial process that can print continuous-tone originals without having them first converted into a pattern of dots, by screening.

Photogravure, first developed in 1852, is an intaglio process characterized by rich tones and the absence of regularly-patterned dots. However, the process does involve a form of screening to create the "grains" on the plate or cylinder. On etching, the grains are eaten away in proportion to the tone values on the original – the blacks become the deepest and the whites the shallowest. On printing, the darker areas are created by a greater amount of ink being deposited on the paper, and the grains are obliterated by the spread of the ink. The process relies on quick-drying spirit-based inks, and for this reason many of the early reproductions appeared in sepia or green. Photogravure is used widely to this day, and is discussed more fully as a printing process in Chapter 5.

The breakthrough that allowed images to be printed by letterpress was the development of the process block. The line block, for black and white work, was invented in Vienna by Paul Pretsch in 1853 and used a process resembling collotype – the softer portions of sensitized gelatin on the surface of the plate swell into relief. An electrotype cast is made, and the resulting plate is mounted onto a wooden block (hence the name – the block brings it up to the height of the type). This can then be assembled with the type. By the mid-1880s, zinc plates were being etched photographically from original artwork, and the profession of process engraving, or blockmaking, was born.

The early process blocks could handle only relatively simple areas of black and white, and the style of illustrators such as Aubrey Beardsley owes much to the constraints of the process. For the first time, an illustrator was free to draw at larger sizes than the work would be appearing in print.

Tints could be added by the blockmaker (Fig. 1.10), where indicated by the illustrator. Ben Day tints, the first commercially available tints, were introduced in 1901. These were sheets of celluloid stretched in wooden frames. Each sheet was embossed with a pattern and was transferred to the block, before etching, using a roller inked with lithographic ink. Areas not requiring a tint were first painted out with gum to repel the ink.

1.10 The line art of William Heath Robinson was as much influenced by the invention of the process block as by the importation of Japanese art at the end of the 19th century. At last an artist's spontaneity could be reproduced directly from artwork – as can be seen in this illustration from Hans Andersen's *Fairy Tales* (1913).

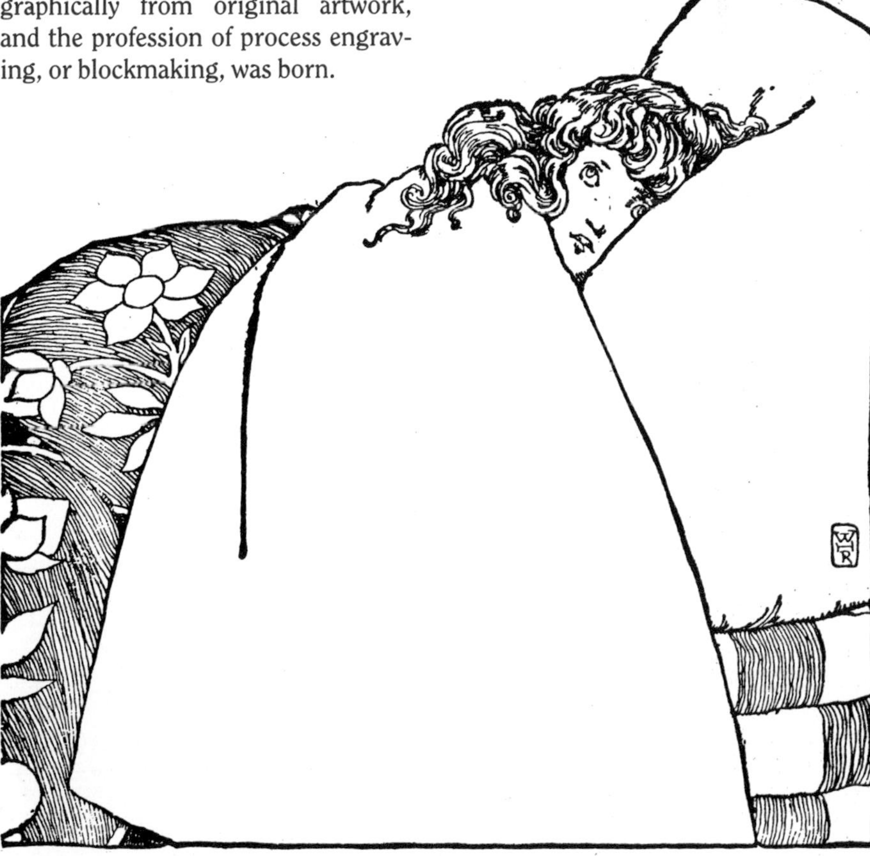

The reproduction of continuous tone by means other than collotype had to await the invention of the halftone screen. The photographer Fox Talbot first suggested in 1852 that tones could be reproduced by means of "photographic screens or veils." But it was Frederick Ives of Philadelphia who patented a method of converting a photograph into dots. This was refined in 1882 by George Meisenbach, who used a single-lined screen that was turned 90 degrees during exposure. Ives, in collaboration with Louis and Max Levy, replied in 1890 with the first cross-lined screen. Now illustrations and photographs could be freely combined with type on the same page, and printed together at the same time.

The invention of the halftone screen also paved the way for full-color printing, using three and later four "process" colors to reproduce all the colors of the rainbow (see p. 85).

The first rotary offset lithography machine for printing on paper was introduced in 1906 by Ira W. Rubel, but it was not until the 1950s that it began to take over from letterpress.

Photocomposition systems could set type, not in pieces of lead, but on rolls of photographic bromide paper or transparent film. These could be cut and pasted into designs that could then be transferred directly to a lithographic plate and printed. This technological breakthrough, and the explosion of print that followed, gave a huge boost to the young profession of graphic design. Over the years, the printing industry had become fragmented – there were separate typesetters, process engravers, and printers – and someone had to step in to plan and coordinate printing projects. That job fell to the graphic designer.

There was greater creative freedom too. No longer were graphic designers constrained to what could be done with metal type and process blocks. Type on paper could be positioned anywhere, alongside any images that could be recorded by the camera.

It was the age of camera-ready artwork – the mechanical. And the introduction of display faces in the form of dry-transfer rub-down lettering such as Letraset liberated the adventurous designer even further. What you saw on the mechanical was what you got in the printed product.

It was a natural next step to want to design on the computer screen, once WYSIWYG (what you see is what you get) displays became available in the early 1980s. Both text and graphics could be treated equally in the eyes of the computer, and could be subjected to an almost infinite variety of manipulation (Fig. 1.11). The introduction of Aldus PageMaker for the Apple Macintosh, in July 1985, was just one of the many recent milestones in the history of print production for graphic designers.

As with the invention of lithography, it is often difficult to foresee the effect of an isolated discovery on the overall history of printing. Lithography had to wait for the development of photography before it could become a commercial proposition. In the same way xerography, invented in 1938 by Chester Carlson, has leapt forward with laser and computer technology. Put these together and we can predict, with some confidence, that xerography will become the dominant printing technology of the early 21st century.

1.11 Old meets new. "Dance of death in the print shop" by Mathais Huss of Lyons, France – said to be one of the earliest woodcuts depicting a print shop – is given a contemporary treatment courtesy of computer graphics.

Milestones in the history of print production

AD 105 Paper invented in China by Ts'ai Lun
868 *Diamond Sutra*, first printed book in China
1041 First presses with clay movable type in China
1150 First paper mill opened in Europe, in Xativa, Spain
1400 Koreans printing with metal movable type
1445 Johannes Gutenberg printed first book in Europe
1446 Earliest known copper engraving: *The Scourging of Christ*, by a German artist
1477 William Caxton issued first dated printed book
1638 First American press established by Stephen Daye at Harvard College
1690 First American papermill established in Germantown, Pennsylvania, by William Rittenhouse
1790 Thomas Bewick perfected process of wood engraving
1796–9 Lithography invented by Alois Senefelder
1798 Papermaking machine invented by Nicholas-Louis Robert

1804 Iron press devised by Earl Stanhope
1810 First Fourdrinier papermaking machines in operation
1812 *The London Times* printed on steam press
1822 First photographic image made by J. N. Niepce
1829 Amos H. Hubbard's mill at Norwich, Connecticut, was first American papermill to install a Fourdrinier machine
1837 Invention of Daguerre photographic process
1839 Negative/positive photography invented by Fox Talbot
1852 Photogravure invented by Fox Talbot
1853 Line block invented by Paul Pretsch
1860 Photographically sensitized boxwood process developed by Thomas Bolton
1860 Principle of color separation by filters demonstrated by Clerk Maxwell
1861 First color photograph by Clerk Maxwell
1872 Process line block invented by Alfred Dawson
1875 Offset litho used for printing on tin
1881 Halftone process invented by Frederick Ives
1884 Punch-cutting machine invented by Linn Boyd Benton
1886 Linotype machine invented by Ottmar Mergenthaler
1886 First Linotype installed at *New York Herald Tribune*
1887 Monotype machine invented by Tolbert Lanston
1890 Four-color separation process invented
1890 Aniline coal-tar process (later called flexography) demonstrated at Bibby, Baron & Sons in Liverpool, England, but later abandoned

1901 Ben Day mechanical tints introduced
1906 First rotary offset litho machine invented by Ira W. Rubel
1920s Aniline process developed for printing on non-absorbent stock such as cellophane
1938 Xerography invented by Chester Carlson
1948 Color scanner invented by Kodak
1952 Name flexography coined for aniline coal-tar process
1955 Linofilm photocomposing system introduced
1959 First Linofilm installation at *National Geographic*
1960 Laser invented at Hughes Laboratory
1967 Computerized Linofilm typesetter introduced
1968 Crosfield Magnascan four-color scanner introduced
1981 IBM personal computer announced
1982 Apple introduced Lisa, the precursor to the Macintosh
1984 Apple Macintosh and Linotronic 300 laser imagesetter launched
1985 Adobe PostScript used to set type on LaserWriter and Linotronic imagesetter at different resolutions
1985 Aldus PageMaker launched, and term "desktop publishing" coined by Aldus founder Paul Brainerd
1987 Mac II and Quark XPress launched
1991 TrueType format and System 7 introduced by Apple

Part 2: getting started – studio equipment

Some graphic designers claim to get by with just a pad of layout paper, a pencil, and a book of type specimens. The typographer Erik Spiekermann used to boast (before he bought his Apple Macintosh computer) that he could communicate clearly with his typesetter by means of a written set of instructions. This was a type specification that could be dictated down the telephone, if need be – with no graphic layout necessary. Well, you may argue that typographers have it a lot easier than graphic designers. They don't have to deal with pictures, or color.

So, maybe in the past the more unprofessional graphic designers just sent rough layouts covered in keylines and instructions to the printer and hoped for the best. These days, designers will often be sending finished, typeset presentations that can go under the printer's camera, with no additional work required. That way they will be sure to know what they will get back. And tomorrow, it is more likely that you will present your design to a bureau on floppy disc, removable hard disc, or down the telephone wire via modem. And you will already have a very good idea of how the printed result is going to look.

What do you need to get started? A sturdy tabletop or, better, a drawing board, with an adjustable angled surface and built-in parallel motion (a straight edge that moves up and down, always perfectly horizontally). The drawing board has become synonymous with the cyclic nature of the design process. How many times have you heard the phrase "back to the drawing board," when pernickety clients changed their mind about what they really wanted? Even in design studios with computers, drawing boards are still seen – they are good places at which to plan and think, to scale and crop illustrations, and are ideal for spreading around the design elements during the sketch stage of design.

A surgical scalpel and a heavier duty craft knife (such as an X-acto) are useful for cutting paper and board. Use a cutting mat with a "self-healing" surface for trimming artwork and typesetting, and clean any stickiness off regularly with lighter fuel. For sticking and mounting you will need rubber cement, which can be spread thinly with an applicator or spatula. Surplus gum can be removed cleanly when dry using a homemade "eraser" of dried-up gum. Some designers prefer aerosol adhesive, such as Scotch Spray Mount, for wrinkle-free mounting. For safety's sake, adequate ventilation is essential while using spray glue. Buy a brand that uses a CFC-free propellant, to protect the environment. Many graphic designers now prefer hot-wax coaters, such as Letraset's Waxcoater, for sticking paper to board; they will also keep the studio warm in the winter! Low-tack masking tape and matte frosted "magic" tape are useful for mending, and for attaching tissue or acetate overlays to delicate artwork.

Other accessories include plenty of non-reproducing light-blue pencils, including some greasy pencils (Chinagraphs) for writing on glossy surfaces, and maybe an electric pencil sharpener. A large soft brush is indispensable for removing debris from the work in progress, and a supply of talcum powder will come in handy for degreasing and "lubricating" surfaces. However, keep it away from finished work! A bulk stock of paper towels is useful to mop up spillages. It is always good policy to keep things clean and tidy.

Paint called process white is used by designers for correcting mistakes and adding highlights to drawings. It is still considered good advice to buy the finest quality sable brushes (sizes 00, 1, and 3 would be a good selection). Look after them – they should be washed and rinsed straight after use (they must never be left point down in a jar of water) and stored with the points upward. There are some very good synthetic substitutes available.

A loupe, linen tester, or eyeglass (Fig. 1.12) is a mounted magnifying glass that will prove its worth over and over. It can be used to check the dots in a halftone, examine a color transparency for suitability and any defects, and to scrutinize proofs for printing problems.

A lightbox that fits on the tabletop, and comprises a translucent surface illuminated from below by fluorescent lights conforming to the **standard lighting conditions** used by printers, is invaluable for properly examining the color temperature of transparencies. It is also a great aid to experimentation. You can try out different designs on a lightbox, tracing

1.12 A loupe, or linen tester, is a magnifying glass which is useful for examining transparencies and proofs for imperfections, often in conjunction with a lightbox.

over those parts of an original design you wish to retain. A lightbox can also be used to check the registration on color separations. Some corner of the studio, too, should be set up according to **standard viewing conditions**, with the light source surrounded by neutral gray, if you are to be checking and correcting color proofs.

A proportional scale, or just a plain old calculator, will help you work out percentage reductions and enlargements. And there are all kinds of other measurement devices. A stainless-steel pica rule will become a lifelong companion, and there are plastic rules available for measuring the depth of type in different sizes, useful for casting off (calculating the length of a text) and copy fitting (making sure your typesetting will fit the space you have left for it in the layout). A transparent grid will assist you in checking that design elements are square, and well aligned. And you may wish to obtain a device called a cadograph, which enables you to draw your own grids.

Bigger studios will have their own darkroom with a process camera and a PMT (photomechanical transfer) processing machine, a Grant enlarger (opaque projector) for sizing illustrations and drawing them onto layouts, and a sink with a water supply. A photocopier capable of enlarging and reducing is a very useful addition to any studio, as is a fax machine to keep in visual touch with the client and printer.

Then there's the computer (Fig. 1.13), so important that it warrants a whole chapter to itself. And here's a word of warning, right at the start of the book. A computer can be a tireless and uncomplaining assistant, but you cannot talk to it in such subjective terms as "increase the spacing here," or "less orange there," as you would with a typesetter or the scanner operator at your repro house. Compositors and scanner operators have had years of experience in delivering results they think you want. They can almost read your mind. They have a common understanding of what is acceptable, and what is good. The computer, on the other hand, can do either nothing or anything – depending on what instructions you give!

The computer might never question your unusual requests and never charge you for changes of mind. But it will expect you to do all the thinking, and be able to tell it exactly, to the thousandth of an inch, centimeter, or percentage point, where things should be moved. Not only does that make more work for you, but you have to know in minute detail exactly what you want – and you will have to take responsibility for the outcome.

Typesetters were in fact some of the first users of desktop publishing systems – they could recognize a good thing when they saw it. Your computer is not going to replace the typesetter and printer, and they will probably always be one step ahead of you. So think of your system as complementing their computers, acting as a front end to their systems.

Use your computer responsibly, to improve the quality of design communication between your studio – the ideas house – and the typesetters or printers – the production house. Their centuries of hard-won expertise are there to be used. And they will appreciate the knowledge you have of their processes, gained from reading this book.

1.13 The computer has transformed the landscape of the graphic designer's studio, replacing (or, more often, supplementing) the traditional drawing board and drawing instruments.

JKLMNOPQRSTUVWXYZ
W&
e
e
A
OPQRSTU
opqr
n
p
6
abcdefghi

2. Text and Type

The ability to use type effectively is an essential skill for successful graphic design. Just a few basic principles open the way to an infinite variety of design possibilities for all kinds of printed products. Graphic designers must make type work hard, in harmony with other graphical elements, such as illustration, photography, and color. They are dealing with practical situations, in the real world of tight deadlines, specific briefs, and competitive pitches.

Since the introduction of desktop publishing (**dtp**), the graphic designer has been confronted with a bewildering choice of typefaces, and the means to manipulate them. It has never been more important for graphic designers to become familiar with the craft and knowledge of the printers and typographers who have gone before.

People like Gutenberg designed their own type, cut the steel to make it, cast it into lead type, composed it into pages, printed their own books, and bound them. They concocted their own ink, and probably made their own paper as well.

Desktop publishing gives graphic designers the opportunity to take back the responsibility for almost as much of the production process as they are willing, or capable enough, to handle. But to go forward, one must first know what is possible.

This chapter aims to give the graphic designer an insight into type and how it is used. It will explain the vocabulary of print and typography, both ancient and modern. For in print production we commonly use both terminology handed down through generations of printers and typesetters, and jargon introduced from computing and desktop publishing.

The chapter is divided into three parts. Part 1 talks about type itself – letters and words, the basic building blocks with which graphic designers work. We see how type originated, and learn the all-important methods of measuring it.

In Part 2 we look at text and house style, investigate how different typefaces are recognized, and discover how to choose the best typeface for the job.

Part 3 is concerned with how type is created. Here we discuss the systems of typesetting – from hot metal, through photosetting, to the desktop publishing systems that make the craft of typography accessible to anyone possessing a power socket.

WHAT EQUIPMENT DO YOU NEED TO GET STARTED?

- a sturdy tabletop or drawing board
- type specimens
- a pad of layout or tracing paper
- a supply of fibertip pens (ballpoints may damage artwork) and soft black pencils
- a pencil sharpener
- a non-reproducing light-blue pencil
- a stainless-steel pica rule or plastic typescale
- a set of standard proofreaders' marks
- a calculator

AND OPTIONALLY:

- a process camera, in a darkroom or behind heavy black lightproof curtains
- a PMT (photomechanical transfer) processing machine
- a Grant enlarger (opaque projector)
- a sink with a water supply
- a photocopier capable of enlarging and reducing
- a fax machine to keep in visual touch with the client and printer

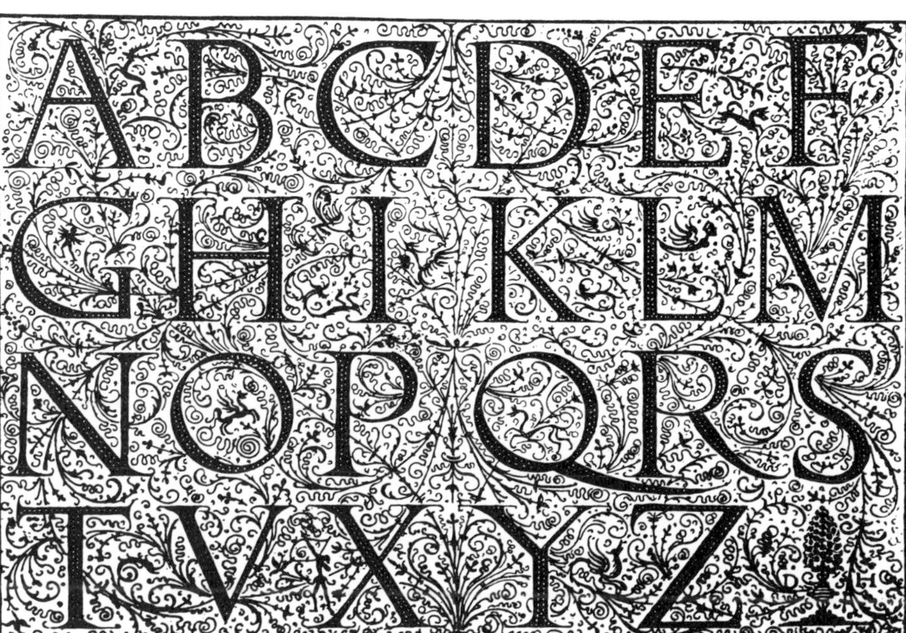

2.1 A decorative alphabet drawn as a sampler by Daniel Hopfer of Nuremburg, Germany, dated 1549. The letterforms are based on the lettering on Trajan's Column in Rome. Note the absence of J, U, and W.

Part 1: type

2.2 Some medieval books were illustrated or "illuminated" with watercolors and gold embellishments. The names of the artists and scribes are long forgotten, and those with recognizable styles are now known only by the names of their patrons – the Master of Mary of Burgundy, for example. To squeeze as many words as possible onto a page, most scribes used the up-and-down form of writing called textura lettering, as on this French Annunciation. Other manuscripts, like this 15th century one for the Duc d'Orléans, used a freer, open, rounded form of script more akin to uncial, or roman lower case, writing.

The essence of writing and lettering, according to typographer Fernand Baudin, is to make language visible and retrievable. Spoken words pass away; written words are here to stay.

Type is the basic building block of print production. The design of type is a very subtle craft, dealing with the sometimes microscopic details that distinguish one typeface from another. It is also a thankless and humbling profession. "The best typography never gets noticed," American typographer Herb Lubalin has been quoted as saying. (Typographer means here a person who designs type and designs with type. The term **compositor** is used for someone who sets type.)

Or, as another famous American typographer Beatrice Warde has pointed out, perhaps more eloquently: "Good typography is like a crystal wine glass, thin as a bubble and just as transparent, its purpose to reveal rather than hide the beautiful thing it is meant to contain. Good graphic design and typography should help people communicate with all the clarity an idea deserves."

When we are taught to write the alphabet at school, it probably never occurs to us that there are thousands of ways that 26 simple letters can be constructed. It is only through looking at printed matter in later life that we begin to realize that a letter g, for example, comes into two main varieties: g and g.

And while an alphabet with 26 letters and eight punctuation marks will be adequate for a message on a noticeboard, a set of over a hundred different characters and marks may still fall short of some tasks facing the graphic designer.

SENATVSPOPVLVSQVEROMANVS
IMPCAESARIDIVINERVAEFNERVAE
TRAIANOAVGGERMDACICOPONTIF
MAXIMOTRIBPOTXVIIIMPVICOSVIPP
ADDECLARANDVMQVANTAEALTITVDINIS
MONSETLOCVSTAL
IBVSSITEGESTVS

ABCDEFGHIJ
KLMNOPQR
STUVWXYZ&
1234567890$

Some history

Our Western alphabet was invented by the Phoenicians around 1100 BC somewhere on the eastern shores of the Mediterranean Sea. Capital letters derive from Roman incised lettering, with its distinctive serifs (the little marks made by the chisel to neaten the ends of letters), slanted stress, and variations in stroke thickness. The chiseled capital letters carved on Trajan's Column in Rome (Figs. 2.1 and 2.3) in around AD 114 are still regarded as the "perfect" roman letters. Lower-case lettering comes from a more rounded form of handwriting, known as the uncial, developed for everyday use in the fourth century.

In the Middle Ages, scribes created all books by hand, usually copying from existing books (Fig. 2.4). They were beautiful objects, often "illuminated" with ornamental letters, paintings, and gold blocking (Fig 2.2).

The commonest form of writing in those days was called textura, or black letter, and sometimes Gothic because of its resemblance to the pointed architecture in fashion at the time.

2.3 (opposite) The lettering on Trajan's Column is the prototype for most present day roman typefaces, including Adobe's display typeface for desktop publishing (above) designed in 1989 by Carol Twombly and called, appropriately enough, Trajan. Note how our serifs derive from the chiseled finishing-off marks made by the Roman stonecutter.

2.4 (right) In medieval times all books were created individually, copied out slowly but lovingly by scribes. Books could only be afforded by the very rich.

2.5 Johannes Gutenberg is credited with the invention of movable type in the western world. No portraits survive from the period; this artist's impression in woodcut, made much later from the carvings on his tomb, shows him reading proofs while his assistant works the printing press.

The first movable type in the western world, invented by Johannes Gutenberg (Fig. 2.5), closely imitated the writing of the scribes. He created a set of over 300 characters, to accommodate all the variations of letterforms and **ligatures** (joined letters, such as fi and fl) that a scribe might need to use (Fig. 2.6).

Gutenberg's masterpiece, known as the 42-line Bible, was an impressive achievement by any standards. Each two-volume work (48 copies survive from an estimated print run of 200) comprises 1286 pages, and was probably Gutenberg's financial undoing.

But his major legacy was the process of **hot-metal setting**. The first step is the cutting of a steel punch for every character and punctuation mark. This punch is then struck into a softer metal to form the **matrix** in which the type is cast. Finally lead, with the addition of some antimony for hardness and tin for toughness, is poured into the mold and the type cast.

Lead was used because it melts easily, flows evenly into the matrix, and expands slightly to make an exact replica of the punch. It hardens sufficiently to print repeatedly with acceptable levels of wear. Type for letterpress was always designed "the wrong way round" in mirror image,

2.6 To imitate the lettering of the scribes, Gutenberg's font had to contain a set of over 300 characters, whereas a modern printer's alphabet might contain only 50 or so.

the production sequence being: drawing (wrong), pattern (right), punch (wrong), matrix (right), type (wrong), print (right) (Fig. 2.7).

The fact that, in letterpress, characters have initially to be carved from steel has had a strong influence on type design ever since. It was only with the introduction of photosetting, in the 1950s, that some of the constraints were lifted.

The condensed upright and angular letters of "black letter" type have almost no curves. Paper and vellum (the prepared skins of calves, sheep, or goats) were expensive then, and the scribes were encouraged to fit as many letters to a line as possible. The result is a closely packed page, with much more black than white.

In Italy, however, the Humanist scholars favored the lighter roman style of lettering. As the skills of printing spread across Europe, craftspeople adapted their type to match the kind of lettering their customers preferred. William Caxton, the first printer in England, learnt his craft in Cologne, Germany, and bought Flemish equipment, so his books adopted the textura type.

Caxton's first book was printed in 1477. By 1509, English printers were already using roman type, mainly because of French influence. Shakespeare's plays were first printed in roman type (Fig. 2.8), and "black letter" is now rarely seen – outside of German-speaking countries – except on newspaper mastheads, certificates and diplomas, and on signs advertising "Ye Olde Worlde Shoppes."

Italics began life as separate typefaces in their own right. They were a derivation of the "chancery script" practiced by Italian legal scribes as a speedy alternative to regular writing. The first italic face was cut in Venice by Aldus Manutius in around 1500. It was not until two centuries later that it became partnered with roman, or plain text, and an essential part of the type family.

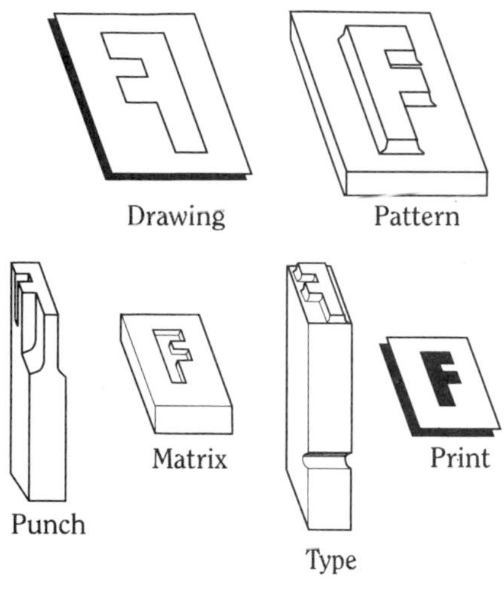

2.7 The design for a hot-metal letterform had to go through many stages on its way to the printed page, and at each successive stage the image had to be reversed (laterally inverted).

2.8 The title page of a Shakespeare edition of 1623. By the time his plays were being published, the more readable roman humanist style of type – still in common use today – had replaced the denser textura faces of the scribes.

The language of type

A **font** is a complete set *in one size* of all the letters of the alphabet, complete with associated ligatures (joined letters), numerals, punctuation marks, and any other signs and symbols (Fig. 2.9). The word font, or fount as it is spelt in Europe, derives from "found" as in type foundry, and reminds us of the days when molten metal type was cast in molds.

Typeface, often shortened to **face**, is the name given to the *design* of the alphabet and its associated marks and symbols. Every typeface has a name. This can be the name of its designer, for example Garamond, Bodoni, or Baskerville. It can take the name of the publication it was originally designed for, for example Times New Roman or Century. Or it may just have a fanciful name intended to convey the "feel" of the face, for example Optima, Perpetua, and Futura.

The letters of the alphabet, the numerals, and all the associated marks and symbols are collectively known as the **alphanumeric character set**. Individually, they are known as **sorts**. The expression "out of sorts," meaning unwell or depressed, comes from the typesetters finding that they have run out of a particular sort when composing a job.

The two words "font" and "typeface" are often used interchangeably. This has come about because in hot metal there will be a different font for each size of type. In photosetting, as we shall see later, it is common for one design to be enlarged or reduced to make all the sizes. This confusion is compounded in desktop publishing (dtp), where a computer menu item labeled "font" will display to the user a list of typefaces.

2.9 A complete font. This font – ITC Clearface – is based on a face originally designed for American Type Founders by Morris Fuller Benton in 1907, and was redesigned in 1979 by Victor Caruso.

ABCDEFGHIJKLMNOPQRSTUVWXYZ
abcdefghijklmnopqrstuvwxyzfifl.,"‘-:;()Ææ
Œœ?&–$£1234567890

ABCDEFGHIJKLMNOPQRSTUVWXYZ
abcdefghijklmnopqrstuvwxyzfifl.,"‘-:;()Ææ
Œœ?&–$£1234567890

ABCDEFGHIJKLMNOPQRSTUVWXYZ
abcdefghijklmnopqrstuvwxyzfifl.,"‘-:;
()ÆæŒœ?&–$£1234567890

A complete set of sorts will also include some or all of the following:

- alternative letters, for the ends of lines, for example, and ornamented or "swash" capitals, such as

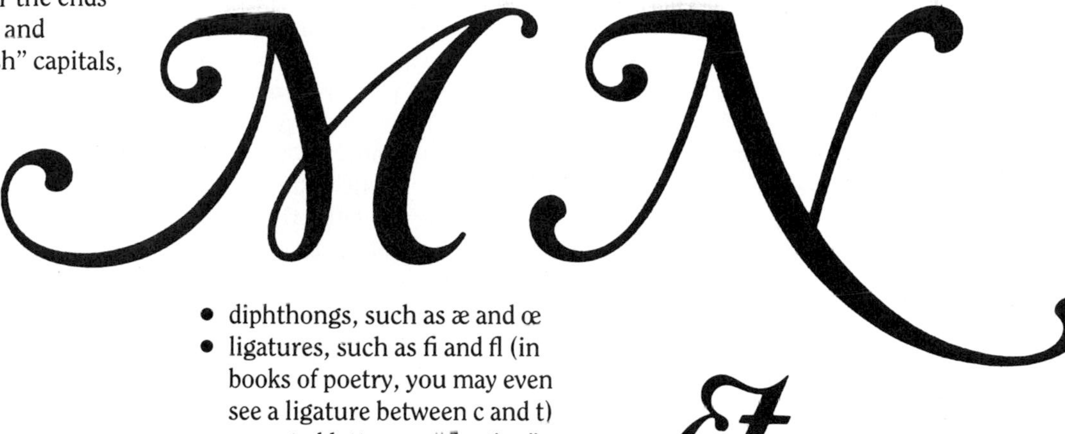

- diphthongs, such as æ and œ
- ligatures, such as ﬁ and ﬂ (in books of poetry, you may even see a ligature between c and t)

ct

- accented letters or "floating" accents for setting foreign languages, such as à (grave), é (acute), ô (circumflex), ü (diaresis), ç (cedilla), ñ (tilde)
- numerals or figures, which can be lining or non-lining (sometimes called "old style" numbers). Some fonts have both (Fig. **2.10**)

1234567890 1234567890

2.10 Lining and non-lining ("old style") numbers. The old style ones have more charm, but lining numerals are easier to incorporate into tabular matter.

- punctuation marks, such as , (comma) and ; (semi-colon)
- reference marks, such as * (asterisk) and ¶ (paragraph)
- fractions and mathematical signs, also known as **pi characters**, such as + (plus) and = (equals)
- and other signs and **dingbats**, such as & (ampersand), ☞, and © (copyright)

A font of roman type will comprise three alphabets:

- capitals, also called majuscules or upper case, named thus because of the position of the letters in the compositor's typecase (abbreviated to caps or u.c.)
- small letters, also known as minuscules or lower case (abbreviated to l.c.)
- and perhaps small capitals, which are the height of a lower case letter

ABCDEFGHIJKLMNOPQRSTUVWXYZ

abcdefghijklmnopqrstuvwxyz

ABCDEFGHIJKLMNOPQRSTUVWXYZ

Italic and bold fonts contain just two alphabets: capitals and lower case.

A **family** is a set of fonts related to the basic roman typeface which may include italic and bold plus a whole spectrum of different "weights" (Fig. 2.11). These range from ultra light to ultra bold. It will also include different widths, ranging from ultra condensed to ultra expanded.

Univers, for example, was designed by Adrian Frutiger in 1957 to have 21 fonts, in five weights and four widths (Fig 2.12). In the original numbering system for Univers, the tens figure indicates the weight, the units figure the width. Odd numbers are roman, even numbers italic.

A **series** is a complete range of sizes in the same typeface.

How type is measured

The way type is measured dates back to the days of hot metal. Type sizes used to have quaint names such as nonpareil, long primer, minikin, minion, and brevier. Only "pica" remains in common usage.

In 1737, the Frenchman Pierre Fournier *le jeune* invented the **point** system of measurement, by dividing the French inch into 12 "lines" which were further subdivided into six points. Some half century later, around 1785, another Parisian, François-Ambroise Didot, settled on a standard – the **didot point** – that is used in Europe to this day.

In the USA, the point was standardized by the American Type Founders' Association in 1886 to be 0·013837 inch (or 0·3759mm). In dtp, the point has been further rationalized to make it exactly 1/72 inch (0·01389in or 0·3528mm). This may seem like splitting hairs, but it means in practise that the pica rules and typescales (Fig. 2.13) designed for traditional typesetting will give inaccurate readings when used for dtp.

There are 72 points to the inch. A **pica** is 12 points, thus measures 1/6 inch. (The didot equivalent to the pica is the cicero.) Although with computerized dtp systems type can be of any height, its size is still generally measured in points, abbreviated to pt.

The use of points to specify size refers back to metal letterpress type. When a font is described as 6pt or 18pt, what is really being measured is the height of the body of lead that the letter sits upon (Fig. 2.14). This is the total height from the lowest extremity of a **descender** (the long vertical stroke of a p or q) to the top of the tallest **ascender** (the long vertical stroke of a k or d), with a little extra space top and bottom. Thus in Linotype Times, for example, the distance from the top of a 10pt letter k to the bottom of a letter p (the **k–p distance**, Fig. 2.15) is not 10pt but only 7·973pt. The k–p distance of a named face can vary depending on its source, so the only sure way to identify type size is to compare your sample with suppliers' example settings.

A more exact way of defining point size is to say that it is the distance from **baseline** to baseline when type is set solid (without leading – see p. 40).

Some typefaces have longer ascenders and descenders than others, so it is quite possible for two typefaces to be exactly the same point size but to appear smaller or larger. A more visually accurate method for describing size is to use the **x-height** (Fig. 2.16). The letter x is used because all its terminals touch a line of measurement.

Type below 14pt is called **body type**, text, or book type. Type above 14pt is called **display type**. Some display types are so decorative as to be unsuitable for text setting and are available in capitals only.

Clearface Regular
Clearface Italic
Clearface Bold
Clearface Bold Italic
Clearface Heavy
Clearface Heavy Italic
Clearface Black
Clearface Black Italic

2.11 A type family contains all the fonts associated with a particular design.

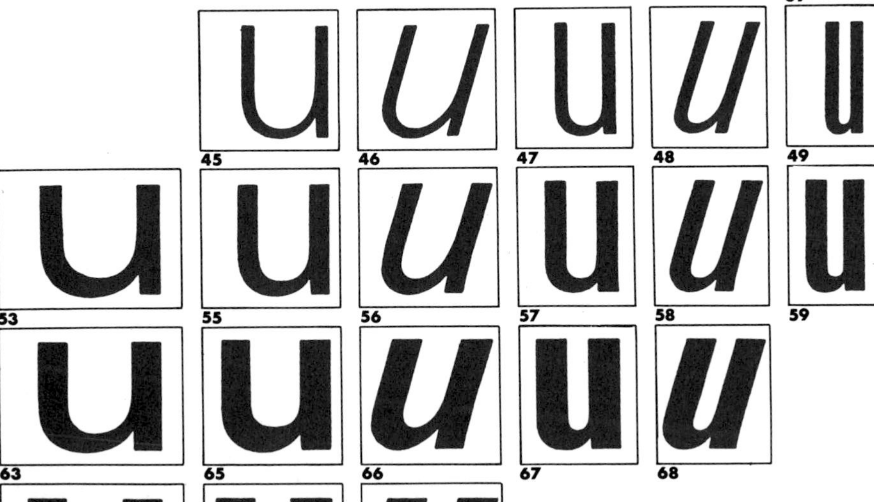

2.12 Univers is a typeface family that was especially designed to comprise a comprehensive set of variants, each of which is identified by a two-digit code number. The tens refer to the weight, the units to the width. Odd numbers are roman, even numbers italic.

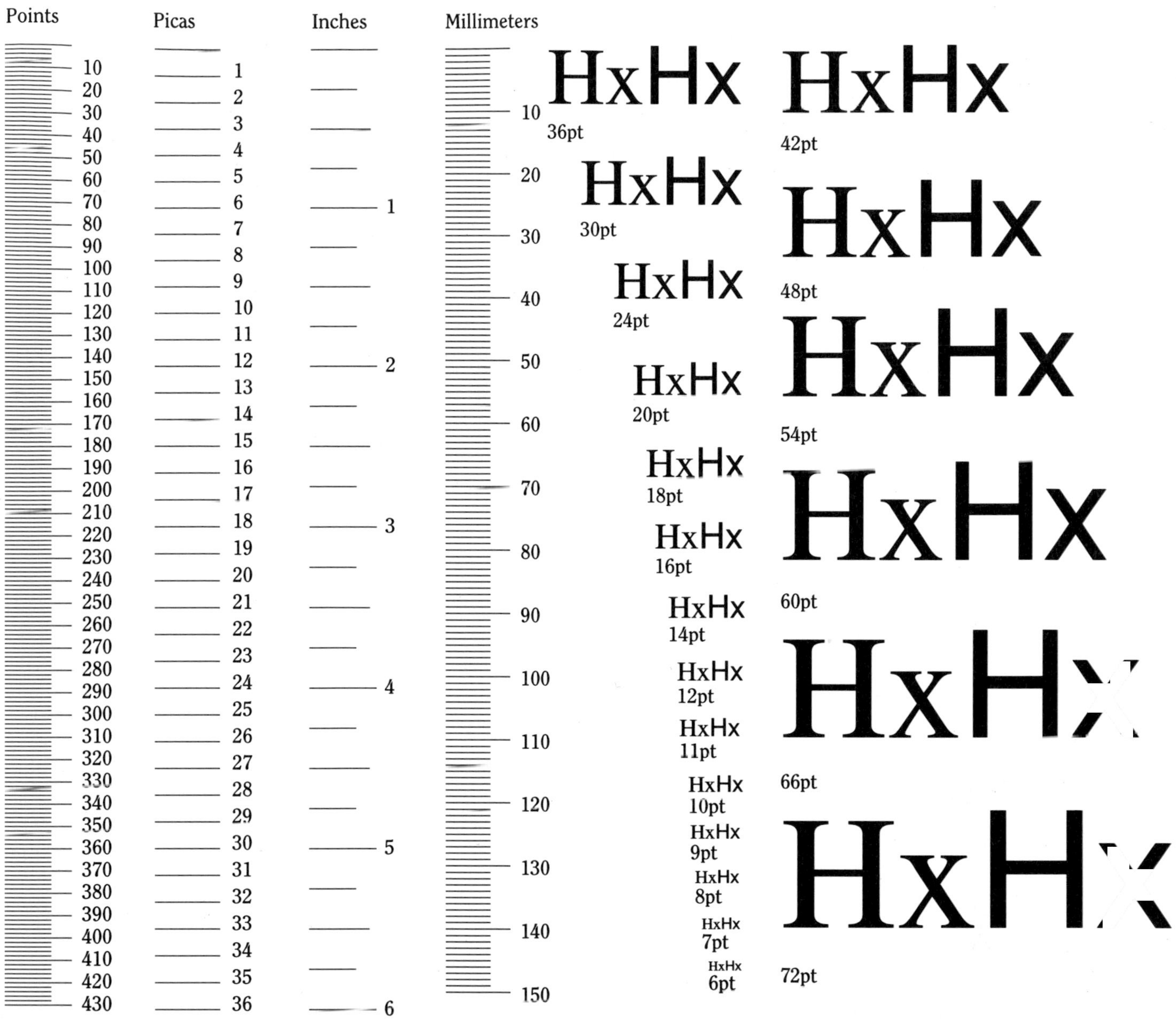

Points

10 20 30 40 50 60 70 80 90 100 110 120 130 140 150 160 170 180 190 200 210 220 230 240 250 260 270 280 290 300 310 320 330 340 350 360 370 380 390 400 410 420 430

Picas

1 2 3 4 5 6 7 8 9 10 11 12 13 14 15 16 17 18 19 20 21 22 23 24 25 26 27 28 29 30 31 32 33 34 35 36

Inches

1 2 3 4 5 6

Millimeters

10 20 30 40 50 60 70 80 90 100 110 120 130 140 150

HxHx 36pt

HxHx 30pt

HxHx 24pt

HxHx 20pt

HxHx 18pt

HxHx 16pt

HxHx 14pt

HxHx 12pt

HxHx 11pt

HxHx 10pt

HxHx 9pt

HxHx 8pt

HxHx 7pt

HxHx 6pt

HxHx 42pt

HxHx 48pt

HxHx 54pt

HxHx 60pt

HxHx 66pt

HxHx 72pt

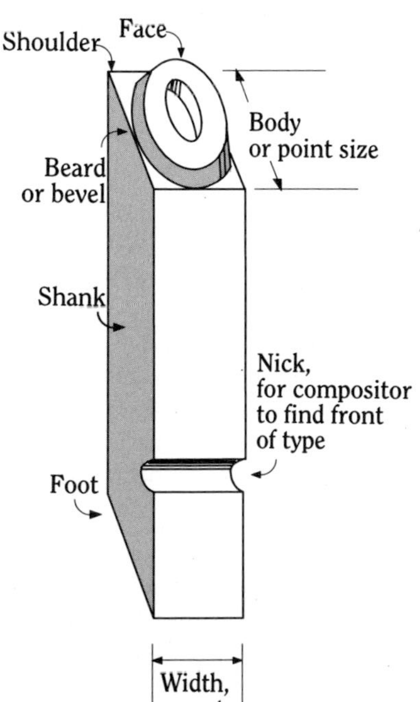

2.13 (above) Type is still mainly measured in points and picas. There are 12 points to the pica, and 72 points to the inch. Here the two most commonplace fonts – Times New Roman and Helvetica – are shown in various point sizes.

2.14 (left) The point size of a font refers back to metal type – to the top-to-bottom size of the body that the letter sits upon, not the distance from the uppermost part of a letter to the lowermost.

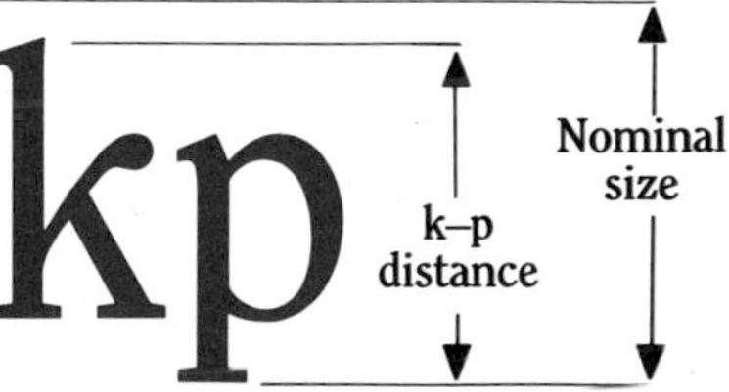

2.15 (above) A more logical method for measuring the size of type is to measure from the top of a letter k to the bottom of a letter p: the so-called k–p distance.

2.16 (above) Different typefaces have different proportions of ascender/descender in relation to the bowl, say, of a letter b. So two faces of the same point size may appear to be different sizes in print. The x-height – the height of a typical lower case letter – is a good guide to the apparent size, and thus legibility, of a particular typeface.

2.17 In a typewriter face such as Courier, all the letters are of equal width – note how the i is elongated to match the m. In more sophisticated typefaces, the width of letters varies, from the slimline l to the more expansive w. Thus different letters are allocated different numbers of units according to their set, or width.

Width and spacing

The width of a letter is called the **set**. Every character sits on a body (real in hot metal, imaginary in photosetting or dtp) that is a number of "set points" wide, each set point being the same as the point which defines the height of the type. Typefaces with a narrow set, such as Bembo, will fit more words per page than wider typefaces, such as Baskerville.

On a regular typewriter, each letter, whether it is a thin i or a fat W, occupies the same width. The carriage moves forward the same distance each time a key is struck. The design of a typewriter font accommodates that shortcoming to some extent. Look at the length of the serifs on a typewritten i, for example, or on a t (Fig. 2.17).

Some letters are naturally wider than others so, in typesetting, the "body" (the letter itself plus some space either side) is divided into vertical slices or **units**. In hot metal, an 18-unit system is employed. Thus the letter i occupies 5 units, whilst an M occupies the maximum of 18. Numerals are normally all 9 units wide, for ease of setting tables.

A regular typewriter uses a 1 unit system. A "proportionally spaced" typewriter, such as the IBM Selectric, uses a 9-unit system. In comparison, photosetting systems use as many as 96 units, the subtleties being apparent only in the very largest sizes of type.

In graphic design, the space around type is often as important as the letterform itself. When characters are allocated units, they are also given units either side to prevent consecutive sorts from touching. These are called **side bearings**, and the information about horizontal spacing built into a typeface is known as its **font metrics**.

EMS AND ENS

The width of a line of setting, or the column width of a publication, is called the **measure**, and is usually measured in picas. Other dimensions, particularly relating to page size and the positions of blocks of type, are generally measured in inches or millimeters.

Another convenient method of measurement is the **em**. This is the width of a capital M (or, strictly speaking, the width of a square space called an em **quad**). Half an em is an **en**, which is the width of a capital N. A complete font also provides the graphic designer with two types of dash, an en rule and an em rule – this book uses spaced en rules.

The em is not an absolute measurement like the pica. Its size will vary depending on the set of the typeface and its point size. A one em indent in 10pt type is 10 points; a one em indent in 18pt type is 18 points. But it is often convenient to ask the typesetter for a paragraph indent of say an em, so that it will always be in proportion with the rest of the setting. A column width should never be specified in ems, however, for it will be different for each different font used. A 12pt em is called a **pica em** – not to be confused with a regular pica!

KERNING AND TRACKING

By overriding the unit allocation for pairs of certain letters, such as L and T, it is possible to bring them closer together and improve their visual appearance. This is called **kerning** (Fig. 2.18).

In hot metal, kerning is only possible by physically cutting, or mortising, away the metal body of the type. Kerning characters are made with portions of the face overhanging the body (Fig. 2.19). With photosetting and dtp, there are no restrictions on the extent of kerning possible. Most systems have routines already pre-programmed to adjust the spacing between kerning pairs automatically.

Adjusting the spacing between *all* the letters is called **tracking** (Fig. 2.20). Tracking should not be confused with kerning, which only takes place between pairs of letters.

Tracking was never really feasible with hot-metal setting, except in special places such as the title pages of books. On the rare occasions when it was, different materials were used to make spaces between letters: brass for 1pt, copper for ½pt, stainless steel for ¼pt, and paper for the finest letterspacing of all.

In photosetting and dtp, it is now common practise to use negative tracking to tighten up the spacing of text, particularly with sans-serif faces.

Jo was very busy in the garret, for the October days began to grow chilly, and the afternoons were short. For two or three hours the sun lay warmly in the high window, showing Jo seated on the old sofa, writing busily, with her papers spread out upon a trunk before her, while Scrabble, the pet rat, promenaded the beams overhead, accompanied by his oldest son, a fine young fellow, who was evidently very proud of his whiskers. Quite absorbed in her work, Jo scribbled away till the last page was filled, when she signed her name with a flourish, and threw down her pen, exclaiming:

"There, I've done my best! If this won't suit I shall have to wait till I can do better."

CLEARFACE 12/13PT NORMAL TRACKING

Jo was very busy in the garret, for the October days began to grow chilly, and the afternoons were short. For two or three hours the sun lay warmly in the high window, showing Jo seated on the old sofa, writing busily, with her papers spread out upon a trunk before her, while Scrabble, the pet rat, promenaded the beams overhead, accompanied by his oldest son, a fine young fellow, who was evidently very proud of his whiskers. Quite absorbed in her work, Jo scribbled away till the last page was filled, when she signed her name with a flourish, and threw down her pen, exclaiming:

"There, I've done my best! If this won't suit I shall have to wait till I can do better."

CLEARFACE 12/13PT NEGATIVE TRACKING

Jo was very busy in the garret, for the October days began to grow chilly, and the afternoons were short. For two or three hours the sun lay warmly in the high window, showing Jo seated on the old sofa, writing busily, with her papers spread out upon a trunk before her, while Scrabble, the pet rat, promenaded the beams overhead, accompanied by his oldest son, a fine young fellow, who was evidently very proud of his whiskers. Quite absorbed in her work, Jo scribbled away till the last page was filled, when she signed her name with a flourish, and threw down her pen, exclaiming:

"There, I've done my best! If this won't suit I shall have to wait till I can do better."

CLEARFACE 12/13PT POSITIVE TRACKING

Yo! World.
Yo! World.

2.18 To improve the visual spacing between certain pairs of letters, especially those with overhanging parts, they are kerned according to rules laid down by the type designer. It is also possible to fine-tune the kerning later, by eye, depending on the context and on the size of the type.

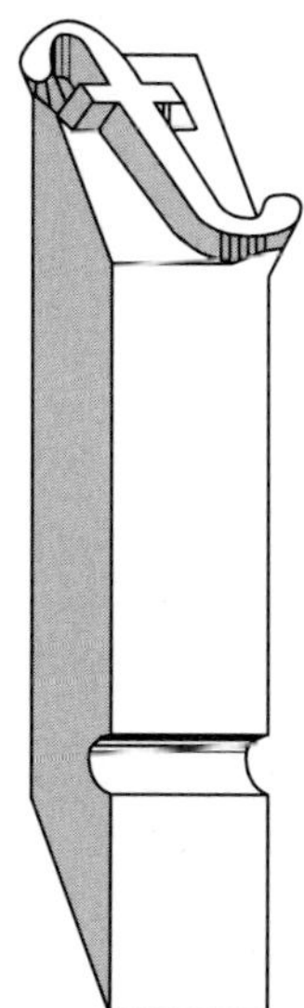

2.19 Letterpress type was kerned by cutting away parts of some metal sorts, and by placing parts of others to overhang the body of the type.

2.20 Normal tracking leaves the spaces between letters as the type designer intended them to be. Negative tracking puts the letters closer together; positive or open tracking spaces them out.

LEADING

Spacing between lines of type is called **leading**, pronounced "ledding," and named after the strips of lead that were placed between lines of type in hot-metal setting (Fig. 2.21). Set **solid** means without leading, for example, written 10/10pt and spoken ten on ten point. To write 10/11pt means to ask for 10pt type with a 1pt space (leading) between the lines, although in hot metal it actually meant to cast 10pt type onto an 11pt body. To aid legibility (see below) it is now common always to use 1pt or 1½pt leading in text setting.

With photosetting and dtp systems, it is now allowable to specify all measurements in inches or millimeters, or even mixtures of the two. However, against all odds, the point and pica persist!

Jo was very busy in the garret, for the October days began to grow chilly, and the afternoons were short. For two or three hours the sun lay warmly in the high window, showing Jo seated on the old sofa, writing busily, with her papers spread out upon a trunk before her, while Scrabble, the pet rat, promenaded the beams overhead, accompanied by his oldest son, a fine young fellow, who was evidently very proud of his whiskers. Quite absorbed in her work, Jo scribbled away till the last page was filled, when she signed her name with a flourish, and threw down her pen, exclaiming:

"There, I've done my best! If this won't suit I shall have to wait till I can do better."

CLEARFACE 12/11PT

Jo was very busy in the garret, for the October days began to grow chilly, and the afternoons were short. For two or three hours the sun lay warmly in the high window, showing Jo seated on the old sofa, writing busily, with her papers spread out upon a trunk before her, while Scrabble, the pet rat, promenaded the beams overhead, accompanied by his oldest son, a fine young fellow, who was evidently very proud of his whiskers. Quite absorbed in her work, Jo scribbled away till the last page was filled, when she signed her name with a flourish, and threw down her pen, exclaiming:

"There, I've done my best! If this won't suit I shall have to wait till I can do better."

CLEARFACE 12/12PT

Jo was very busy in the garret, for the October days began to grow chilly, and the afternoons were short. For two or three hours the sun lay warmly in the high window, showing Jo seated on the old sofa, writing busily, with her papers spread out upon a trunk before her, while Scrabble, the pet rat, promenaded the beams overhead, accompanied by his oldest son, a fine young fellow, who was evidently very proud of his whiskers. Quite absorbed in her work, Jo scribbled away till the last page was filled, when she signed her name with a flourish, and threw down her pen, exclaiming:

"There, I've done my best! If this won't suit I shall have to wait till I can do better."

CLEARFACE 12/13PT

Jo was very busy in the garret, for the October days began to grow chilly, and the afternoons were short. For two or three hours the sun lay warmly in the high window, showing Jo seated on the old sofa, writing busily, with her papers spread out upon a trunk before her, while Scrabble, the pet rat, promenaded the beams overhead, accompanied by his oldest son, a fine young fellow, who was evidently very proud of his whiskers. Quite absorbed in her work, Jo scribbled away till the last page was filled, when she signed her name with a flourish, and threw down her pen, exclaiming:

"There, I've done my best! If this won't suit I shall have to wait till I can do better."

CLEARFACE 12/14PT

2.21 The space between lines of type is called leading after the strips of lead that were used in letterpress. This 12/12pt is said to be set solid. The 12/13pt has 1pt leading. Type can also be set with negative leading, producing lines with ascenders and descenders touching.

JUSTIFICATION AND HYPHENATION

A regular typewriter produces rows of type that line up on the left-hand side but give a ragged appearance on the right. In typesetting, this is called ragged right, **ranged left**, or flush left. Type can also be set ragged left, **ranged right**, centered, or asymmetrical (Fig. 2.22).

In books and magazines, it is usual to see columns of type with neat edges on both sides. This is called **justified** setting, and it is achieved by introducing variable amounts of space between the words. More often than not, especially with the narrow columns used in newspapers and magazines, it is not possible to justify a line merely by increasing the space, and so words must be divided, or **hyphenated**.

Compositors have been taught to break words according to certain rules, as found in handbooks such as *Hart's Rules for Compositors and Readers*. A word is usually hyphenated between syllables, pairs of consonants, or pairs of vowels. The part of the word left at the end of a line should also suggest the part commencing the next line. Thus starva-tion is to be preferred to star-vation. Other rules instruct to hyphenate before -ing, except in ring, and unless preceded by d, t, or h.

Rules for hyphenation can be programmed into photosetting and dtp systems, along with tables of exceptions to avoid **bad breaks**. However, it is still common to see howlers. Some careless word breaks can create unwanted meanings: the-rapist is a memorable example.

For two or three hours the sun lay warmly in
the high window, showing Jo seated on the old
sofa, writing busily, with her papers spread
out upon a trunk before her, while Scrabble,
the pet rat, promenaded the beams overhead,
accompanied by his oldest son, a fine young
fellow, who was evidently very proud of his
whiskers.

RANGED LEFT

For two or three hours the sun lay warmly in
the high window, showing Jo seated on the old
sofa, writing busily, with her papers spread
out upon a trunk before her, while Scrabble,
the pet rat, promenaded the beams overhead,
accompanied by his oldest son, a fine young
fellow, who was evidently very proud of his
whiskers.

RANGED RIGHT

For two or three hours the sun lay warmly
in the high window, showing Jo seated
on the old sofa, writing busily, with her papers
spread out upon a trunk before her,
while Scrabble, the pet rat, promenaded the
beams overhead, accompanied by
his oldest son, a fine young fellow, who was
evidently very proud of his whiskers.

CENTERED

For two or three hours the sun lay warmly
in the high window, showing Jo seated on
the old sofa, writing busily, with her
papers spread out upon a trunk before
her, while Scrabble, the pet rat, promenaded
the beams overhead, accompanied by
his oldest son, a fine young fellow, who was
evidently very proud of his whiskers.

ASYMMETRICAL

For two or three hours the sun lay warmly in the high window, showing Jo seated on the old sofa, writing busily, with her papers spread out upon a trunk before her, while Scrabble, the pet rat, promenaded the beams overhead, accompanied by his oldest son, a fine young fellow, who was evidently very proud of his whiskers.

JUSTIFIED

2.22 Type is commonly set ranged left (ragged right). It can instead be ranged right, centered, or asymmetrical. If type is to be set justified – neatly aligned on both left and right sides – variable spaces must be introduced between words to make each line the same length. Failing this, some words must be broken, or hyphenated.

RAMBLING NEWS

FILING CAN BE FUN!

by Ivor System

There can be few of us who are not feeling the cruel tweak of recession about our Gucci waistbands at the moment, and there are even some of our membership who are OUT OF WORK! Of course, certain individuals would do well to get out of bed before the crack of noon on a weekday. Still, we'll say no more: some people are at their most creative when they're asleep, or at least I presume that must be the case.

Oh dear! Some orphans!

However, it was only when I was in Kensington Gardens deliberating over which was the better bargain at the Dodgy Deli – the rusty tins with no labels or the out-of-date shellfish from Poland – that I saw our Club Secretary go by, leading a dog of dubious parentage by a grimy length of macramé yarn, and I realized just how bad things really are.

Being between jobs myself at the moment, I wondered how I could pass the

Sketching can be fun!

(continued from page 5)

It's great! This is what you do:

1) Nip down to your local art supplies store and buy lots of Japanese handmade paper. Also purchase some cartridge paper, as the Japanese gear is far too expensive to waste.

2) Skulk about the art museum a while until you can lift one of their folding seats without being seen.

3) Take it back and pay the fine.

4) Whatever else you do, try to avoid creating

widows!

5) Drive the car to an out-of-town supermarket and get a picnic together. Need a few hints?

- Chocolate-chip cookies – several packs
- a pot of spicy Nutrasweet dip and some sponge fingers
- brie, French bread, wine, etc
- a Swiss army penknife
- a warm woolly jumper

Now you're all set! Let's go sketching! Of course, you can just sit in front of the television and run off a few workmanlike studies of the aspidistra, but half the fun is getting your orange shellsuit on, tucking your trousers into your socks, finding your

It is also generally considered good design to avoid too many consecutive hyphens. Three lines ending with hyphens or other punctuation marks is the maximum that can be tolerated. The designer should also be on the look out for **rivers** of space running vertically in the middle of chunks of type. And for **widows** and **orphans** (Fig. 2.23).

A widow is a single word on the last line of a paragraph carried over to the top of a column, and is best avoided by asking the copywriter or author to lose a word from earlier on in the paragraph. Orphans are single words, or small groups of words, left at the ends of paragraphs. There will be more discussion on the principles of layout in Chapter 4.

A revival from medieval manuscripts is the **drop cap** (Fig. 2.24), mainly because it is easy to do on a dtp system. A drop cap is an initial letter signaling the beginning of the text. It is usually enlarged to a size equivalent to three or more lines of type, with the type adjacent to the drop cap indented to make room. Drop caps work best when the first sentence begins with a single letter, such as A or I. Failing that, avoid short words, especially ones with only two letters. And take care with those words that form different words when the initial letter is removed, such as T-he, E-very and S-elf. Another common error is to forget to remove the first letter of the body text that follows.

2.23 (opposite) One of the general rules of good layout is to avoid creating "orphans" – one or a few words alone on a line at the end of a paragraph – or worse still, a "widow" – a single word floating at the top of a new page or column.

Actum hoc nonū et infrascri
ptum beate Marie virginis
psalteriū ad honorē omnipotē
tis dei ad eiusdē beatē Marie
virginis celestis et terrestris
glo'se Imperatricis Illustrissi-
mi Friderici tercij Imperatoris
et maximi Maximiliani glori
osissimi nostri regis ab earun
dem Illustrissimarum regiarum
maiestatū humillimo Cappella
no Hermāno Nitzschewitz
ex Brandeburgēsi Margia
Trebbinensi vtriusque Iuris consultu magno Cir
ca Oderam Franckfordensis ciuitatis prothono-
tario ad teucrorum cōtentōrum denoue legis dulcissi
mis mirabilibus diuini amoris flore vberrime refer
tis perfectū Annodomini Millesimoquadringē-
tesimooctuogesimo Nono Illustrissimo Impa
tori Friderico ex Lunenborch delatū Et Anno
Nonagesimosecūdo in mense Septēbri ad Il-
lustrissimas cesarias regiasque man' pricialit' pre
sentatū Nutu regio cesario iussu Ab illustrissi-
ma Romana Friderici Imperatoris tercij Can
cellaria examinatū Cesareo sumptu ad imprimē
dum commissum Nūc et in Tzenna Cisterciensis
ordis deuoto claustro subprincipatu domini. dn̄i
Nicolai abbatis spiritualis patris ac domini dō
m sui graciosi singularis in huius glo'se virginis
laudibus sui et toci' Cistersiensis ordinis dulcis-
sime patronisse deuoti ad alti celsi sacri diui pij

For two or three hours the sun lay warmly in the high window, showing Jo seated on the old sofa, writing busily, with her papers spread out upon a trunk before her, while Scrabble, the pet rat, promenaded the beams overhead, accompanied by his oldest son, a fine young fellow, who was evidently very proud of his whiskers.

For two or three hours the sun lay warmly in the high window, showing Jo seated on the old sofa, writing busily, with her papers spread out upon a trunk before her, while Scrabble, the pet rat, promenaded the beams overhead, accompanied by his oldest son, a fine young fellow, who was evidently very proud of his whiskers.

2.24 A drop cap is an embellishment found at the beginning of a chapter in a book or in the opening paragraph of a magazine article, in which the first letter is enlarged and set into the body of the text. Its historical precedent can be found in illuminated medieval manuscripts like the ornamented title page of 1496 from the Cistercian monastery at Zinna reproduced above.

Part 2: text

Text is the "meaning" part of type: just plain words plus the spaces between them, devoid of any information about the typefaces, sizes, measures, or weights being used. In print production, raw text is called **copy**.

One of the designer's tasks is **copy preparation**: adding the instructions that define how the text is going to look, either by keying them directly into the computer or by **marking up** the manuscript for the typesetter (Fig. 2.25).

For type to remain consistent within a long document, or from issue to issue of a magazine, the graphic designer will write down and send to the compositor a **style sheet** or **type specification** (Fig. 2.26). This will define the size, typeface, and measure of the body text, captions, headlines, and so on. In this book, for example, the text is set in 10/12pt Clearface justified to 13 picas, with captions in 9/10pt Clearface, headlines in various sizes of News Gothic Bold, and chapter titles in 72pt Alternate Gothic No. 1.

The type spec may also lay down a **grid** (see pp. 102–3) which restricts type to certain areas of the page.

B

Correcting text proofs

~~Proofing and proof correction~~

Once type has been set, it must be checked to make sure that it has been keyed correctly. The old proofreaders on newspapers were adept at reading type back to front, but for mere mortals, a proof must be taken. The first proof is called the galley proof. Several pulls are taken so that the various professionals involved in the production can each read the proof. The printer's reader is the first, and ~~he or she~~ marks the printer's mistakes to be corrected, usually in green ink.

run on

One proof of the galley is designated the **master proof**, and others go to the author or copywriter and to the copy editor, who decides which corrections should be incorporated onto the master proof. So-called **author's corrections** are marked in blue and have to be paid for, while any other printer's errors are marked in red. Typing errors such as transposed letters are called **literals**, and probably constitute the bulk of the corrections. Note that it is possible in hot metal and photosetting to introduce new, more serious errors into a text when attempting to correct a relatively trivial one! So that there can be no chance of misunderstanding between the copy editor and the compositor, corrections are marked neatly both in the setting and with an accompanying marginal symbol, according to an internationally agreed convention (Fig. 2.52). If something is wrongly corrected and needs to be reinstated, it should be marked with dotted underlining and the word stet in the margin.

bold bold bold n.p. ¶

Although there are no physical galleys in photosetting, the

Typography in design

A Heads in 30/32pt. (w. 22.5) News Gothic Bold u/l.c. Range left in 27½ picas

18pts#

Our Western alphabet was invented by the Phoenicians around 1100BC somewhere on the Eastern shores of the Mediterranean sea. Capital letters derive for Roman incised lettering, with its distinctive serifs (the little marks made by the chisel to neaten the ends of letters), slanted stress and variations in stroke thickness. The chiselled capital letters carved on Trajan's column in Rome around AD114 are still regarded as the 'perfect' Roman letters. Lower-case lettering comes from a more rounded form of handwriting, known as the uncial, developed for everyday use in the fourth century.

In the middle ages, scribes created all books by hand, usually copying from existing books. They were beautiful objects, often 'illuminated' with ornamental letters, painting and gold blocking.

Set running text in 10/12pt Clearface Reg. u/l.c. Justify to 13 picas Indent first line of new paragraphs by 1½ picas (Hyphenate to even out word spacing)

18pts#

Some history

B Heads in 18/20pt. (w. 13.5) News Gothic Bold u/l.c. Range left in 13picas

12pts#

Our Western alphabet was invented by the Phoenicians around 1100BC somewhere on the Eastern shores of the Mediterranean sea. Capital letters derive for Roman incised lettering, with its distinctive serifs (the little marks made by the chisel to neaten the ends of letters), slanted stress and variations in stroke thickness. The chiselled capital letters carved on

9pts#

EMS AND ENS

C Heads in 12pt. (w. 9) News Gothic Bold Caps Range left in 13picas.

3pts#

Our Western alphabet was invented by the Phoenicians around 1100BC somewhere on the Eastern shores of the Mediterranean sea. Capital letters

2.25 An author's manuscript must be marked up by a copy editor before it goes to the printer for typesetting. This process brings the raw text into house style, corrects any errors, and can involve some degree of rewriting. Either the editor or the designer will also need to instruct the compositor as to which typefaces, sizes, and measures to use when converting the text into type.

2.26 The style sheet for this book.

Correcting text proofs

Once type has been set, it must be checked to make sure that it has been keyed correctly. The old proofreaders on newspapers were adept at reading type back to front, but for mere mortals, a proof must be taken. The first proof is called the galley proof. Several pulls are taken so that the various professionals involved in the production can each read the proof. The printer's reader is the first, and marks the printer's mistakes to be corrected, usually in green ink. One of the galley proofs is designated the **master proof**, and others go to the author or copywriter and to the copy editor, who decides which corrections should be incorporated onto the master proof. So-called **author's corrections** are marked in blue and have to be paid for, while any other printer's errors are marked in red.

Typing errors such as transposed letters are called **literals**, and probably constitute the bulk of the corrections. Note that it is possible in hot metal and photosetting to introduce new, more serious errors into a text when attempting to correct a relatively trivial one! So that there can be no chance of misunderstanding between the copy editor and the compositor, corrections are marked neatly both in the setting and with an accompanying marginal symbol, according to an internationally agreed convention (Fig. 2.27). If something is wrongly corrected and needs to be reinstated, it should be marked with dotted underlining and the word **stet** in the margin.

Although there are no physical galleys in photosetting, the same procedure applies. The designer and/or copy editor will usually receive a set of photocopies of the bromide print, which is treated in exactly the same way as the hot metal galley proof. Once corrected, another proof may be sent, but it is more likely that the next chance to check that the corrections have been made will be on the **page proof**, a proof of the mechanical complete with running headlines, captions, and line illustrations in place.

With a dtp system, it is tempting to go straight to page layout once the text has been input. It is much safer to print out the text and to read it as if it were a galley proof. In this way there is **hardcopy** – a record of the corrections made. Better still, get a colleague to read the proof – mistakes are often invisible to those who make them.

BOOKWORM TYPESETTING
4 Harthill Street, Manchester
☏ 061-832 3034

Calmann & King W9808FIG.FOL
Production for Graphic Design
8.5.1992 [Own Disc & Pi]
David Newton [254G]

Correcting text profs

Once typo has been set, it must be checked to make sure that it has been keyed correctly. The old proof readers on newspapers were adept at reading type back to font, but for mere mortals, a proof must be taken. The first proof is called the gallery proof. Several pulls are taken so that the various proffesionals involved in the production can each read the proof. Several pulls are taken so that the various proffesionals involved in the production can each read the proof. The printers reader is the first, and marks the printer's mistakes to be corrected, usually in green ink.

One of the galley proofs is designated the **master proof**, and others go t the author or copywriter and to the copy editor, who decides which corrections should be incorporated onto the master proof. So-called **author's corrections** are marked in blue and have to be paid for, while any other **printer's errors are marked in red.**

Typing errors such as trasnposed letters are called *literals*, and probably constitute the bulk of the corrections. NOte that it is possible in hot metal and photosetting to introduce new, more serious errors into a text when attempting to to correct a relatively trivial one! so that there can be no chance of misunderstanding between the copyeditor and the composer, corrections are marked nearly both in the setting and with an accompanying marginal symbol, according to an internationally agreed convention (*Fig.* 2.27. If something is wrongly corrected and needs to be reinstated, it should be marked with dotted underlining and the word stet in the margin Although there are no physical galleys in phototosetting, the same procedure applies. The designer and/our copy editor usually will recieve a set of photocopies of the bromide print which is treated in exactly the same way as the hotmetal galley proof. Once correcd, another proof may be sent, but it is more likely that the next chance to check that the corre-ctions have been made will be on the page proof, a proof of the mechanical complete with runnning headlines, captions, and line illustrations in palace.

With apologies to Bookworm Typesetting, who set the galley proofs very cleanly.

2.27 Once the marked-up copy returns from the typesetter in the form of galley proofs, it must be read, checked, and marked for correction using standard proof correction signs, as shown overleaf. Here we show the original marked-up copy (Fig. **2.25**), the typesetting after being marked for correction (right), and, after another journey to the typesetters, the resulting "clean" setting (above), incorporated into the layout.

STANDARD PROOF CORRECTION SIGNS

EXPLANATION	MARGINAL MARK	TEXT MARK
Delete letter(s) or word(s)	₰	I've doner my best
Close up; delete space	⁀	I've done my best !
Delete, and close up word	₰	I've done may best
Let it stand as it is	stet	I've done my best
Insert space	#	I've donemy best
Equalize spacing	eq #	I've done my best
Insert hair space	hr #	1398 1468
Letterspace	ls	I'VE DONE MY BEST
Begin new paragraph	¶	I've done my best! If
Don't begin new paragraph; run on	no ¶	I've done my best If this won't suit
Move type one em	☐	I've done my best
Move type two ems	☐☐	I've done my best
Move right	]	I've done my best
Move left	[	I've done my best
Center	][	I've done my best
Move up	⌐¬	I've done my best
Move down	└┘	I've done my best
Flush left; range left	fl	I've done my best
Flush right; range right	fr	I've done my best
Straighten type; align horizontally	=	I've done my best
Align vertically	||	I've done
Transpose; swap the order	tr	I've done my bset
Set in *italic* type	ital	I've done my best
Set in roman type	rom	*I've done my best*
Set in **bold** type	bf	I've done my best
Set in lower case	lc	I've done MY best
Set in UPPER CASE (capitals)	cap	i've done my best
Set in SMALL CAPITALS	sc	I've done my best
Remove blemish	×	I've done my best
Make superscript figure	10	1024 is 210
Make subscript figure	2	10102
Insert comma	^	There I've done my best
Insert apostrophe or single quotation mark	'	Ive done my best
Insert period	⊙	I've done my best
Insert question mark	(set) ?	Have I done my best
Insert colon	:/	She exclaimed "I've done
Insert hyphen	-/	Black and-white print
Insert en dash	1/N	1398 1468
Insert em dash	1/M	I've done my best
Insert parentheses	(/)	I've done my best
Insert brackets	[/]	I've done my best

Collectively, a text document is called a **manuscript**, abbreviated to Ms. A single sheet is called a **folio**. (A folio is also the term given by publishers to the page numbers in books.) Each folio should be numbered and identified with a tag or catchline, usually the name of the author or job, in case the Ms is dropped or blown about by a passing breeze. It is also customary for short pieces of setting to indicate on each folio whether *(more follows* or that the copy *(ends*.

Copy should always be clean and legible, typed on one side of the paper in double spacing with wide margins, leaving enough room for the copy editor's corrections. Some publishers provide authors with templates, sheets printed with faint blue guidelines, for the purpose. Any matter not to be printed, such as instructions to the typesetter, should be encircled.

Casting off and copy fitting

Casting off is estimating the number of words in a manuscript. **Copy fitting** is assessing how much space text will take up in a printed document. Both are tedious and produce only approximate results, but are important in ensuring that you do not end up with pages of **overmatter**. Traditionally, one would encourage the author to type the same number of lines per page, and across a measure containing a round number of characters that is simple to calculate.

A regular typewriter does not have proportional spacing, so each letter takes up the same amount of space. Rule a pencil line down the right-hand edge of the typing, placed so that the visual area of the type to the right of the line equals the area of white space to the left. This establishes the average number of characters per line. A less accurate method is to count the number of characters per line for the first, say, ten lines and find the average. Then count the number of lines, marking, say, every hundredth line in pencil. It is assumed that, in English, an average word is five letters plus one space long, so the number of characters divided by six gives the number of words.

Most word processors use proportional spacing which makes character counting more difficult. However, most now have built-in word counters. These are often approximate, depending on what the program decides constitutes a word. Different programs can give different word counts for the same piece of text.

The amount of space required when the text is set into type will vary depending both on the type size and the typeface. For hot metal and photosetting, the type foundries supply copy-fitting tables (Fig. 2.28), which will give you the information that, for example, 11pt Bembo averages 66 characters (11 words) in a line 24 picas long. It is thus possible to find out how many pages the copy will fill once set in type.

For smaller jobs, a plastic type gauge can be used to measure the number of lines that a particular size of type will occupy. If you calculate that five lines of text will give you seven lines of type, for example, it is possible to count them off using the gauge. Many type gauges also have scales with which to count typewritten characters. On typewriters, the number of characters per inch is called the **pitch**: the normal 10 pitch is called pica (no relation to the typographic pica!), and the smaller 12 pitch is called elite. Always overestimate the number of words, to be on the safe side. It is easier to deal with white space than to find room for unexpected text.

In dtp, there is a lot of variation in set width between the same named typeface from different suppliers. The only way to be safe is to base your calculations on a piece of sample setting from your chosen font and use *exactly* the same font for the eventual setting. This is particularly important when using a bureau which may claim to hold the same font; when the proof arrives you may find the words are not where you wanted them.

With dtp, it is all too easy to make copy fit an awkward space by altering the tracking, the size of type, or the leading, by just the tiniest amount, with a resulting inconsistency of "color" within the document. This is a temptation that should be resisted.

House style

There are few absolutes in life, and in some cases a usage is neither right nor wrong. But **house style** is a way of standardizing spelling and codifying the way, say, that ships' names, like the *USS Enterprise*, are always italicized. There will normally also be guidelines to avoid sexist and racist usages creeping into print.

House style will regulate how the date should be written, and will also include instructions as to whether acronyms should be given periods or not (dots per inch as d.p.i or dpi, or even dots/in), set all caps or all lower case (both WYSIWYG and wysiwyg, for example, could be used to stand for "what you see is what you get").

The keyword is consistency – within a publication, and within an organization.

Characters per line

Font size	*Pica Measure*												
	18	*19*	*20*	*21*	*22*	*23*	*24*	*25*	*26*	*27*	*28*	*29*	*30*
8 pt.	59	62	65	68	72	75	78	81	85	88	91	94	98
9 pt.	52	55	58	60	63	66	69	72	75	78	81	83	86
10 pt.	46	48	51	53	56	58	61	64	66	69	71	74	76
11 pt.	42	44	47	49	51	54	56	58	61	63	65	68	70
12 pt.	38	40	43	45	47	49	51	53	55	57	60	62	64

2.28 Copy-fitting tables help estimate the space needed by copy in a particular typeface and point size. The above old-style table is for Century. In the two-part table below, each typeface is given a value. A number from the first table is used to read off characters per pica from the second.

Alphabet lengths for different sizes
Laufweitenkennzahl für verschiedene Schriftgrößen
Longueur d'alphabet pour différents corps

alphabet length ref. no. at 10 pt / Laufweitenkennzahl in 10 pt / Référence de longueur d'alphabet en 10 pt	pt 6 mm 2,25	7 2,63	8 3,00	9 3,38	10 3,75	11 4,13	12 4,50	14 5,25	16 6,00	18 6,75	20 7,50	24 9,00	30 11,25	36 13,50	42 15,75	48 18,00
85	51	59	68	76	85	93	102	119	136	153	170	204	255	306	357	408
87	52	60	69	78	87	95	104	121	139	156	174	208	261	313	365	417
88	52	61	70	79	88	96	105	123	140	158	176	211	264	316	369	422
90	54	63	72	81	90	99	108	126	144	162	180	216	270	324	378	432
92	55	64	73	82	92	101	110	128	147	165	184	220	276	331	386	441
93	55	65	74	83	93	102	111	130	148	167	186	223	279	334	390	446
95	57	66	76	85	95	104	114	133	152	171	190	228	285	342	399	456
97	58	67	77	87	97	106	116	135	155	174	194	232	291	349	407	465
98	58	68	78	88	98	107	117	137	156	176	196	235	294	352	411	470
100	60	70	80	90	100	110	120	140	160	180	200	240	300	360	420	480
102	61	71	81	91	102	112	122	142	163	183	204	244	306	367	428	489
103	61	72	82	92	103	113	123	144	164	185	206	247	309	370	432	494
105	63	73	84	94	105	115	126	147	168	189	210	252	315	378	441	504
107	64	74	85	96	107	117	128	149	171	192	214	256	321	385	449	513
108	64	75	86	97	108	118	129	151	172	194	216	259	324	388	453	518
110	66	77	88	99	110	121	132	154	176	198	220	264	330	396	462	528
112	67	78	89	100	112	123	134	156	179	201	224	268	336	403	470	537
113	67	79	90	101	113	124	135	158	180	203	226	271	339	406	474	542
115	69	80	92	103	115	126	138	161	184	207	230	276	345	414	483	552
															491	561
															495	566
															504	576
															512	585
															516	590
															525	600
															533	609
															537	614
															546	624
															554	633
															558	638
															567	648
															575	657
															579	662
															588	672
															596	681
															600	686
															609	696
															617	705
															621	710
															630	720
															638	729
															642	734
															651	744
															659	753
															663	758
															672	768
															680	777
															684	782
															693	792
															701	801
															705	806
															714	816
															722	825
															726	830
															735	840

Characters per line (Pica)
Zeichen pro Zeile (Pica)
Caractères par ligne (Pica)

determined alphabet length ref. no. / ermittelte Laufweitenkennzahl / Référence de longueur d'alphabet déterminés	Pica 1.00	10	12	14	16	18	20	22	24	26	28	30	32	36	40	45
50	6.74	67	81	94	108	121	135	148	162	175	189	202	216	243	270	303
52	6.48	65	78	91	104	117	130	143	156	168	181	194	207	233	259	292
54	6.24	62	75	87	100	112	125	137	150	162	175	187	200	225	250	281
56	6.02	60	72	84	96	108	120	132	144	156	168	181	193	217	241	271
58	5.81	58	70	81	93	105	116	128	139	151	163	174	186	209	232	261
60	5.62	56	67	79	90	101	112	124	135	146	157	168	180	202	225	253
62	5.43	54	65	76	87	98	109	120	130	141	152	163	174	196	217	245
64	5.27	53	63	74	84	95	105	116	126	137	147	158	168	190	211	237
66	5.11	51	61	71	82	92	102	112	123	133	143	153	163	184	204	230
68	4.96	50	59	69	79	89	99	109	119	129	139	149	159	178	198	223
70	4.81	48	58	67	77	87	96	106	116	125	135	144	154	173	193	217
72	4.68	47	56	66	75	84	94	103	112	122	131	140	150	168	187	211
74	4.55	46	55	64	73	82	91	100	109	118	127	137	146	164	182	205
76	4.43	44	53	62	71	80	89	98	106	115	124	133	142	160	177	200
78	4.32	43	52	60	69	78	86	95	104	112	121	130	138	156	173	194
80	4.21	42	51	59	67	76	84	93	101	110	118	126	135	152	168	190
82	4.11	41	49	58	66	74	82	90	99	107	115	123	131	148	164	185
84	4.01	40	48	56	64	72	80	88	96	104	112	120	128	144	160	181
86	3.92	39	47	55	63	71	78	86	94	102	110	118	125	141	157	176
88	3.83	38	46	54	61	69	77	84	92	100	107	115	123	138	153	172
90	3.74	37	45	52	60	67	75	82	90	97	105	112	120	135	150	168
92	3.66	37	44	51	59	66	73	81	88	95	103	110	117	132	147	165
94	3.58	36	43	50	57	65	72	79	86	93	100	108	115	129	143	161
96	3.51	35	42	49	56	63	70	77	84	91	98	105	112	126	140	158
98	3.44	34	41	48	55	62	69	76	83	89	96	103	110	124	138	155
100	3.37	34	40	47	54	61	67	74	81	88	94	101	108	121	135	152
102	3.30	33	40	46	53	59	66	73	79	86	92	99	106	119	132	149
104	3.24	32	39	45	52	58	65	71	78	84	91	97	104	117	130	146

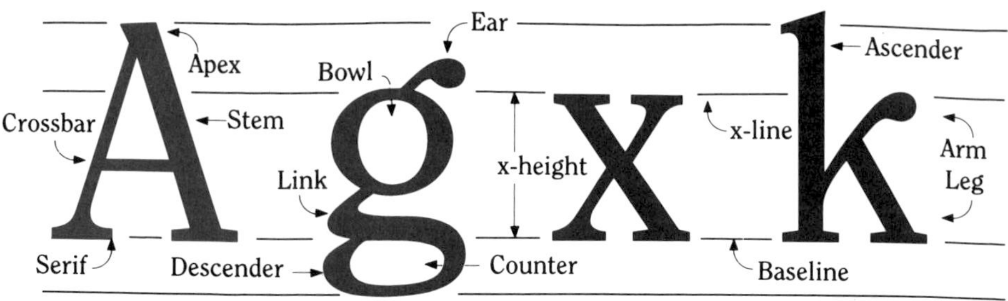

Choosing and recognizing typefaces

To be able to choose the right typeface for the job, one must first know something about how typefaces are constructed and classified (Fig. 2.29).

Each face has its own personality (Fig. 2.30), and typefaces are described by typographers in the same hallowed tones used by connoisseurs to talk about wine. Garamond is said to be "quiet"; Bodoni "sparkles."

Each has its place in the graphic designer's toolkit: for a bank's annual report, for example, you may wish to use a well established "classic" face like Garamond to convey tradition and solidity; a music magazine aimed at young people will look better with a fashionable type like Futura. Some typefaces are chosen for practical reasons. Newspapers tend to use faces with large x-heights and open counters, because the ink spread on low grade paper would fill in less robust faces.

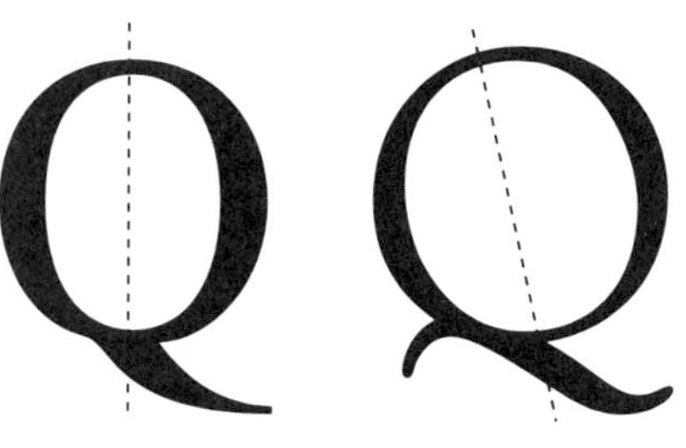

2.29 (above) Each letter has its own anatomical details, and knowing the names for the component parts of a letterform is a great aid to identifying and specifying a particular typeface.

Establishment

Times New Roman

Professional

Clearface

Fun and Friendly

Cooper Black

Bland but safe

Helvetica

Traditional

Baskerville

Powerful

Gill Sans Ultra Bold

Fashionable

Futura

Elegant

Garamond Italic

2.30 Some typefaces are so familiar as to be virtually invisible – Times and Helvetica are the main culprits – while others, such as Futura and Gill, come regularly in and out of fashion every few years.

2.31 All typefaces can be classified according to whether they do or do not have serifs. Some serifs have brackets – smooth "fillets" between the horizontal and upright – and some do not. The size of the serif can range from slab to hairline.

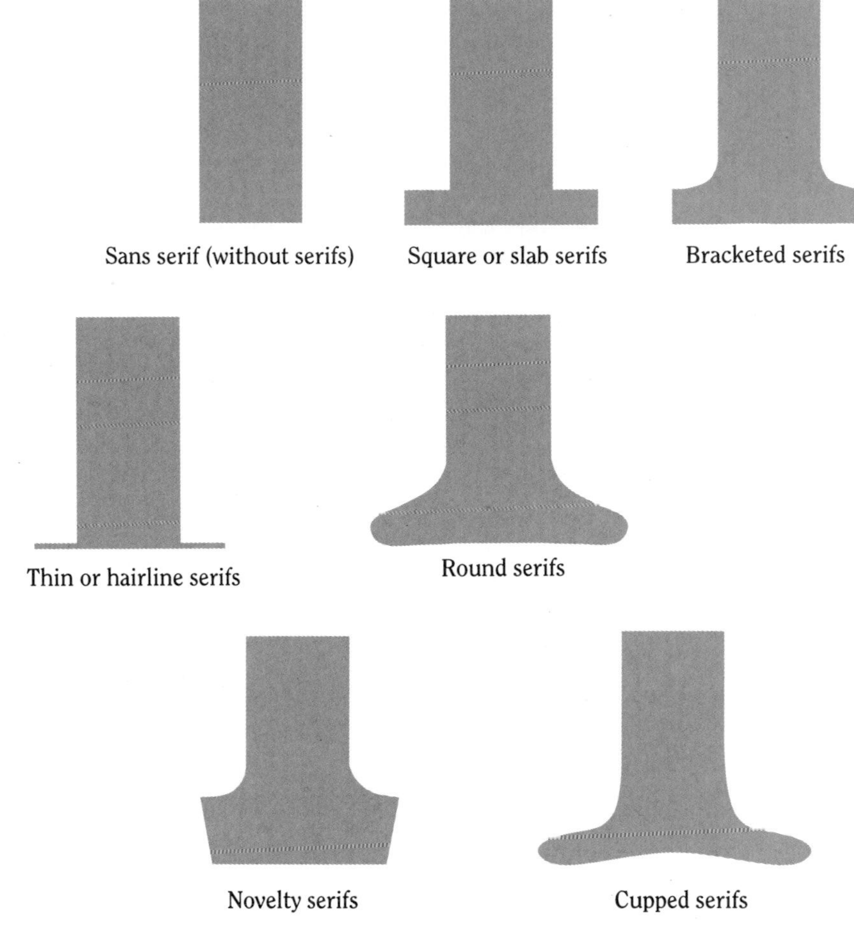

SERIF OR SANS SERIF?

The most obvious distinguishing feature of a typeface is whether it has a serif or not (Fig. 2.31). **Serifs** are marks or flourishes around the extremities of letters, on the baseline and at the top, usually at right angles to the direction of the stroke. They help to make type more readable (see below), and take several different forms: bracketed, with a smooth curved "fillet" between the serif and stem; slab, with sharper corners and almost the same thickness as the stem; hairline; or wedge.

A typeface without serifs is called **sans serif**, or just sans. The old name was grot, from grotesque, and in America they are also known as Gothic faces. The first sans typeface for text was cast in 1835 and called Seven Lines Grotesque, though sans faces have long been used for display setting and for signwriting. It did not become popular until the beginning of this century, first with Edward Johnston's 1916 typeface – still in use – for London Transport. Later came Univers, and Max Miedinger's Helvetica, perhaps one of the most popular typefaces currently in use.

EARMARKS

Each typeface has its own distinctive characteristics, called **earmarks** (Fig. 2.32), named after the distinctive "ear" on the lower case g. These enable us to identify one design from another. To distinguish Helvetica from Univers, for example, look for the vertical downstroke in the capital G, the curly tail of the lower case y, and the angled tail through the bowl of the Q.

Soon you will be spotting the more subtle differences. For other typefaces, a good strategy is to start with the Q (a letter so infrequently used that typographers often have fun with it, making it their trademark), then the ampersand, then the J, G, and W. Try the lower case g, then a, j, and y. For numbers, look first at 3, then 7, 5, and 2. Real italics, not the sloped oblique versions of roman type found in dtp systems, are usually distinctive and easy to identify.

GyQa&3
Helvetica

GyQa&4
Clearface

GyQa&3
Univers

GyQa&4
Times

GgQa&3
Futura

GgQaP&3
Baskerville

GgQa&3
Gill

GgQaP&3
Garamond

2.32 Earmarks are the distinguishing features of a typeface design. Easily identifiable letters include the capital Q and the lower case g, and don't forget the ampersand.

Other features that help distinguish different typefaces are the overall proportions (the relation of x-height to ascenders and descenders, for example), the stress (is it oblique or vertical?), the contrast between thick and thin strokes, the formation of the serifs. Are the characters wide and loose fitting, or compact and tight? Some are easy: script and "black letter" faces, for example, stand out from all the others. To the untrained eye, others look virtually indistinguishable.

Type has long been classified into groups, such as "old face," "transitional," and "modern." These sometimes vague classifications have been codified, first by French typographer Maximilien Vox, and later by national and international standards, into nine groups (Fig. 2.33). The categories may not seem at first sight to be of great use to the graphic designer when choosing type, but they are a considerable aid to communicating with the typesetter and printer.

GROUP 1: HUMANIST

These faces are characterized by an inclined bar on the lower case e, which points to their calligraphic origins. They are light in weight, with bracketed serifs, and an oblique stress. Also known as Venetian. An example is Centaur.

2.33a Humanist: Centaur.

Mind your Ps & Qs

ABCDEFGHIJKLMNOPQRST

UVWXYZ

abcdefghijklmnopqrstuvwxyz

1234567890

(.,:;*?$["&"]'%'!)

It was after sun-up now, but we went right on and didn't tie up. The king and the duke turned out by and by looking pretty rusty; but after they'd jumped overboard and took a swim it chippered them up a good deal. After breakfast the king he took a seat on the corner of the raft, and pulled off his boots and rolled up his britches, and let his legs dangle in the water, so as to be comfortable, and lit his pipe, and went to getting his "Romeo and Juliet" by heart.

GROUP 2: GARALDE

The faces in this group still have an oblique stress, but are less script-like, with a horizontal bar on the e. The name Garalde is a contraction of *Gara*mond and *Ald*us, though where the e comes from is a mystery. Other examples include Bembo, Plantin, and Caslon (Fig. 2.34).

Collectively, humanist and garalde are called "old face" or "old style." Old style, however, does not mean old fashioned: Galliard is a face designed with the aid of a computer by Matthew Carter in 1978–81.

2.33b Garalde: Caslon.

Mind your Ps & Qs

ABCDEFGHIJKLMNOPQ

RSTUVWXYZ

abcdefghijklmnopqrstuvwxyz

1234567890

(.,:;*?$["&"]'%'!)

It was after sun-up now, but we went right on and didn't tie up. The king and the duke turned out by and by looking pretty rusty; but after they'd jumped overboard and took a swim it chippered them up a good deal. After breakfast the king he took a seat on the corner of the raft, and pulled off his boots and rolled up his britches, and let his legs dangle in the water, so as to be comfortable, and lit his pipe, and went to getting his "Romeo and Juliet" by heart.

Declaration of Independence

In Congress, July 4th, 1776.

The Unanimous Declaration of the Thirteen United States of America.

When, in the course of human events, it becomes necessary for one people to dissolve the political bands which have connected them with another, and to assume among the powers of the earth, the separate and equal station to which the laws of nature and of nature's God entitle them, a decent respect to the opinions of mankind requires that they should declare the causes which impel them to the separation

We hold these truths to be self-evident — that all men are created equal ; that they are endowed by their Creator, with certain unalienable rights ; that among these are life, liberty, and the pursuit of happiness. That to secure these rights, governments are instituted among men, deriving their just powers from the consent of the governed ; that whenever any form of government becomes destructive of these ends, it is the right of the people to alter or to abolish it, and to institute new government, laying its foundation on such principles, and organizing its powers in such form, as to them shall seem most likely to effect their safety and happiness. Prudence, indeed, will dictate, that governments long established, should not be changed for light and transient causes ; and, accordingly, all experience has shown that mankind are more disposed to suffer, while evils are sufferable, than to right themselves by abolishing the forms to which they are accustomed But when a long train of abuses and usurpations, pursuing invariably the same object, evinces a design to reduce them under absolute despotism, it is their right, it is their duty, to throw off such government, and to provide new guards for their future security. Such has been the patient sufferance of these colonies, and such is now the necessity which constrains them to alter their former systems of government. The history of the present king of Great Britain, is a history of repeated injuries and usurpations, all having in direct object the establishment of an absolute tyranny over these states. To prove this. let facts be submitted to a candid world.

He has refused his assent to laws, the most wholesome and necessary for the public good.

He has forbidden his governors to pass laws of immediate and pressing importance, unless suspended in their operation till his assent should be obtained ; and when so suspended he has utterly neglected to attend to them.

He has refused to pass other laws, for the accommodation of large districts of people, unless those people would relinquish the right of representation in the legislature — a right inestimable to them, and formidable to tyrants only.

He has called together legislative bodies, at places unusual, uncomfortable, and distant from the depository of their public records, for the sole purpose of fatiguing them into compliance with his measures.

He has dissolved representative houses, repeatedly, for opposing with manly firmness his invasions on the rights of the people.

He has refused, for a long time after such dissolutions, to cause others to be elected ; whereby the legislative powers, incapable of annihilation, have returned to the people at large, for their exercise ; the state remaining, in the meantime, exposed to all the dangers of invasion from without, and convulsions within.

He has endeavored to prevent the population of these states ; for that purpose obstructing the laws for naturalization of foreigners ; refusing to pass others to encourage their migrations hither, and raising the conditions of new appropriations of lands.

He has obstructed the administration of justice, by refusing his assent to laws, for establishing judiciary powers.

He has made judges dependant on his will alone for the tenure of their offices, and the amount and payment of their salaries.

He has erected a multitude of new offices, and sent hither swams of officers, to harass our people, and eat out their substance.

He has kept among us, in time of peace, standing armies, without the consent of our legislatures.

He has affected to render the military independent of, and superior to, the civil power.

He has combined with others to subject us to a jurisdiction, foreign to our constitution, and unacknowledged by our laws ; giving his assent to their acts of pretended legislation.

For quartering large bodies of armed troops among us :

For protecting them, by a mock trial, from punishment for any murders which they should commit on the inhabitants of these states :

For cutting off our trade with all parts of the world :

For imposing taxes on us without our consent :

For depriving us, in many cases, of the benefits of trial by jury :

For transporting us beyond seas, to be tried for pretended offences :

For abolishing the free system of English laws in a neighboring province, establishing therein an arbitrary government, and enlarging its boundaries, so as to render it at once an example and fiti instrument for introducing the same absolute rule into these colonies :

For taking away our charters, abolishing our most valuable laws, and altering fundamentally the forms of our governments :

For suspending our own legislatures, and declaring themselves invested with power to legislate for us in all cases whatsoever.

He has abdicated government here, by declaring us out of his protection, and waging war against us.

He has plundered our seas, ravaged our coasts, burnt our towns, and destroyed the lives of our people.

He is at this time, transporting large armies of foreign mercenaries to complete the works of death, desolation, and tyranny, already begun, with circumstances of cruelty and perfidy scarcely paralleled in the most barbarous ages, and totally unworthy the head of a civilized nation.

He has constrained our fellow-citizens, taken captive on the high seas, to bear arms against their country, to become the executioners of their friends and brethren, or to fall themselves by their hands.

He has excited domestic insurrections among us, and has endeavored to bring on the inhabitants of our frontiers, the merciless Indian savages, whose known rule of warfare is an undistinguished destruction of all ages, sexes, and conditions.

In every stage of these oppressions, we have petitioned for redress in the most humble terms ; our repeated petitions have been answered only by repeated injury. A prince whose character is thus marked by every act which may define a tyrant, is unfit to be the ruler of a free people.

Nor have we been wanting in attention to our British brethren. We have warned them from time to time of attempts by their legislature, to extend an unwarrantable jurisdiction over us. We have reminded them of the circumstances of our emigration and settlement here. We have appealed to their native justice and magnanimity, and we have conjured them by the ties of our common kindred to disavow these usurpations, which would inevitably interrupt our connexions and correspondence. They, too, have been deaf to the voice of justice and consanguinity. We must, therefore, acquiesce in the necessity which denounces our separation, and hold them, as we hold the rest of mankind — enemies in war — in peace, friends.

We, therefore, the representatives of the United States of America, in general congress assembled, appealing to the Supreme Judge of the world for the rectitude of our intentions, do, in the name and by the authority of the good people of these colonies, solemnly publish and declare, that these United Colonies are, and of right ought to be, free and independent states — That they are absolved from all allegiance to the British crown, and that all political connexion between them and the state of Great Britain is, and ought to be, totally dissolved; and that, as free and independent states, they have full power to levy war, conclude peace, contract alliances, establish commerce, and to do all other acts and things which independent states may of right do. And for the support of this declaration, with a firm reliance on the protection of Divine Providence we mutually pledge to each other our lives, our fortunes, and our sacred honor

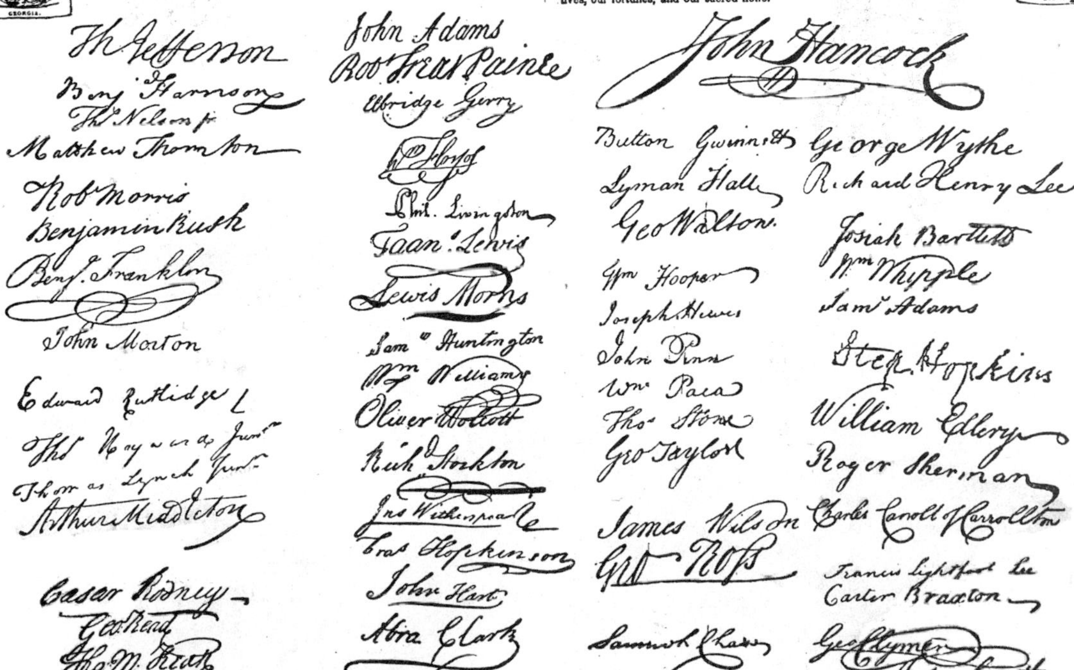

2.34 The US Declaration of Independence, 1776, set in Caslon.

GROUP 3: TRANSITIONAL

Here the axis of the curves has become vertical, with bracketed oblique serifs. The construction of each letter is on a mathematical basis, and the major example is Baskerville, which is wide for its x-height.

2.33c Transitional:
Baskerville.
Mind your Ps & Qs
ABCDEFGHIJKLMNOP
QRSTUVWXYZ
abcdefghijklmnopqrstuv
wxyz
1234567890
(.,:;*?$[“&”]‘%’!)

It was after sun-up now, but we went right on and didn’t tie up. The king and the duke turned out by and by looking pretty rusty; but after they’d jumped overboard and took a swim it chippered them up a good deal. After breakfast the king he took a seat on the corner of the raft, and pulled off his boots and rolled up his britches, and let his legs dangle in the water, so as to be comfortable, and lit his pipe, and went to getting his “Romeo and Juliet” by heart.

GROUP 4: DIDONE

There is an abrupt contrast between the thick and the thin strokes; the axis of the curves is completely vertical; and serifs are horizontal, unbracketed, and hairline. This grouping is also called “modern.” The name is a contraction of *Did*ot and Bo*doni*, and other examples include Caledonia.

2.33d Didone: Bodoni.
Mind your Ps & Qs
ABCDEFGHIJKLMNOPQRS
TUVWXYZ
abcdefghijklmnopqrstuvwxyz
1234567890
(.,:;*?$[“&”]‘%’!)

It was after sun-up now, but we went right on and didn’t tie up. The king and the duke turned out by and by looking pretty rusty; but after they’d jumped overboard and took a swim it chippered them up a good deal. After breakfast the king he took a seat on the corner of the raft, and pulled off his boots and rolled up his britches, and let his legs dangle in the water, so as to be comfortable, and lit his pipe, and went to getting his “Romeo and Juliet” by heart.

GROUP 5: MECHANISTIC

Also known as slab-serif or Egyptian, these faces have heavy square ended serifs, with or without brackets. Examples include Clarendon, Melior, and Rockwell.

2.33e Mechanistic:
Rockwell.
Mind your Ps & Qs
ABCDEFGHIJKLMNOPQR
STUVWXYZ
abcdefghijklmnopqrstuv
wxyz
1234567890
(.,:;*?$[“&”]‘%’!)

It was after sun-up now, but we went right on and didn’t tie up. The king and the duke turned out by and by looking pretty rusty; but after they’d jumped overboard and took a swim it chippered them up a good deal. After breakfast the king he took a seat on the corner of the raft, and pulled off his boots and rolled up his britches, and let his legs dangle in the water, so as to be comfortable, and lit his pipe, and went to getting his “Romeo and Juliet” by heart.

GROUP 6: LINEAL

Better known as sans serif, these faces are further subdivided into:

- Grotesque, the original 19th-century faces with a “closed” appearance, e.g. Grot and Headline
- Neo-grot, which are rounded and open with a monoline weight, e.g. Helvetica and Univers

2.33f Neo-Grot sans serif:
Helvetica.
Mind your Ps & Qs
ABCDEFGHIJKLMNOPQ
RSTUVWXYZ
abcdefghijklmnopqrstuv
wxyz
1234567890
(.,:;*?$[“&”]‘%’!)

It was after sun-up now, but we went right on and didn’t tie up. The king and the duke turned out by and by looking pretty rusty; but after they’d jumped overboard and took a swim it chippered them up a good deal. After breakfast the king he took a seat on the corner of the raft, and pulled off his boots and rolled up his britches, and let his legs dangle in the water, so as to be comfortable, and lit his pipe, and went to getting his “Romeo and Juliet” by heart.

GROUP 6: LINEAL continued

- Geometric, based on the geometric shapes of the Bauhaus, such as circles and straight lines, e.g. Futura
- Humanist sans serif, based on more classical proportions, e.g. Gill Sans and Optima

2.33g Geometric sans serif: Futura.
Mind your Ps & Qs
ABCDEFGHIJKLMNOPQ
RSTUVWXYZ
abcdefghijklmnopqrstu
vwxyz
1234567890
(.,:;*?$["&"]'%'!)

It was after sun-up now, but we went right on and didn't tie up. The king and the duke turned out by and by looking pretty rusty; but after they'd jumped overboard and took a swim it chippered them up a good deal. After breakfast the king he took a seat on the corner of the raft, and pulled off his boots and rolled up his britches, and let his legs dangle in the water, so as to be comfortable, and lit his pipe, and went to getting his "Romeo and Juliet" by heart.

GROUP 7: GLYPHIC

These faces look chiseled rather than written, with blunt elephant's foot serifs. The example here is Albertus.

ABCDEFGHIJKLMNOPQ
RSTUVWXYZ
abcdefghijklmnopqrstuvwxyz
1234567890

GROUP 8: SCRIPT

Script faces imitate cursive or "copperplate" writing. They can be formal, e.g. the Palace Script shown here, or informal, e.g. Flash. They are not normally used as text faces, but are reserved for jobs such as wedding invitations or menus.

ABCDEFGHIJKLMNO
PQRSTUVWXYZ
abcdefghijklmnopqrstuvwxyz
1234567890

GROUP 9: GRAPHIC

This group includes faces that look as if they have been drawn, rather than written. Examples are Cartoon (shown here) and Klang.

ABCDEFGHIJKLMN
OPQRSTUVWXYZ
1234567890

To this classification scheme ought to be added a group to include the digital faces created recently on dtp systems (see later) mainly for the style magazines of the 1980s, e.g. Modula and Emigré, and the so-called "intelligent" faces such as Beowulf.

Despite the best efforts of the classifiers, there still remain some typefaces that defy categorization, and which can only be described as being "hybrids." These include the best known typeface of all – Times New Roman – which has to be described as a Garalde/Didone hybrid. There are two other points to make about typefaces: first, not all versions of a named typeface are the same (Fig. 2.35). There are many versions and interpretations of Univers and Times for example, and if you are not precise in specifying a particular vendor's Univers, you may be in for a surprise, especially when an accurate cast-off has been attempted.

Second, for copyright reasons, the same design of typeface may have a different name (often thinly disguised to give a clue to its origin) when obtained from a source other than its originator. For example, Bitstream's version of Plantin is called Aldine 721, Linotype's Futura Book is called Spartan Book, and Compugraphics' Helvetica is renamed Helios.

2.35 Many classic letterpress typefaces have been redesigned over the years, first for phototypesetting and lately for dtp. Note how recent versions often have greater x-heights, thicker serifs, and a more condensed appearance. This is to accommodate changing needs in both technology and fashion. Shown contrasted here are Monotype's Century Old Style and ITC's Century Book, and both Monotype and ITC versions of Garamond and Garamond Italic. (ITC faces are printed in red.)

ABCDEFGHIJKLMNOPQRSTUVWXYZ
abcdefghijklmnopqrstuvwxyz

ABCDEFGHIJKLMNOPQRSTUVWXYZ
abcdefghijklmnopqrstuvwxyz

ABCDEFGHIJKLMNOPQRSTUVWXYZ
abcdefghijklmnopqrstuvwxyz

ABCDEFGHIJKLMNOPQRSTUVWXYZ
abcdefghijklmnopqrstuvwxyz

ABCDEFGHIJKLMNOPQRSTUVWXYZ
abcdefghijklmnopqrstuvwxyz

ABCDEFGHIJKLMNOPQRSTUVWXYZ
abcdefghijklmnopqrstuvwxyz

CAUTION.

Whereas, it is understood that the Practice of

SELLING BEER

IN PRIVATE HOUSES,

Without a Licence, prevails to a considerable extent in this neighbourhood.

Now, I GIVE NOTICE and WARNING, that if the Occupier of any House erected on the Property of the late EDMUND WILLIAMS, Esq., of Maesruddud, be detected in the above illegal Practice, he will not only be proceeded against for the Penalty, but measures will be taken to forfeit the Lease under which the Premises may be held.

Dated this 8th October, 1851,

A. WADDINGTON,

SOLICITOR TO THE ESTATE.

H. HUGHES, PRINTER, BOOKBINDER, AND STATIONER, PONTYPOOL.

2.36 Maximum legibility is always required for warning signs. This poster, dated 1851, was printed by letterpress – the word "CAUTION" using wooden type, the rest in metal.

LEGIBILITY AND READABILITY

One of the most important concerns of the graphic designer is to ensure that any type used is legible and readable. The intention, after all, is to communicate the author's or copywriter's ideas to the reader as efficiently as possible. If the type makes an aesthetically pleasing "picture" on the page as well, then that's a bonus.

For legibility, context is everything (Fig. 2.36). Novels, cookery books, and telephone directories are all read in different ways. The designer has to know the conditions in which the type will be read, who will be reading it, and why.

Faces with quirky letters, like the Q in Bookman and the g in Galliard Italic, can begin to annoy when set in continuous text. And a display face for advertising or a logo has a completely different purpose to that of a face for a children's book. A logo, for example, may initially be harder to read, but in the long term is more memorable and recognizable. The instant legibility of type on freeway signs is a matter of life and death.

Legibility, however, is a cultural matter. Unless they are German-speaking, many people find "black face" lettering difficult to understand. Graffiti on subway trains are unreadable by most people over 15.

There has been much research on the legibility of sans versus seriffed faces. The outcome seems to be that faces with serifs are easier to read continuously over long periods than those without. Serifs serve several purposes. They help letters to keep their distance. They link letters to make words, for we read by recognizing the shapes of words. They also help to differentiate letterforms, particularly the top halves, which are apparently more critical for rapid recognition. Faces with a large x-height, favored by newspapers, do not guarantee legibility, for the relatively short ascenders and descenders may have a negative effect on the overall shape of a word.

Sans serif faces, especially geometric ones like Futura, have a (purposely) high degree of similarity between sorts. Try to distinguish for example 1, I, and l out of context! For some faces there are versions specially designed for continuous setting. Futura Book, for example, is just such a version of Futura. But the matter is highly subjective. Some assert that sans serif faces set in blocks of text look monotonous and hence intrinsically less attractive.

Italic is said to be less legible than roman, so much so that the typographer Sir Francis Meynell recommended that poetry be set in italic because it ought to be read slowly!

For print to be legible, words should be set close to each other, and certainly closer than the space between lines of type. If the gap between words is too great, the eye will skip to the next line rather than the next word. So all continuous text matter is made easier to read by increasing the leading. Of course, there are some exceptions to this rule – for television graphics and on traffic signs, for example.

Legibility also has a part to play in deciding the width of columns. If the line is longer than about 12 words (or seven words in newspaper setting), the eye will have difficulty in returning to find the next line.

Black on white setting, too, is considered to be more readable than reversed out white on black (abbreviated WOB), where hairline serifs, for example, can be lost and horizontal spacing can look too cramped. Text all set in capitals, as in telexes, can be very tiring on the eye.

Legibility can be achieved by observing common-sense rules like these. Readability is something else. It entices readers to continue reading what you have designed, and that takes care, skill, and talent!

Part 3: typesetting systems

There are many ways of producing type. Most graphic designers will eventually be using offset lithography for print, and this process demands input in the form of film – a photographic image of the page to be printed. This may be made from a mechanical (see Chapter 4) or come direct from a dtp system. The typesetting used as raw material in compiling the mechanical may in turn come from metal type, in the form of a reproduction proof, or it may be a bromide print from a phototypesetting machine, or a piece of hand lettering.

Other print technologies, such as flexography and silkscreen rely on similar processes – some newspapers even print on letterpress machines from phototypeset mechanicals. Each method of typesetting has its role and its place, though some methods (e.g. so-called "strike-on" from the IBM Selectric typewriter) are rapidly becoming obsolete, and are discussed here only for the sake of completeness.

Hand lettering and calligraphy

It is an amusing exercise to try to work out the very least expensive way to produce a book, magazine, or any other publication. If you have all the time in the world, the cheapest production method of all must be to handwrite every single copy.

Since the development of photolithography and, more recently, the introduction of fast high-quality photocopying machines, the idea of handwriting a whole book is not as crazy as it may first appear. Many books have been produced this way, and curiously it is typographers who tend to favor this quirky approach. Fernand Baudin's book *How Typography Works (and Why it is Important)* has been produced almost entirely by reproducing the author's best handwriting (Fig. 2.37).

2.37 Text does not necessarily have to be typeset. Typographers like Fernand Baudin are very fond of their own handwriting, as demonstrated in these pages from his manual *How Typography Works (and Why it is Important)*.

Above: letters with a small x-height. On the facing page letters with a large x-height. The size is identical in both cases. The difference is in the contrast between the normal letters and the ascenders & descenders. All ascenders line at the top. All descenders line at the bottom. But the normal letters are much deeper on the facing page: And the descenders & ascenders are shorter accordingly. Traditionally the smaller x-height is for book-typography. The Italian Renaissance marks a return to the Carolingian alphabet & the progressive elimination of Gothic letter-forms. The black-letter, however, was never totally eliminated. In Germany, in Switzerland it is ever-present. Nor is it absent in Britain & the U.S. It would be a real loss for typography & calligraphy if it were to disappear altogether. A larger x-height has been popularised by newspapers. The poor quality of newsprint & the speed of the printing process combine to fill in the bowls of a b d e g o p q. Technology may change. Not so the letterforms, the text columns. For more than a century the newspaper has met the expectations of millions. It is therefore easier to carry on than to try to change their visual habits.

NEW

ADZIDO
PAN AFRICAN DANCE ENSEMBLE

Shakespeare Alabama

CLOUD NINE

Books of Bale

BODY

BOO YAA T·R·I·B·E

ACHEQUE BY RETURN

ALL ABOUT EVE

Vicinanza

Auberge

The Complete Calligrapher

fashion

anima

Reflexe

The WEAVER'S DAUGHTER

Menuhin
EDITION

Signature

The Queen

PAUL YOUNG

DICKENS SECOND HAND BOOK SHOP

Merry Christmas Southsiders!

MICHAEL BALDWIN HOLOFERNES

BLACK SWAN

Cuvée Marie d'Ecosse

2.38 (opposite) Calligraphy can be mixed effectively with typesetting in advertisements and on book covers, as in these examples by Carol Kemp.

2.39 (below) Dtp software can turn your handwriting into a usable font, as demonstrated by these commercially available typefaces from two Dutch designers: Erik van Blokland's Erikrighthand and Just van Rossum's Justlefthand.

Calligraphy is handwriting's beautiful cousin (Fig. 2.38), and is often used on the title pages of books. A grounding in calligraphy is essential for a proper understanding of good typography and graphic design, and its practise is to be encouraged. The famous German designer Jan Tschichold wrote in 1949, "All my knowledge of letter spacing, word spacing, and leading is due to my calligraphy, and it is for this reason that I regret very much that calligraphy is so little studied in our time."

Handwriting and calligraphy have long been copied in type. Script and brush faces are "cleaned up" versions of hand lettering. And with dtp it is possible to invent your personal font based on your own hand (Fig. 2.39).

JUST LEFTHAND : A B C D E F G H I J K L M
N O P Q R S T U V W X Y Z A B C D E F G H
I J K L M N O P Q R S T U V W X Y Z 1 2 3 4 5
6 7 8 9 0 ! @ # £ $ % ^ & * ( ) _ + < > ?

Eric Righthand : A B C D E F G H I J K L M N O
P Q R S T U V W X Y Z a b c d e f g h i j k l m
n o p q r s t u v w x y z 1 2 3 4 5 6 7 8 9 0
! @ # £ $ % ^ & * ( ) _ + < > ?

ERIC RIGHTHAND CAPS : A B C D E F G H I J K L
M N O P Q R S T U V W X Y Z A B C D E F G H I
J K L M N O P Q R S T U V W X Y Z 1 2 3 4 5 6
7 8 9 0 ! @ # £ $ % ^ & * ( ) _ + < > ?

"Strike-on" or "cold-metal" setting

Cutting and pasting of existing type, as in the punk blackmail-style designs of album covers by Jamie Reed in the late 1970s, is a form of **cold-metal setting**. Another form is the rub-down dry-transfer lettering used for display type from vendors such as Letraset. The vinyl letters are transferred one by one onto paper or board, and then pressure is applied through the backing sheet to "fix" the lettering in place. This is called **burnishing** (Fig. 2.40).

With **strike-on setting**, the marks made at the time of setting are those that will go under the camera for printing by the offset litho process. There is no intermediate processing required.

Type *can* be set using a regular typewriter (for menus, for example). Typeset-quality typewriters designed for the purpose were introduced during the 1960s. The IBM Selectric has fonts of 88 characters arranged around a "golfball" print head. It uses a 9-unit system of proportional spacing, and has "real" fonts such as Univers and Times. For justified setting, each line has to be typed twice, as the first attempt is used to calculate the amount of space needed between words.

The VariTyper has an open carriage, to tackle greater widths of setting than the IBM, and can handle two fonts at a time, each of 99 characters. These machines represented a breakthrough at the time, and replaced hot metal for many low cost jobs, but by today's standards the setting looks crude and poorly spaced.

2.40 Rub-down lettering, from suppliers such as Letraset, revolutionized graphic design in the 1970s and remains a cost effective way of originating display type, borders, textures, and symbols. It must be applied carefully to prevent break-up.

Hot metal: hand and machine setting

The method of setting type from hot lead remained virtually unchanged from the time of Gutenberg until the invention of the punch-cutting machine by the American Linn Boyd Benton in 1884. This paved the way for the Linotype machine in 1886 and the Monotype machine a year later.

But whereas machine setting has been superseded by phototypesetting, handsetting is still used whenever beautiful typography is demanded for high-quality publications and limited-edition poetry books.

For handsetting, the compositor takes individual metal sorts and spaces from a typecase and places them one by one into a **composing stick** (Fig. 2.41) that has been adjusted to the correct measure. Capital letters are taken from the upper case, and small letters from the lower case. The sizes of the compartments in the typecase reflect the popularity of certain sorts. You will need more "e"s for example than "z"s in an average job. Less frequently used fonts are kept in drawers under the typecase.

When the composing stick is full, the setting is transferred to a **galley** on the **imposing table**, and the compositor returns to the typecase to set the next couple of lines. When the galley is full, a **proof** is taken on a hand-operated **proofing press**, and any mistakes are picked up and corrected by the proofreader, the designer, or copy editor.

A galley proof is a long thin strip of paper, and gives the designer an opportunity to see the setting before it is divided up into pages. This proof, when corrected, may be good enough to be used as a **reproduction proof**, or **repro**, if the setting is going to be cut up using a scalpel and incorporated into a mechanical.

2.41 (above) Inserting sorts from the lower typecase into the composing stick, where type is set, line by line, before being transferred to the chase.

If the setting is going to be printed – and hot-metal setting is the only kind of setting discussed here that *can* be printed directly – then the type is taken from the galley and placed into a page-sized contraption called a **chase**, and "locked up" (Fig. 2.42). The spaces and leading used to fill up the rest of the chase, often of wood, are collectively known as furniture. The locked-up chase is called a **forme**.

2.42 When the type, leading, and any process blocks are all flat and in place, the chase is packed with metal or wooden "furniture" and locked up. It is now called a forme and is ready to be inked and printed.

For small runs, the printing is made direct from the type in the chase. But for large jobs, and for newspapers and magazines, for example, where the type must be wrapped around a cylinder, a one-piece duplicate of the type, called a **stereotype** or **stereo** (Fig. 2.43), has to be made from a *papier-mâché* mold called a **mat** or **flong**.

Once the stereo has been made, or the pages printed, the type is then cleaned and returned (the word used in the trade is "distributed") to the typecases. Extra care has to be taken to get this right, compositors being told "to mind their 'p's and 'q's."

The **Linotype** machine (Fig. 2.44) was invented by Ottmar Mergenthaler of Baltimore in 1886 to automate the casting of type. Whole lines of type (hence the name from line o' type) called **slugs** are set in one operation. A compositor keys in the text, and as it is typed, molds of the letters to be cast fall into place. Wedge-shaped spacers are inserted between words, and when a line is complete, the compositor pulls a lever and these push the words apart to fill out the justified measure. Lead pours into the assembly, and out comes a slug of type. After the setting has been used, the slugs are melted down for re-use.

The **Monotype** machine, developed by Tolbert Lanston of Washington DC in 1887, sets type in individual sorts and, unlike the Linotype, uses a two-stage process. The compositor sits at the keyboard and inputs the text which is coded onto a perforated roll of paper. When the end of a line approaches, a bell rings and it is left to the compositor's skill to calculate the spaces needed between words to justify the line. This information is keyed in at the end of each line. When the job is complete, the roll of paper is inserted into a typecasting machine *back to front*, so that the spacing information precedes the text it adjusts, and the type is cast individually.

2.43 (above) Metal type cannot be used directly on a rotary letterpress machine. It must first be made into a curved plate known as a stereotype, which is then wrapped around the press cylinder ready for printing.

The advantage of the Monotype machine over the Linotype one is that corrections can be made using pre-cast sorts. This is especially useful for book production. With the Linotype method, the whole line has to be reset and replaced. As a consequence, Linotype machines are mostly used for newspaper and magazine work where speed is of the essence, and where the effect of spilling the type, a catastrophy known as "printer's pie," is minimized.

2.44 The Linotype machine automated hot-metal setting. As the compositor keyed in the text, matrixes would fall into place and the type was set line by line from molten lead.

Phototypesetting

The popularity of offset litho as a printing process led to the development of new ways of setting type. With letterpress it is not easy to mix text with illustrations and photographs, and the opportunities for creative design are limited.

Phototypesetting, or **photosetting**, was first demonstrated to the American Newspaper Publishers' Association in 1949 by Rene Higgonet and Louis Marius Moyroud, but did not become popular until the 1960s. Like a Monotype system, it comprises two separate parts. The compositor sits at a keyboard and generates paper or magnetic tape. This is then transferred to the **imagesetter**, where the bromide or film is exposed. In the earliest systems, light was projected through a matrix of tiny photographic negative images of the font's sorts onto photosensitive bromide paper or film. Later, the fonts were stored digitally, and reconstructed using CRTs (cathode ray tubes); now lasers are used (Figs 2.45 and 2.46).

Photosetting gives the designer many advantages over hot metal. Letters can be set closer together. They can be set touching, or even overlapping.

It is also possible, by means of mirrors and prisms, to distort type. Oblique (slanted) letters can be created from roman type, and headlines can be condensed or expanded to fit a given width.

Type produced by photosetting is sharper than the equivalent hot-metal setting. Hot metal is always proofed to paper, and no matter how carefully the ink is applied, it will be squeezed between the face of the type and the paper and there will be some spread. A typeface such as Bodoni, with its extremely fine serifs, was designed to be pressed into paper – photoset versions of Bodoni had to be redesigned with thicker serifs.

With photosetting, type can be set ahead of a type specification – the text is keyed in and the size, face, and measure are added later. The same text can be used over and over, in different forms. Any metal type to be re-used had to be stored as "standing matter." This was costly and took up lots of space. With photosetting, type for dictionaries and telephone directories, for example, can be stored on tape, and updated later.

2.45 A screen shot of a letter outline being designed for phototypesetting. Note that the space between the letter n and the next letter is an integral part of the design of the "font metrics."

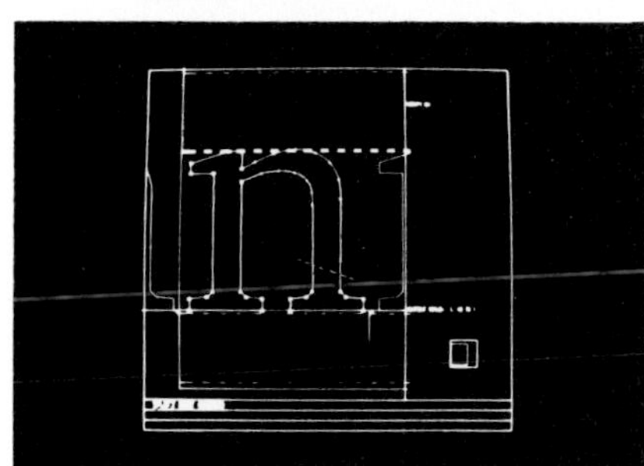

2.46 A bitmap of a Baskerville Bold capital B, showing how individual pixels are edited for optimum appearance at the laser printer resolution of 300 dpi.

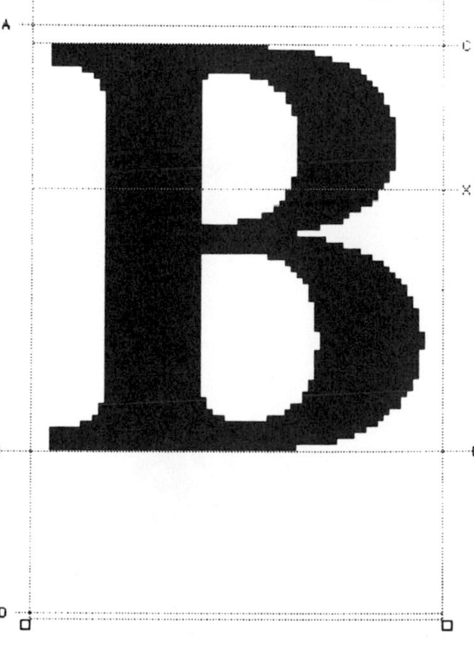

Desktop publishing

A photosetting machine may look like a regular computer, but setting is all it can do. A dtp system, on the other hand, makes use of a standard off-the-shelf computer to produce a floppy or hard disc full of information that is then input to the imagesetter that generates the bromide paper or film. It does much more besides.

MORE CHOICE OF TYPEFACES

Perhaps the most apparent effect of dtp on graphic designers is that they have a much greater range of typefaces to choose from. With early photosetting, and even more so with strike-on technology, the user was offered any typeface . . . so long as it was Times, Univers, or Helvetica. There are currently some 6000 different typefaces available that can be used with dtp systems. So-called "expert sets" add ligatures, small caps, swash caps, non-aligning numerals, fractions, and superior/inferior figures to the basic fonts.

To produce a typeface in hot metal was an enormous and costly undertaking, requiring a huge investment in both time and money. Most of the great typographers of the past are known for just one or maybe two typefaces. The same is true for photosetting. Particular typefaces were tied to particular machines. Thus if you had a Linotype machine, you could use only faces from the Linotype library. Similarly, if you had a Berthold machine, you could use only type from Berthold.

If a typographer went to Berthold with a new idea for a typeface, its production would be extremely expensive and its distribution limited to the number of Berthold machines worldwide.

But with dtp it is possible to design a brand new face, copy it onto a floppy disc or CD-rom, and distribute it for use by thousands of other designers within weeks.

QUALITY AND FLEXIBILITY OF DTP

The pace of progress in dtp means that the few advantages of other technologies are fast disappearing. Dtp is being adopted by both the printing and the design industries. Yet hot metal has always held one advantage over photosetting, that of visual quality.

In hot metal, each size of a typeface has been designed individually. Thus, for legibility, the small sizes have a relatively larger x-height and a wider set width. Bigger sizes have daintier serifs and more subtle distinctions between the parts of the letterform, created by enlarging or reducing one of these **font masters**.

In dtp and photosetting, all sizes are created by **scaling** (enlarging or reducing) one font master, usually 12pt, designed as the best compromise. There have been some concessions to creating different designs for different sizes. Times Ten Roman, for example, is a version of Times New Roman that works better at small sizes. But the problem of legibility at smaller sizes has usually been solved by a more widespread use of tracking.

Photosetting machines can be used to expand and condense type, but this always distorts the overall proportions of the letterform. A Futura E, for example, when condensed will have a vertical stroke thinner than the horizontals.

By sloping roman letterforms, a photosetting system can create an oblique – but not an italic – version of the typeface. A true italic font has entirely different designs for many of its letters. Look at the a, f, and g of an italic face (Fig. 2.47).

Roman & afg

Oblique & afg

Italic & afg

2.47 Photosetting and dtp software can concoct a kind of italic by slanting the roman font. This is better termed an oblique variant, as a true italic has different designs from the roman for most letters, with more cursive serifs.

Any dtp system can perform these kinds of distortions. They can embolden letters too, and produce combinations of italic, bold, outline, and shadow (Fig. 2.48). But the results bear little aesthetic relationship to the original "plain" letterforms. The design intention of the typographer will have been lost.

MultiMaster from Adobe is a technology that incorporates non-linear scaling into dtp typefaces. It uses mathematical formulas to retain relationships between the stroke weights of individual letterforms, and intercharacter spacing is adjusted appropriately. It is possible to encode a font master with information that describes the shapes of small, medium, and large versions of the typeface, and the computer will interpolate all the gradations in between.

With photosetting and dtp, the graphic designer has never been restricted to the standard list of point sizes available from the hot-metal type foundries. In PageMaker 4, for example, type can be any size from 4pt to 650pt in 0·1pt increments; leading can be defined in 0·1pt increments; and letters can be kerned to within 0·01 of an em. Type can be stretched or condensed from 5 to 250 percent. MultiMaster automatically generates the correct weight/width shape for any specified size.

2.48 Desktop publishing software can also take a roman font and "style" it in various ways. Most programs can create bold, outline, shadowed, and reversed out variants. More specialized software, such as FreeHand, can be used, for example, to set type along a curve, and to apply "fill and stroke" to a letterform.

BOLD

STROKE & FILL

SHADOW

SET ALONG A CURVE

OR AROUND A CIRCLE

ZOOM

OUTLINE

REVERSE

FANCY FILLS

TYPE MANIPULATION AND CUSTOM FONT DESIGN

Dtp systems, such as Aldus PageMaker and Quark XPress, are able to adjust the size of type to fit a certain space, condensing or expanding it to the limits of legibility.

Drawing programs (more of which in Chapter 3) such as Aldus FreeHand and Adobe Illustrator allow text, for example, to be set around an ellipse or along a freeform curve. More specialized packages, such as LetraStudio, permit more extreme distortions (Fig. 2.49). The designer creates graphical "envelopes" into which the text is squeezed and contorted to fit.

With programs such as Fontographer and FontStudio (Fig. 2.50), you can tweak existing faces to your own preferences – FontStudio, for example, has a "serif bay" with which the serif style of a face can be changed quickly. Alternatively, you can create entirely new faces from scratch. A "tween" function in FontStudio allows a new font to be created from two similar existing fonts by interpolating their features. It is this power of dtp that horrifies traditional typographers. Here, a knowledge of typography, however rudimentary, is essential to prevent the novice from falling into the pitfalls learnt the hard way throughout the history of type.

2.49 Software such as LetraStudio can be used to distort letters and words mathematically. Previously, the lettering would have to have been drawn laboriously by hand.

2.50 (below) New custom fonts can be designed letter by letter using programs such as Fontographer and FontStudio. These programs can also import existing typefaces, which can then be adapted to your own taste.

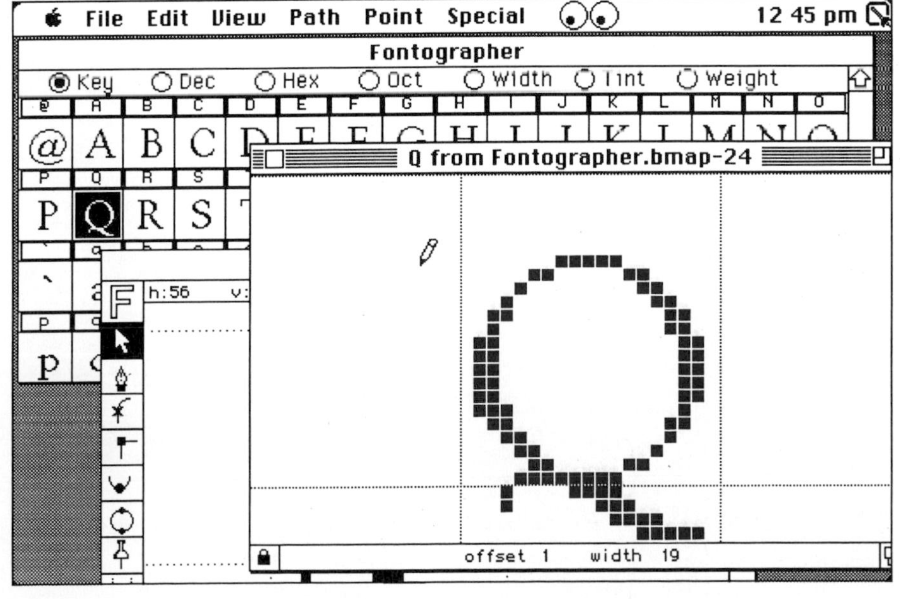

David Collier of DeCode Design recommends that faces be invented in the following order. First, design the capital I to establish the stem thickness and overall "weight" of the font. Next, the O establishes the weight of the curves and the angles of stress. The E defines the weight of the crossbars, and the V the relative thickness of the downstrokes. These are ideally followed by W, S, R, and P. Be aware of optical variations in the other letters – L, for example, should be narrower than E because of the extra space within it. The capital Q is rarely used, so offers scope for artistic flair. For lower case letters use a keyword, such as Hamburgers, that features letters with the ascenders, descenders, bowls, ears, and cross strokes used in the rest of the alphabet. Once that word looks right, the elements created can be used to design the rest of the sorts.

McVAY S.T,
18 Swan Copse,Mansfield Rd 25...708 0761
T, 9 Hollington Cres 33 ... 784 7037
McVEAGH J.G.R, 211 Castle La,Solihull ... 743 3266
W, 69 Damson La,Solihull ... 705 7866
McVEICH S, 171 Jayshaw Av 43 ... 357 5933
McVEIGH A, 63 New Coventry Rd 26 ... 742 8955
D.F, 5 Bernard Pl,Brookfield Rd 18 ... 554 2068
G, Warwick Rd,Solihull ... 705 6922
J, 16 Harvington Rd,Oldbury ... 422 4789
J.D, 17 Winton Gro,Sutton Coldfield ... 351 4406
J.M, 99 Miranda Clo 45 ... 453 9681
J.P, 49 Round Moor Wlk 35 ... 747 8542
M.F.P, 27 Prospect La,Solihull ... 744 5227
R.M, 8 Chiseldon Croft 14 ... 474 5165
McVEIGHTY D, 82 Audley Rd 33 ... 786 2946
D, 39 Este Rd 26 ... 783 0454
D, 67 Hilleys Croft 37 ... 770 1737
R, 62 Clarence Rd 13 ... 444 4088
McVEITH T, 37 Frankley La 31 ... 478 0534
MACVENAN M, 15 Overbrunton Clo 31 ... 477 2547
McVERRY B.P, 4 Chalybeate Clo 45 ... 453 8277
D, 24 Goodrest Croft 14 ... 430 4084
D.J, 17 Duncalfe Dv,Sutton Coldfield ... 308 5672
McVEY C.F, 19 Brownley Rd,Shirley ... 745 1015
J, 31 Beeches Wy 31 ... 477 8434
J, 158 Jayshaw Av 43 ... 357 4988
McVICAR A.J, 158 Swan Gdns 23 ... 373 0289
E.W, 38 Moorfield Dv,Sutton Coldfield ... 373 8366
McVICKER N.M, 78 Northdown Rd,Solihull ... 705 8822
R.P, 43 Heybarnes Rd 10 ... 773 7558
MACVIE F.E,
Fiddlers Gn,Blackford Hl...**Henley-in-A** 2819
Mrs M.H, 72 Marsh Hl 23 ... 373 2702
McVITTY P.J, 312 Sarehole Rd 28 ... 777 5775
McWALTER I.M,
30 Upper St. Mary's Rd,Smethwick...429 1297
J.W, 66 Hawkstone Rd 29 ... 475 6246
S.G, 207 Court Oak Rd 17 ... 427 9694
McWALTERS S.B,
11 Chadwick Rd,Sutton Coldfield...378 3693
McWATTS A.C,
6 Bannersgate Rd,Sutton Coldfield...355 1647
McWEE R.M, 29 Stanmore Gro,Halesowen ... 422 7767
McWEENEY L, 114 Junction Rd 21 ... 523 3828
McWHINNEY S.J, 6 Longmore Rd,Streetly ... 353 7526
McWHINNIE J.R.K,
282 Eachelhurst Rd,Sutton Coldfoield...351 2022
J.R.K,
282 Eachelhurst Rd,Sutton Coldfield...351 3382
W.R, 22 Widney Manor Rd,Solihull ... 705 8842
McWHIRTER D,
9 Spring Ho,Cooks Ct,Chester Rd 36...770 0970
D.C, 30 Greenfield Rd 17 ... 427 9679
D.L, 24 Fugelmere Clo 17 ... 429 4883
J, 28 St. Michaels Rd,Sutton Coldfield ... 354 6521
John D, 23 Maxholm Rd,Streetly ... 353 2850
P.J.K, 92 Devon Rd,Smethwick ... 429 1213
R, 17 Aldbourne Wy 38 ... 459 4503
R.M, 127 Manor La,Halesowen ... 550 1718
W.H.P, 188 Northfield Rd 17 ... 427 1736
McWILLIAM A.R, 30 Waldrons Moor 14 ... 444 2414
I, 38 Corbridge Rd,Sutton Coldfield ... 354 2558
I.R, 50 Meriden Rd ... **Hampton-in-A** 2015
J.W, 55 Colesbourne Rd,Solihull ... 742 3228
R, 108 West Av 20 ... 554 4261
R.C, 20 Galton Tower,Civic Clo 1 ... 236 4901
McWILLIAMS A.G,
32 Sandhills Cres,Solihull...704 9547
B, 126 Kingswood Rd 31 ... 477 6225
B.V, 4 Dornton Rd 30 ... 444 3788
C, 203 Albert Rd 6 ... 328 4676
C.P, 20 Hatherton Gro 29 ... 427 6854
E, 20 Somerset Rd 23 ... 384 4951
G, 306 Prince of Wales La 14 ... 430 3917
J.B, 18 Milner Rd 29 ... 472 7085
J.D, 3 Newells Rd 26 ... 742 1801
K, 103 Ashbrook Rd 30 ... 472 5807
N, 98 Manor Ho La 26 ... 743 2498
P.W, 56 Hodge Hill Rd 34 ... 783 7477
R, 28
R, 5 C
R, 14
S, 48
W.K,
MACWI

MACZK
MADAH
J.S, 1
T, 84
MADAN
V.P,
MADDA
MADDA
A.D,
B.M,
D.G,
G.W,
H, 41
J, 21
J.L, 2
M, 1 Chantry Dv,Halesowen ... 422 4339
R.G, 714 Hagley Rd Wst,Oldbury ... 422 7826
Sidney C, 4 Griffins Brook Clo 30 ... 459 3814
T.A, 212 Highters Hth La 14 ... 430 2472
MADDEN A, 54 Strathdene Rd 29 ... 472 1469
A, 2 Wilford Gro,Sutton Coldfield ... 351 3998
A, 256 Witton Ldg Rd 23 ... 350 6119
A.C, 41 Galton Tower,Civic Clo 1 ... 233 2935
B, 113 Heather Rd 10 ... 771 2140
C, 4 Sycamore Terr,Vicarage Rd 14 ... 444 0919
C, 257 West Boulevard 32 ... 427 6313
C.A, 548 Bromford La 8 ... 786 2021
C.W, 6 St Johns Rd,Oldbury ... 544 7941
D, 23 Court Oak Gro 17 ... 427 9851
D, 12 Elmwood Rd,Sutton Coldfield ... 353 3807
D, 40 Middle Dv 45 ... 445 2002
D, 73 St. Agathas Rd 8 ... 327 2379
D, 4 Sunnydale Wlk,W Bromwich ... 525 1518
D.M.J, 40 Sheldonfields Rd 26 ... 743 4350
D.S, 134 Kingsdown Av 42 ... 357 6662
E, 23 Eileen Rd 11 ... 449 0807
E, 105 Manor Ho La 26 ... 742 6515
E, 1/4 Ward End Pk Rd 8 ... 327 6308
F, 34 Cecil Rd 24 ... 373 4542
F, 19 Greswolde Ho,Cole Hall La 34 ... 784 9304
F.D, 71 All Saints Rd 14 ... 444 7512
G, 78 Spiceland Rd 31 ... 475 3988
G.S, 69 Woodcote Rd 24 ... 382 5991
H, 169 Douglas Rd 27 ... 706 7444

MADDEN H.A, 85 Naseby Rd 8 ... 327 5567
I, 11 Boldmere Clo,Sutton Coldfield ... 350 6027
I.M, 74 Worlds End Rd 20 ... 554 7649
J, 44 Amberley Gro 6 ... 356 8558
J, 266 Galton Rd,Smethwick ... 429 6179
J, 140 Knowle Rd 11 ... 777 8672
J, 3 Minster Dv 10 ... 773 3675
J, 37 Roughley Dv,Four Oaks ... 308 4882
James, 347 St. Benedicts Rd 10 ... 772 0748
J, 68 Tomey Rd 11 ... 772 0813
J, 137 Wellsgreen Rd,Solihull ... 743 2015
J, 5 Welwyndale Rd,Sutton Coldfield ... 373 6653
J, 61 Windmill La,Smethwick ... 565 3634
J, 21 Windsor St Nth 7 ... 359 0115
J.A, 91 Pinewood Dv 32 ... 422 0066
J.E, 64 Pitts Fm Rd 24 ... 350 5780
J.T, 100 Alston Rd,Solihull ... 704 1390
K.W, 37 Varlins Wy 38 ... 458 6997
L, 26 Chartley Rd 23 ... 328 3751
L, 7 Clodeshall Rd 8 ... 328 3186
L, 51 Ercall Clo 23 ... 356 0845
L, 331 Yardley Wood Rd 13 ... 449 8241
M, 12 Cecil Rd 24 ... 373 8447
M, 323 Guardian Ct,
Francey Beeches Rd 31...477 5078
Michael, 101 Livingstone Rd 20 ... 356 0701
M, 55 Norfolk Rd 23 ... 373 0753
Michael, 232 Somerville Rd 10 ... 773 9922
M, 7 Yew Tree La 26 ... 706 6797
Michael A, 51 Courtenay Rd 44 ... 360 4605
M.A, 75 Harrow Rd 29 ... 472 1056
M.J, 48 Brookvale Rd,Solihull ... 706 3076
M.J, 29 Link Rd 16 ... 454 7864
M.J, 50 Moorend La 24 ... 384 4518
N, 88 Pritchett Tower,Arthur St 10 ... 773 8947
P, 21 Ebley Rd 20 ... 523 9924
P, 7 Rawlins Croft 35 ... 749 3961
P.B, 101 Clodeshall Rd 8 ... 328 7530
P.J, 48 Broadway Ave,Halesowen ... 550 7879
P.J, 135 Oxhill Rd 21 ... 523 9704
R.F, 55 Hill La,Sutton Coldfield ... 308 4990
R.J, 3 Whitwell Clo,Solihull ... 744 7724
R.N, 303 Dovedale Rd 23 ... 382 7236
S, 27 Gladstone Rd 26 ... 706 5469
S.D, 14 St. Michaels Rd,Sutton Coldfield ... 355 5701
S.J, 376 Queslett Rd 43 ... 360 1421
T, 228 Millhouse Rd 25 ... 784 0182
T, 30 Station Rd 21 ... 554 2344
Timothy, 16 Westbury Rd,Wednesbury ... 526 3558
T.A, 22 Avenue Rd 14 ... 444 1597
T.H, 53 Allcroft Rd 11 ... 778 1379
T.J, 68 Hazelbeach Rd 8 ... 326 0974
T.S, 8 Daniels Rd 9 ... 773 1741
W, 7 Hilldrop Gro 17 ... 426 3667
W.A.L, 340 Hagley Rd Wst,Oldbury ... 422 8554
MADDERS G.R, 37 Quarry La,Halesowen ... 550 5409
G.T, 23 Rowton Dv,Streetly ... 353 6668
J.L, 9 Stourton Clo,Sutton Clodfield ... 329 3193
Max A, 6 Selly Clo 29 ... 472 1670

41 Moundsley Ho,Baverstock Rd 14...474 5139
MADDIX C, 8/8 Broadmeadow Clo 30 ... 459 4724
D, 33 Calder Tower,Birchfield Rd 20 ... 356 5853
Martin, 15 Heanor Croft 6 ... 328 3670

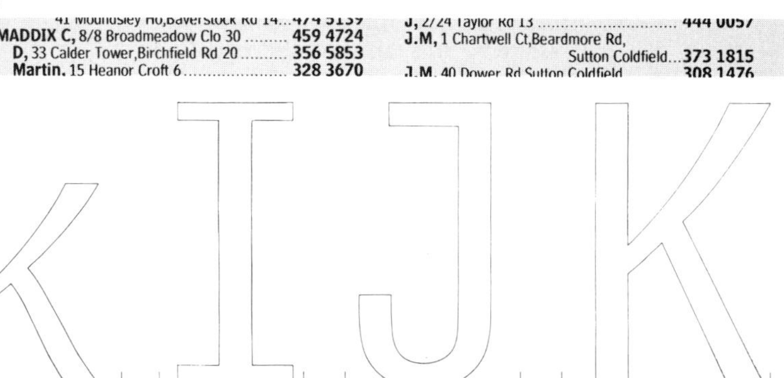

E.L, 16 Harbury Rd 12 ... 440 2185
F.M, 512 Kingsbury Rd 24 ... 350 2007
G, 31 Daimler Clo 36 ... 747 0199
I.F, 824 Pershore Rd 29 ... 472 2636
J, 1 Denise Dv 17 ... 427 2395
J, 28 Tinmeadow Cres 45 ... 453 5355
J.C, 1 Overbury Clo,Halesowen ... 550 4642
M, 8 Raven Hays Rd 31 ... 477 2201
N, 29 Marsham Rd 14 ... 430 5180
P, 38 Daisy Fm Rd 14 ... 474 5939
P, 46 Middle Pk Rd 29 ... 476 9146
P, 1 Pagnell Gro 13 ... 443 3851
R.A, 178 Franklin Rd 30 ... 458 7198
R.C, 119 Bell Holloway 31 ... 477 3973
R.S, 178 Gregory Av 29 ... 477 3372
S, 34 Hodgetts Clo,Smethwick ... 429 2362
S, 25 Pettit Clo 14 ... 430 5011
S.C, 48 Rowheath Rd 30 ... 459 0944
V, 8 Cherry Tree Ct,Woodfall Av 30 ... 451 3284
W, 73 Longford Rd 44 ... 354 5745
W.L, 129 Kineton Gn Rd,Solihull ... 708 2684
MADDON J, 229 Manningford Rd 14 ... 430 6295
MADDOX A, 192 Farnborough Rd 35 ... 747 8584
A, 12 The Hurstway 23 ... 382 5280
A.A, 84 Hales Rd,Wednesbury ... 556 1092
A.F, Plot B36,Hollywood Grange 47 ... 474 4057
A.J, 36 Cartwright Rd,Four Oaks ... 308 3020
A.J, 64 Park La,Wednesbury ... 556 2535
A.T, 42 Grosvenor Av,Streetly ... 353 4619

MADDOX B.T, 235 Hay Green La 30 ... 475 6050
C.D, 347 The Ridgeway 23 ... 331 4687
C.R, 37 Coniston Av,Solihull ... 743 6397
C.R, 26 Libbard Ho,Stonebow Ave,Solihull ... 705 8876
D, 1 Alcombe Gro 33 ... 784 9496
D, 20 Ashton Rd 25 ... 784 5873
D, 73 Newlands Rd 30 ... 451 2736
D.C, 38 Duncumb Rd,Sutton Coldfield ... 378 3508
D.M, 71 Babbington Rd 21 ... 523 0145
E, 139 Garretts Green La 26 ... 742 5777
E, 149 Nuthurst Rd 31 ... 476 6364
E, 2 Arbor Ct,Penns La,Sutton Coldfield ... 351 5636
E.S, 89 Monmouth Rd 32 ... 475 1892
F.C, 49 Milstead Rd 26 ... 784 6434
G, 54 Harleston Rd 44 ... 360 2212
G, 57 Surrey Cres,W Bromwich ... 502 1184
G, 26 Elm Croft,Windmill La,Smethwick ... 565 1169
H, 15 Bucknall Cres 32 ... 550 5836
H, 5 Middleton Rd,Shirley ... 744 4732
I, 41 Ansell Rd 24 ... 373 1003
J, 8 May La 47 ... **Wythall** 824209
J.R, 142 Birdbrook Rd 44 ... 360 1132
John W, 18 Elmfield Rd 36 ... 747 5667
K, 2 Ingram Gro 27 ... 778 2433
K.A, 28 Britwell Rd,Sutton Coldfield ... 355 3522
K.J, 2 Linford Gro 25 ... 783 5073
L, 801c Warwick Rd 11 ... 706 1305
L.L, 9 Ferndale Rd,Streetly ... 353 7885
M.E, 83 Stanton Rd 43 ... 358 7530
M.I, 510 Chester Rd 36 ... 770 5083
M.K, 42 Teesdale Ave 34 ... 730 2350
M.P, 48 Amberley Gro 6 ... 356 7517
N, 3 Western Rd,Sutton Coldfield ... 354 9278
P.W, 31 Marlborough Rd 36 ... 747 2149
R, 78 Grestone Av 20 ... 554 0267
R, 197 Newton Rd 43 ... 357 1863
Roy A, 182 Northfield Rd 17 ... 427 3322
R.L, 33 Wharf Rd 30 ... 459 2660
S, 2 Greenway Clo 43 ... 360 5791
S, 50 Vimy Rd 13 ... 444 1945
S.L, 12 Boldmere Clo,Sutton Coldfield ... 373 3765
W, 3 Westholme Croft 30 ... 472 8782
MADDRELL Simon, 48 Ellesmere Rd 8 ... 326 8979
MADDY K.P, 3 Merehill Av,Solihull ... 745 5813
MADELEY A, 128 Dudley Rd Est,Oldbury ... 552 4887
A, 7 Walton Ct,High Farm Rd,Halesowen ... 503 0184
A.C, 98 Triumph Wlk 36 ... 749 2685
A.E, 56 Farnhurst Rd 36 ... 328 3619
B, 7 Dauntsey Covert 14 ... 458 6910
B.W, 27 Leaford Rd 33 ... 784 0412
C.E, 17 Marldon Rd 14 ... 444 7677
D, 89 Braemar Rd,Solihull ... 706 0366
D, 30 Macmillan Rd,Rowley Regis ... 559 2793
D.H, 252 Coleshill Rd 36 ... 747 4575
E, 5 Pryor Rd,Oldbury ... 544 4518
E.A, 17 Mynors Cres 47 ... **Wythall** 826651
E.G, 27 Queens Ct,Alderham Clo,Solihull ... 705 6750
E.S, 117 The Ridgeway 23 ... 356 7835
J, 2/24 Taylor Rd 13 ... 444 0057
J.M, 1 Chartwell Ct,Beardmore Rd,
Sutton Coldfield...373 1815
J.M, 40 Dower Rd,Sutton Coldfield ... 308 1476
T, 449 Lugtrout La,Solihull ... 704 9849
Theo M, 38 Redthorn Gro 33 ... 783 7684
W.E, 126 Spouthouse La 43 ... 357 6503
MADELIN A.E,
305 Beaconview Rd,W Bromwich...588 2099
D, 152 Powis Av,Tipton ... 557 7026
H, 55 Glebefields Rd,Tipton ... 557 9450
K, 415 Sycamore Rd,Tipton ... 520 4748
M, 20 Kipling Clo,Tipton ... 557 5572
MADEN M.A, 44 Steel Rd 31 ... 476 6493
MADER R, 107 Birmingham Rd 48 ... 445 2366
MADEW E.A, 39 Witton Ldg Rd 23 ... 350 0522
J.T, 226 Rectory Rd,Sutton Coldfield ... 378 3905
MADGE A,
60 Bampfylde Pl,Thornbridge Av 42...358 2139
C, 19 Andrew Rd,W Bromwich ... 588 6693
C.J, 5 Rectory Pk Av,Sutton Coldfield ... 378 0353
G, 1 Ravenhill Clo 34 ... 748 7534
G.H, 78 Hathersage Rd 42 ... 360 2845
H, 118 Finchley Rd 44 ... 355 4840
H.E, 36 Homecroft Rd 25 ... 783 4867
H.S, 11 Parkhall Croft 34 ... 747 0129
J, 27 Walsham Croft 34 ... 748 5736
J.E, 86 Preston Rd 26 ... 708 0883
J.M, 42 Cambridge Dv 37 ... 770 4121
J.M, 2 Mayhurst Rd 47 ... 474 3720
J.R, 6 Lodge Clo,Walsall ... 358 6816
L.G, 84 Elmcroft,Windmill La,Smethwick ... 558 4783
M.J, 95 Kingstanding Rd 44 ... 356 0782

MADGE M.J, 1 Station Approach,Vesey Ldge,
Sutton Coldfield...353 6347
W.H, 68 Drayton Rd 14 ... 443 2047
MADGWICK D.J,
239 Ulverley Green Rd,Solihull...706 1349
G, 3 Beresford Cres,W Bromwich ... 553 3637
H.A, 78 Coopers La,Smethwick ... 558 8623
MADHAL C.S, 11 Raglan Rd,Smethwick ... 565 1487
MADHAS N, 34 Chantry Rd 21 ... 554 7075
MADHOO G, 10 High Trees 20 ... 523 8532
MADIGAN A, 693 Hagley Rd Wst 32 ... 421 3971
E.G, 183 Bucklands End La 34 ... 747 8988
E.J, 206 Gravelly La 23 ... 350 7814
J.J, 48 Cranmore Rd,Shirley ... 745 4407
J.J, 48 Shakespeare Rd,Shirley ... 745 1712
M, 711 Kingstanding Rd 44 ... 355 5221
M.J, 4 R.A.F Houses,Chester Rd 35 ... 748 6327
S, 175 Balden Rd 32 ... 429 3689
W, 18 Blakeland Rd 44 ... 356 9967
MADILL W, 64 College Rd,Sutton Coldfield ... 354 8566
MADIN J, 34d Wentworthrd 17 ... 427 7430
M.L.K, 182 Lightwoods Hl,Smethwick ... 429 2530
W.H, 131 Park Hl Rd 17 ... 427 1634
MADISON J.O, 132 Raglan Rd,Smethwick ... 558 4789
N.A, 34 Teesdale Av 34 ... 748 1201
MADKINS A.H,
76 Somerville Rd,Sutton Coldfield...355 3613
A.J, 39 South Gro 23 ... 350 8551
P.E, 20 Hinton Av 48 ... 445 2966
T.W, 433 Birmingham Rd,Walsall ... 358 1512
W.E, 110 Meadthorpe Rd 44 ... 360 3535
MADLAM K, 73 Caldwell Gro,Solihull ... 711 1215
MADLEY Gwyn, 48 Neville Rd,Shirley ... 744 4881
MADOURIE C, 31 Glendower Rd 42 ... 356 1081
MADRELL K.W, 95 Silhill Hall Rd,Solihull ... 705 2477
MAECHER Pictureproducts
Ltd...**Snodland** 243450
MAEER C.W, 5 Lingard Ho,Fox Hollies Rd,
Sutton Coldfield...351 7629
F.W.C, 70 Clay Pit La,W Bromwich ... 553 2571
G, 3 Park La 21 ... 525 3628
J.E, 12 New St,W Bromwich ... 556 0285
K.M.F, 81 Riland Rd,Sutton Coldfield ... 378 5549
M.A, 42 New St,W Bromwich ... 502 1718
MAEERS G.A, 119 Kingsbury Rd 24 ... 373 3909
MAER G.J, 14 Spiral Ct,Monkskirby Rd,
Sutton Coldfield...378 1979
MAESE R, 34 Southcote Gro 38 ... 459 8562
MAETINEAU B.E,
Good Rest Camp Site,Good Rest La 38...459 1481
MAFFIN R.W, 64 Woodgate Gdns 32 ... 422 1769
MAFLAHI M, 11 Birkdale Gro 29 ... 471 4011
M.S, 22 Aubrey Rd 10 ... 773 8415
MAGAHRAN E, 46 Doveridge Rd 28 ... 744 5756
MAGAR K.S, 2 Greenside Rd 24 ... 373 3709
MAGDZIARZ A, 14 Hamstead Rd 19 ... 554 1014
MAGEE A, 20 Holte Rd 6 ... 327 0796
7957
9226
8046
2119
0339
8640
1630
1666
5134
0260
1923
5979
9070
7482
8897
6654
R, 20 The Scotchings 36 ... 747 9215
R.H, 153 Castle La,Solihull ... 743 9893
T, 11 Pavillion Av,Smethwick ... 429 5635
GEEAN J.J, 9 Leatherhead Clo 6 ... 359 8471
GEED R, 27 Whetstone Clo 15 ... 454 3927
GEN J.W, 80 Coronation Rd 43 ... 358 6283
GENIS I, 52 Oxford St 30 ... 459 8501
GGS B.E, 389 Warwck Rd,Solihull ... 704 3235
.D, 20 Greenwood Clo 14 ... 443 4936
.I, 10 Harleston Rd 44 ... 350 5654
, 32 Pitleasow Clo 30 ... 451 2997
.O, 3 Garnett Av 43 ... 360 3103
.D, 7 Meerhill Av,Shirley ... 745 9427
.R, 21 Whitley Ct Rd 32 ... 422 0127
V.J.T, 17 Nevison Gn 43 ... 325 0098
V.S, 24 Cherrywood Ct,Solihull ... 743 5528
GILL B, 11 Inkberrow Rd,Halesowen ... 550 4366
.R, 24 Morven Rd,Sutton Coldfield ... 354 2746
red, 172 West Hth Rd 31 ... 475 4518
, 201 Wyndhurst Rd 33 ... 783 2748
, 114 Clent View Rd 32 ... 422 1576
.G, 2 Bishbury Clo 15 ... 455 0101
GINLEY T.H, 57 St. Peters Rd 20 ... 523 3415
GINNIS A.F, 10 Chapel St,Halesowen ... 501 3269
A.R, 22 Cross St,Halesowen ... 550 4024
J.E, 14 Grosvenor Rd,Solihull ... 704 2707
L.A, 43 Barcheston Rd ... **Knowle** 6840
T.W, 676 Chester Rd 36 ... 770 7022
MAGNAY Dr A.R, 18 Crosbie Rd 17 ... 427 3433
MAGNER P.F, 74 Fredas Gro 17 ... 427 9846
R.D, 10 Lottie Rd 29 ... 472 7916
MAGNESS C.R,
50 Slater Rd,Bentley Hth...**Knowle** 3189
MAGONS F, 61 Burney La 8 ... 783 6389
MAGOR D.C,
6 Linden Ct,Hampton La,Solihull...704 9722
M, 7 The Avenue,Rowley Regis ... 559 1674
MAGOWAN S.C, 21 Tansy Badgers Bank Rd,
Sutton Coldfield...308 3265
MAGRATH G.F, 90 Wentworth Rd 17 ... 426 2485
MAGRAW W.L,
42a Maney Hl Rd,Sutton Coldfield...354 5063
MAGRI S, 69 Tedstone Rd 32 ... 427 5127
MAGRIS G.L,
5 Far Highfield,Sutton Coldfield...378 2470
MAGSON A.G, 109 Stoney La 25 ... 783 0170
A.M, 243 The Avenue 27 ... 707 3712
D.C, 26 Scott Rd,Olton ... 706 9854
G, 172 Stoney La 25 ... 783 4842
H, 34 George Rd 43 ... 357 9641
K.H, 2551 Stratford Rd,Hockley Hth ... **Lapwth** 2700
P.J, 52 Ascot Rd 13 ... 449 0285

Most dtp fonts are revivals of traditional fonts, adapted to the limitations of the technology. There are also several fonts designed specifically for the process, and for the changing needs of the graphic designer. Erik Spiekermann's Meta (Fig. 2.52) is described as an ecological face, designed to look attractive even in small sizes on problematic papers such as coarse, thin, and recycled stocks. Designers Banks and Miles developed an economical typeface for British Telecom's telephone directories and managed to achieve savings in paper of over ten percent (Fig. 2.51).

Some typographers are using the power of the computer to incorporate "intelligence" (or rather, chaos) into their typefaces. Beowulf from Dutch designers Erik van Blokland and Just van Rossum, for example, is a "random" font in which the letterforms mutate subtly each time a character is produced (Fig. 2.53). Three versions of Beowulf have differing levels of randomness built in, and they imitate the effects of wear and tear on metal and wooden type.

In a way, faces like Beowulf are a modern counterpart to Gutenberg's efforts to emulate the scribes' humanized typography. A similar point could be made about computer simulations of hand lettering in comics.

2.51 (opposite) The new condensed typeface designed by Colin Banks of London-based designers Banks and Miles also addresses green issues. It allows four columns per page of the telephone directory and this, along with the decision not to repeat surnames, has resulted in huge savings in both paper and ink. As only one size (5·75pt) was required, Banks was able to design the bitmaps pixel by pixel. Note the **"traps"** in some letters to prevent ink spread from filling in the junctions.

2.53 (right) Building randomness into a font's characteristics creates subtly mutating type. Beowulf from Dutch designers Erik van Blokland and Just van Rossum is the first "anarchistic" dtp font.

Meta Normal : A B C D E F G H I J K L M N O P Q R S T U V W X Y Z a b c d e f g h i j k l m n o p q r s t u v w x y z 1 2 3 4 5 6 7 8 9 0 ! @ # £ $ % ^ & * ( ) _ + ‹ › ?

META CAPS : A B C D E F G H I J K L M N O P Q R S T U V W X Y Z A B C D E F G H I J K L M N O P Q R S T U V W X Y Z 1 2 3 4 5 6 7 8 9 0 ! @ # £ $ % ^ & * ( ) _ + ⇣ ⇡ ?

Meta Bold : A B C D E F G H I J K L M N O P Q R S T U V W X Y Z a b c d e f g h i j k l m n o p q r s t u v w x y z 1 2 3 4 5 6 7 8 9 0 ! @ # £ $ % ^ & * ( ) _ + ⇠ ⇢ ?

2.52 (above) Erik Spiekermann's ecological face Meta was designed as a reaction to the overuse of Helvetica, which he describes as "the Federal font."

R21 : ABCDEFGHIJKLMNOP QRSTUVWXYZabcdefghijk lmnopqrstuvwxyz1234567 890!@#£$%^&*()_+ < > ?

R22 : ABCDEFGHIJKLMNOP QRSTUVWXYZabcdefghijk lmnopqrstuvwxyz1234567 890!@#£$%^&*()_+ < > ?

R23 : ABCDEFGHIJKLMNOP QRSTUVWXYZabcdefghijk lmnopqrstuvwxyz1234567 890!@#£$%^&*()_+ < > ?

ABC ABC ABC

POSTSCRIPT AND TRUETYPE

Almost every machine or device in print production encountered today – from computer screens and scanners to high-resolution imagesetters – works on the **raster** principle. A raster (from the Latin for "rake") is the line that makes up the picture on a television screen. On digital devices like a computer screen, each line is divided into a series of dots called **pixels**, and the **resolution** of the screen is described in terms of the number of pixels horizontally by the number of lines vertically. Thus the screen of an Apple Macintosh Classic has a resolution of 512 × 342.

Another way of measuring resolution is by the number of dots per inch, or **dpi**. Thus, measured in this way, the Mac's screen has a resolution of 72 dpi.

The higher the resolution, the better the quality. A laser printer typically has a resolution of 300 dpi. A production-quality imagesetter, such as the Purup 7100, has a resolution of 2540 dpi.

The same type has to look good (or at least be recognizable) on all kinds of different devices with all kinds of resolutions. A designer may work initially on the computer screen, proof the results on a laser printer, and then send a disc containing all the type information off to a bureau for high-quality bromide prints or film.

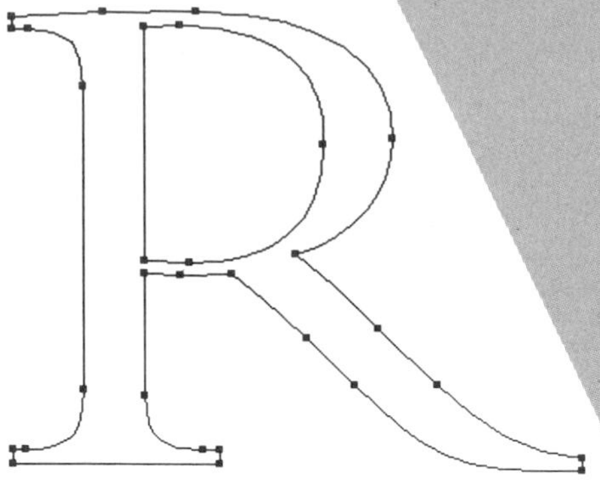

2.54 PostScript is an outline description format, developed by Adobe and adopted worldwide as a *de facto* standard. Letterforms are described in terms of outlines using the math of Bézier cubic spline curves. These outlines are then converted to bitmaps appropriate to the resolution of the output device.

Type descriptions have to be stored in a device-independent format, and converted to a form readable by the particular device as and when necessary. **PostScript**, developed by Adobe, is such a format (Fig. 2.54).

PostScript describes the outline of the letterform in terms of vectors (lines and curves) rather than dots, and this outline is converted by software into a pattern of dots specific to each output device. PostScript is, strictly speaking, a page-description language (more in Chapter 3; see p. 93) that describes not only letterforms, but also drawings created in the computer, and the layouts of type and drawings on pages.

As PostScript is a proprietary piece of software, anyone wanting to make PostScript-compatible typefaces or printing devices has to pay Adobe a license fee. To try to break Adobe's monopoly, Microsoft, the developers of Windows 3 for the PC (personal computer), and Apple have developed a rival format called **TrueType** (Fig. 2.55).

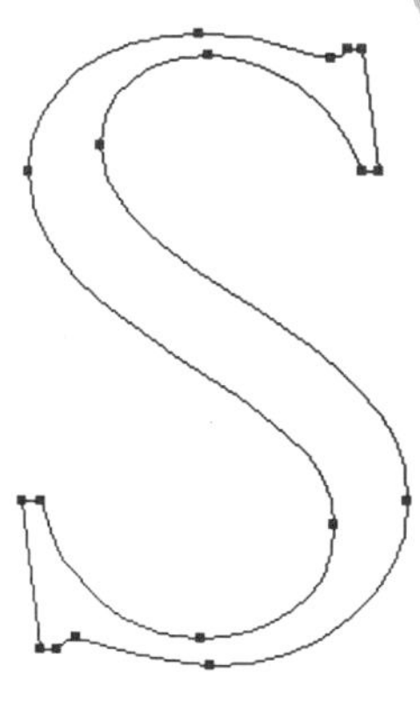

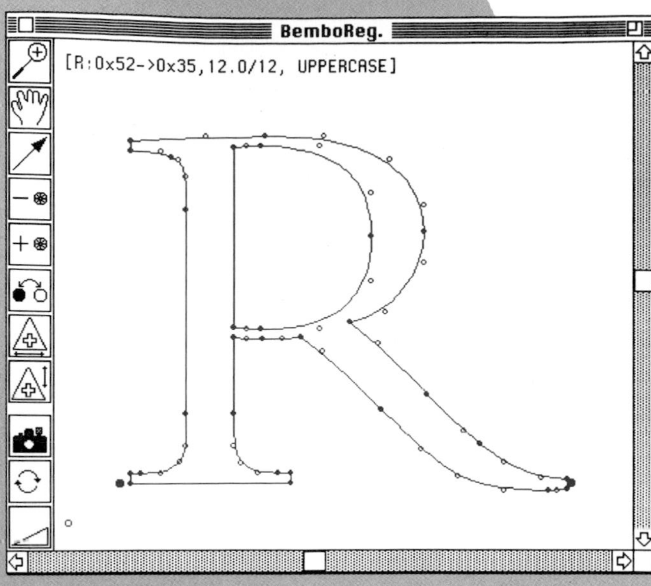

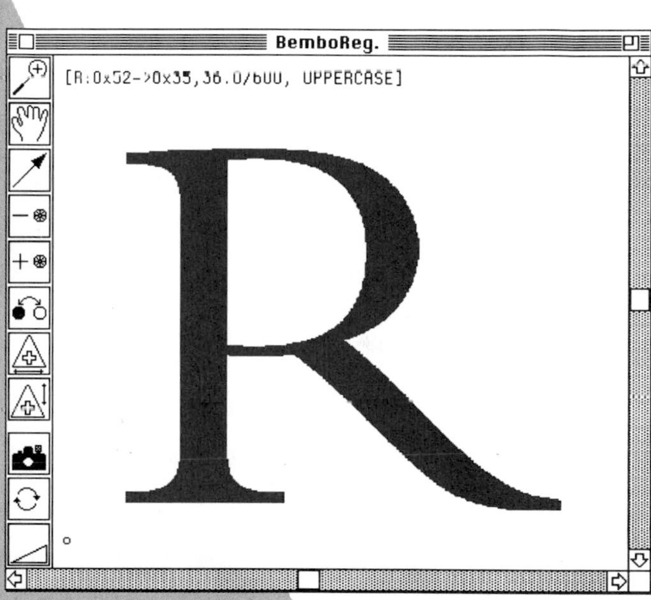

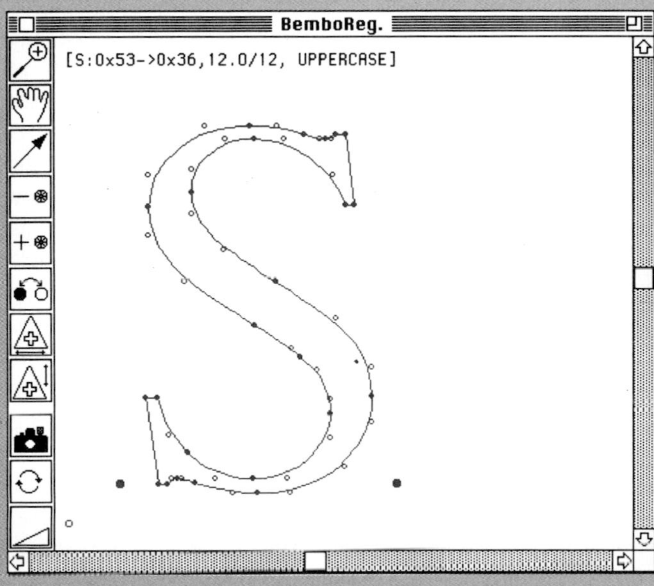

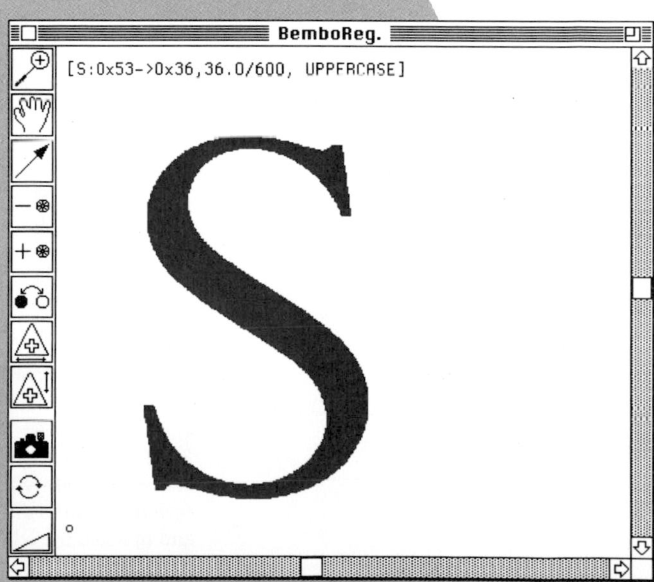

2.55 TrueType is a rival format to PostScript, developed jointly by Apple and Microsoft. It is similar in principle to PostScript, but its mathematical basis is different – it uses quadratic curves. It is linked to Apple's System 7 operating system, but also runs under Windows on an IBM PC. These samples were produced using TypeMan from Type Solutions, Inc.

The two systems will work together in the same dtp document, but PostScript fonts will not print on the cheaper TrueType printers. There are other pieces of software, such as FontMonger, that are said to convert fonts between the formats.

Before PostScript and TrueType, fonts were stored as arrays of dots called **bitmaps** (Fig. 2.56). These can, when printed, be every bit as good as the equivalent PostScript version, but you will need a separate bitmap for every font and every resolution of target device. With PostScript you need just two: a screen font to give an idea of the look of the typeface on the relatively low resolution of the computer screen; and a printer font, to cover all the different kinds of output device. A format called Display PostScript uses the printer font to generate the screen font, as does TrueType.

2.56 A bitmap is a pattern of dots that approximates the outline of a letterform. On a low-resolution device, such as a computer screen or dot-matrix printer, a bitmap looks crude and jagged. But on a high-resolution device, such as an imagesetter, the dots would be too small to see.

72 dpi

144 dpi

300 dpi

Inconsistent weights

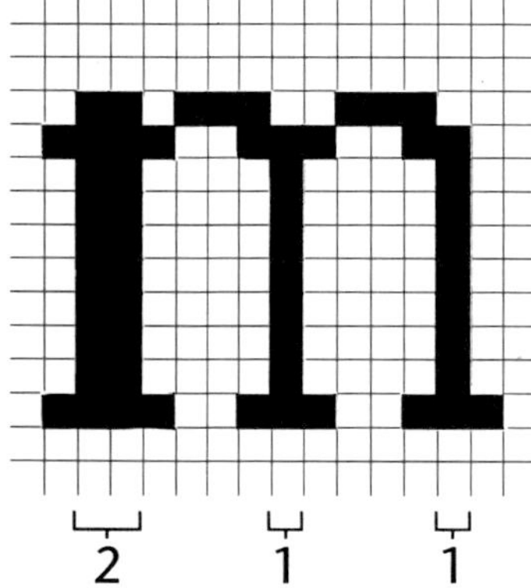

Consistent weights

144 dpi, 12 point bitmap scaled

Without hints

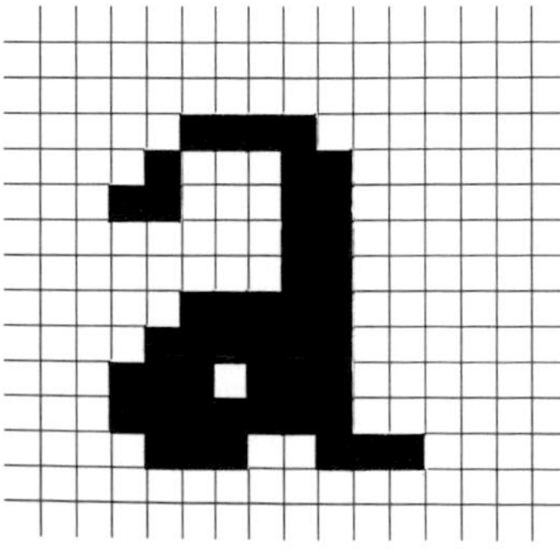

With hints

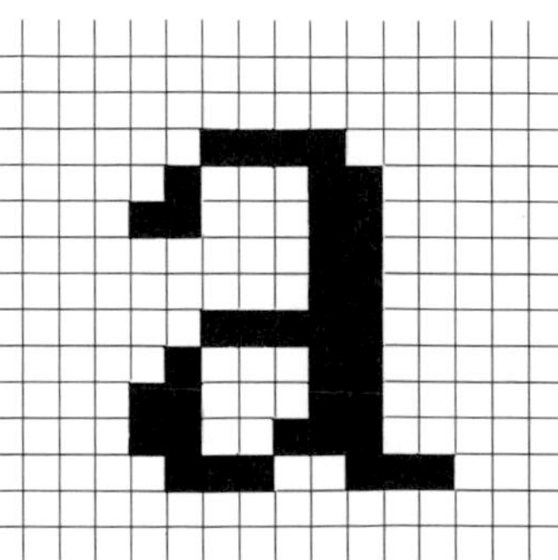

144 dpi, 12 point bitmap scaled

2.57 Hinting is the name given to the process of slightly adjusting the pixels in a scaled bitmap to give a consistent weight and to make the letterform more legible at smaller sizes.

Adobe Type Manager is a package that improves the appearance of scaled-up fonts on the computer screen and on low-resolution printers. It has been developed purely for use with Adobe's own fonts or those from Adobe licensed suppliers such as Linotype, Monotype, Agfa, and AM Varityper.

Adobe's licensed fonts are called Type 1 PostScript fonts. Other PostScript fonts are called Type 3. There is no Type 2! Type 1 fonts have **hinting** (Fig. 2.57), which subtly changes the shape of a character so that it better fills the pixel grid of the target device. It is not the same as non-linear scaling.

Summary

What, then, are the pros and cons of the various typesetting technologies?

HOT METAL OR LETTERPRESS

Advantages Quality: each font designed specifically for its particular size; printed result gives an impressed look and feel which conveys care and expense. Uses original type designs. Can be quick to set up for small jobs such as business cards. Corrections easy to make. Reserved mainly for short-run prestigious invitations, overprinting diplomas, and for private press editions of poetry books.
Disadvantages Handsetting is labor-intensive, and thus costly. Must hold a large inventory of metal type, which takes up space. Can run out of sorts in the middle of a job. Machine setting is noisy and highly skilled. Metal type is inflexible, does not enlarge well, and cannot be set close. Limited availability.

COLD METAL OR STRIKE-ON

Advantages Quick and direct setting by relatively unskilled operators. Inexpensive. Justified setting difficult.
Disadvantages Poor selection of typefaces, crude intercharacter spacing. Low quality.

PHOTOSETTING

Advantages Fast and relatively inexpensive. Wide range of typefaces. Letters can be set closer than in hot metal. Set by skilled compositors, ensuring a good quality result.
Disadvantages All sizes produced by one font master. More "sterile" look than hot metal. Mechanicals usually needed to produce pages.

DTP

Advantages Wide range of typefaces available. Type can be adjusted and manipulated in different ways. Type can be imported directly to page make-up systems, so no intermediate mechanical stage required. Possibility of "do it yourself" setting, so no typesetting costs.
Disadvantages Designs of traditional typefaces vary between suppliers. Unless set by skilled compositor, possibility of errors going unchecked. Choice of sizes, leading, tracking can result in unimaginative use of defaults. New skills to be learnt.

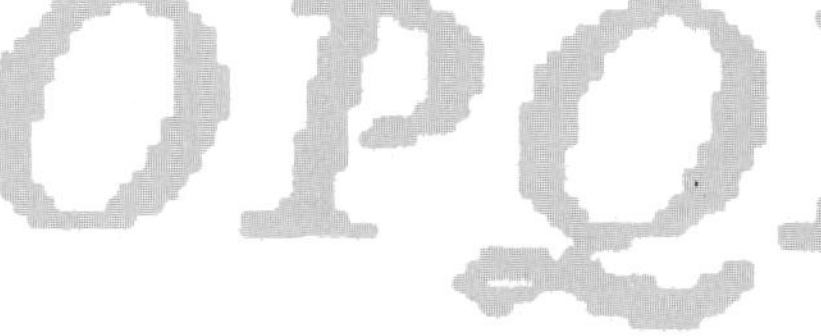

3. Illustration

"A picture is worth more than a thousand words," says the ancient Chinese proverb. Well, that may be a gross undervaluation in our image-rich and visually literate society. And while beautifully set typography can have "shape," "form," and "color," there is nothing to compare with the real thing.

Words and pictures are the raw material of the graphic designer. We have looked at the print production of words, and now it is the turn of images in all their diversity.

Until the middle of last century, there were very few ways that images could be combined with type. Today, any image is immediately accessible to the resourceful graphic designer. How individual designers choose to communicate the message of their particular publication is no longer limited by printing technology. But an understanding of the process is essential if designers are to realize their dreams.

We explore the differences between line and tone, the finer points of flat color and the four-color process, and learn how the process camera and electronic scanner "see" the copy we put before them. We discover practical methods of sizing and cropping images. We find out the best ways of preparing artwork and photographs for the printer, and pick up some tips for developing winning ways with our professional colleagues, the illustrators and photographers.

WHAT EQUIPMENT DO YOU NEED TO GET STARTED?

- a sturdy tabletop or drawing board
- a pad of layout paper
- a supply of fibertip pens and soft black pencils
- a pad of tissue or acetate for overlays
- a non-reproducing light-blue pencil
- a blue waxy pencil (Chinagraph) for writing on glossy surfaces
- low-tack masking tape or matte frosted "magic" tape
- a loupe, linen tester, or eyeglass
- a lightbox conforming to standard lighting conditions
- a proportional scale, or calculator
- a stainless-steel pica rule or plastic typescale
- a Pantone color fan and swatches

AND OPTIONALLY:

- a process camera, in a darkroom or behind heavy black lightproof curtains
- a PMT processing machine
- a Grant enlarger
- a photocopier capable of enlarging and reducing

Part 1: line and tone

Line, to the printer, is any copy that will print in a single color requiring no other intermediate treatment. When the printer mixes ink, the machinery is not capable of diluting it to produce grays, or tints of a color. Black cannot become gray; dark green cannot become pale green. The ink is either there on the paper or it's not. Line means solid areas, dots, or lines of a single color, with no gradation of tone.

There are ways of fooling the eye into perceiving tints and tones. Illustrators use techniques such as stippling or cross-hatching to simulate tones. Victorian engravings can look almost photographic, but look closely and you will see only lines and dots of one color (Fig. 3.1).

3.1 Line art includes much more than just black lines on paper, as can be seen in this Victorian engraving of Prince Albert by D. J. Pound, from an original photograph by Mayall. Look closely at the full picture and at the detail opposite and you will not be able to see anything that cannot be reproduced directly.

The line process is both the cheapest and the most satisfactory for printing on inferior papers. As mentioned in Chapter 1, the line block for letterpress was invented by Paul Pretsch in 1853, and, by the mid 1880s, zinc plates mounted on wooden blocks were being used to reproduce black-and-white illustrations in newspapers and books.

For the first time, an illustrator was able to work at larger sizes than the image would appear in print; any imperfections of the line would thus be proportionally reduced. It became common, therefore, to work "half-up" – at 45 × 30 to become 30 × 20 – or "twice-up" – at 60 × 40 to become 30 × 20. Too great a reduction, however, can lose much of the original quality and spontaneity of the work, and over-reduced lines may break up or disappear under the pressure of printing.

From 1901 onward, the blockmaker could add Ben Day **mechanical tints** to a line drawing as indicated (usually with a blue wash on the original) by the illustrator (Fig. 3.2). Later, self-adhesive film such as Letratone, printed with various tints and patterns, could be added to line work to achieve the same effect.

For offset litho, line illustrations are reproduced photographically on high-contrast **bromide** paper, usually reduced down in size from the original. This print is then pasted onto a board along with the typesetting. Bromide prints can also be produced as **PMTs** (photomechanical transfers), or **diffusion transfers**, by a proprietary method developed by Kodak (Fig. 3.3). It is a much drier process than the original method, in which the bromide paper was processed in trays of photographic chemicals in a darkroom.

To produce a PMT, original artwork is exposed on special negative paper through a process camera. This negative is then fed into a processor which activates the inbuilt developer and then laminates it to a receiving sheet of paper or film. After a short delay, the two sheets are peeled apart and the line image is revealed. It is also possible to obtain reversed out (white on black) images using appropriate paper.

3.2 (above) "Overcoming the difficulties of serenading in New York City," a cartoon with a mechanical tint, from William Heath Robinson's 1934 collection *Absurdities*.

3.3 Most graphic design studios use a combination of process camera, like this WLTC 184, and PMT machine to produce enlarged or reduced copies of line art good enough to use on the mechanical.

If more than one copy is required, or there is a need for the image to be retouched, a negative film is first made from the original. (It is easier, for example, to clean marks on the white areas of an image by opaquing out the black areas on a negative.) This is then used to produce contact prints on bromide paper, by means of the conventional messy method of processing.

For low-cost work, it is also possible (and much cheaper) to reduce artwork on a laser photocopier. The results are getting better all the time.

Screens and halftones

A **halftone** is any photograph or piece of artwork that contains tonal values other than just plain black and white (Fig. 3.4). Before an original containing continuous or intermediate tones can be printed, it must first be converted to "line" – into a form in which there can be either ink on the paper or not. The most common method is to use a **halftone screen**, which converts the continuous tone original into a pattern of single-colored dots (Fig. 3.5).

This is achieved by placing a screen between the lens of the process camera and the bromide paper or film being exposed. As mentioned in Chapter 1, the method devised by George Meisenbach in 1882 used a single-lined screen that was turned 90 degrees during exposure. The first cross-lined screen was introduced in 1890 by Frederick Ives, in collaboration with Louis and Max Levy.

Halftone screens come in two varieties: glass screens and the cheaper plastic contact screens. Glass screens have a finely ruled grid pattern and are situated between the lens and the film. Contact screens contain a pattern of vignetted holes and are placed in direct proximity with the film. The term halftone is perhaps a misnomer: they are thus named because half of the tone is eliminated during the process. Half the image maybe – but *all* of the tone.

The optics of how this happens is not really important to know. Suffice to say that different tones are converted into dots varying in size, shape, and number, which when viewed from a distance seem to melt back into continuous tone.

3.4 Tone art has to be converted into a pattern of dots before it can be printed, by a process called screening. (Annabella Lwin, who fronted the post-punk pop group Bow Wow Wow in the early eighties.)

3.5 (below) A conventional halftone contains dots of different sizes, but in a regular array conforming to the screen being used. Light areas are represented by small black dots. At 50%, you will see a checkerboard of black and white squares, while the darker tones appear as white dots on black. It is rare to find either pure white (no dots at all) or pure black (a solid area of black) on a halftone.

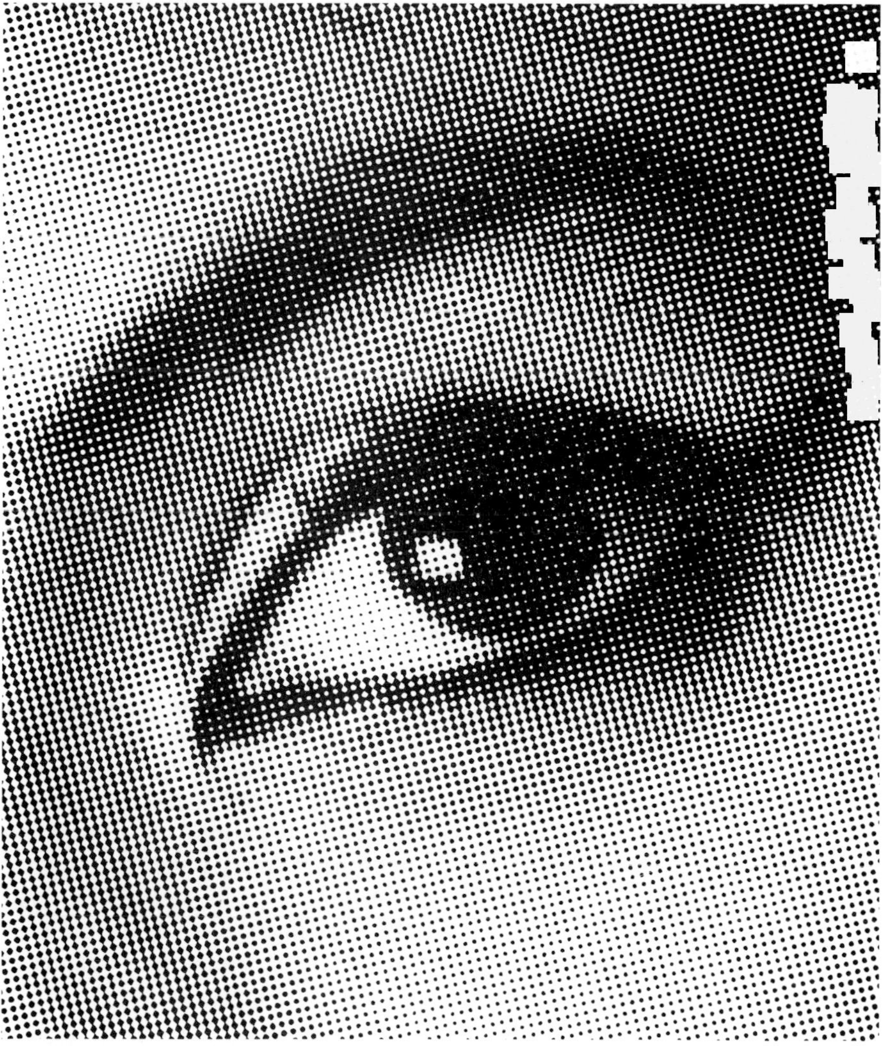

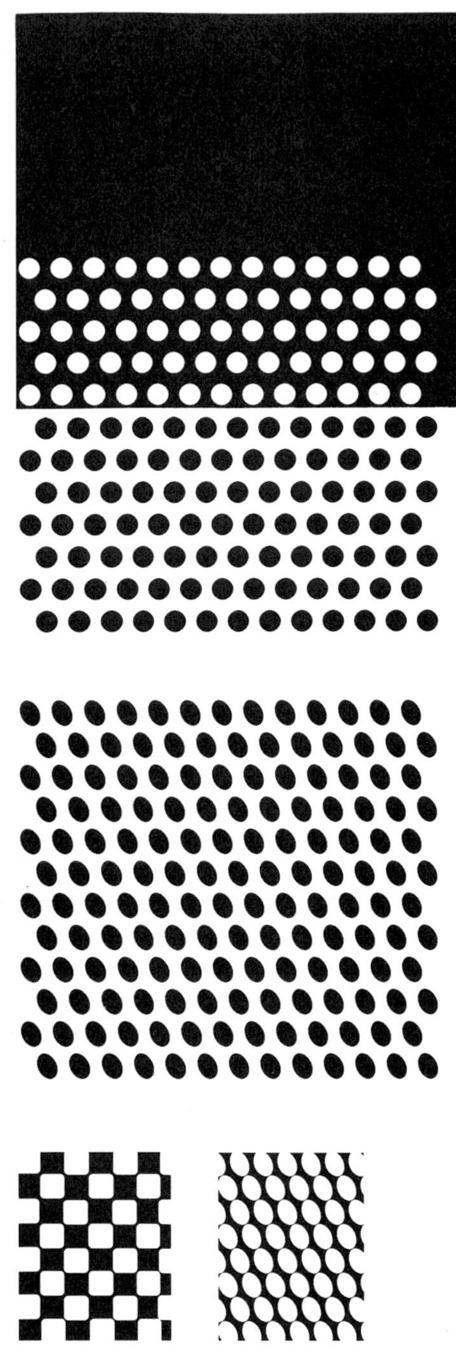

3.6 Imagesetters can make various shapes of dot electronically. Elliptical dots score over conventional ones, as they are less prone to dot gain – the abrupt darkening of areas where the dots are beginning to join up.

The traditional crossed-line screen of 1890 gives a round dot, which becomes a square in the midtones – a checkerboard pattern at 50 percent density. More recently, various shapes of dot have been tried. An improvement on the conventional screen is one with elliptical holes that produce kite-shaped dots that join first in one direction, then the other, giving a much smoother gradation in the middle tones.

On modern electronic imagesetters, the dots are "written" onto the bromide paper or film directly by a laser beam – no screen is involved. These machines are capable of producing any shape of dot you like: square, round, or elliptical (Fig. 3.6). The operator at the repro house will choose the best type of dot for the printing process and paper stock being used, and the tonal quality of the original.

Halftone screens are measured in lines per inch (lines per cm in continental Europe), usually abbreviated to **lines** (Fig. 3.8). The higher the number of lines, the finer the dot pattern, and the better the quality of the reproduction. But there is a trade-off. Newspapers, for example, use cheap rough paper and thin ink that is prone to spread. Too fine a screen, and the dots in the darker areas of the image will merge and **fill in**. Thus, for newsprint, a coarse dot pattern of 55 or 65 lines for letterpress and 100 or 120 lines for offset is standard. Magazines are printed on smoother papers, and so a finer screen of, say, 150 lines can be used. The very finest screens are reserved for glossy art papers (see Chapter 5 for more on paper).

3.8 (opposite) Detail of Rajarani Temple at Bhuvanesvar, India, at screen rulings of 65 (coarse), 120 (general purpose), and 175 (the ruling used throughout this book).

The lines of the screen are usually aligned at 45 degrees to the horizontal, as this seems to produce the pattern that is easiest on the eye. There are dangers, however, when screening photographs containing regular patterns, on a person's clothing, for example. The screen dots and the pattern in the picture can interfere with each other to produce **moiré** (wavy or basket-weave) patterns (Fig. 3.7). This can be avoided or lessened by adjusting the angle of the screen. The moiré effect is put to good use in devices that can tell you what screen is being used in a printed publication.

3.7 When two screens are superimposed and are not quite in alignment, there is a good chance that moiré patterns will result. This happens most commonly when a previously screened halftone, cut from a magazine, for example, is put through another screening process.

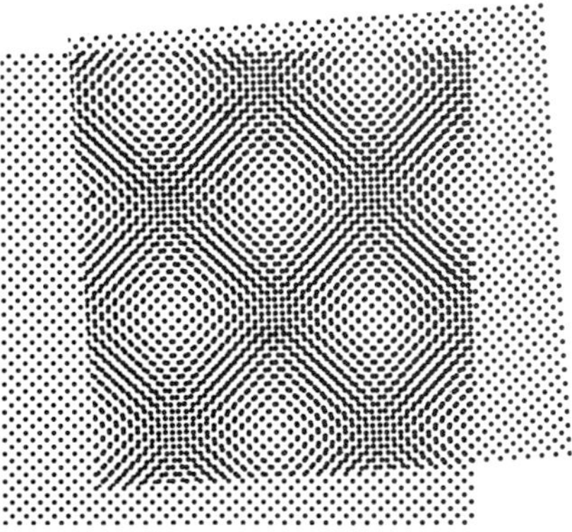

"Anyone who has a library and a garden wants for nothings."
-Cicero
Mark your calendar
Book Sale
9a.m.-noon
2nd Saturday of the month at the Pasadena Central Library
285 East Walnut
Friends of the Pasadena Public Library

3.9 It does not have to be dots! But use special effect screens with discretion! (Ronald Reagan, Warner Bros publicity shot.)

There are also special-effect screens available that convert continuous tone into straight lines of varying weight, wavy lines, concentric circles, and textures that simulate canvas, linen, and random grain (Fig. 3.9).

Halftones are generally squared up, i.e. rectangular in shape. Sometimes you might want to specify a thin black line around them to define the edge. There are other effects that can be used by the discerning graphic designer (Fig. 3.10). These include **cut-outs**, in which extraneous matter is opaqued out (by hand, or optically by machine); **drop-outs**, in which the dots in the very whitest areas are eliminated to accentuate the highlights; and **vignettes**, usually oval, in which the image fades gradually to nothing at the edges.

In work destined for offset lithography, halftones are usually made into negative film and are "stripped-in" later, occupying the clear holes on the negative page left by black squares placed on the artwork. For some jobs, however, it is cheaper and more convenient to be able to put correctly sized halftones into place along with the type and line, and shoot the whole page in one operation.

A **velox** is the halftone equivalent of a PMT – a halftone on bromide paper. Do not be alarmed if a velox appears slightly lacking in contrast, because each time an image is copied, it gains contrast. It will look fine when printed. The screen for veloxes should be as coarse as can be accepted, and should never exceed 120 lines.

Sometimes it may be necessary to produce a halftone from copy that has already been screened. It may not be possible to locate the original of an old illustration from a book, for example. To put a screened picture directly under the camera will more often than not result in unwanted moiré patterns, but there are ways of avoiding this.

Use your **loupe** (eyeglass) to see if the dots on the original are sharp and black. If the screen does not exceed 120 lines, it can be shot as line copy. This is called **dot-for-dot** reproduction, and will often result in an increase of contrast. Where this method is not possible, try rotating the screen angle 30 degrees from the original and shooting slightly out of focus. If all else fails, shoot an unscreened copy print first. This can be retouched before being screened in the regular way.

Where lines and tones appear on the same piece of artwork, for example in a pencil drawing or an ink and wash illustration, a compromise has to be made. Either the whole illustration is treated as tone, in which case the white of the paper will appear light gray and the black lines will lose their crispness. Or the artwork is shot twice, as line and as tone, and combined at the film or platemaking stage as a **line and tone combination**.

3.10 A halftone is not always "squared-up." It can also be cut-out around a profile, have the highlights dropped-out, or it can be made into a vignette with the usually elliptical edges fading away to white. (Bartholdi's Statue of Liberty at the entrance to New York harbor.)

Part 2: color

The use of color in printing is almost as old as printing itself, but the process has always been labor-intensive and has required painstaking amounts of skill. The chromolithographs of the mid-19th century sometimes used as many as 12 separate hand-drawn plates. This created correspondingly enormous problems of positioning the successive printings into correct alignment, one on top of the other – what printers call **registration**.

Flat color

Printers can mix up any color of ink you like – you will just be charged for the cost of special ink and for cleaning up the machine afterward.

An additional color used as a design element in a layout is called **flat color**, or sometimes **match** or **spot color**. In theory, you could use any number of different colors in a design. In practise, most printing presses are designed to handle two, four, or even six colors in one printing, and the more printings you ask for, the higher the cost of the job.

Printers can match almost any color – from a color chart, a piece of printed work, or even the color of your eyes. But if it is consistency you're after, between jobs and other related printed items, you're going to have to be a little more scientific.

The **Pantone Matching System** (PMS) is an industry-standard collection of over 1000 colors that printers recognize and are comfortable using. It is worth purchasing a color guide, in the form of a fan chart or **swatch book**. It will show you all the shades, along with the formulas for mixing the ink, and the effect of colors printed on both coated and uncoated paper (Fig. 3.11). The easiest way of specifying flat color is to give the printer the Pantone number and perhaps one of the tear-off samples that come with the swatch book.

Any color chosen from the Pantone range is made from a mixture of

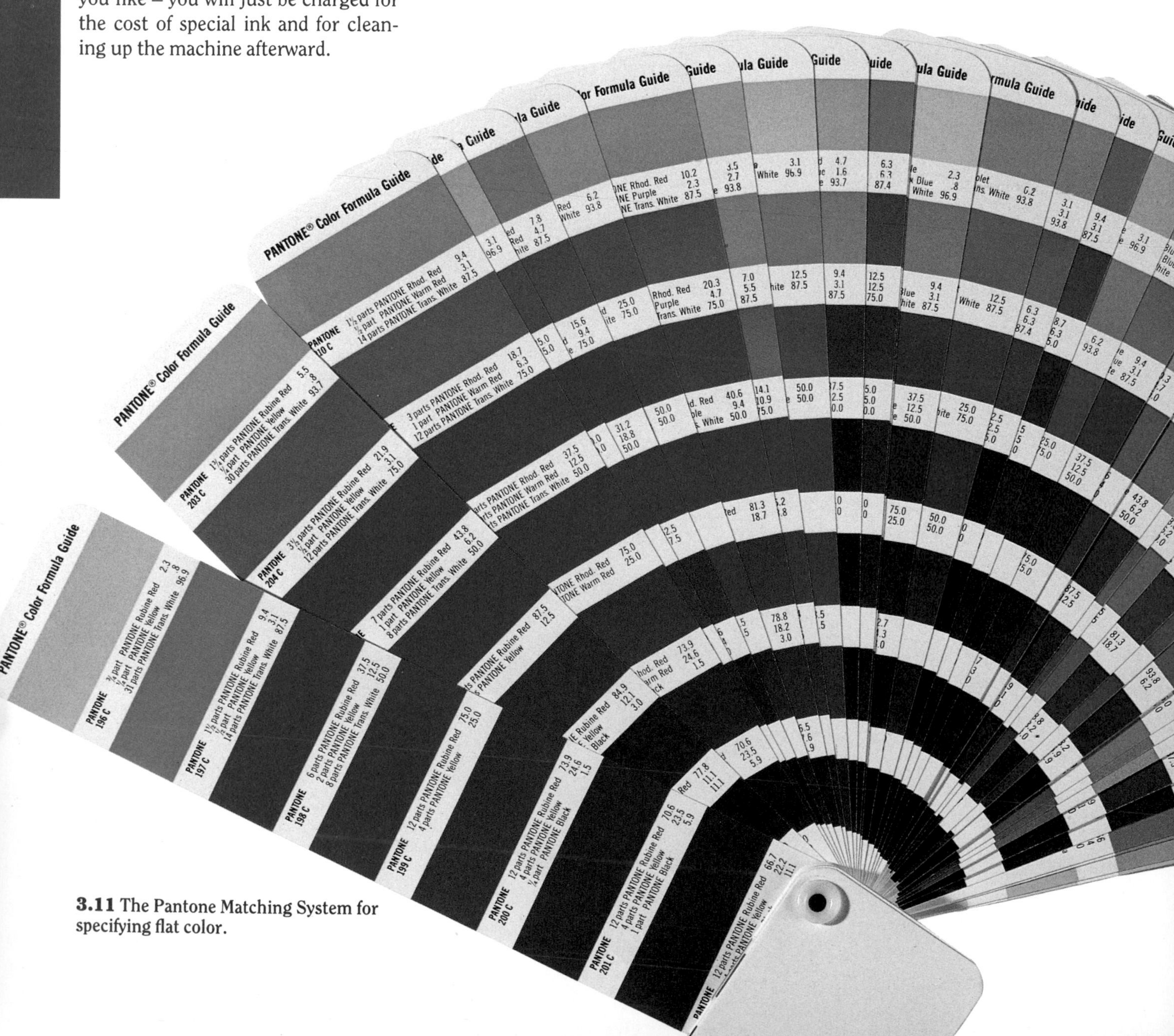

3.11 The Pantone Matching System for specifying flat color.

two or more from a set of nine basic colors: yellow, warm red, rubine red, rhodamine red, purple, violet, reflex blue, process blue, and green, supplemented by transparent white and black. There are also complementary sets of colors incorporating metallic inks, and specialist selections, such as pastel colors for packaging designers.

Flat color can be printed solid or as a percentage **tint** (Fig. 3.12). Books are also available that show Pantone colors in a range of percentage tints. Type can be combined with a tint of flat color in three ways: **surprinted**, with the tint and in the same color; **reversed out** of a tint block; or **overprinted** in another color (Fig. 3.13). Legibility is an issue, so check with printed samples to see what will work with different percentages of tint.

Printers do not like to have flat colors overlapping, because it slows down the rate of drying of the inks and introduces the possibility of smudging. A color will change shade, too, when printed over another one. But adjacent areas of flat color will need to overlap to a small extent to allow for misregistration (misalignment of successive printings). This allowance is called **trapping** (Fig. 3.14) and is particularly important where, say, lettering is reversed out of a block of one color and printed in another. Without trapping, the slightest amount the printing slips **out of register** will cause a thin white line to appear around part of the boundary, resulting in an unwanted bas-relief effect. Generally, it is the lighter color that is extended into the area of the darker color.

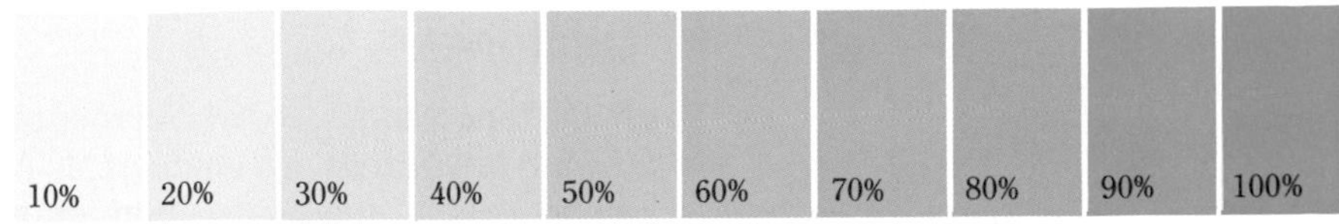

3.12 Color tints are effective when used under typesetting to draw attention to a particular passage, quotation, or checklist.

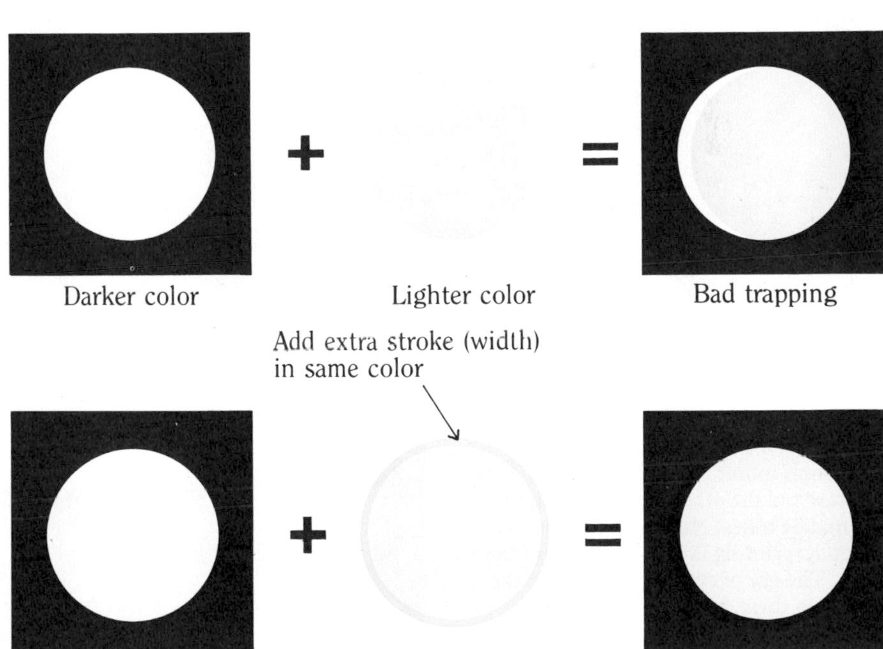

3.13 Text surprinted, dropped out of a tint of the same color, and overprinted in a different color.

3.14 If a graphic or type in one flat color has to fit with a background of another color, there is always the possibility that misregistration might cause a sliver of white where they should abut – this is called bad trapping. The prevention and cure is to add a "stroke" width all round the lighter component, which will be hidden when the darker ink is overprinted.

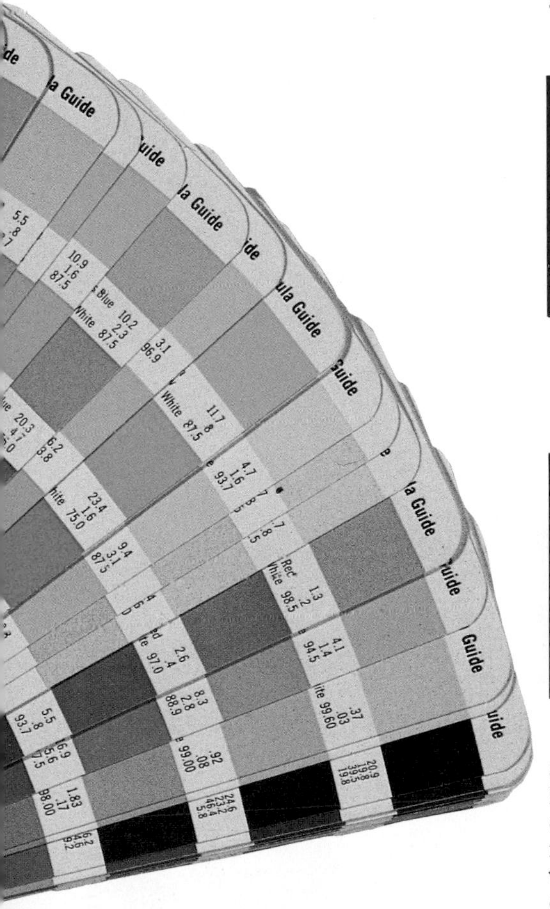

Duotones

A halftone cannot always reproduce the full tonal range of a photograph. A **duotone** is a superimposition of a contrasty black halftone over a one-color halftone, which is shot for highlights and middle tones (Fig. 3.15), using the same image. The most commonly used colors are yellows, browns, and reds. The intention is to create a rich range of tones, and at the same time add a colored tint to the result. For high-quality work, where cost is not a constraint, a duotone may even comprise two printings in black, or in black with a shade of gray. A basic shot with the screen at 45 degrees is used for the black plate, and a second shot at 15 degrees is used for the second color.

For very high-quality publications, three passes of black or gray ink may be used to reproduce the full tonal range of a halftone. A less impressive duotone effect can be achieved by printing a black halftone over a color tint of the same size. This is called a **flat-tint halftone**. The tint must be kept quite light, as the highlights in the halftone can only ever be as light as the underlying tint.

3.15 A duotone is a halftone reproduction comprising two (or sometimes more) printings – one for contrast and the other for the highlights and middle tones. More often than not, the underprinting is in a color other than black. The use of cyan here enhances the sparkle in these Art Deco glass panels, now housed in the Metropolitan Museum of Art, New York, from the ocean liner *Normandie*.

Full-color reproduction

It is neither economic nor practical to mix up ink and print every individual color to be found in a piece of artwork or color photograph, so another method has to be used. It should be possible to create any color from a mixture of the three primary pigments: red, yellow, and blue. Mix any two primary colors and you have the secondaries. Thus blue and yellow produce green, red and yellow produce orange, and blue and red produce purple. Theoretically, if you mix all three, you get black. Experience tells us, however, that what we really end up with is an unpleasant muddy brown. These combinations apply to **reflected light**.

With **transmitted light** (Fig. 3.16), things are a little better. Here, the three primaries are red, green, and blue-violet; the secondaries are yellow, **magenta** (reddish purple), and **cyan** (turquoise). Mix three such primary beams of light, and the result is pure white. Grass is green because it absorbs the red and blue-violet components of white light and retransmits the green.

The secondary colors of transmitted light – yellow, magenta (process red), and cyan (process blue) – are the ones used by printers to reproduce full-color work. In 1860, Clerk Maxwell demonstrated how colored filters could be used to record the blue-violet, green, and red constituents of any full-color subject. Filters of red, green, and blue-violet – the primaries of transmitted light, also known as **additive colors** – are used to produce **separation** negatives (Fig. 3.17). The red filter allows only the blue and green components through, creating cyan. The green filter allows through only red and blue, creating magenta. And the blue filter lets through only the red and green, creating the yellow. The negatives taken through these filters, known as **color separations**, are screened and the positives are then used to make plates to be printed in sequence and in register (correct alignment) in the **process colors** of yellow, magenta, and cyan.

In theory, all the colors added together should produce black, but in practise printing ink, like school paint, never does produce a pure enough black. So a fourth color – black – is added to deepen the dark areas and increase contrast. This makes the scheme a **four-color process**. In print jargon, black is referred to as **key**, so the system is known as **CMYK**. Other systems of defining color include **RGB** (red, green, blue) used for computer displays, and the more theoretical **HLS (hue, luminance, saturation)**. Hue is the part of the rainbow the color occupies – whether it is red or blue. Luminance, or **value**, is the amount of black or white that has been added, to make yellow into brown, or red into pink. Saturation, or intensity, is a measure of the color's position in the range from neutral gray to fully saturated, or bright, color.

3.16 Pure white light contains all the colors of the rainbow. Add together the three primaries – red, green, and blue-violet – and you get white. Where the primaries overlap, the secondaries appear: yellow, magenta, and cyan.

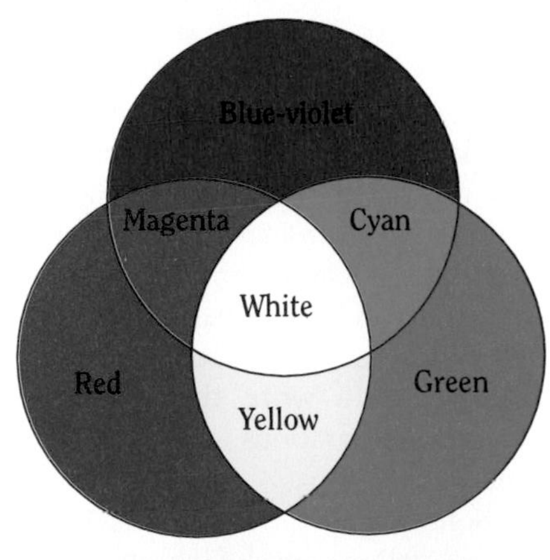

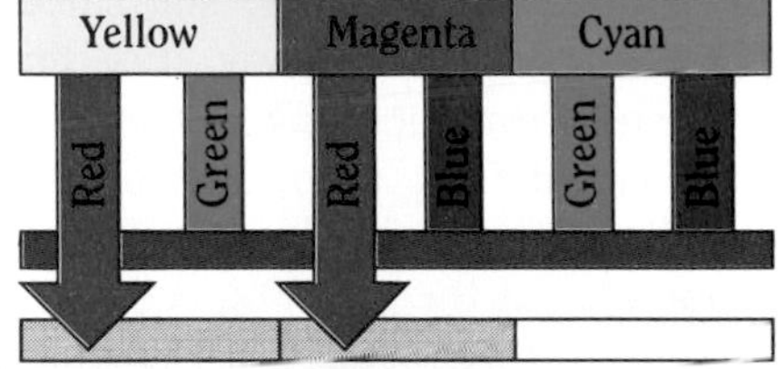

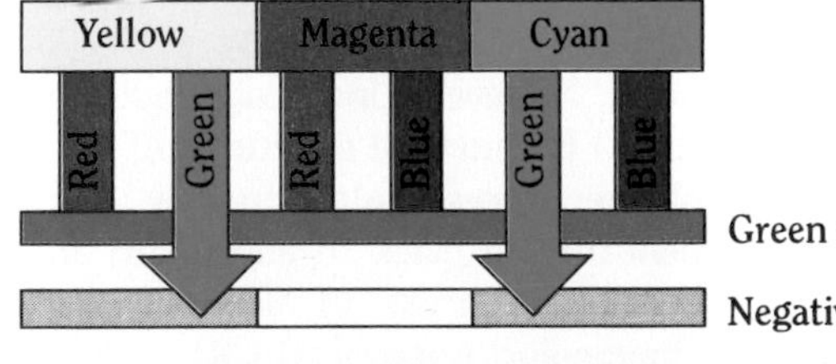

3.17 All the colors in full-color copy can be reproduced from a mixture of the secondaries – yellow, magenta, and cyan – and these components of any color can be extracted using filters of the primaries red, green, and blue-violet.

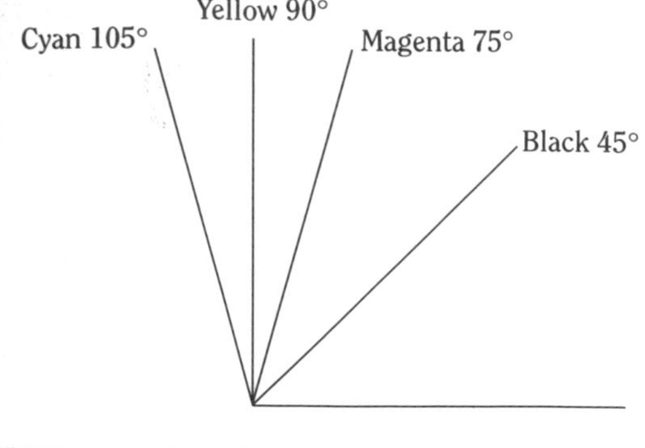

3.18 (above) To prevent moiré patterns, the screens for the different color printings are set at specific angles: 45 degrees is easiest on the eye, so that is reserved for black; 90 degrees is the least satisfactory angle, so it is used for the relatively pale yellow.

3.19 (right) In theory, any color can be reproduced from a combination of yellow, cyan, and magenta. In practise, though, black is added for extra punch. Electronic scanners are able to trade some of the neutral gray created by combinations of the process colors for tints of black. This is called gray component replacement – it saves ink and quickens drying. Detail of *Scene in Harlem (Simply Heavenly)* by Edward Burra (1905–76).

Color separations

A color tone original can be separated either in the **process camera** or, most commonly these days, by an electronic **scanner**. Separations by camera are made onto continuous tone film using the three color filters, and these are then converted into halftones by exposure through screens. The screens are laid out at different angles, so that the dots are kept separate – the "mixing" of the colors is done by the eye – and in a pattern designed to eliminate moiré effects (Fig. 3.18). The screens of the main colors are orientated at 30 degrees to each other, with the stronger colors at 45, 75, and 105 degrees, and the less intrusive yellow at the "difficult" angle of 90 degrees.

Scanners work by reading the artwork as a series of horizontal lines, or rasters. The **transparency** or artwork is wrapped around the scanner's transparent drum, which revolves at around 90 miles per hour (150 km/h). A beam of light is used to pick up the three color components. These split beams are digitized, and pass into a computer where color correction and some manipulation of the image can take place. Finally, a laser is used to "write" the dots of the screened separations directly onto film.

Some combinations of the three process colors cancel each other out to produce neutral grays, and since black is being used anyway, this can be seen as overkill. **Gray component replacement** (Fig. 3.19), also known as **achromatic stabilization**, is a technique used at the scanning stage for cleaning up the color and reducing the amount of ink that gets to the paper. Not all the "chromatic" gray is removed and replaced by a tint of black, however. **Undercolor addition** (UCA) is a method of returning some of the process color, usually cyan, beneath the black to add depth and density to areas of deep shadow. **Undercolor removal** (UCR) reduces the amount of color in areas of shadows, to save ink and prevent problems that may occur if a new layer of ink is printed onto ink that is not quite dry.

Dee Dee's
OLD CROW
KENTUCKEY

Dee Dee's
OLD CROW
KENTUCKEY

Dee Dee's
OLD CROW
KENTUCKEY

Dee Dee's
OLD CROW
KENTUCKEY

Dee Dee's
OLD CROW
KENTUCKEY

Dee Dee's
OLD CROW
KENTUCKEY

Dee Dee's
OLD CROW
KENTUCKEY

If a solid area is to be printed in a Pantone shade along with four-color illustrations, it will be cheaper to match the color by using a combination of tints in two or more of the process colors. Pantone publishes charts illustrating various combinations of process tints printed one over the other (Fig. 3.20). But if you plan to substitute in this way, check first with your clients. They may have strict rules about the use of color for corporate-identity work – the color of a company logo, for example – and may be willing to stand the cost of an extra printing in a specially mixed Pantone shade.

To prevent potential muddiness when too many colors are mixed together, a rule of thumb has evolved that the sum of percentage components of the process colors should never exceed 240. A color comprising 30% yellow, 10% cyan, and 60% magenta (=100%) is fine, but one containing 70% yellow, 100% cyan, and 80% magenta (=250%) would not be allowed on the press. The color bar on a color proof has checks for this (see p. 112).

3.20 Charts showing combinations of various percentage tints help you make the most effective use of flat color in layouts. This chart shows the effect of changing the percentages of magenta and cyan while keeping yellow constant at 60 percent. Along the axes, 50– refers to dots that are not touching and 50+ refers to ones that are.

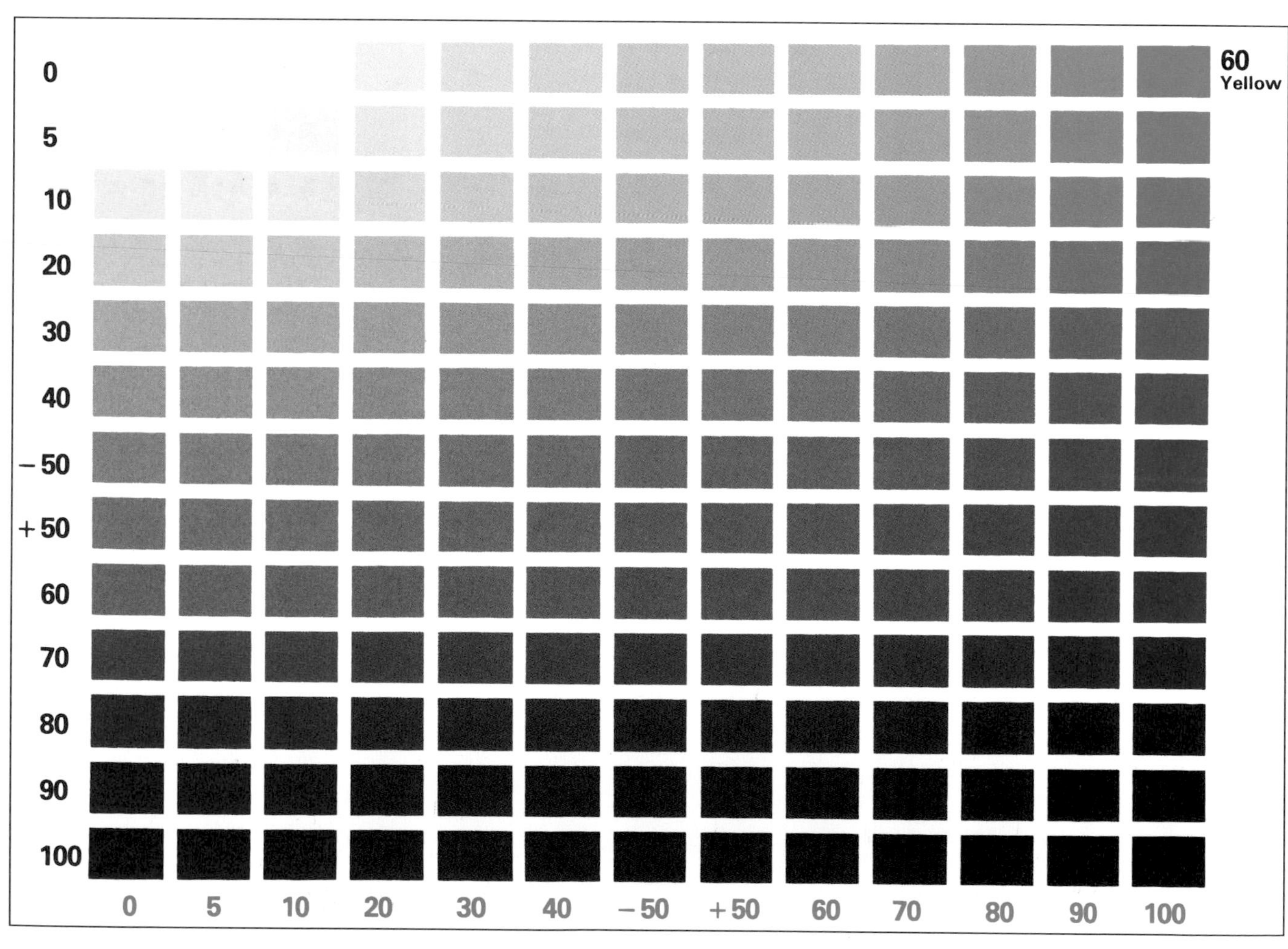

Part 3: choosing and preparing illustrations

Briefing an illustrator or photographer

Graphic designers and illustrators have much in common. The most famous illustrator turned graphic designer, Milton Glaser, has always encouraged illustrators to do as he has done. Not only will you earn more money as a graphic designer, but you can then commission yourself to do the illustrations! Be that as it may, not every graphic designer can draw as well as he, nor is every illustrator as passionately interested in type.

A graphic designer may commission artwork and photography, or may be presented with a package of words and pictures to put together according to a design brief. If the graphic designer is involved at an early stage with the commissioning of illustration and photography, a careful eye can be kept on the quality and content of the finished job.

Perhaps the two most important pieces of information an illustrator needs to know are the deadline date, and the size of the artwork required. The content and style will be different for each job, and the choice of a particular illustrator or photographer will be made on their ability to deliver what you want, on time, and to a professional standard. There are, however, some further general principles that can be outlined.

There are two kinds of original copy. Flat artwork from the hand of the illustrator, photographic prints, and PMTs are termed **reflection copy**; they are viewed by reflected light. Color transparencies and film positives are known as **transmission copy**.

In general, black-and-white copy goes under a process camera, whereas color originals are separated on a drum scanner. Transparencies of color photographs and full-color artwork are thus preferred, because they are more easily scanned.

Many illustrators like to work on rigid board. There is a kind of board available with a surface that can be peeled off from a rigid base and then wrapped around the drum of a scanner. Originals sometimes get damaged and some kinds of paint crack, so it is wise to have a transparency made first, and for this to be used in the scanning process. Bear in mind, however, that there will be a loss of quality whenever an original is copied. Alternatively, the artwork can be separated conventionally under the process camera.

Where you do have commissioning power, and when selecting images that already exist – from picture libraries, for example – insist on the following:

- Line reflection copy, such as cartoons, should be in black Indian ink on good quality artboard, with any corrections made in process white paint. The original should be drawn no larger than twice-up, unless the lines are simple and thick enough to withstand reduction below 50 percent. Scratchboard illustrations, with their sharp lines, generally reduce well. If a line-and-tone effect is required, as in comic book illustration, the line work and lettering should be drawn on an acetate overlay, in register, over the tonal element.
- Halftone reflection copy, such as photographic prints or airbrush drawings, should have a wide tonal range with not too much contrast. Check for the correct exposure, the graininess, and whether the part of the image you require is correctly in focus. The original should ideally be same size and, at any rate, not more than half-up. Photographs should be printed on glossy paper. Never risk scratch marks by attaching anything to a photograph with a paperclip or staple. If color copy is to be reproduced in black and white, be prepared for a loss in clarity and contrast, and be aware that certain colors are "seen" by the process camera differently from the way the human eye perceives them. Red, for example, will print black, but light blue may not print at all. Flesh tones, particularly, will have to be compensated for. If in doubt, you can have a black-and-white internegative and print made.

Artwork intended for flat color should be supplied in black on a baseboard, with each color drawn, in register, on a separate overlay. Artwork in which the separate flat colors do not touch or overlap can be drawn on the same board, provided that the portions to be printed in different colors are clearly indicated on an overlay.

Artwork in full color should not contain any fluorescent paints or inks, as they do not reproduce well when separated into process colors. Nor do very pure secondary colors, such as purples and lime greens.

- Halftone transmission copy, such as photographic transparencies, should be chosen on a lightbox equipped with standard lighting conditions. Transparencies come in various formats: 35mm, 5in × 4in, and 10in × 8in, for example. Because they will undergo considerable enlargement when reproduced, choose as large a format as you can afford. Check for graininess – it will increase as the transparency is enlarged. And because a transparency's tonal range will be compressed by the printing process, look for detail in both shadow areas and highlights. Check for correct exposure (ask the photographer to "bracket" the exposures, by shooting at apertures above and below the optimum f-stop, and choose the best result). Look, too, for the **color cast** found on a subject photographed against a strongly colored background. Also, scrutinize the transparencies for fingerprints, scratches, and other blemishes. Colors can be corrected to some degree at the repro house, and some retouching can be done, but beware – you will be charged for the service.

Ensure that each transparency is right reading – the repro house will assume that the image is correct when the transparency is viewed with the **emulsion side** facing away from you. This is not always the case, especially if the "original" is a duplicate. Double check by supplying them with a sketch of the subject.

Scaling and cropping

Copy to be reproduced at exactly the same size as the original is called same size and marked S/S. More often than not, artwork will have to be reduced in size to fit your layout, and transparencies enlarged. This is called scaling, or reproportioning.

The simplest and clearest way to indicate the required size of artwork or photographs is to mark the limits of the image with a double-headed arrow and write "Reduce to 4 inches," or whatever you want the width (or height) to be. To avoid damaging the artwork, this is best done on an **overlay**, or flap, of layout paper or tissue. If you are using only a portion of the photograph or artwork, the area you need can also be outlined on the overlay. This is called **cropping**, or recomposing.

It must be said, however, that few photographers and probably no illustrators like to have their work cropped by a graphic designer. Some sensitivity and diplomacy is required if it just has to be done. It is much better to have the size and shape of the illustration or photograph worked out in advance so that the illustrator or photographer can be briefed thoroughly. Obviously, photographs come in standard formats, and some cropping is inevitable. But give the photographers a chance to crop their images and you will be rewarded with better results.

If you are ever tempted, for the sake of a composition, to invert a photograph laterally, i.e. turn it into a mirror image of itself (and it can be done quite simply at the stripping-in stage), get out your loupe and watch out for the giveaways. These include obvious ones such as lettering and signs, but also more subtle telltales such as clocks and maps in the background, or the position of a man's suit breast pocket, or specialized equipment with controls and buttons that the reader will recognize as inverted. Some of these can be retouched, but it is often better to prevent potential embarrassment by leaving well alone, or paying out to have the photograph reshot.

It is difficult to draw **crop marks** accurately on such a small area as a portion of a 35mm transparency, and it is better to make an enlarged velox or photocopy, and to mark that with your instructions. These copies can be placed in position and at the correct size on the artwork (more on this in Chapter 4).

It is often useful to know the size an image will appear once it has been reduced or enlarged, so that you can plan your layout with confidence that the PMT or dropped-in color separations will fit. There are two methods for making this calculation. The first is to use a **reproduction calculator** or **proportional scale** (Fig. 3.21). This is a kind of circular slide rule, comprising two discs that rotate relative to each other. Find the width of the original on the inner wheel, line up the width of the space into which it has to fit on the outer wheel, and you will be able to read off the corresponding reduction or enlargement in height. It will also give you another useful figure – the percentage reduction or enlargement.

An ordinary pocket calculator can also be used to determine the size of an illustration after reduction or enlargement – just substitute your figures into the following formula:

$$\frac{\text{height after reduction or (enlargement)}}{\text{height of original}} = \frac{\text{width after reduction}}{\text{width of original}}$$

Suppose you have a photograph 10 inches high by 8 inches wide that you have to reduce so that it will fit a column 3 inches wide. What will be the resulting height after reduction? How much room should you allocate in the layout?

Using the above formula: $\frac{x}{10} = \frac{3}{8}$

Now, cross-multiply and divide to find x, thus:

$8x = 30$

$x = 30 \div 8 = 3{\cdot}75\text{in}$

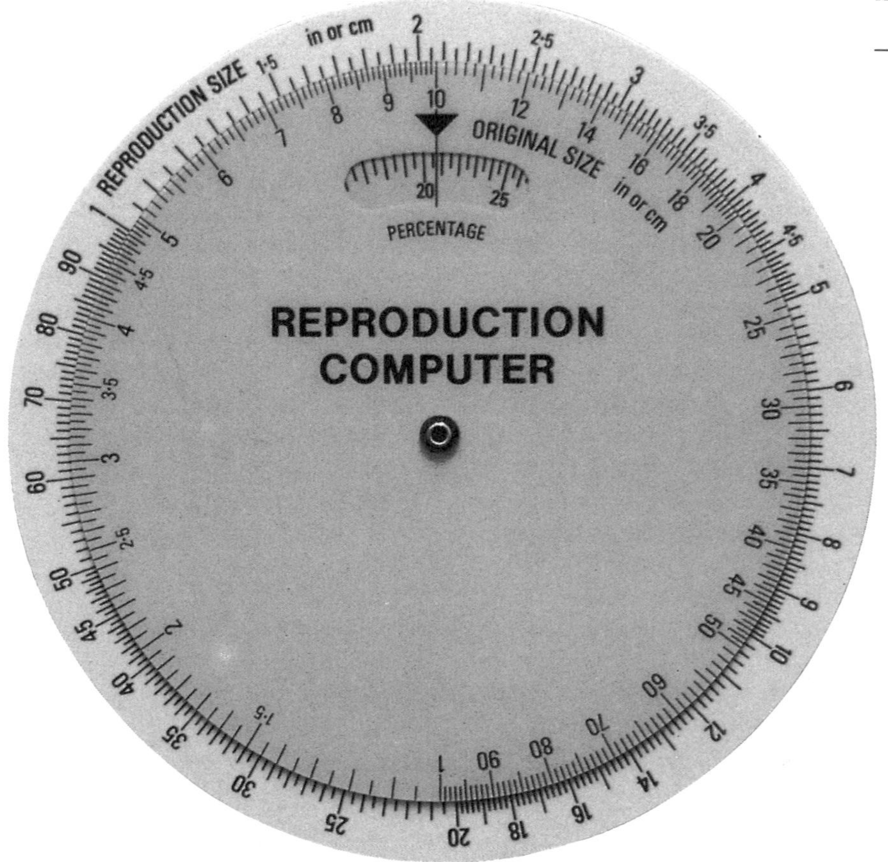

3.21 A reproduction calculator – a device for working out the size an illustration will appear on the page once it has been reduced or enlarged.

The main thing to remember when using a regular pocket calculator is to ensure that your units of measurement are consistent. *All* units must be in either inches, millimeters, or picas – but never a mixture!

To calculate the percentage reduction or enlargement, divide the intended width (or height) by the width (or height) of the original and multiply the result by 100. In this example:

$$\text{percentage reduction} = 3/8 \times 100 = 37{\cdot}5\%$$

A process camera can handle images within a range of 16 percent reduction and 600 percent enlargement.

Percentages can seem confusing at first: 100 percent, for example, is same size; 50 percent is half the width or height, but a quarter the area; 200 percent is twice the width or height, but four times the area. If you increase or reduce the width, do not forget that the height will also be increased or reduced, in direct proportion. When in doubt, always mark the copy with the width (or height) at which you want the image to appear. Writing exact measurements on the copy will also make it easier to check that the correct reduction or enlargement has been made when you receive your picture proofs.

The diagonal method (Fig. 3.22) uses geometry to help you to work out the final size of your scaled artwork. Draw a rectangle around the cropped area on the overlay, using a setsquare (triangle) or transparent grid to make sure that the corners are square. Protect the original, and draw a diagonal from the bottom left corner to the top right. If the artwork is to be reduced, measure the width you want it to appear along the bottom edge of the rectangle using the bottom left corner as your starting point, and draw a vertical from the other end, up to meet the diagonal. Where these two lines intersect, draw a horizontal line to meet the left vertical edge of your original box. This is the height that your scaled artwork will appear when reproduced.

If the artwork or transparency is to be enlarged, trace the crop outline to the bottom left corner of a piece of paper, draw the diagonal as before, but extending it beyond the crop rectangle. Also extend the bottom edge of the box and the left vertical. Now measure off the intended width of the enlargement, draw a line vertically to meet the extended diagonal, and read off the enlarged height.

Most pictures have to fit a specified width – a column width, for example. This method can, however, be used to calculate the width of an image that has to fit a specific height.

A Grant enlarger, or opaque projector, is a great help in scaling artwork. A lightbox, too, will make the process a lot easier.

Always label illustrations, and do so in soft pencil, preferably a non-reproducing light-blue one, or in felt tip pen (checking first that it will not bleed through the overlay). Do not stack photographs while the marks on the back are still wet without first protecting the front, and never write on the back of a photograph with a ballpoint pen. A greasy pencil, such as a Chinagraph, is best for writing on glossy surfaces. If you will be handling a lot of transparencies, invest in some lint-free cotton gloves to avoid introducing fingerprints onto the images. And always remove transparencies from glass mounts before sending them to the printers – they will break, damaging the transparency, and showering the recipient with thin shards of glass.

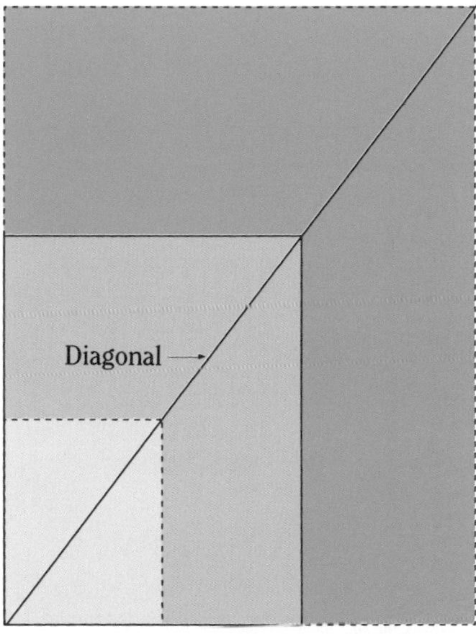

3.22 Diagonal scaling is a quick and easy way of estimating the space an enlarged or reduced illustration will occupy.

Dtp and desktop scanning

Users of desktop publishing (dtp) systems can bypass the PMT stage by directly scanning black-and-white artwork, using a desktop or hand-held scanner. The quality of the scanned images produced by these devices is much lower than that of illustrations originated on the drum scanners found in repro houses, but they are improving, and coming down in price all the time.

Desktop color scanners and special slide scanners are not yet considered to be up to repro quality, but they do have a place in giving the graphic designer an idea of how the layout is going to work. And they are being used as a creative tool by a new breed of computer graphics illustrators. With video stills cameras (Fig. 3.23), it is possible to bypass even the scanning process, and input digitized images direct to the computer.

3.23 Video stills cameras, such as this Logitech FotoMan, do not use film – they capture photographic images digitally. The digital information can then be input to a computer system directly, and no digitizing, scanning or other processing is necessary.

Drawing and painting by computer

On a computer such as the Macintosh, there are two different ways of producing illustrations, referred to as "draw" and "paint" (Fig. 3.24). A "paint" document is stored in the computer's memory as a bitmap, a one-to-one array corresponding to the pixels (dots) appearing on the screen. In a **paint program**, a circle intersected by a line, say, is just a pattern of dots and can only be moved en bloc. It is not possible to edit "globally" – modify every circle in a picture, for example – using just one command.

A "draw" document has more in-built "intelligence." It is stored in the computer's memory as a display list of the points and lines that make up the illustration, plus the formulas for any circles, ellipses, and curves. This is also known as object-oriented graphics, because every object – a circle, line, or curve – can be accounted for separately. In draw programs, it is possible to move the

3.24 The main difference between "paint" and "draw" software lies in how the image seen on the screen is stored in the memory. A paint document is a bitmap – just a representation of the screen – whereas a draw document is stored in terms of the points, lines, and formulas used to create it. Thus a draw document is not restricted to the resolution of the screen, and the image can be "deconstructed" for editing and amendment.

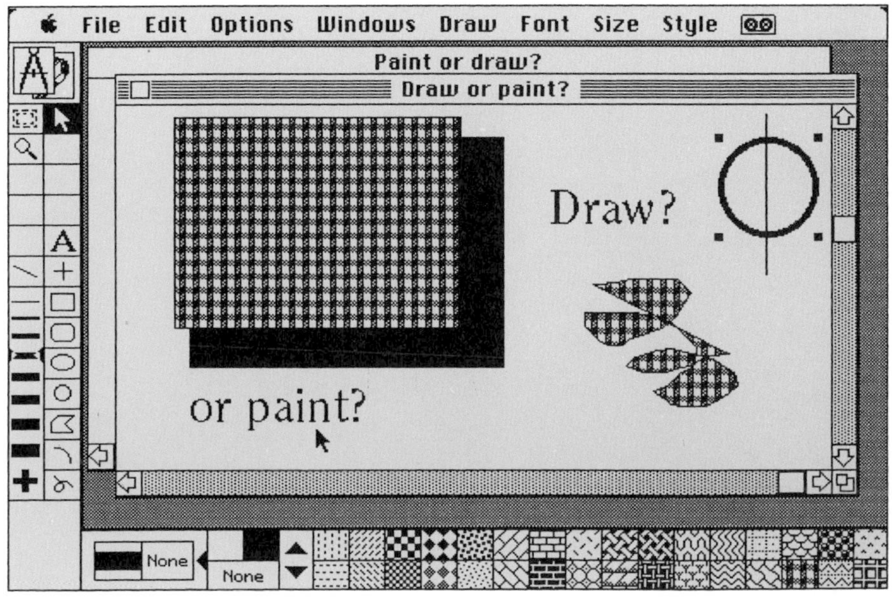

line without affecting the circle. And because they are not stored in terms of bitmaps, the output resolution to, say, a PostScript plotter is independent of the screen resolution.

MacPaint was the first program for the Macintosh to use bitmapped graphics, and is good for producing freehand irregularly shaped objects and airbrush effects. MacDraw, now completely rewritten, was the original object-oriented program. Some programs, such as Aldus's (formerly Silicon Beach's) SuperPaint, use both techniques, on separate layers (like overlays). Images can be transferred from the draw layer to the paint, but not vice versa. The early draw packages were restricted to drawings made up of simple geometric primitives, such as lines, boxes, circles, polygons, and arcs, which could be combined and grouped together.

Paint systems, such as the Quantel Paintbox (Fig. 3.26), are best known for their use in graphic design and for producing special effects for broadcast television. There are paint systems around that do their best to emulate real paint. Time Art's Oasis, for example, can simulate the wet appearance of oilpaint and produce convincing chalk and pastel effects through the use of a pressure-sensitive stylus.

It is as a medium of photomontage, however, that paint systems such as PixelPaint Professional and Studio 32 are being put to work in most design studios (Fig. 3.25). Similarly with **retouching** systems such as Digital Darkroom and PhotoShop. Here so-called source or "reference material" (beware of copyright infringement!) can be scanned into the system, or "framegrabbed" by a video camera, to be combined, manipulated, and recolored. This is analogous to sampling and remixing musical quotations to produce today's electronic dance music.

3.25 This "paint" illustration by David Wood, for an EMI Classics recording of Wagner's *Die Walküre*, was created on PC-based equipment at London's Central St Martin's College of Art and Design.

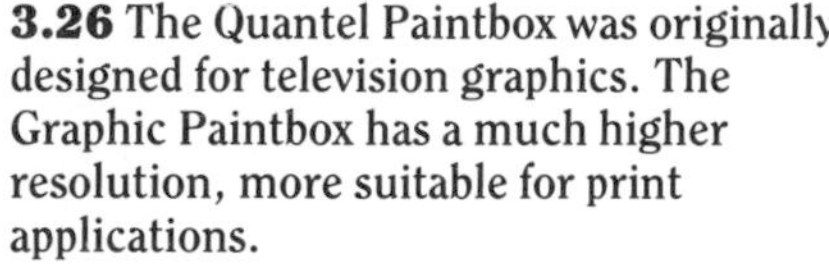

3.26 The Quantel Paintbox was originally designed for television graphics. The Graphic Paintbox has a much higher resolution, more suitable for print applications.

Some graphic designers also use paint systems as a concept design tool. If you are designing packaging for a new range of TV dinners, for example, a convincing illustration can be montaged from illustrations "grabbed" from cookery books or other sources. When the concept has been approved for go-ahead by the client, these roughs can be used as a brief for the commissioning of original illustration or photography.

The power of the computer as a conceptual tool is grossly underestimated. Some designers use it for nothing else, preferring to produce finished artwork traditionally, by hand. The computer allows you to play around with ideas – trying out different type, alternative positioning of elements, another color, and so on – for as long as your schedule will allow. As West Coast designer April Greiman says: "The paint never dries." And so long as you save the different versions, there is no chance of ever spoiling the original.

Retouching covers a multitude of sins: it can be as innocent as adding a few crocuses to a countryside scene, or it can be used to subvert reality completely, placing well known characters in compromising positions, for example (Fig. 3.27). Thankfully, it is mainly used to clean up images or as a purely creative medium – in fact, just as graphic designers use any other form of illustration. What is certain, however, is that as desktop scanners become more affordable and programs such as PhotoShop and Digital Darkroom are ever improved, photographs will be retouched routinely because it will be so easy to do so. And the adage that "the photograph never lies" will have even less credibility than it has now.

3.27 Paint systems are not only used to make "paintings" from scratch; they are more usually put to work retouching or montaging photographs. This illustration was created by Broder Brodersen at BB Video Graphics in Hanover using Quantel's Graphic Paintbox.

Draw programs such as Adobe Illustrator, MacDraw, and Aldus FreeHand are now closely linked to page layout packages. They can be used not only for black-and-white or color illustration, but to manipulate type too (Fig. 3.28).

Adobe Illustrator's objects are mostly controllable freeform curves (called Bézier curves) which can be manipulated to produce complex drawings. Scanned images or bitmapped drawings from a paint program can be "imported" and traced over. Aldus FreeHand uses a join-the-dots approach to create Bézier shapes, but it is not always clear what is going on until you move to preview mode. Apart from the Bézier tool, others are used to create boxes, lines, ellipses and corners at any angle. FreeHand has 200 layers (overlays) available, so that the drawing can be split up into separate elements which can be displayed and edited individually. Line attributes, pattern fills, and colors can be saved on a computer style sheet and applied to other elements later to maintain a consistency throughout a series of illustrations. There are commands for rotating, scaling, mirroring, skewing, and stretching elements. Text can be wrapped around a line or shape. Drawings thus created can be exported directly, as EPS (Encapsulated PostScript) files to page layout packages such as Quark XPress, Aldus PageMaker, or Xerox's Ventura. There they can be combined with text originated on a word processing system.

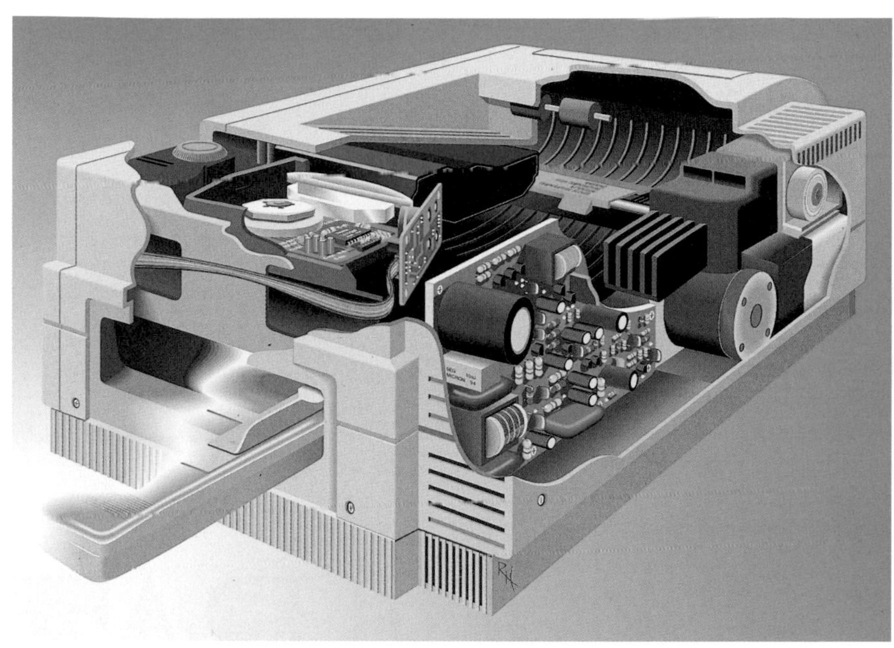

3.28 Illustrator Bob Harrington used Adobe Illustrator to produce this technical drawing of the Apple LaserWriter laser printer. Output is direct to film separations. A completely different use of a "draw" program is shown in this image by Henry Lyndsey – a dodo containing the names of 2000 endangered animals. It is a virtuoso demonstration of Aldus FreeHand's ability to set text along freeform lines.

3.29 Samples of dtp clip art from the Clipper Creative Art Service.

Clip art (Fig. 3.29) is copyright-free artwork that can be bought ready-made and en masse on a floppy disc or compact disc (CD-rom) and incorporated into your layouts. It has always been around in book form, to be copied at will, but with dtp has proliferated. Some is good, most is awful, and none of it is either original or unique. It should be used with discretion, and never in work where clients are under the impression that they are paying for original artwork. Maps can be copied with confidence, especially when they are to be customized in a program such as FreeHand or Illustrator.

Three-dimensional design programs, such as Swivel–3D, are also increasingly being used by illustrators, especially in comic books where cartoon characters are viewed from different angles and against different backgrounds (Fig. 3.30).

More and more, illustrators will be creating work on computer – images that can be shipped directly to page make-up programs with no intermediate artwork needed. There will always be a place, however, for original illustration and photography produced using traditional materials, and today's graphic designer will need to know how to make the best use of both, for a long time to come.

3.30 Pepe Moreno used three-dimensional graphics combined with paint software to produce the artwork for the DC Comics graphic novel *Batman: Digital Justice*.

Summary

Illustrations can be line or tone. If tone, they must be screened to convert the image into a pattern of dots for reproduction. Artwork can be drawn or painted conventionally, or created on a computer. Photographs can come in one of two forms: as reflection copy prints, or as transmission copy transparencies. Before origination, they will need to be scaled, and maybe cropped, so as to fit the size and shape of their position on the page layout. And they can be manipulated by computer, either on the level of merely correcting or changing colors, or in terms of undergoing more drastic treatment, using the image as a basis for a photomontage.

Whether you choose the manual or the mechanical method for the production of your designs will depend quite a lot on the processes being employed, and on the type of project. Conventionally drawn line work, such as cartoon illustrations, will have a sparkle and a fluidity that a computer program is unable to replicate. On the other hand, the consistent line weights and perfect geometry of a computer "draw" program are ideal for technical diagrams.

The constraints on black-and-white and color illustrations are different. Conventional black-and-white line drawings can be made into PMTs and simply be pasted directly onto mechanicals (see Chapter 4), ready for the next stage of production. If you are using a dtp system, it is easy enough to scan in black-and-white artwork and place it straight onto your page layout. Where photographs are concerned, the desired quality will be the decisive factor as you choose between scanning in a coarsely-screened picture or leaving its origination to the repro house. With a computer-generated or -stored illustration, there is the distinct advantage that the all-important artwork cannot get lost or damaged in the mail. It can even be sent to its destination down the telephone lines. And once the image is inside the system, it can be used over and over in different shapes and forms.

For color work, illustrations usually arrive in the form of transparencies, though original artwork can produce much better results. Whichever form they take, they must be flexible enough to be wrapped around the drum of the scanner at the repro house or printer. Desktop scanners can be used to input images intended for photomontage and other forms of creative retouching. Or the scanner can produce low-resolution scans to indicate positions and crops for illustrations that will later be processed at the repro house, on better quality equipment, as we shall discover in the next chapter.

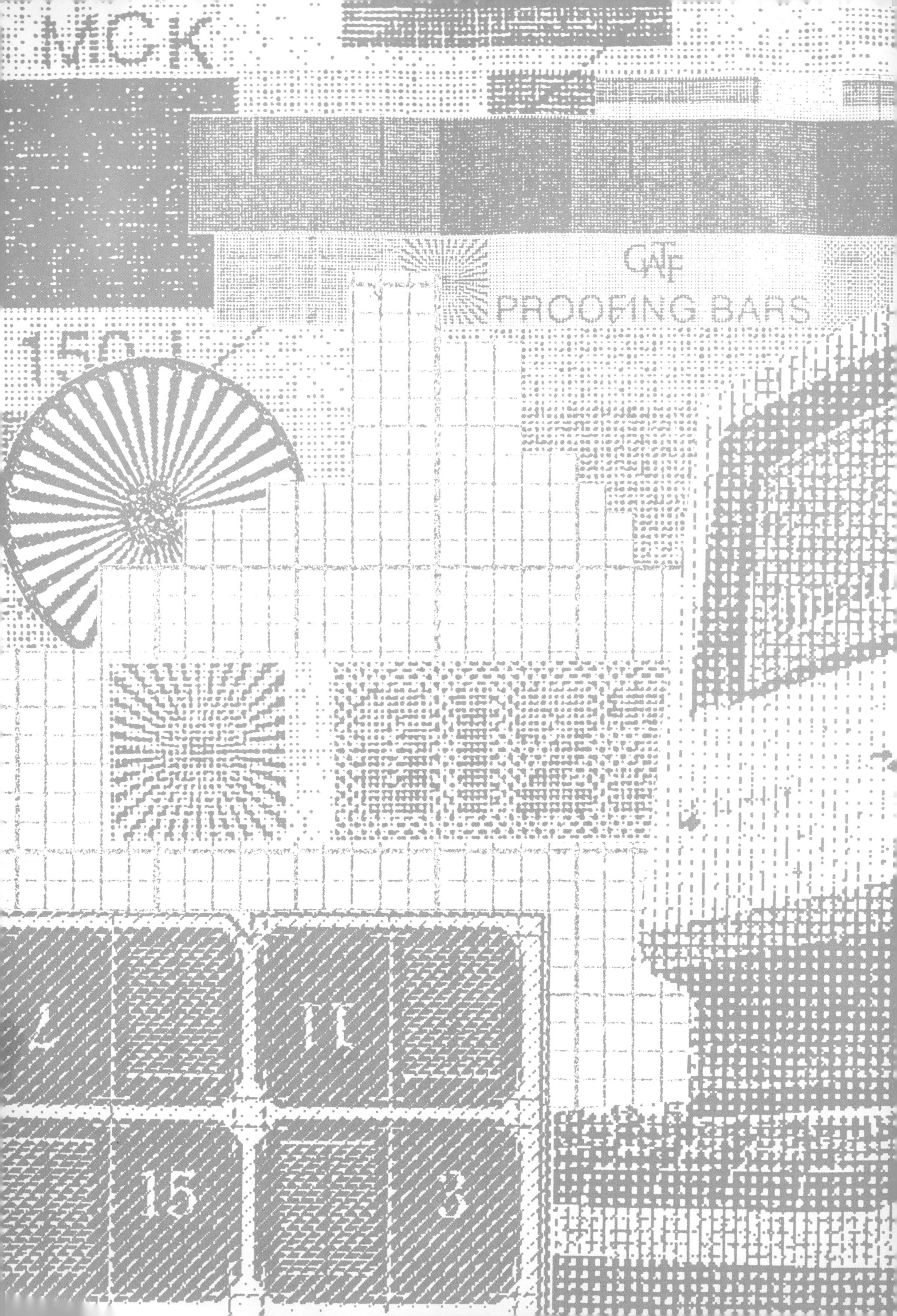
MCK
GATF
PROOFING BARS
11
15
3

4. Prepress

Prepress is the part of the print process in which all the design elements – the words and the pictures – are assembled into a unified whole. It is the stage in print production that ends with the making of lithographic plates, silkscreens, or gravure cylinders. This marks the point of no return, after which the presses begin to roll.

But in recent years that decisive moment has shifted. The involvement of the graphic designer has been extended, and is now much more closely tied to the outcome. A publication used to be "put to bed" with the dispatch of the mechanicals to the printer or repro house. Now, as all the data that makes up a page is digitized and stored electronically, it is feasible (though not always desirable) to make essential changes much later in the process – right up until the exposure of the final film, in some cases.

This chapter begins by covering the principles and terminology of layout, with tips for avoiding common design pitfalls. We take a look at grids and their usefulness in providing structure to a page. They save time too. Then imposition schemes are explained – a good grounding in how and where pages are arranged on printing plates or cylinders is important for effective prepress planning. Next, a practical task: preparing the mechanical, or the camera-ready artwork. This may not be what a lot of graphic designers actually do – many leave the neat work to the typesetter. But a good knowledge of producing precise mechanicals will stand you in good stead for working on the more flexible electronic equivalent: the desktop publishing package.

In Part 2 we move on to repro, and look at film montage. We discuss the various methods of checking picture proofs, and outline what you can discover from a detailed examination of the proof's color bar.

Finally, we take a look at the top-end full-color prepress systems, with which it is possible to produce final film straight from the screen, with no intermediate hand work necessary.

WHAT EQUIPMENT DO YOU NEED TO GET STARTED?

- a sturdy tabletop or drawing board
- a supply of smooth white mounting board
- a pad of layout paper
- a supply of fibertip pens and soft black pencils
- a clean plastic eraser
- a pad of tissue or acetate for overlays
- a non-reproducing light-blue pencil
- a blue greasy pencil (Chinagraph) for writing on glossy surfaces
- a surgical scalpel or craft knife (such as an X-acto)
- a “self-healing” cutting mat
- a straight metal edge
- rubber cement and spatula, spray mount aerosol adhesive, or a hot-wax coater
- low-tack masking tape or matte frosted “magic” tape
- a large soft brush
- talcum powder for de-greasing and “lubricating” surfaces
- paper towels to mop up spillages
- process white for correcting mistakes
- sable or synthetic sable brushes, sizes 00, 1, and 3
- a loupe
- a lightbox conforming to standard lighting conditions
- a proportional scale, or calculator
- a stainless-steel pica rule or plastic typescale
- a geometry set with compasses, setsquare (triangle), and protractor for measuring angles
- circle and ellipse templates
- a transparent grid to check alignment
- a selection of type specimens
- a selection of paper samples
- a Pantone color fan and swatches

AND OPTIONALLY:

- a process camera, in a darkroom or behind heavy black lightproof curtains
- a PMT processing machine
- a Grant enlarger
- a sink with a water supply
- a cadograph, for drawing your own grids
- a photocopier capable of enlarging and reducing
- a fax machine to keep in visual touch with the client and printer

Part 1: layout

In design, all rules are there to be broken. But first you have to know what they are. Most graphic designers are, so to speak, in the fashion business, and if asymmetrical or off-center designs are in vogue this year, then maybe a symmetrical or centered design will get noticed (Fig. 4.1). Whenever someone writes down the rules, you can bet that someone

4.1 Layouts can be symmetrical – with almost everything centered – or asymmetrical or can combine elements of both approaches. The look you decide upon is very much dependent on the sort of job in hand, the message you wish to get across, and the fashion at the time.

RAMBLING NEWS

SKETCHING CAN BE FUN!

by Ivor Pencil

There can be few of us who are not feeling the cruel tweak of recession about our Gucci waistbands at the moment, and there are even some of our membership who are OUT OF WORK! Of course, certain individuals would do well to get out of bed before the crack of noon on a weekday. Still, we'll say no more: some people are at their most creative when they're asleep, or at least I presume that must be the case.

However, it was only when I was in Kensington Gardens deliberating over which was the better bargain at the Dodgy Deli – the rusty tins with no labels or the out-of-date shellfish from Poland – that I saw our Club Secretary go by, leading a dog of dubious parentage by a grimy length of macramé yarn, and I realized just how bad things really are.

Being between jobs myself at the moment, I wondered how I could pass the time cheaply yet creatively. I thought: "I know what! I went to art college – I'll go out and do some sketching!"

It's great! This is what you do:

1) Nip down to your local art supplies store and buy lots of Japanese handmade paper. Also purchase some cartridge paper, as the Japanese gear is far too expensive to waste on mere outdoor sketching.

2) Skulk about the art museum a while until you can lift one of their folding seats without being seen.

3) Take it back and pay the fine.

4) Drive the car to an out-of-town supermarket and get a picnic together.

Need a few hints?

• Chocolate-chip cookies – several packs
• a pot of spicy Nutrasweet dip and some sponge fingers
• brie, French bread, wine, etc
• a Swiss army penknife
• paracetamol
• a warm woolly jumper
• some pencils

Sketching can add a new dimension to your rambling holidays – just try it and see!

Now you're all set! Let's go sketching! Of course, you can just sit in front of the television and run off a few workmanlike studies of the aspidistra, but half the fun is getting your orange shellsuit on, tucking your trousers

7

RAMBLING NEWS

Sketching can be fun!

by Ivor Pencil

"I wondered how I could pass the time cheaply yet creatively. I thought: I know what! I went to art college – I'll go out sketching!"

There can be few of us who are not feeling the cruel tweak of recession about our Gucci waistbands at the moment, and there are even some of our membership who are OUT OF WORK! Of course, certain individuals would do well to get out of bed before the crack of noon on a weekday. Still, we'll say no more: some people are at their most creative when they're asleep, or at least I presume that must be the case.

However, it was only when I was in Kensington Gardens deliberating over which was the better bargain at the Dodgy Deli – the rusty tins with no labels or the out-of-date shellfish from Poland – that I saw our Club Secretary go by, leading a dog of dubious parentage by a grimy length of macramé yarn and I realized just how bad things really are.

Being between jobs myself at the moment, I wondered how I could pass the time cheaply yet creatively. I thought: "I know what! I went to art college – I'll go out sketching!"

It's great! Here's what you do:

1) Nip down to your local art supplies store and buy lots of Japanese handmade paper. Also buy some cartridge paper as the Japanese gear is far too expensive to waste on sketching.

2) Skulk about the museum a while until you can lift

Sketching in the open air! What bliss!

7

else will come along before the ink is dry to rewrite them.

Having said that, however, there are some rules that endure and, for the majority of jobs, the desire will not be to shock, but to communicate ideas clearly, in a visual language accessible and understandable to all.

Very few designers are given a completely free hand – an open brief – to design what they will. There are always constraints, and therein lies the challenge: how to be different and eye-catching, while getting the message across, to time and to a budget. The client will expect the design to relate to the job it has to do – an annual report for a prestigious company will look very different, for example, from a newspaper advertisement for a cut-price corner store.

Designers must develop skills in communicating their concepts to the client clearly and unambiguously, through presentations, which may include rough sketches and more polished visualizations. Designers are also sometimes asked to help "sell" an idea to a client's clients by producing highly finished mock-ups or dummies that will convey a flavor of how the printed product will look.

There are technical constraints in planning your layout. Paper comes in stock sizes, and so do printing plates. Insisting on so-called **bastard sizes** and non-standard shapes is wasteful of resources. Folding machines have their limitations too. Packaging designers, in particular, may be restricted by the print technology – for example, only two non-overlapping colors may be allowable when printing a plastic container by flexography (see p. 149).

Thankfully, the offset litho process has given designers almost complete freedom over where the design elements – the type, line illustrations, and photographs – can be positioned on the page. And desktop publishing (dtp) offers the chance to try out many more potential design solutions. So where do we start?

For magazine and book work, there are certain conventions to be observed. Here we are dealing with pages. Most pages are the shape of an upright rectangle, and this orientation is sometimes called **portrait**. A page with a width greater than its height is denoted **landscape**.

Page sizes are written thus: US Letter is 8½ inches wide and 11 inches tall, and is written 8½ × 11in. The European equivalent is called A4 (see p. 135), and its dimensions are written 210 × 297mm. In inches, that is 8¼ × 11¾in. In the USA and most of Europe, it is usual to write the width before the height; in the UK and the Far East the opposite is the case – the height precedes the width.

The white areas that frame the printed portion of the page are called the **margins** (Fig. 4.2). The one at the top is the **head**; the one at the bottom is the **foot**. On the outer edge of the page is the **fore edge**; and the space between the printed material and the spine or fold is the **back edge**. The combined back edges of a double-page spread is called the **gutter**. It is also a term used for any vertical space – between two columns, for example.

4.2 The page has a vocabulary of its own to describe the various parts of its anatomy. The blank spaces – the margins – are as important as the image and type areas: at the top is the head; at the bottom, the foot; nearest the inside, the back edge; and nearest the extremities, the fore edge.

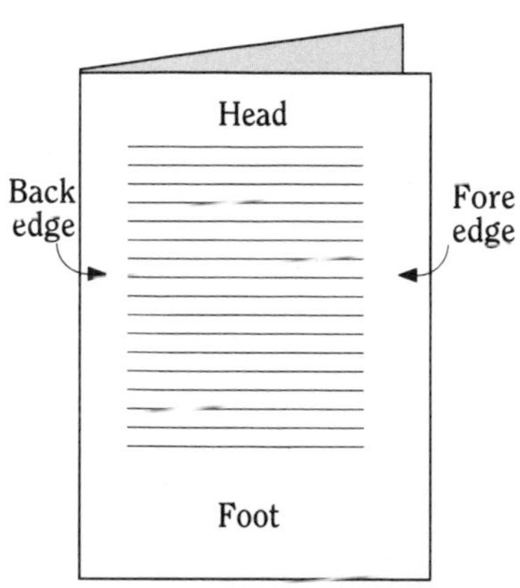

4.3 The standard proportions of medieval book pages, as discovered by the German designer Jan Tschichold. The page size and text area are in the ratio 2:3, the depth of text is equal to the width of the page, and the margins are in the proportions 2:3:4:6.

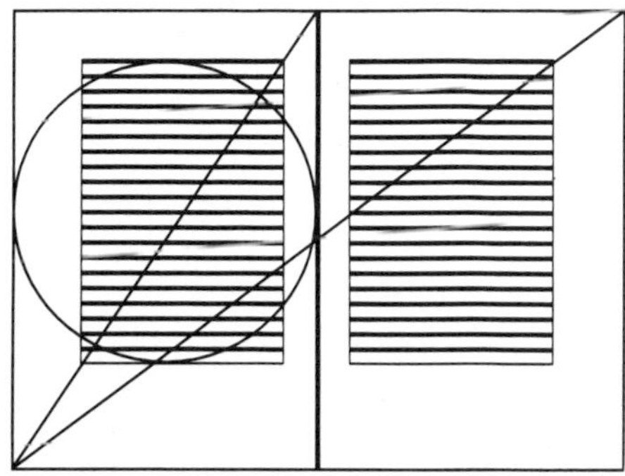

Traditionally, the foot is greater in depth than the head, and the fore edge around twice the width of the back edge so that two facing pages will be united as a spread.

Much has been written about what constitutes "good" and "elegant" design. Our response to a layout is embedded in our cultural background. The German designer Jan Tschichold discovered that the margins of medieval manuscripts followed certain rules of proportion, which are still thought pleasing today (Fig. 4.3). The page size was of the ratio 2:3; the depth of the printed area was the same as the width of the page; and the head:back:fore edge:foot margins were of the ratio 2:3:4:6.

The famous **golden section** format of the Renaissance has proportions of 34:21 or 8·1:5. Superimposed onto a sheet of US Letter stock, the golden section is just over 1¾ inches narrower (Fig. 4.4).

4.4 The golden section is a proportion (34:21) that people through the ages and in different cultures have found pleasing. It has many parallels in nature – the way a snail's shell grows, for instance. Here a sheet of paper to golden section proportions is compared with US Letter and A4 sizes.

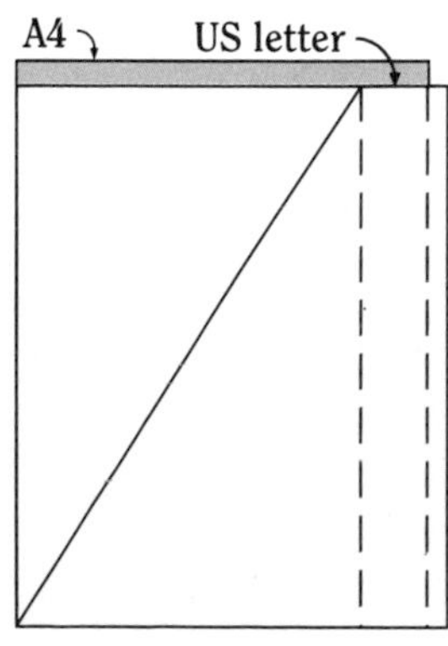

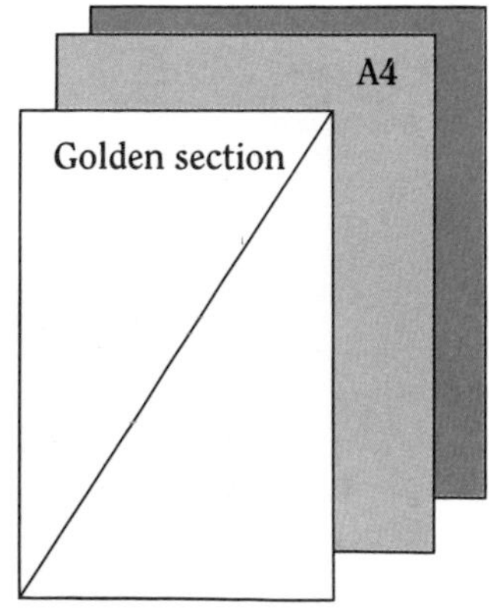

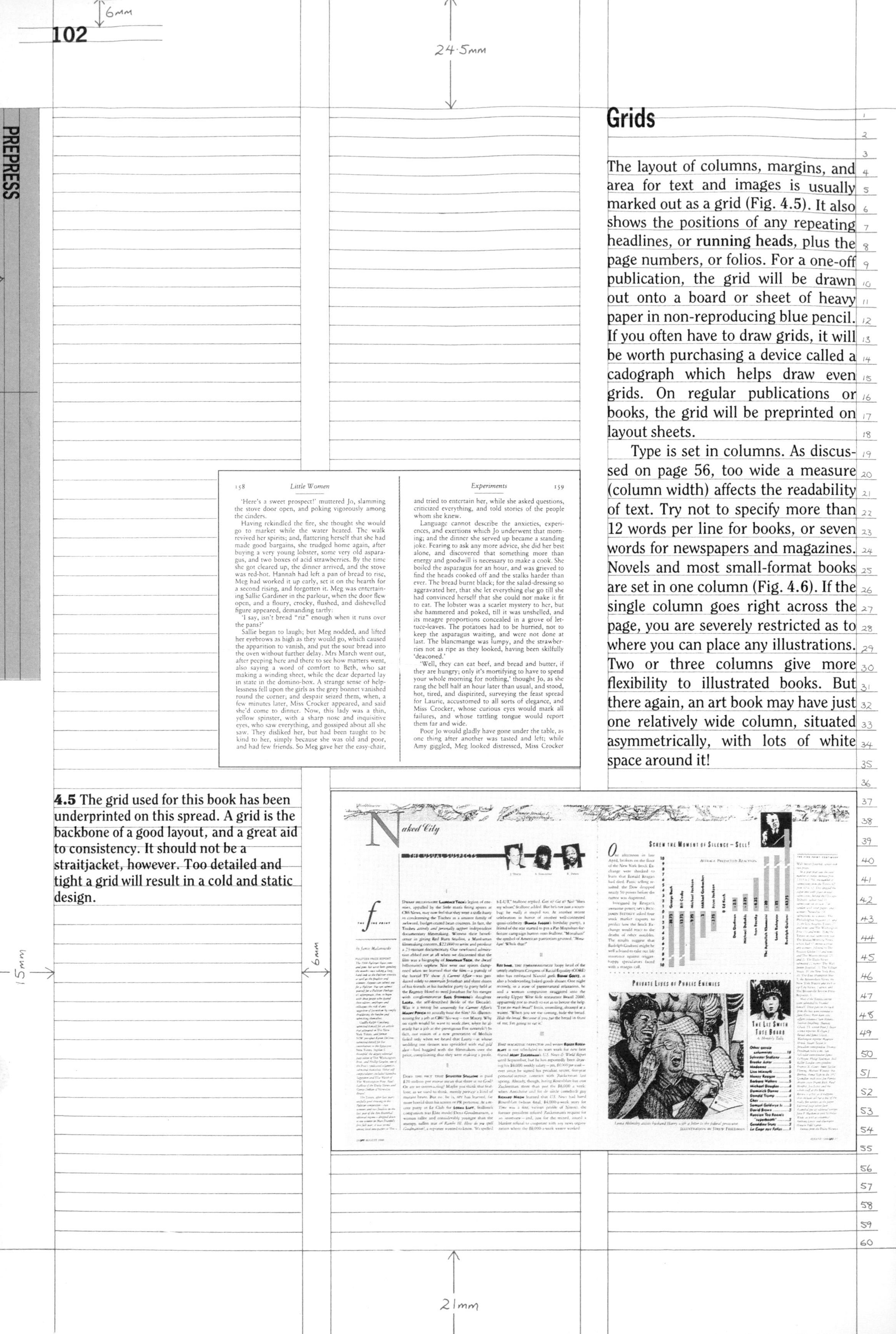

Grids

The layout of columns, margins, and area for text and images is usually marked out as a grid (Fig. 4.5). It also shows the positions of any repeating headlines, or **running heads**, plus the page numbers, or folios. For a one-off publication, the grid will be drawn out onto a board or sheet of heavy paper in non-reproducing blue pencil. If you often have to draw grids, it will be worth purchasing a device called a cadograph which helps draw even grids. On regular publications or books, the grid will be preprinted on layout sheets.

Type is set in columns. As discussed on page 56, too wide a measure (column width) affects the readability of text. Try not to specify more than 12 words per line for books, or seven words for newspapers and magazines. Novels and most small-format books are set in one column (Fig. 4.6). If the single column goes right across the page, you are severely restricted as to where you can place any illustrations. Two or three columns give more flexibility to illustrated books. But there again, an art book may have just one relatively wide column, situated asymmetrically, with lots of white space around it!

158 *Little Women*

'Here's a sweet prospect!' muttered Jo, slamming the stove door open, and poking vigorously among the cinders.

Having rekindled the fire, she thought she would go to market while the water heated. The walk revived her spirits; and, flattering herself that she had made good bargains, she trudged home again, after buying a very young lobster, some very old asparagus, and two boxes of acid strawberries. By the time she got cleared up, the dinner arrived, and the stove was red-hot. Hannah had left a pan of bread to rise, Meg had worked it up early, set it on the hearth for a second rising, and forgotten it. Meg was entertaining Sallie Gardiner in the parlour, when the door flew open, and a floury, crocky, flushed, and dishevelled figure appeared, demanding tartly:

'I say, isn't bread "riz" enough when it runs over the pans?'

Sallie began to laugh; but Meg nodded, and lifted her eyebrows as high as they would go, which caused the apparition to vanish, and put the sour bread into the oven without further delay. Mrs March went out, after peeping here and there to see how matters went, also saying a word of comfort to Beth, who sat making a winding sheet, while the dear departed lay in state in the domino-box. A strange sense of helplessness fell upon the girls as the grey bonnet vanished round the corner; and despair seized them, when, a few minutes later, Miss Crocker appeared, and said she'd come to dinner. Now, this lady was a thin, yellow spinster, with a sharp nose and inquisitive eyes, who saw everything, and gossiped about all she saw. They disliked her, but had been taught to be kind to her, simply because she was old and poor, and had few friends. So Meg gave her the easy-chair,

Experiments 159

and tried to entertain her, while she asked questions, criticized everything, and told stories of the people whom she knew.

Language cannot describe the anxieties, experiences, and exertions which Jo underwent that morning; and the dinner she served up became a standing joke. Fearing to ask any more advice, she did her best alone, and discovered that something more than energy and goodwill is necessary to make a cook. She boiled the asparagus for an hour, and was grieved to find the heads cooked off and the stalks harder than ever. The bread burnt black; for the salad-dressing so aggravated her, that she let everything else go till she had convinced herself that she could not make it fit to eat. The lobster was a scarlet mystery to her, but she hammered and poked, till it was unshelled, and its meagre proportions concealed in a grove of lettuce-leaves. The potatoes had to be hurried, not to keep the asparagus waiting, and were not done at last. The blancmange was lumpy, and the strawberries not as ripe as they looked, having been skilfully 'deaconed.'

'Well, they can eat beef, and bread and butter, if they are hungry; only it's mortifying to have to spend your whole morning for nothing,' thought Jo, as she rang the bell half an hour later than usual, and stood, hot, tired, and dispirited, surveying the feast spread for Laurie, accustomed to all sorts of elegance, and Miss Crocker, whose curious eyes would mark all failures, and whose tattling tongue would report them far and wide.

Poor Jo would gladly have gone under the table, as one thing after another was tasted and left; while Amy giggled, Meg looked distressed, Miss Crocker

4.5 The grid used for this book has been underprinted on this spread. A grid is the backbone of a good layout, and a great aid to consistency. It should not be a straitjacket, however. Too detailed and tight a grid will result in a cold and static design.

In newspapers and most popular magazines, white space means wasted space, and space is at a premium. So there will typically be many narrow columns to the page, with the possibility of photographs straddling two, three, or more of them.

Horizontal lines built into the grid can be used to impose further discipline on the layout, allowing you to align the edges of photographs, say, with blocks of text. Six to eight horizontal divisions should be sufficient. Too many, and the layout will seem fussy, with no apparent thought-out design. Too few will not allow enough variety in the layout – it will appear static if the illustrations always fall in the same positions. Some grids may show a numbered horizontal line marked out for each line of type.

A grid can seem confusing at first sight, but not all the lines and divisions have to be used on every page. Seen as an underlying structure, however, the grid can become an indispensable time-saving aid to producing clear and consistent layout, quickly and painlessly.

Design elements such as cross-**headings** (subheadings within a block of text), boxed copy, captions, rules, borders, and tint blocks are all devices for adding "color" to an otherwise "gray" layout. They will assist the readers' eyes, helping them follow the flow of the text, especially if it has been split to accommodate the placement of illustrations. And, if the copy does not fit exactly, they are useful and unobtrusive space fillers.

RAY KERRISON

METS RAPE SUSPECT GIVES BLOOD SAMPLE

It's one long High Noon for sheriff

He's under the gun for doing his job

Ind. court KO's Tyson's bid for bail during appeal

The untruth and nothing but the untruth

MIKE McALARY

Brown wins Vermont caucuses

BILL & JERRY SQUARE OFF IN BRONX DEBATE

Brown ripped over boast he slashed Calif. taxes

4.6 Magazines and newspapers have relatively complex grids, so as to look busy and up-to-the-minute, and thus have the option to use illustrations at different shapes and sizes. The spread from *Spy* magazine opposite uses a versatile five-column grid, with text at either one- or two-column measure. Note the map bleeding off the top. Newspapers avoid white space, so use even more columns to cram as much text onto the page as possible. But while magazines and newspapers are meant to be browsed, books are generally intended for reading sequentially and calmly, hence the simple and comforting one-column format found in most fiction.

A **bleed** is any area of flat color, a halftone, or a rule that goes right off the edge of the page. Any design element meant to bleed should exceed the trim line of the page by at least ⅛ inch (3mm). Check with your printers, however, if you are to introduce a bleed, in case their recommended overlap is different. In any case, for practical reasons try to avoid a layout that demands an exact trim.

Lastly, a word of caution. When pasting down type, try to keep a tidy desk. There is nothing worse than having completed a tight and attractive layout, only to find an odd paragraph that has been carelessly left out of the grand design. Keep a complete copy of the galley proofs (see Chapter 2) for reference, to check that paragraphs have not been pasted down out of sequence, and make any adjustments to the layout to avoid widows and orphans (see p. 43). The rest – is up to you!

Imposition

Unless you are designing a solitary jar label, or a single-sided folder, it will help the printer considerably if you know about imposition. **Imposition** is the term used for the planning of **pagination** in folders, magazines, or books in a pattern such that when the printed sheet of paper is folded and trimmed, the resulting pages **back up** correctly and run consecutively.

A sheet of paper has two sides: front and back (Fig. 4.7). Fold it once and – to the printer, at least – it becomes a four-page folder. Fold it again, and once one of the short sides has been cut, it becomes an eight-page folder, comprising two folded sheets, one nesting inside another. Fold a third time, and the result after trimming is a 16-page folder. It is a curious fact of the printing world that it is impossible to fold paper more than seven times, regardless of the size of the original sheet, or the thickness of the paper stock.

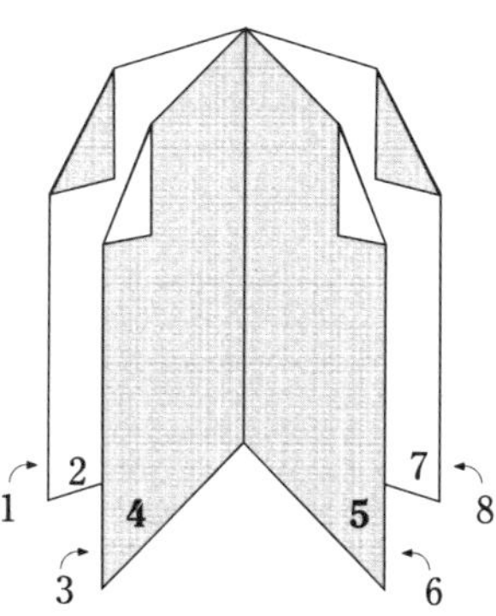

4.7 Imposition schemes can look complicated in diagram form, but all should become clear if you make a folded dummy in miniature – for your own benefit and to show the printer.

Most printers work in 16-page sections, with plates that print eight pages on each side. If your 16-page folder is numbered consecutively, with the first right-hand page as page 1, the first left as page 2, the numbers will fall as follows:

front: 1 4,5 8,9 12,13 16
back: 2,3 6,7 10,11 14,15

It is important to know which page numbers are on which side of the sheet, because you may wish to introduce flat color, or full color, into the publication. It will save you money if you can restrict it to one side of the sheet (Fig. 4.8).

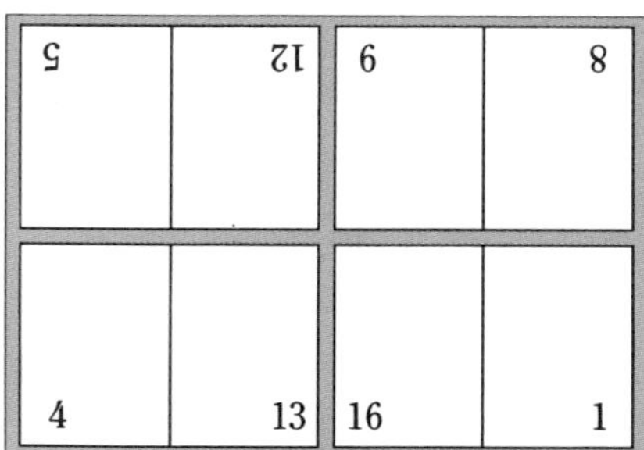

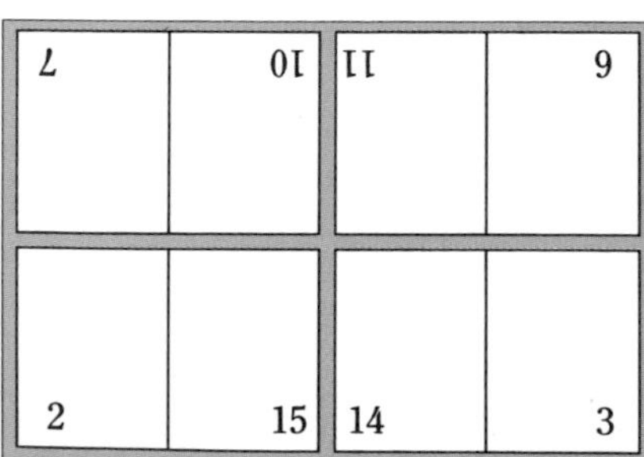

4.8 Sheetwork – the simplest form of imposition. Several pages are printed on one side of a sheet of paper, which is then turned over and printed again on the other side.

The odd numbers are always, by convention, on the right-hand side; the even numbers on the left. In bookwork, right or front is called **recto**; left or back is called **verso**. A 16-page section of a book is called a **signature**, and each signature will usually be marked with a **backstep mark** – a letter, number, or black strip to help the binder **collate**, or assemble, the signatures in the correct order.

If the cover of a 16-page folder is to be printed in the same stock as the rest of the publication, as a **self cover**, the first page will be the outside front cover (or OFC), page 2 will be the inside front cover (or IFC), page 15 will be the inside back cover (or IBC), and page 16 will be the outside back cover (or OBC). If, however, the cover is to be printed in heavier stock, or if it alone is to be printed in color, then it will be treated as a four-page section, printed separately. This leaves you with 16 pages for the inside, making a 20-page publication.

Generally speaking, printers like to handle only 4-, 8-, or 16-page sections (though novels are often printed in 32s and 64s). A 64-page magazine with a separate 4-page cover comprises four 16-page sections, which is convenient and economical. If you increase the pagination to 68, a 4-page section would have to be added somewhere. It is possible to add a two-page section, but not recommended. If the publication is to be saddle-stitched, this would leave an unsightly strip of paper at the other side of the wire staples. It would probably be just as economic to create another two pages.

To help you find your way around an imposition scheme, it is common to draw out a **flatplan** (Fig. 4.9). This shows diagrammatically what goes where in a publication. It also makes clear which sections or signatures can accommodate flat or full color to best effect. It is a good medium of communication on a magazine, for example, between the editorial, advertising, and design staff.

There are many ways of drawing up a flatplan, and it is best to consult your printers first, so as to take into account the way they are used to working, and any peculiarities of their folding machines. If in any doubt about imposition, do not be afraid of making up a folded **dummy** out of scrap paper. This would be a miniature version of your publication marked with page numbers and the position of any color.

There are two distinct ways of feeding paper through printing presses. It can be done either with pre-cut single sheets (**sheetwise**) or with a roll of paper (for **web** printing). The sheetwise method uses one plate to print the front of a sheet, and another for the back. Both sides share a

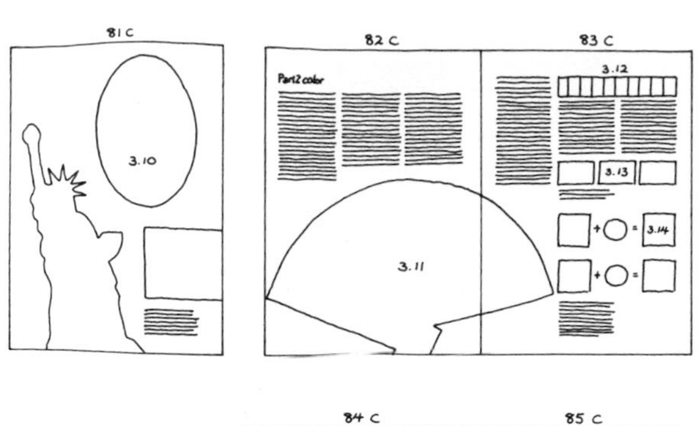

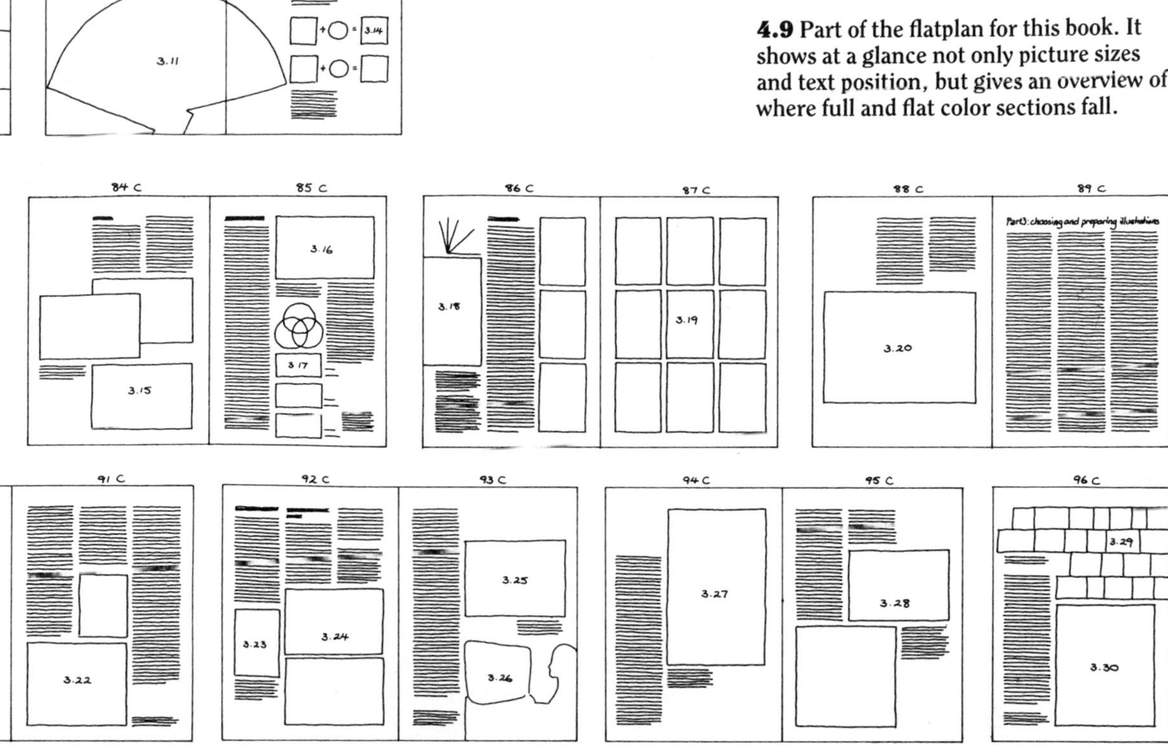

4.9 Part of the flatplan for this book. It shows at a glance not only picture sizes and text position, but gives an overview of where full and flat color sections fall.

common **gripper edge** (Fig. 4.10). The gripper edge is the leading end of the sheet, and is held in place on the press by finger-like grippers. An allowance of ½ inch (15mm) must be made on this edge when estimating the printed area of a sheet. Opposite the gripper edge is the **leave edge**, and the left side of the sheet as it passes through the press is called the **lay edge**.

An alternative, and a method used when printing booklets or sections of publications with fewer than 16 pages, is to put both sides of the sheet on the same plate. This may sound crazy, but when it is cut and folded correctly you end up with twice as many half-size sheets.

Work-and-turn (Fig. 4.11) is a technique in which the sheet goes through the machine first one way, then the paper is turned over sideways and printed once more, such that page 2 prints on the back of page 1. The gripper edge remains the same. The sheet is cut in two, and the result is two piles of paper printed on both sides that can be folded and trimmed as in sheetwise imposition. **Work-and-tumble** (Fig. 4.12) is similarly ingenious, but the paper is flipped head over heels, and the gripper edge changes ends.

Using work-and-turn or work-and-tumble is economical. This is not only because just one plate is made and there is less **spoilage**, but also because for smaller jobs the printer can **step-and-repeat** (duplicate), a set of pages and print **two-up** – twice as many again in one printing.

4.10 The way a sheet of paper goes into the printing press has a bearing on the layout. The gripper edge, for example, must contain an area free of all text or graphic material.

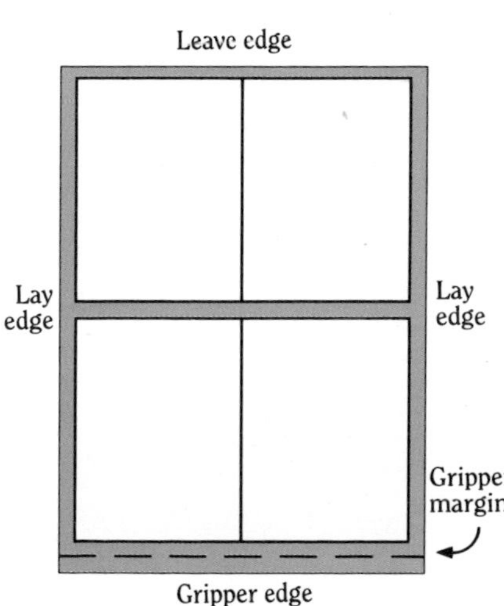

4.11 Work-and-turn is an ingenious imposition scheme that gives twice as many products as you would expect using just one plate. It is often more economical to use large plates, so one side of the sheet is put on one half of the plate, the other side on the other half. The sheet is printed, and the pile is turned over and printed again on the other side. Later the pile of sheets is cut down the middle to give you two identical half-size piles of printed sheets. Both sides share the same gripper edge.

4.12 Work-and-tumble is similar to work-and-turn, except the pile is flipped head over heels and the gripper edge changes ends.

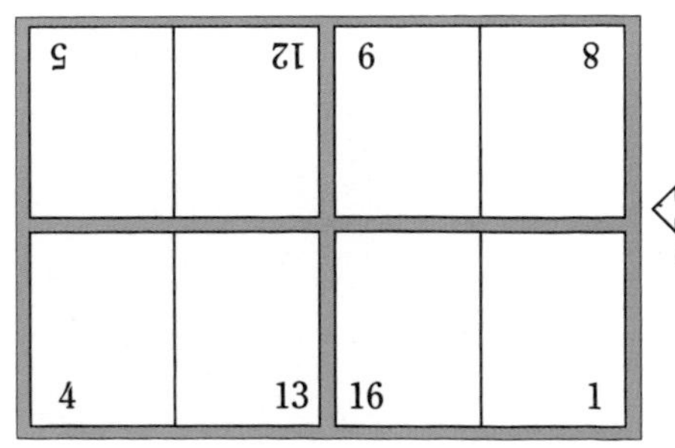

With a knowledge of imposition, it is possible to arrange two or more pages of a publication on the same mechanical, saving the printer time and effort. If you are designing a whole range of stationery, to be printed in the same colors and on the same paper stock, you can make similar savings by **ganging up** the individual items onto one plate and printing **one-up**.

Web printing is usually reserved for large print runs. The possible imposition schemes are quite different from those for sheetwork. If you are going to use this method, it is best to consult the printers at the outset.

There are other design considerations relating to the imposition scheme. A double-page spread (DPS) will be a problem if text or an image runs across two facing pages. They will only align correctly on a center spread, and even here you must take care to keep anything important – the eyes in a portrait, for example – well away from the position of a magazine's wire staples. For consistency of print density, it is best to have DPSs printed on the same side of the same section, if at all possible. **Starvation ghosting** is an unwelcome effect that results in uneven printing and is due, to some extent, to the placement of dense black elements in certain positions on the plate. If you think you may have problems, check with the printer about an alternative imposition.

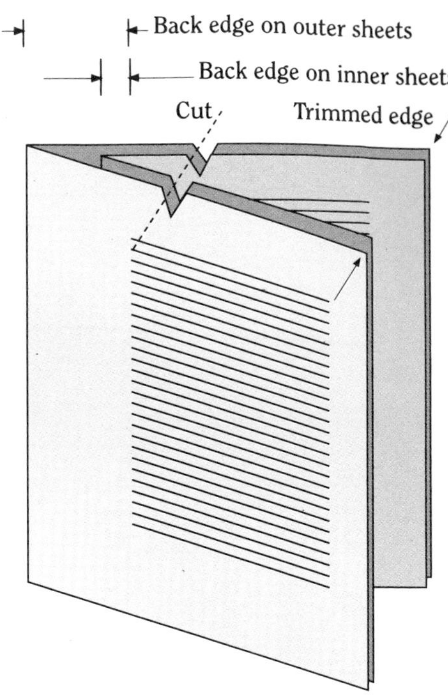

4.13 Paper creep allowance – made to counter the effect caused by the thickness of the paper in the fold of saddle-stitched publications with lots of pages. Otherwise, after the pages have been trimmed the text area will creep nearer the fore edge as the center of the publication is approached.

There are all kinds of other imposition schemes that relate to non-standard folders and booklets – those with fan or **accordion folds**, for example, and those having unusual shapes and sizes. For very large projects, keep your ears to the ground for the latest developments in computerized imposition, on systems such as Opticopy and Misomex.

Factors that influence the choice of a particular imposition scheme include: the total number of pages, the print run, the untrimmed page size, and the type of folding and binding. Discuss all these with the printer before you start on the mechanicals, and together you will be able to plan for the most economical sheet size, the most cost-effective press, the lowest spoilage, the highest quality, and the fastest turnaround.

PAPER CREEP ALLOWANCE

A book will be bound stitched or glued in 16-page sections. A saddle-stitched publication, however, may have quite a number of sections nested one within the other. When these sections are collated, the thickness of the paper at the fold will add up to make pages toward the center stick out more than those near the covers. More paper will be trimmed from these pages, making them significantly narrower than those near the covers. To allow for this paper creep, you will need to vary the position of the margins, especially those at the outer edges.

A simple method of **paper creep allowance**, or shingling, is as follows (Fig. 4.13). Make a folded dummy, using the same paper stock as the proposed publication. Looking down at the top edge of the dummy, measure off the inner margin of the center pages and make a scalpel cut through the rest at the same point. Disassemble the dummy and use the position of the scalpel cuts as an inner margin reference on the mechanicals. It will appear to move toward the fold as you approach the center pages. It is not necessary to make an allowance on every page – a cumulative allowance can be made every few pages. Trim and center marks must remain to the same measure on all the boards, and remember to mark each mechanical "paper creep allowance made" in case a "helpful" printer decides to straighten up your seemingly wandering margins.

Preparing a mechanical

The **mechanical**, also known as **camera-ready copy** (CRC) or artwork (A/W), is the graphic designer's very own domain. It is what the canvas is to the fine artist. It is where all the line copy – both text and illustration – comes together, under the control of the graphic designer, as artwork, at the right size and ready to go under the process camera (Fig. 4.14).

Some designers **paste up** their own finished artwork. Others merely provide a rough cut-and-paste of photocopies to indicate their ideas to another professional, known as a **finished artist**, who does the neat job of preparing the boards for the camera. For the purpose of simplicity, we assume here that you the graphic designer are preparing the finished mechanical yourself. The principles underlying the neat and rough work are exactly the same.

Preparing a mechanical is a manual operation using text galleys plus PMTs of line art and perhaps veloxes of halftones (see p. 80). These are cut to shape using a scalpel, preferably on a "self-healing" cutting mat, and pasted onto a baseboard marked with a grid (Fig. 4.15).

The high-contrast film used in platemaking is **orthochromatic**, i.e. sensitive only to the blue end of the spectrum. The process camera "sees" red as black, and blue as white. As discussed in the previous chapter (see p. 89), the printer may have trouble with a color photograph that is to be reproduced in black and white. **Panchromatic** film, i.e. film sensitive to all colors, will have to be used if skin tones, for example, are to record correctly.

A mechanical will consist of many different kinds of paper, and the paste will have to contend with them all. Photosetting paper comes in two varieties: resin-coated (RC) bromide paper, and the cheaper stabilization paper that discolors with time (it should be avoided if the mechanical is to be used again). Typesetting from typewriters, laser printers, and photocopiers comes on plain paper, and repro proofs from letterpress setting usually come on heavy smooth art paper called **baryta**.

4.14 A mechanical layout can contain all kinds of design elements: text on bromide paper, PMTs of line art, rules and boxes, and maybe even headlines created using rub-down lettering.

One commonly used type of paste is rubber cement, spread thinly with an applicator or spatula. Surplus gum can be removed cleanly when dry using a homemade "eraser" of dried-up gum. But if any remains on the mechanical, it can pick up dust and grit. It is an even worse catastrophe if gum gets onto the process camera's copyboard glass. The result is that the next few halftones processed contain annoying blemishes.

Many graphic designers use an aerosol adhesive, such as Scotch Spray Mount, which may be convenient but, unless you use a spray booth with an extractor fan, can mess up your working environment. An alternative is wax, applied to the paper from a hot-wax coating machine, such as Letraset's Wax-coater. Wax gives a firm and even bond with no spread, and paper elements can be peeled off relatively easily to be placed elsewhere on the mechanical. Wax does not have as strong a bond as gum or spray mount, and there is a danger of small pieces falling off the mechanical.

4.15 Paste-up is the act of cutting graphic elements to size with a scalpel, and pasting them down onto the mechanical using rubber solution, hot wax, or aerosol adhesive.

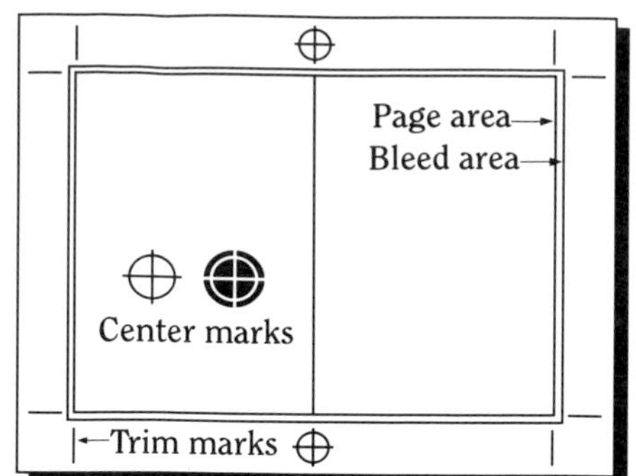

4.16 Trim and center marks are an aid to alignment of graphic elements and show the printer the extent of the printed page – everything the wrong side of the trim marks will be guillotined off and discarded.

You will need to put **trim and center marks** (Fig. 4.16) on the mechanical to indicate to the printer where the sheet is to be trimmed by the guillotine and folded. For hot-metal printing, these marks always had to be kept well away from the "visible" area of the page, so that they would disappear after trimming. For offset litho, the printer uses the marks to help join several pages together, and thus a visible cross-hair mark is preferred. These will be removed before printing.

Indicate any tints on an **acetate overlay**, using a **keyline** (Fig. 4.17), accompanied by the written message, "Keyline – do not print." A keyline marks out any area to be printed in a flat color or a tint for which you are not providing separate artwork. It can also show the position of a halftone, to be stripped-in later, or can indicate a bleed.

Tints can be cut from self-adhesive sheets, from vendors such as Letraset, but once in place over text are difficult to remove if you decide that the type has been rendered illegible. This operation is best left to the printer.

For most black-and-white work, with perhaps a single underprinting in flat color (see p. 83), the mechanical will go straight under the camera. If your halftones have a screen below 100 lines (see p. 78), veloxes will suffice. Above 100 lines, it is common for the designer to draw a black square or place a piece of red film called **Rubylith** in the position the halftone will occupy, to make a **mask**. When the negative film is made, these appear as **windows**, into which the negative halftones can be placed. But to avoid any ambiguity, it is best to stick down photocopies of the halftones, marked "for position only" – they will have to be cut out anyway, as we shall see below.

Rules (lines) and boxes can be drawn directly onto the boards using a technical pen filled with Indian ink (but never onto a substrate that might stretch or distort). Or printed rules can be pasted in place – they usually look neater on the final product. Do not cut them too thinly, or they will be prone to distortion. This is also true for rules that come in dispenser rolls on transparent carrier tapes. A great deal of practise and skill is needed to lay these down well. To create boxes, overlap the rules at the corners and cut miters through both rules, then trim away the excess.

Rule width is generally measured in points. A **hairline rule** is one narrower than half a point.

When the boards are complete, use a transparent grid lined up against the trim and center marks to check the alignment of all the pasted-down design elements. Label the boards with the name of the job and any page number. Then send them to the printer, with all the photographs and any artwork requiring special treatment, color swatches for any flat color, a folding dummy and/or flat-plan to tell the printer exactly how individual pages are to be arranged, and any spare bromides or repro proofs of the typesetting for emergency repairs.

If any small-scale corrections have been made to the boards – individual letters cut and transposed, a comma added, and so on – it is prudent to circle them on the overlay. That way, the printer won't brush them onto the floor by mistake, and you will know which areas of the page proof to pay particular attention to. It is better, in any case, to replace the entire paragraph, if you have the time. There is the risk of any scalpel cuts showing up as visible shadows under the camera. They appear as white lines on the negative film, and can easily be opaqued-out using a substance called ox-blood, just so long as they are kept well away from any typematter.

If the black-and-white mechanical has been prepared at the typesetters from your rough layouts, it is most likely to be proofed on a photocopy machine. The photocopier will be sensitive to the blue lines of the grid and will show scalpel marks too. The printer is well aware of all this, and the marks should be ignored. They won't be there when the mechanical is printed.

At the printers, a negative film is made from the mechanical. After retouching work to opaque-out scalpel marks and any other imperfections, it is contact printed direct to a negative-working plate. Alternatively, it may first be contact printed to film to produce a positive, which is then used to produce a positive-working plate (see the next chapter for a fuller explanation of platemaking).

Text and Type

Do not print keylines
Color photo (A) to bleed at left
20% black tint
Text and Type
Title wording in 100% magenta + 100% yellow
All text to print in black

4.17 A keyline shows the printer where halftones, bleeds, and areas of flat color or tints are to be positioned. If they are not to print, they should appear on an overlay marked "keyline – do not print."

Part 2: repro

Film make-up

For most high-quality work, and all multicolor printing, the **make-up** of the full mechanical will be bypassed, and the design elements will be assembled together on **film** (Fig. 4.18). Paper-based mechanicals are good enough for black-and-white work, but are not considered **dimensionally stable** enough for close register work. (They will stretch and distort on their travels from the studio to the printers, as they are subjected to different environmental conditions. The amounts are tiny, but sufficient to cause the different printings to be out of register.) It is unlikely that the average graphic designer will ever be asked to do film make-up – the **assembly** will be done by a professional called a "stripper." But graphic designers effectively have to brief the strippers with their roughs, and check the results, so it is important to know what is going on.

Film used by printers has a high-speed high-contrast emulsion on a polyester base. The emulsion side of the film is slightly duller than the other side, and it may be possible to see the image on the film if it is held up to the light and viewed at a shallow angle. If in doubt, scratch the film – well away from the image area, naturally – to discover which side the emulsion is on.

Film can be right reading, or wrong (reverse) reading. As you can view film from either side, it is important to specify "emulsion up" or "emulsion down" as well.

When the printing plates are made, the film is always put in contact with the plate for maximum sharpness. The emulsion touches the plate, i.e. the film is emulsion side down.

The type of film most commonly used is **right-reading emulsion down (RRED)**, also known as **wrong-reading emulsion up (WREU)**. The image appears the correct way round (is right-reading) when the film is viewed from the shiny side, and wrong-reading from the dull emulsion side. RRED film is used for offset litho printing – and for all offset processes. When the film is contacted with the plate, the image is transferred so that it is right-reading. During printing, the ink on the plate transfers as wrong-reading to the rubber blanket, and then as right-reading to the paper (Fig. **4.19**; there is more about the offset litho process on p. 141).

Wrong-reading emulsion down (WRED) film, also known as **right-reading emulsion up (RREU)**, has a wrong-reading image when viewed from the shiny side and is right-reading when viewed from the dull emulsion side. WRED film is used for direct printing processes, such as gravure. When the cylinder is made, the image is wrong-reading. It transfers ink to the paper directly, and right-reading (see p. 146 for further information on gravure).

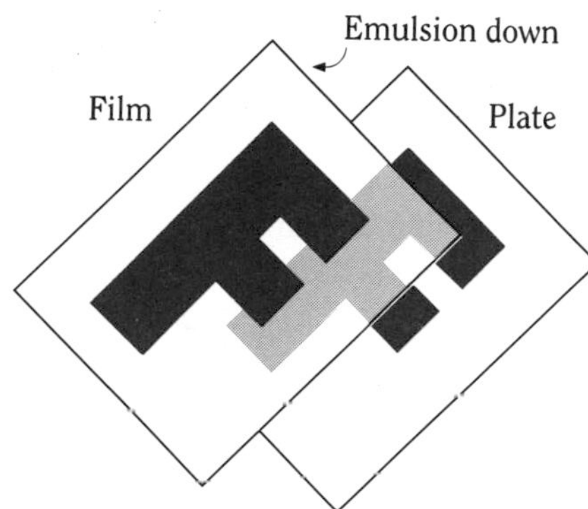

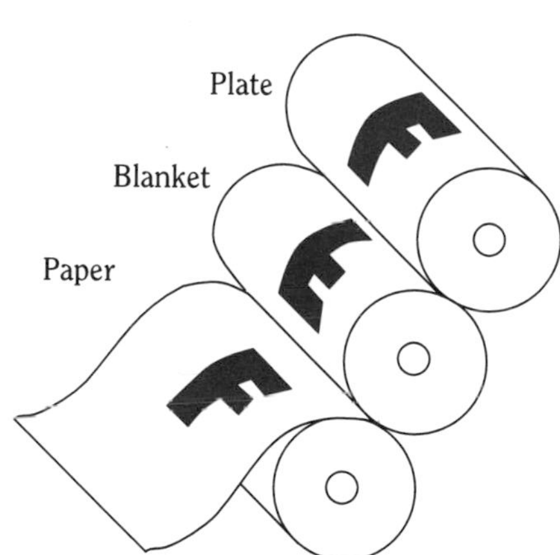

4.19 (above) For offset litho work, strippers most often use positive right-reading emulsion down film. Thus the emulsion comes into contact with the surface of the plate; the blanket is wrong-reading; and the final printed image is right-reading.

4.18 At the printers, halftones and tints are "stripped in" to the spaces left in the text films. Opaque material such as Rubylith is used to blank out black or solid flat color areas on positive film or white areas on negative film.

Pages can be assembled using positive or negative film. Negative film, with all the white space turned to black, is often too dense to use accurately. So most color **stripping in** is done using positive film. The stripper uses a white board, onto which the grid (or layout) plus all the trim and center marks have been drawn or preprinted. A clear carrier sheet of polyester or acetate is laid onto this guide, and for each page the design elements (type, line illustrations, and halftones) on film are assembled into place with the emulsion side uppermost. The film elements are cut to size with a scalpel and attached to the base sheet with pressure-sensitive tape, so as to leave a uniformly flat surface, with none of the elements overlapping.

If the layout is quite complex, with lots of design elements stuck down with tape, a copy is made onto positive-working daylight film. This is called the **final**. Every time a duplicate is made, however, there is a slight degradation in quality. The best results are obtained when film is copied emulsion to emulsion. Using normal negative-working film, the image would be reversed and another copy would have to be made to right it. Special **auto-reversing film** is used instead to keep the number of steps to a minimum.

For multicolor work, a separate clear carrier sheet is used for each of the process colors. The registration (alignment) between the separate finals has to be observed meticulously, using a **pin-register** system to line up the trim marks and multicolor elements (see below). Color tints are laid down according to the formulas given in the Pantone charts.

As discussed earlier, it is generally most economical to print several pages together, in one pass of the printing press. Putting together the **flat** (Fig. 4.20), or forme, to make a 16- or 32-page plate is the stripper's job, and here's how it is done.

A single-color flat with no registration problems to worry about is usually made-up from film negatives, assembled together on an opaque orange-colored paper called **Goldenrod**. Goldenrod contains a dye that prevents ultraviolet (UV) light from passing through it, and acts as a mask to protect the non-printing areas of the flat. The negative film is placed in position emulsion side up, and the whole assembly is turned over. Windows are then cut into the Goldenrod to allow UV light to pass through the image areas. The assembled flat is placed on the press plate and exposed in a **printing-down frame**.

Goldenrod can stretch, so, for work requiring close registration, the negatives are assembled first onto clear acetate or polyester sheets, emulsion side up. The assembly is turned over and non-printing areas are masked using either Goldenrod or a red/amber masking film.

For multicolor printing, a positive flat is made for each of the process colors. To ensure close registration, these are pin-registered (Fig. 4.21) with pins and a special punch used to make holes in the flats. They can be correctly located with pins on the press plate, and again the plates can be located on the press cylinder with further pins and clamps.

An alternative method is called **blue and red keys**. The first flat is assembled using either the cyan or the magenta elements. This is exposed in contact with a sheet of blue or red **dyeline** film, which produces a key image of the original image in blue or red. With blue keys, each color flat is registered in position using the blue to give accurate sightings. When complete, the flat is used for platemaking in the normal way, as the blue does not record on the plate. Red does record, so when red keys are used, the flat is assembled onto a clear acetate sheet with the red keys underneath, acting as a guide.

4.20 The stripper assembles all the pages for one printing into a flat ready for platemaking, opaquing out any blemishes or marks not to be printed.

4.21 (below) For color work, each printing must be in close register. Pin registration is a system of precisely placed holes and corresponding pins which ensure that all the films, flats, and plates are correctly aligned.

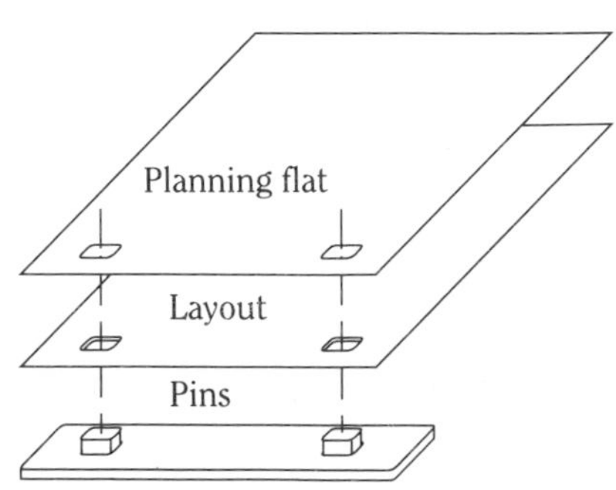

Picture proofing

Film for a single color is commonly proofed as a positive dyeline or **diazo print** (contact ammonia prints), called **ozalids, brownlines, blueprints,** or **blues.** Blues (which may also be gray, brown, or other colors) often give the only opportunity to check the **alignment** of halftones and other elements. This is absolutely the last chance to make any changes before the job is "put to bed."

It may be necessary to see the printed quality of halftones, either all together in random order, as **scatter proofs,** or – probably more expensively – in their correct position on the page, as page proofs.

Color separations of illustrations and photographs can be proofed photographically, as **inkjet, dye-sublimation,** or **thermal-transfer prints,** or on plastic laminate systems. These are called **prepress proofs,** or **dry proofs,** and are all approximations to the finished printed result, but will give you an idea of what to expect.

Photographic systems work by exposing each process color separation in turn onto a three-layer photographic paper, using filters. The material is then processed to produce the color proof.

One-off transfer or integral proofs, such as Du Pont's **Cromalin,** 3M's **Matchprint,** and Agfa's **Agfaproof,** take colored powders or pre-coated sheets representing the process colors. They are laminated in register onto white paper (Fig. 4.22). With some systems it is possible to use the same stock as you will be using for the final printing, which is useful for checking color and inking accurately.

Plastic laminate proofs, such as 3M's **Color-Key** and Du Pont's **Cromacheck,** build up an image layer by layer onto a plastic substrate using mylar or acetate overlay film, one for each process color.

Digital proofing systems are proliferating, and are discussed further in Chapter 6. These produce proofs direct from the computer's memory, using inkjet, thermal-transfer, dye-sublimation, or electrostatic technologies.

A form of proofing that can be more expensive requires four plates to be made from the separations and printed on a flatbed proofing press. This should produce the most realistic representation of the finished job, and allows several sets of proofs to be made. Ensure that a complete set of color bars are run with the proof – these can later be compared with the values being recorded on the press. And ask for standard inks to be used.

A full set of **progressives** (Fig. 3.19) can be obtained in this way. Progressives are color proofs printed in the same order in which the process colors will be applied at press time. Each color printing is shown separately and also surprinted with the other colors. A typical set comprises the individual process colors of yellow, magenta, cyan, and black, accompanied by the cumulative combinations: magenta on yellow; cyan on yellow and magenta; and finally black on yellow, magenta, and cyan. Some printers vary the sequence by running the cyan printing before the magenta. If progressives are required, ask for them to be made in the **laydown sequence** – the order in which the finished job will be printed.

For flat color, the printer may offer a **drawdown** – a smear of ink from a smooth blade on a particular paper stock. This should not be relied upon, however, to give an accurate impression of how a particular color will print on the press.

As mentioned above, it is important to ask for the same paper stock as will be used for the final printing. Always make allowance for the fact that **press proofs** pulled from a proofing press will be sharper and show less dot gain (see p. 157) than a high-speed production press.

Check the proofs to see that the images are the right way round – it's amazing how often they are upside-down or reversed (**flopped**) left-to-right, or both. Check also for the correct crop, size, position, sharpness, and mark any obvious imperfections such as spots and scratches. Black-and-white proofs need to be checked for contrast – they should have the full tonal range from shadow to highlights.

4.22 A Cromalin color proof is a "dry" proprietary system from Du Pont which gives a good idea of how a set of color film separations are going to work together on the press.

When it comes to marking proofs for color correction, tell the printer as plainly as possible what you think is wrong. Color judgment is subjective, and there may be many routes to a better end result. Just because something has a blue cast, it does not necessarily mean that there is too much cyan – the cyan may be alright but the other colors may need taking up. It is better to say "too blue" than to instruct the printer with technical certainty to "take down the cyan."

COLOR BARS

Color bars (Fig. 4.23) yield vital information about the performance of both the press and the inks being used. To be able to interpret them arms you with the knowledge to improve the quality of the job without being "blinded by science" at the printers. They contain a whole range of tests: some are visual checks; others require special instruments such as a **densitometer**. And they are totally independent of the job, thus representing a consistent guide to the standard of printing you can expect.

Color bars comprise most or all of the following components:

1 Printing-down controls. There will be a series of microlines and highlight dots to assess how accurately the job has been printed down from film to plate.

2 Solid density patches for each color. These monitor ink film thickness, and should be read using a densitometer.

3 Trapping patches. These show solid process colors printed on top of others in different combinations, and they test how ink is being accepted in **wet-on-wet** printing. There will also be a dense black made up from 100% black, 55% cyan, 42·5% yellow, and 42·5% magenta (=240%, the maximum recommended percentage of tints; see also p. 88).

4 Screen patches. Patches for each process color at different screens are used to monitor **dot gain**. Dot gain happens as the ink spreads around just joined-up dots in the middle tones, tending to make these areas look darker than they should be. At one tone lighter, where the dots are not yet touching, density does not gain to the same extent. This effect can cause a visible jump in an otherwise smooth gradation of tone. Elliptical dots can help alleviate the problem.

5 Coarse and fine halftone scale. This quick visible check comprises ten steps in the form of the numerals 0 to 9 set using a screen of 200 lines, which are dropped out of a background tint screened at 65 lines. Dot gain shows as the numbers fill in and become visible – the theory is that fine tints are more sensitive to dot gain than coarser ones.

6 Slur gauge. These patches reveal any directional dot gain caused by **slurring** or **doubling**, and take the form of star targets and/or oblongs containing horizontal and vertical lines.

7 Gray balance. If all is well, a 50% cyan, 40% magenta, and 40% yellow, printed on top of each other, should produce a neutral gray.

4.23 A color bar is used by printers to assess the performance of their presses – giving information, for example, about dot gain and slurring. It appears away from the image area and is trimmed off the sheets later.

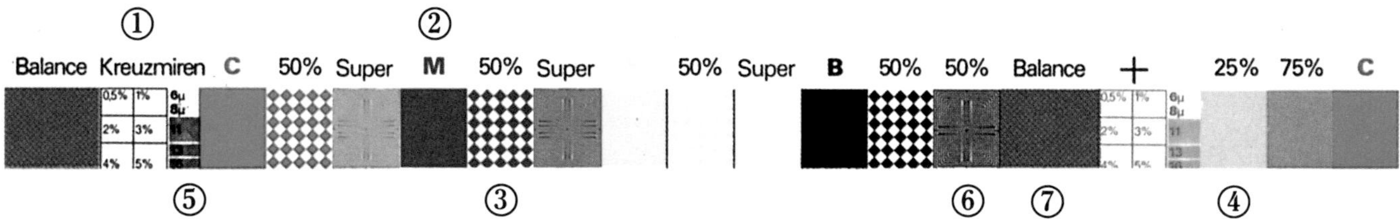

Part 3: desktop publishing and digital make-up

If you follow the conventional prepress procedure, you will have to prepare text for the typesetter, deciding on the typeface, size, and measure in advance. You will receive back a photocopied galley to use for layout. Alternatively, the galley will be on bromide paper, and you will use this to paste-up the finished artwork. If you change your mind, or find that the copy does not fit your meticulously planned layout, then you will have to start over, and ask for the text to be reset, or at least rerun. This can all be very time-consuming and costly.

With a dtp system, it is possible to design "on the fly," though this methodology is not always recommended! What is certain with dtp, though, is that you will be able to try out lots of "what-if?" layouts, and always end up with clean, seamless artwork, with no changes in density where paragraphs have been corrected, no scalpel cuts to be retouched, and no chance of last-minute corrections dropping off the mechanical and onto the printer's floor. That's the theory, of course!

In practise, however, there will be some compromise. Unless the entire process – from idea to press plate – is digital, you will probably have to use a service bureau to produce the bromides of the pages on a high-quality imagesetter. And once the bromide is back in your studio, last-minute emergency repairs may have to be made with scalpel and paste.

Nevertheless, dtp represents a huge advance in the technology available to the graphic designer. It is an immensely powerful tool, which brings with it a great deal of responsibility for the appearance of the finished product. Once the dtp system is up and running, there will be no-one to blame for a less than perfect layout except yourself, or perhaps a bug in the program. And there will be much to learn: about operating the system, making use of the flexibility it offers, and about computers in general (but help is at hand – see Chapter 6).

So how does dtp work, and how does digital make-up differ from preparing mechanicals by hand? Not as much as you may think. As with the totally manual method, it will always pay to sit down with a pencil and paper to plan your layout. A layout pad has been designed for that purpose, with leaves thin enough for you to trace the best parts of a previously attempted design before it is consigned to the trash. Make a sketch layout of the page. It does not have to be completely accurate, but it should be good enough for you to see what a spread is going to look like at full size. This should include the margins, columns, and the position of page numbers and running heads.

Next, select your typeface. This will depend on the type of job, and what's available – both on your system, and at the service bureau. Don't forget practical considerations, such as the number of words per line and the relative x-heights (see p. 36) of the different faces. Try running off some sample lines of type in the face and at the point size and measure that you have chosen, and place it on the layout. That way you will be able to judge whether you require more or less leading and tracking. Try out different sub-headings, and decide now whether the text is to be set justified or ranged left. Remember, type on the screen only approximates the output from the laser printer or imagesetter, so it is important to have an idea of what to expect.

Next, calculate how much space the type will occupy. If the text has been input using a word processor with a word counter, then that figure will be a good guide. Otherwise use one of the methods outlined in Chapter 2 (see p. 46). If it is going to be too long, or fall short, adjust the layout.

Now draw up a grid. Although the dtp system will have built-in rulers and construction lines, the page on the screen – even on a large-format display – will look deceptively different from a piece of board on your desk. So double-check with a ruler and a same-size reference grid. Then you can key the specifications into the computer.

If the publication is mostly words, with few or no illustrations, then you can start to place the text onto the page. If, however, there is a large number of illustrations, it is best to draw up a rough plan showing where you expect them to fall. It is much easier to manage the layout (and make sure that nothing is left out) if you know exactly which elements have to be included, and roughly where.

Finally, make a written record of your specification and keep it nearby. Although it is in the computer somewhere, it can be time-consuming and disruptive to have to stop what you are doing to find a reminder of what measure, margin, or horizontal division you have been using.

Dtp programs

It is possible to make-up complete pages in some of the so-called drawing programs, such as FreeHand and Illustrator. Even off-the-shelf word processing programs can now handle several columns of text integrated with graphics. And there are some packages on the market developed for specific design tasks: Multi-Ad Creator from Studio Box, for example, is aimed at designers producing display advertisements for newspapers and magazines. It is not page-oriented like other dtp programs, and contains built-in modules for text and image origination. If all you do is design ads, then you won't need to buy any other programs.

At the other extreme, there are programs – FrameMaker, Ventura, and Interleaf Publisher, for example – developed to handle very large, but relatively unsophisticated publications, such as technical manuals. There are also dtp packages that seek to emulate the previous generation of computer typesetting systems. Interset's Quoin, for example, requires the user to type codes – ps10ff11qc, for example, means point size 10, film feed (leading) 11, quad center (centered) – among the text. For experienced compositors at typesetting shops moving into dtp, this kind of program seems reassuringly familiar, but it is most unappealing to jobbing graphic designers used to the more intuitive graphical user interface (GUI) of a computer such as the Apple Macintosh (more on computer jargon in Chapter 6).

Most designers come across all kinds of jobs, however, and need a more general-purpose dtp program. The best known and most versatile are Aldus PageMaker (Fig. 4.24) and Quark XPress (Fig. 4.25). Aldus released the first version of PageMaker for the Apple Macintosh in July 1985, and for the IBM PC in January 1987. Quark XPress was not introduced until later in 1987. It was Aldus founder Paul Brainerd who coined the phrase "desktop publishing." PageMaker can thus rightly claim to be the original desktop publishing package.

Both boast a WYSIWYG (what you see is what you get) display, but the term is not strictly accurate. The printed result is far superior to the page you see on the screen, even at full zoom (magnification), because screen fonts are fundamentally different from printer fonts (see p. 68). Nevertheless, what you see is far superior to what compositors have seen on screen at the typesetters in the past. Both XPress and PageMaker make extensive use of the WIMP (windows, icons, mouse, and pull-down menus) facility, with "palettes" of tools (for drawing boxes, for example) and such things as style-sheet information available on the screen all of the time (Fig. 4.26).

Both systems enjoy equal popularity; however, they have different working methods. In general, XPress is favored by magazine designers, PageMaker by designers of publications with fewer pages. But there is no clear division, and designers will argue into the night about the relative merits of *their* program and its suitability to do a particular job.

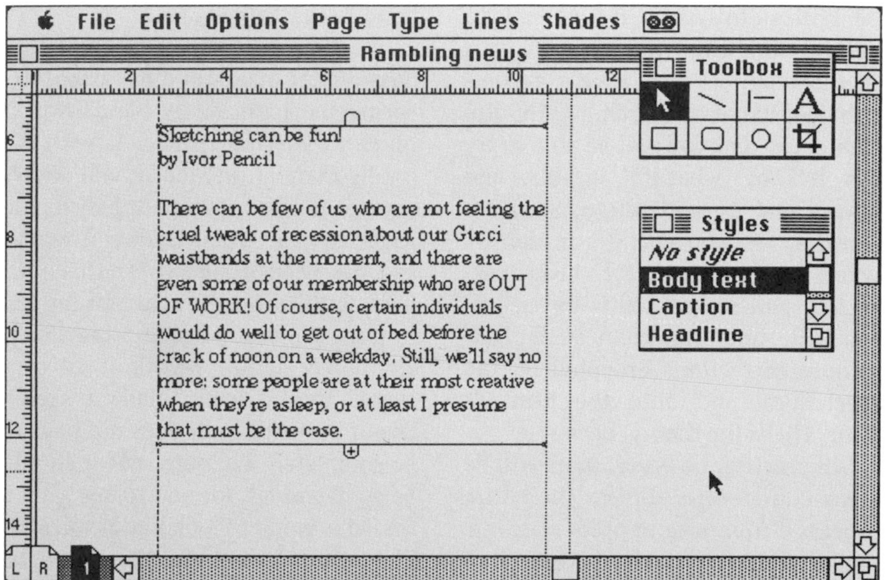

4.24 In a dtp system such as Aldus PageMaker the mechanical is replaced by an "electronic pasteboard." Text is imported from a word-processing system (often on the same machine) and placed onto a grid. The windowshade allows you to pull down more text. Text can also be wrapped around illustrations.

In PageMaker, the user is presented with a picture on the screen of a "pasteboard" for electronically pasting on text or graphics. Any elements not being used can be placed outside the page area until they are needed. When you open a new **document** in PageMaker, you are asked to enter the page size and margins in a "dialog box." (In computer language, any job you are working on is called a document, whether it is a drawing, a piece of text, or a page layout.) You will also be asked how many pages the publication will have. It is then possible to specify the number of columns, their width, and the spacing between them. All of these parameters can be changed later, if need be.

Text is imported from a word processor document, and a symbol is placed in the position you wish the text to start. In "auto-flow" mode it will flow down the columns until all the text is in position. In regular mode, text will flow down the first column, and then stop. The text block takes the appearance of a window-shade (roller blind). A little + sign in the "handle" indicates that there is more text in there. A # sign indicates that all the text is accounted for. Once placed, the text can be moved around en masse, and edited as if it were in a word processing program.

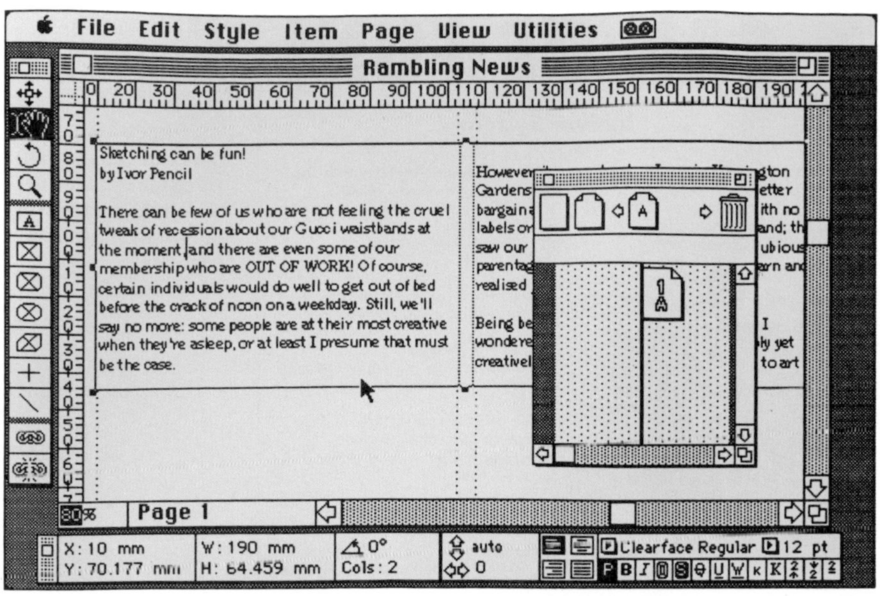

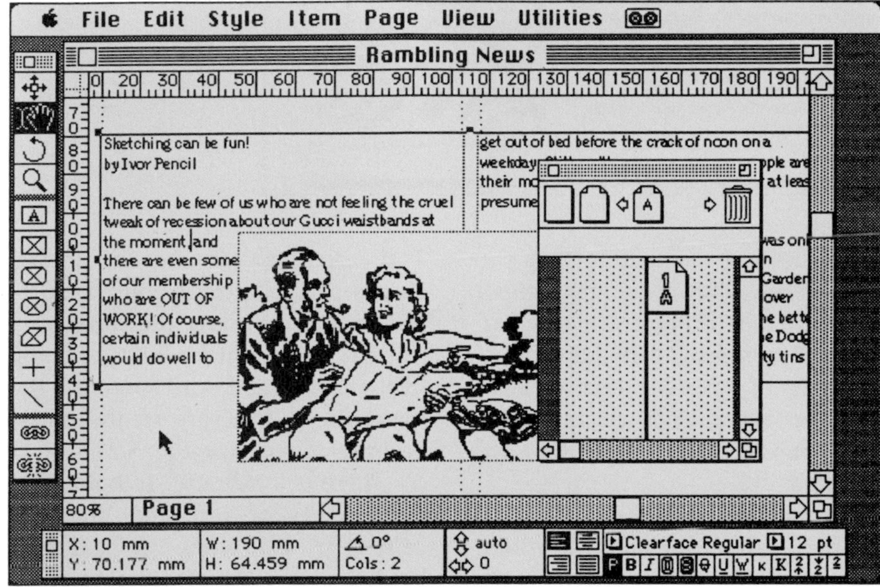

4.25 Quark XPress is similar to PageMaker in many ways, but uses a different approach to placing text and graphics – XPress has linked text and graphic frames.

4.26 Both PageMaker and XPress allow you to compile and edit a style sheet outlining highly specific instructions for components such as the font, leading, and tracking of body text, headlines, and captions. Thus you can maintain consistency between publications.

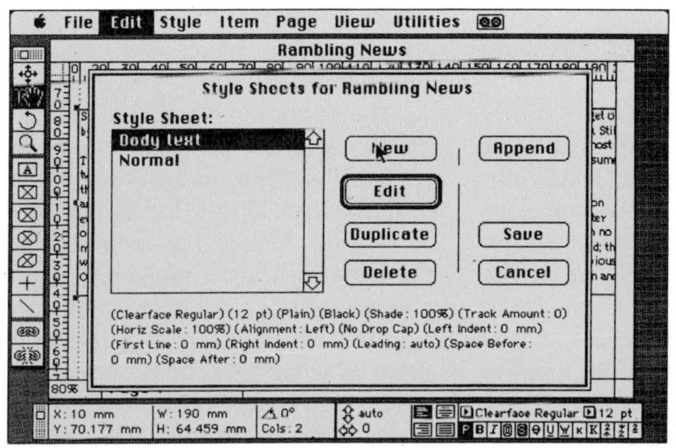

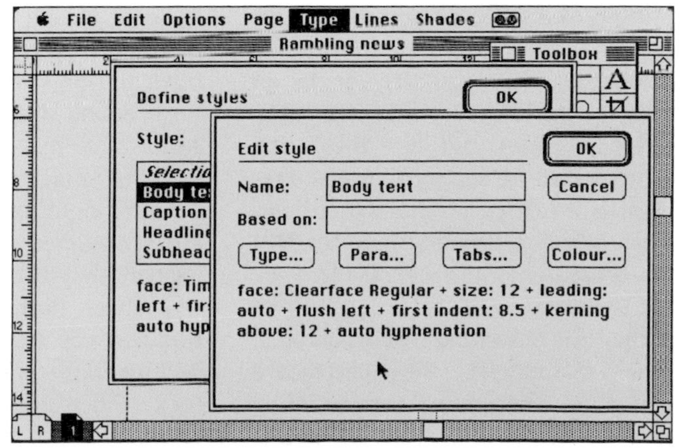

There are several aids to consistency. Anything placed on the two facing "master pages" will appear on every page in the publication. This is useful for positioning construction lines, effectively creating a grid, and for inserting running heads and folios. (Pressing the command, option, and letter p keys together will invoke automatic page numbering throughout the document.) Style sheets allow you to specify body text, captions, headlines, and different grades of subheadings, as well as instructions about indents for paragraphs, kerning, and hyphenation. Entire "skeleton" documents can be saved as templates, which can be used over and over to produce documents that are going to look similar – future issues of a newsletter, for example.

The latest release of PageMaker at the time of writing is Version 4.0. Its biggest change has been the incorporation of a story editor, virtually a word processing package in itself, for fast text entry and editing while you are working on the publication. This includes a spelling checker, and a search-and-replace command. It can rotate text, but only in 90 degree increments. It also has improved kerning, widow and orphan control, and "editors" for generating tables and indexes.

PageMaker can handle flat color, which can be specified by Pantone number or percentages of process colors, and also in terms of red, green, and blue values or hue, luminance, and saturation. It has six halftone screens, and ten tint patterns. Output will generally be to a laser printer or desktop color printer for proofing and low-grade output (for a newsletter, for example), or to an imagesetter for bromide or film. Oversize pages can be "tiled" and printed out in sections. Aldus PrePrint is a related program that helps produce color separations to the **OPI** (open prepress interface) standard.

The latest major release of **XPress** at the time of writing was version 3.0. This introduced the pasteboard metaphor (necessary for handling bleeds), the ability to work on double-page spreads, and the freedom to rotate text and graphics to an accuracy of one thousandth of a degree. (It is a truism in computing that you only realize what something *cannot* do when they bring out a new version.) The original "parent and child" hierarchy of boxes has been replaced by a freer approach of selecting boxes and grouping them in whichever way you wish.

RAMBLING NEWS

FILING CAN BE FUN!

by Ivor System

There can be few of us who are not feeling the cruel tweak of recession about our Gucci waistbands at the moment, and there are even some of our membership who are OUT OF WORK! Of course, certain individuals would do well to get out of bed before the crack of noon on a weekday. Still, we'll say no more: some people are at their most creative when they're asleep, or at least I presume that must be the case.

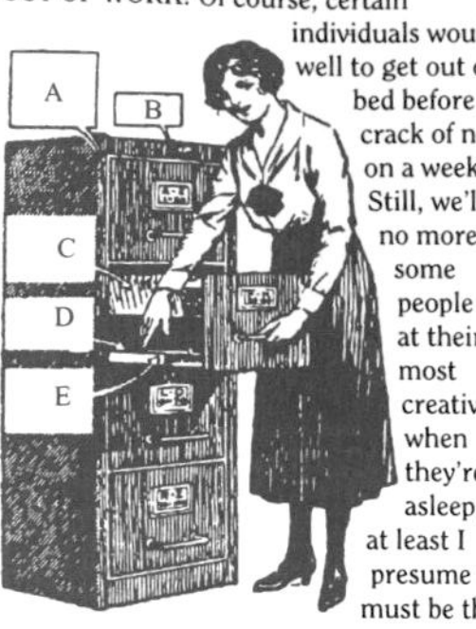

However, it was only when I was in Kensington Gardens deliberating over which was the better bargain at the Dodgy Deli – the rusty tins with no labels or the out-of-date shellfish from Poland – that I saw our Club Secretary go by, leading a dog of dubious parentage by a grimy length of macramé yarn, and I realized just how bad things really are.

Being between jobs myself at the moment, I wondered how I could pass the time cheaply yet creatively. I thought: "I know what! I went to art college – I'll go out and do some filing!"

It's great! This is what you do:

1) Nip down to your local art supplies store and buy lots of Japanese handmade paper. Also purchase some cartridge paper, as the Japanese gear is far too expensive to waste on mere outdoor sketching.
2) Skulk about the art museum a while until you can lift one of their folding seats without being seen.
3) Take it back and pay the fine.
4) Drive the car to an out-of-town supermarket and get a picnic together. Need a few hints?

- Chocolate-chip cookies – several packs
- a pot of spicy Nutrasweet dip and some sponge fingers
- brie, French stick, wine, etc
- a Swiss army penknife
- a warm woolly jumper

Deciding where to file things is such fun!

Now you're all set!

7

4.27 In a program such as PageMaker, the graphic element is surrounded by an area that repels text. The operator can change its shape by inserting and grabbing control points all around the edges of an illustration.

It has also introduced "floating palettes," which include a measurements palette – a long, narrow window that lets you adjust type specifications or graphic elements as you go along – and a document layout palette for setting up and navigating a document. As it is possible to have up to 127 master pages in a single publication, a good means of keeping track of things is essential.

Creating drop caps (see p. 43) is easier in XPress 3.0, with or without hanging indents, to a maximum depth of eight lines. And as drop caps are considered to be a paragraph format, they can be included in the style sheet. Both the font and size of the drop cap (by percentage) and its kerning with the abutting text (to tuck under an overhanging T, for example) can be adjusted too.

The way that text can run around a graphic element, or arbitrary shape, has been improved in version 3.0. Text can flow around, or inside, shapes such as circles and triangles. But try not to abuse the **runaround** feature, and watch out for ugly hyphenations and word spacing if the measure in any part of the shape becomes too narrow (Fig. 4.27).

There is a "library," to hold standard pieces of text and graphics: page-turn indicators, and section headings, for example. And to speed up the program's responsiveness, picture elements on a page can be greeked – represented by a gray tint. **Greeking** is a time-saver most usually used in dtp for type in small sizes, which would be unreadable anyway, and are thus represented on the screen by gray lines.

The essence of dtp is that you can be as rigid or as flexible as you choose. PageMaker is said to be more intuitive than XPress, but at the time of writing XPress has more functionality, with just about every typographic control a designer could wish for. The above can only give you a flavor of what both Aldus and Quark have to offer. Check with a dealer for the specification of the latest update. Both will continually improve, however, and ultimately the choice is going to be a personal one.

Full-color digital prepress

All dtp systems can handle color to some extent. XPress, for example, can separate files imported from Illustrator and FreeHand, or images from retouching programs such as PhotoShop and ColorStudio. But full color is extremely expensive on computer memory and can slow down the most powerful desktop computer to a snail's pace if it constantly has to manipulate and redraw pages with many full-color images.

It is recommended, therefore, that layouts are designed on a dtp system using only low-resolution images, in the same way that photocopies of halftones on a mechanical are used "for position only." Send transparencies to the repro house to be electronically "stripped in" later.

Printers and repro houses have been using digital scanners coupled with computers for many years. This is one of graphic design's best kept secrets. Organizations with digital prepress systems from suppliers such as Scitex, Crosfield, Linotype-Hell, and Dainippon have been able to scan in and retouch color transparencies since the early 1970s. Of course, these systems have been capable of much more, but were so expensive to buy and run that printers, afraid that designers might develop the "bad habit" of asking for alterations to their images, adopted an almost conspiratorial silence.

All this has changed, however. Designers are now able to effect similar changes to their images before the prepress stage, using desktop systems running programs such as PhotoShop and ColorStudio. The scanner manufacturers have also introduced less expensive "front-ends" to their systems specifically for designers to use.

Visionary from Scitex (Fig. 4.28) and Lightspeed from Crosfield (Fig. 4.29) are both examples of such halfway-house systems based on the Apple Macintosh. The designer uses low-resolution images to produce the "electronic mechanicals" on modified dtp systems. High-resolution scans, straight from the original transparencies, are reunited with the layouts at the repro house (Fig. 4.30).

4.29 The Crosfield Lightspeed is a Mac-based designer's front-end to the kind of sophisticated electronic repro system found at the printers.

4.28 The Scitex Visionary system is a front-end to the larger Scitex systems found at the printers. It is a modified version of XPress which allows you to design pages while it keeps track of all the cropping and scaling information of the color illustrations that will eventually be scanned directly into the bigger Scitex.

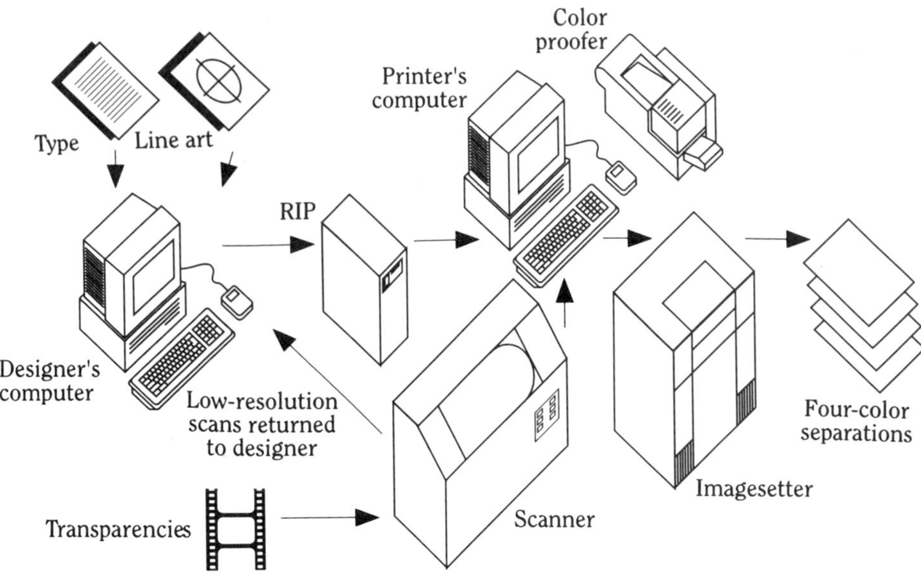

4.30 A regular dtp system can be used as a front-end to the system at the repro house, mixing and matching the abilities of both to the best and most economical advantage. Transparencies are sent to the repro house where both high- and low-resolution scans are made. The low-res scans are used in your dtp layouts and the high-res ones are substituted later, when the final pages are made-up.

Visionary is an enhanced version of Quark XPress that writes its output files in the same format as a Scitex Response system. Lightspeed is based on a program called DesignStudio, formerly Ready,Set,Go! The low-resolution scans used in the computer until the proofing stage can come from your desktop scanner, or they can be "compressed" versions of scans from the repro house's Scitex system. Each one is given a name which can be recognized by the Scitex. A pull-down annotation layer (like an electronic overlay) is available so that you can write related instructions to the repro house.

As you lay out the images in Visionary, the system remembers all the scaling, rotating, and cropping alterations made to the image, and conveys them to the Scitex operator at the repro house. This makes considerable savings on **set-up time** compared with conventional repro techniques, in which the operator has to check and measure position mark-ups on overlays.

Complex cut-outs and masks can be made on Visionary. These are automatically translated into smooth high-resolution masks on the Scitex, using a technique called mask density substitution. In the same way, graduated tints (called degradés in Scitex talk) are recreated automatically in high-resolution versions.

Most dtp programs are output to an imagesetter via a device called a **RIP** (raster image processor) which changes the PostScript outlines of the letters and drawings into a bitmap (an array of dots) that the laser can print out. Unlike most dtp and prepress programs, Visionary does not use PostScript. Instead it uses a method called run-length encoding for transferring and storing data. This is much faster than PostScript and all the design elements remain "live" and editable (whereas a file that has been "ripped" cannot be easily altered).

Using this format also means that different elements of the design can be sent to the repro house at different times – a work method not always recommended, but useful for tight deadlines, where layout may precede last-minute text.

Any PostScript files, such as FreeHand drawings, are converted into Scitex format at the repro site. Screen angles in PostScript files are ignored and patented Scitex or Linotype-Hell angles are applied, ensuring moiré-free color reproduction.

Once you have finished designing on Visionary, with all color and **mono** elements in place, the page can be proofed on a 300 dpi A3-size Mitsubishi thermal printer. Although the quality of the color will be nowhere near the finished result, these quick proofs will give you the opportunity to see the integrated page and perhaps adjust colored backgrounds and the color of type. For near-Cromalin quality, Visionary can produce output on both the Iris inkjet and Du Pont's 4-cast proofing systems.

After corrections and alterations have been made (remember, one of the great advantages of dtp is that no repro or film costs have been incurred at this stage), the file can be sent for repro via floppy disc or down the telephone wire. This assumes, of course, that the repro house already holds the original transparencies. At the repro house, all type, tints, and images are plotted directly onto final output film, with no intermediate typesetting or imagesetting, and no stripping in necessary.

GATF PROOFING BARS

Summary

Prepress is where the text set in type, the illustrations and photographs, and any other graphic elements, such as rules, boxes, and areas of flat color, all come together in a form that can be printed. The prepress process starts with the mechanical – a board onto which are pasted paper-based graphic elements: typesetting on bromide paper, line art on PMTs, and maybe veloxes of photographs too. For simple black-and-white work, the job is done.

For close-registration color work, however, halftones must be processed onto film, and stripped in at the printers onto flats. Paper and board can stretch and distort; film is more dimensionally stable.

For medium- and large-scale jobs, it is important to give some thought to imposition schemes. Early planning in this area can have a substantial effect on the cost-effectiveness and smooth running of a project.

The preparation of type and graphic elements at the prepress stage can also be carried out on a computer. Simple black-and-white work, and some flat color jobs, can be done using the electronic cut-and-paste of desktop programs such as Quark XPress and Aldus PageMaker. It can then be output by laser printers onto plain paper, or by higher-resolution imagesetters as bromide prints or film.

More sophisticated systems from Scitex, Crosfield, and Dainippon, located at the printers or repro house, are used for more complex four-color projects. But there are so-called front-end systems available – such as Scitex's Visionary, which is based on Quark XPress – that can be used by designers to communicate their layouts directly to the computers at the printers.

Whichever method or system is used, it is essential to see and to be able to understand blues, picture proofs, and color bars, so that you can be sure of quality . . . and know that your design is the one that is going to be printed!

Plate
Blanket

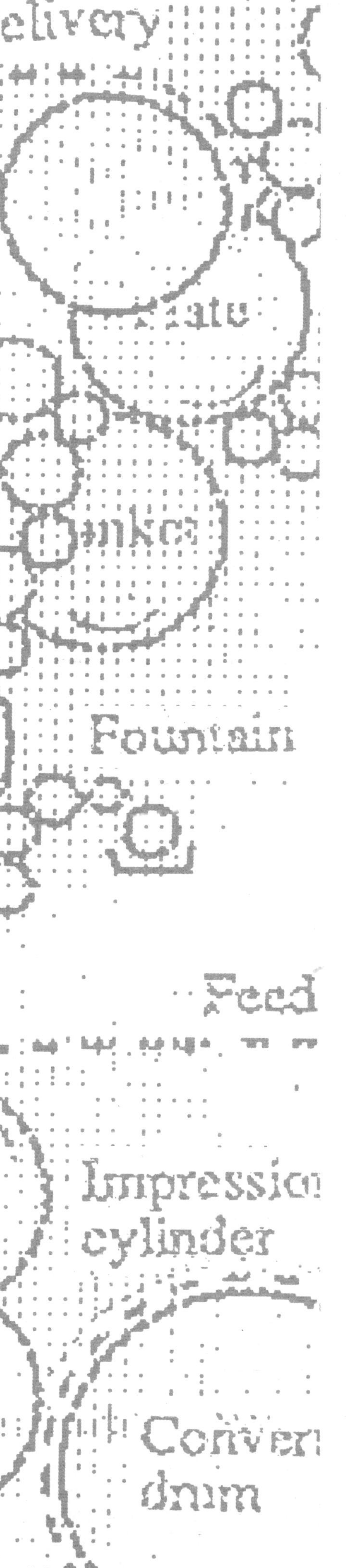

5. On Press

The secret of a successful print job is a well designed mechanical, some good scans for color repro, and the correct choice of paper and ink. Get all these right, and a good printing company can be relied upon to produce a pleasing result.

On press is the one part of the process that the graphic designer scarcely influences. It's now time to say goodbye to the layouts, leaving the printing work in the experienced hands of the printer.

Paper is one of the basic foundations of a good print job, but so often its choice is an afterthought. The first task in specifying paper is to think hard about what the finished item has to achieve. Then, after carefully considering the budget and availability of the stock, the designer can decide which particular characteristics of a paper are required.

Ink, too, plays a crucial role in the printing process, and the right formulation must be used for the right technology. Knowing about how inks perform will allow you to predict accurately how a job will come out. We discuss the effect of varnishing and laminating on an ink's performance, and explain the difference between die-stamping and thermography.

The printing process itself has a profound effect on print quality. The majority of designers will probably use offset litho for most applications. But in some circumstances, gravure can become a cost-effective possibility. And when should you use flexography, or even screen printing? What are the pros and cons? This chapter gives an insight into the process of choosing the right supplier, and suggests how to go about ensuring the best quality job.

Finally, we come to finishing – all those operations of folding, gathering, stitching, and trimming that happen to a printed sheet after it leaves the press. What are the options? Is perfect binding better than saddle-stitching? This chapter explains.

Part 1: paper

5.1 Papermaking in China, from a sequence of miniatures dating from 1811. Note that two people are required to make large sheets, a feat of coordination usually avoided by western papermakers.

Papermaking is older than any of the other printing crafts. Paper is largely a natural product – organic fibers held together by their own molecular forces. It is easy to make, but hard to make well. You can make it at home, with the help of a blender, some torn up paper and other fibrous material (flowers, straw, cotton), and some kind of mesh to let the water drip through. Whether it will have the right degree of absorbency, strength, and surface finish required for fine printing is quite another matter.

The word "paper" comes from the Greek word "papyrus," the name of a plant that grows on the banks of the River Nile in Egypt. The writing material made from papyrus was not the kind of paper we are familiar with today. It was produced from strips peeled from the stem of the plant and pounded together into sheets.

The invention of paper made entirely from vegetable fibers – in this case tree bark, hemp, rags, and fishing nets – was announced to the Emperor of China in AD 105. However, a quasi-paper, made from pulped silk, was being made at least 200 years before that date.

Papermaking flourished in China (Fig. 5.1), but the techniques took a thousand years to reach Europe. The first documented paper mill was established in Spain, at Xativa, in around 1150. Mills were later set up in Italy, at Fabriano (a name still famous for the manufacture of beautiful paper) in around 1260, and in Hertfordshire, England, in around 1490. Papermaking was brought to America by a German, William Rittenhouse. The first American papermill was established in Germantown, Pennsylvania in 1690. Papermills couldn't be built just anywhere. The process depends on huge amounts of pure running water – 150,000 US gallons (120,000 UK gallons or about

500,000 liters) of water, for example, are required to manufacture just one ton (or metric tonne) of handmade paper.

Until the 19th century, all paper was made by hand. The first papermaking machine was invented by Nicholas-Louis Robert in 1798 and built in France. His patents were taken up by Henry and Sealy Fourdrinier, and further developed in England. The Fourdrinier process, as it is known, allowed paper to be made in a continuous operation, producing a web (Fig. 5.2), or roll, at the end of what are still some of the largest machines in existence.

5.2 Papermaking is a continuous process, producing huge webs, or rolls, of paper. These are cut into sheets or made into smaller webs to feed the hugh web litho, gravure, or flexo presses. Here, recycled paper is shown drying, in a mill in Minnesota.

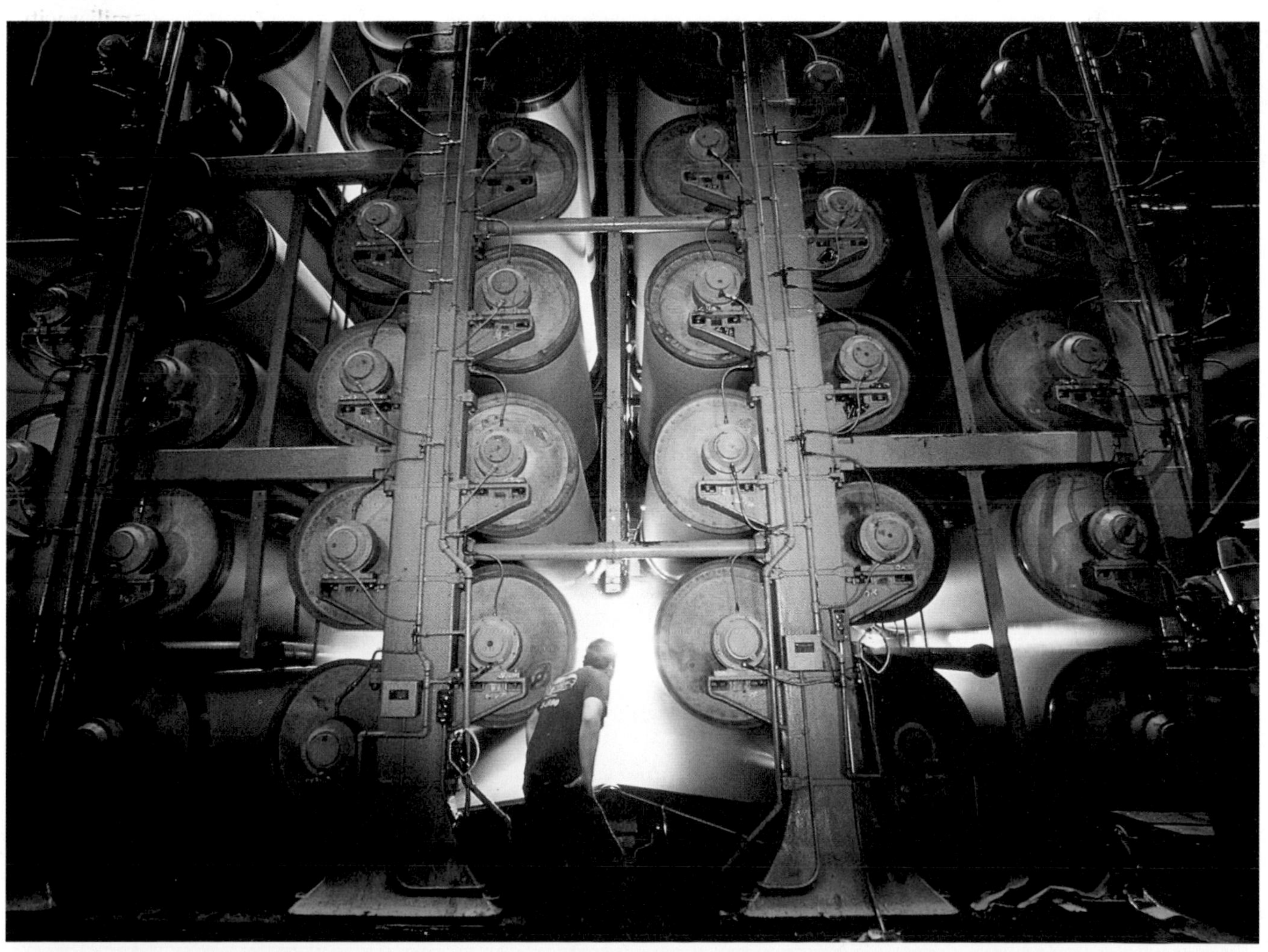

The raw materials

Paper is made from cellulose fibers, and these come from plants or trees. Cellulose is a chemical compound of the elements carbon, hydrogen, and oxygen, and constitutes the cell walls of plants. Cellulose fibers are tubular, and swell when immersed in water. Allowed to dry in close contact with one another, they create their own gelatin "adhesive." Along with the bonding from the fibrillation (splitting and fraying) of the fibers, this produces an extremely strong material. The resulting paper is naturally porous and will absorb the inks and dyes used in printing. And it can be made less porous by adding a substance called **size**. It is also inert enough not to be affected by inks or photographic chemicals. The fibers are colorless and transparent, yet produce paper that is white and opaque.

Early papermills made paper from rags. Textile production requires strong, long fibers for spinning and weaving. Papermaking is not so exacting, so papermills could recycle the shorter fibers from de-buttoned cast-off clothing and offcuts from shirt manufacturers, turning them into paper. Synthetic fibers such as nylon and rayon have put a stop to that. Artificial fibers (and animal fibers such as wool) are much more inert than cellulose. They do not bond as it does, and if they find their way into paper, they weaken it and produce clear specks among the opaque white of the natural fibers.

One remaining source of pure cotton "rags," however, is the T-shirt industry, and its waste clippings are used to produce some of the finest papers. Another source of cotton for papermaking is from **linters**. These are the fibers left on the seed once the longer fibers for yarnmaking have been removed. The best linters come from the southern states of the USA, and from Egypt.

Clippings and linters are sorted, shredded, and placed in a large boiler. Under pressure and steam, any contaminants are removed. The fibers are washed and pulped. The dirty water is then drained off, clarified, and reused. The pulp is bleached, and any chemicals left over are recycled into the next batch. Chlorine bleaches, harmful to the environment, are gradually being replaced by hydrogen peroxide. The pulp is then felted into board-like sheets, for ease of transport to the papermill.

Most paper for general-purpose use is produced from wood. There are two kinds of **woodpulp**: mechanical and chemical. Mechanical, or groundwood, woodpulp is made by grinding logs under a stream of water, after first removing the bark (Fig. 5.3). This results in the cheap but not very strong pulp used in **newsprint** and rougher grades of wrapping paper. It is the lignin left in mechanical pulp that makes the resulting paper turn brown and brittle in sunlight.

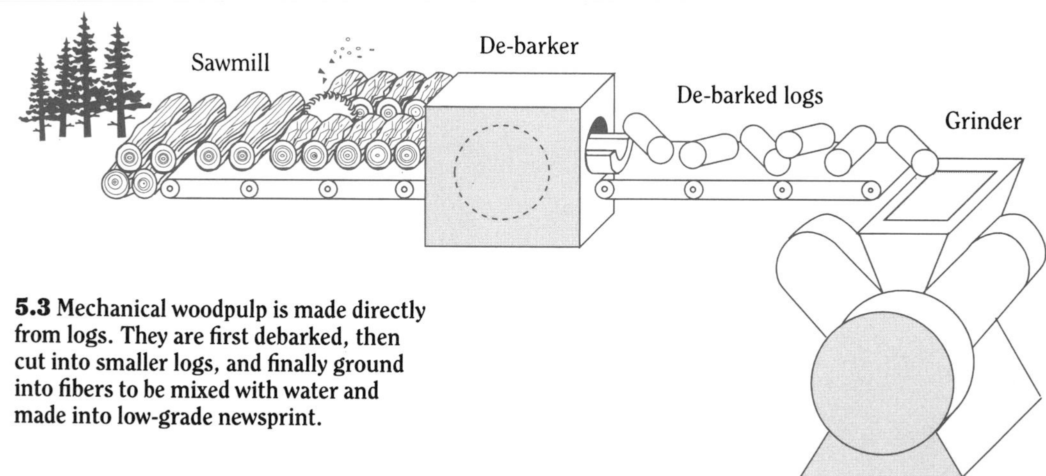

5.3 Mechanical woodpulp is made directly from logs. They are first debarked, then cut into smaller logs, and finally ground into fibers to be mixed with water and made into low-grade newsprint.

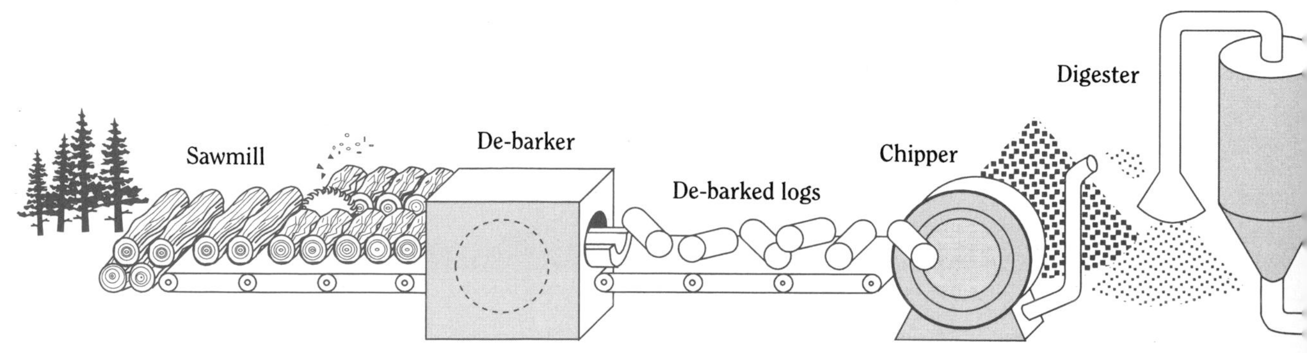

Chemical pulp relies on chemical agents such as calcium or sodium bisulfite to separate the wood fibers (Fig. 5.4). This way they are damaged less than in mechanical pulping, and thus paper from chemical pulp is of a higher quality. Oddly, chemical pulp is sometimes known as **woodfree**.

There are two sources of woodpulp: from softwood (coniferous) and hardwood trees. When softwood is beaten, it loses opacity. Well-beaten softwood is thus used for hard translucent papers, such as glassine (in the windows of envelopes, and also used to wrap after-dinner mints), greaseproof, and tracing papers. Hardwoods, such as eucalyptus, produce more opaque and bulky pulp than softwoods, and can be used to produce a wide range of different papers.

Cotton products and woodpulp are the most common raw materials for papermaking. Other plants are used for producing specialized papers. Esparto grass from North Africa and Spain is used in Europe for the body of the coated papers used in color work, and for good quality writing papers. The fibers are small and flexible, and combine to form a paper with a closeness of texture and smoothness of surface. It also watermarks well. Straw is used for the rough board found in book jackets, and in cigarette papers. Hemp has short fibers that bond well, and is used for papers that must be thin but strong – for Bibles and airmail paper.

Manilla fiber comes from the leaves of a plant that grows in the Philippines. It produces tough, almost untearable, paper mostly used for envelopes and wrapping papers. Other trees and plants that yield fibers for papermaking include corn (maize) stalks, bamboo, bagasse (from sugar cane), and nettles.

Japanese papers are made from a wide range of plants, from the short-fibered *gampi*, which gives a thin, transparent paper with a fine smooth finish, to the longer-fibered and thus stronger *mitsumata*.

5.4 Chemical woodpulp is also debarked, but then the chips are cooked in chemicals to remove the lignin that makes newsprint brittle and turn brown. The pulp is reduced to fibers, washed, screened to remove knots and splinters, bleached, beaten, and mixed with various additives.

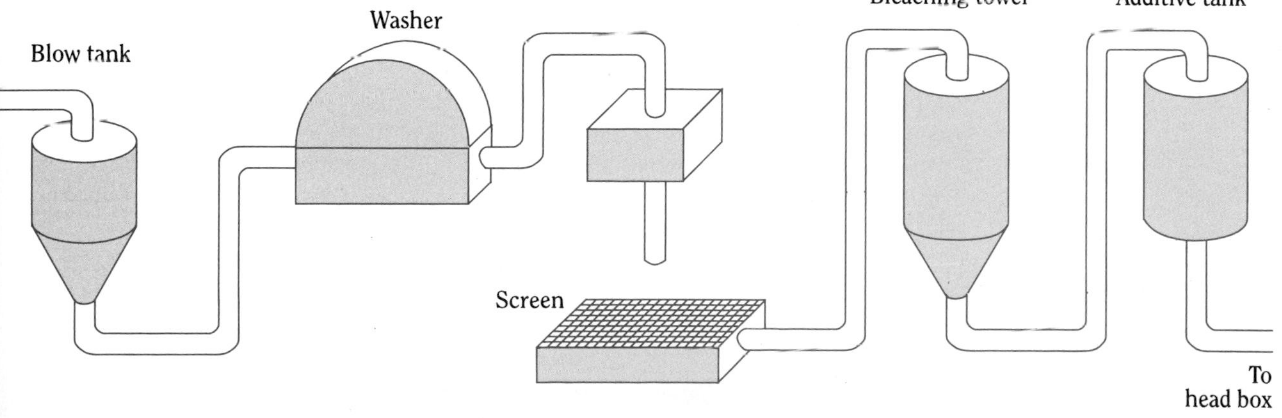

Recycled paper

All paper contains some recycled material, in the form of "broke," the waste from the papermaking process created within the paper mill. This is returned to the refiner, beaten, and turned into more paper. So-called "post-consumer" waste has always been used to manufacture board – the gray kind with specks of ink and sometimes whole letters visible.

Papermills specializing in recycled paper prefer good clean clippings from printers – all the trimmings, with no ink or other "pernicious contraries" present. That apart, the next best source is office or domestic paper. There is not very much demand for newsprint, which is low grade stock to begin with. And what mills definitely do not want are fax paper, self-adhesive envelopes, and plastic-coated papers such as milk and fruit-juice cartons. Problems are also caused by foil-stamped papers, varnishes, and anything containing ultraviolet inks.

Material for recycling is first put through vibrating sieves and centrifuges, where metal objects such as staples and paperclips are removed. Next it is liquefied in a hydro-pulper, and washed to remove the fillers. The sludge then goes for de-inking (Fig. 5.5). Steam and detergents are used to loosen the ink from the fibers. Air is blown through the sludge and the ink flocculates (attaches to the bubbles) and floats to the surface where it is scraped away.

The resulting pulp is mixed with a percentage of virgin stock and printers' waste and made into paper. Virgin pulp is added for strength, for the more times that fibers go through the process, the shorter they become.

5.5 More and more paper is being produced from recycled material, but it is ironical that removing and disposing of the ink can produce an ecological cost of its own.

Recycled paper is never pure white. If the ink from previous usages has not been completely removed but merely redistributed, then the paper will have a grayish tinge. This is something that has to be allowed for in color printing. Good results can be achieved by reducing the black component in four-color work, but do not expect miracles. Recycled paper tends to have greater absorbency than conventional papers. This results in dot gain (see p. 157) and reduced sharpness, and it dries more quickly after printing. It is important that you discuss the use of recycled paper with your printer. Cylinder pressure may have to be adjusted, presses run slower, and different inks be used.

Off-whites and colored recycled paper can, however, have a subtlety of appearance and finish not found in conventional papers. One irony is that recycled papers are getting better all the time, and it is not always obvious to the purchaser that you are using them. Clients who want to demonstrate that they care about the environment by using recycled paper should print a statement to that effect somewhere on the publication.

5.6 Paper is still being made by hand today. Handmade paper is particularly strong and durable. Here the "vatman" is scooping the pulp from the wooden vat to form a sheet of paper in the sieve-like mold at Hayle Mill in Maidstone, England. It takes a minute's rest to change from pulp to paper, it is said, but 30 years to get it right.

Handmade paper

The tradition of handmade paper is still going strong (Fig. 5.6). Handmade products are not only in demand from watercolor artists, but also from designers requiring exceptional strength and that slightly rough traditional finish, for limited edition books, prestigious corporate brochures, and stationery. Decorative papers incorporating plant fibers from linen, onion skins, and vine leaves are used for endpapers and book covers.

Handmade paper is always made from the finest ingredients. After all, producing it is an expensive process, and so it makes no commercial sense to use inferior raw materials. Each sheet is slightly different, and therein lies its charm. Its extra strength comes from the process of manufacture, which requires a "vatman" to shake, or joggle, the mold to the left and to the right – an operation that the machine has been unable to imitate. This gives the paper strength in all directions, and no "grain." One of the most obvious characteristics of handmade paper is its four **deckle** edges. The deckle, another word for the mold, is the name also given to the uneven tapering-off edge of the sheet seen sometimes on untrimmed books of poetry.

The size of a sheet is limited to the size a person can hold, the maximum being Antiquarian at 31 × 53 inches (787 x 1346mm). Larger sheets would need two people to hold the mold.

Handmade paper is available in three finishes: HP (hot pressed), NOT (not hot pressed), and rough.

So-called **mold-made paper** uses a more automated procedure, producing the look and feel of handmade paper in a more consistent and reliable product.

Machine-made paper

Most printing papers are produced on Fourdrinier machines (Figs 5.7 and 5.8). This is a continuous process: pulp goes in at one end, and rolls of paper come out at the other. Fibers, whether from cotton linters or woodpulp, are bought by the papermill in the form of sheets. At this stage they have already undergone a kind of pre-papermaking felting process for ease of handling. These sheets are blended with lots of water for ten minutes or so to form a **slurry**. This is pumped into storage towers and then through conical refiners containing rotating bars. The amount of beating in these refiners determines the length of the fiber and the extent to which individual fibers are fibrillated. This in turn determines the kind of paper that will be manufactured: from highly beaten glassine and tracing paper to soft, bulky blotting paper that receives hardly any beating at all.

From the refiners, the pulp is moved to storage chests, and from there, via a large pump, through an internal sizing process. Next, it is put onto a moving conveyor belt made from a mesh, where the transformation takes place from creamy pulp to solid white paper.

A process called sizing controls the absorbency of the resulting paper, and is responsible for keeping the ink on the surface and preventing **feathering**. Internal sizing does this without blocking the pores or altering the porosity of the fibers. An acidic mixture of rosin (synthetic resin) and alum was traditionally used. More recently it has been replaced by synthetic sizes such as alkyl ketene dimer, which has a neutral pH (i.e. it is neither acidic nor alkaline). The paper may later be surface-sized with starch.

Other additives such as colored dyes are also introduced at this stage. Mineral **fillers**, or loading agents, such as china clay, increase the opacity of the paper and make its surface smooth. Printing papers commonly contain up to 30 percent of fillers.

As the pulp goes through the large pump, it comprises 99 percent water and 1 percent fibers. This is called the **furnish**. From a headbox at the start proper of the papermaking machine, the furnish is released onto the wire mesh of the Fourdrinier. The rate of release and the speed the wire is traveling dictate the resulting weight of the paper. The slower the wire and greater the amount of furnish, the heavier the paper.

After forming on the wire, the paper is still around 70 percent water. Water drains through the mesh, and the screen is vibrated from side to side. The fibers thus tend to align in one direction, along the length of the roll, and this gives machine-made paper its characteristic **grain**. The pattern of the wire mesh gives the paper its texture. **Laid** papers have a pattern of mainly horizontal or vertical stripes. **Wove** papers are created with a woven mesh.

Paper is formed as it lies horizontally on top of the wire. To create texture on the top of the sheet, a hollow dandy roll is located above the wire. It presses a pattern onto the top surface of the paper corresponding to the pattern on the wire.

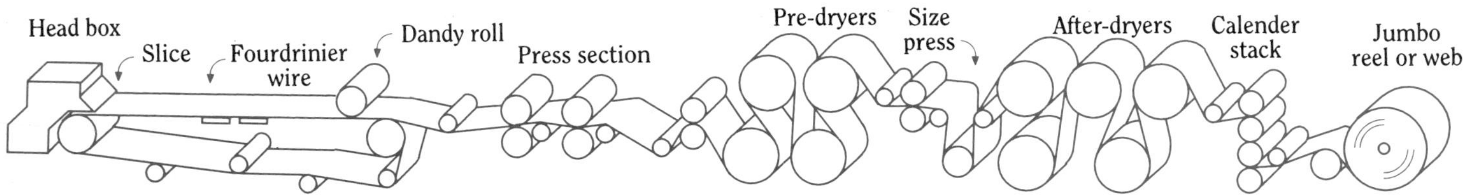

5.7 (above) Fourdrinier machines convert pulp to paper. The first stage is the Fourdrinier wire – a conveyor belt of wire mesh that forms the paper and gives it texture. The rest of the machine is dedicated to drying and smoothing the paper.

5.8 Papermaking machines are among the biggest production machinery in existence – some are over a mile long. This No. 4 machine at James River Fine Papers at St Andrews in Scotland has since been modernized and largely enclosed to conserve heat.

A **watermark** is created by placing a raised symbol, fashioned in wire, on the dandy roll (Fig. 5.10). In handmade paper production, it forms part of the mold. The watermark is thinner and thus more transparent than the rest of the sheet. For large print runs, it may be possible to have your own watermark incorporated into specially ordered paper stock. It can be an attractive design element in its own right (Fig. 5.9), especially if it falls in the margins of a printed publication. But it can interfere with the printing, for example, by weakening a solid area of ink.

From the Fourdrinier wire onward, most of the immense length of a papermaking machine is concerned with drying the damp paper. First, it passes through a series of presses that squeeze out most of the water. These presses can also be used to impart surface texture, and the amount of smoothing affects the final bulk (but not the weight) of the stock.

The paper can then be surface coated or sized with starch, and carried on a felt belt between staggered rows of huge steam-heated cylinders. It must not get too dry, however. After leaving this section, it will still contain two to eight percent of water, necessary to ensure a paper stock with good printing and folding characteristics, and the ability to **cure** in balance with the relative humidity at the printers.

Once dry, the paper is pressed in a vertical row of polished steel calender rolls, or nips. This operation, called **calendering**, increases the smoothness and degree of gloss. The more calenders, the higher the gloss.

The distance from headbox to calenders can be a mile or more. But the elapsed time of a fiber traveling that distance could be as little as two minutes. From the calender stack, the paper is wound into large rolls called webs. These are slit and rewound into more manageable smaller rolls for shipping. If the papermill has the capacity, they may be cut into sheets. Some papers may also require off-machine finishing such as **supercalendering** (polishing), **coating**, or embossing.

Cover paper, or board, is made in much the same way as book paper. The furnish contains more recycled material, and is beaten less, to ensure efficient drainage on the wire. Board can be single-ply, or multi-ply. Multiply board comprises a top liner, under liner, middle, and back liner. Generally, the liners are given conventional amounts of beating to develop strength. The middle stock, which is there as padding, is given very little. The plies may be combined on the machine or off it.

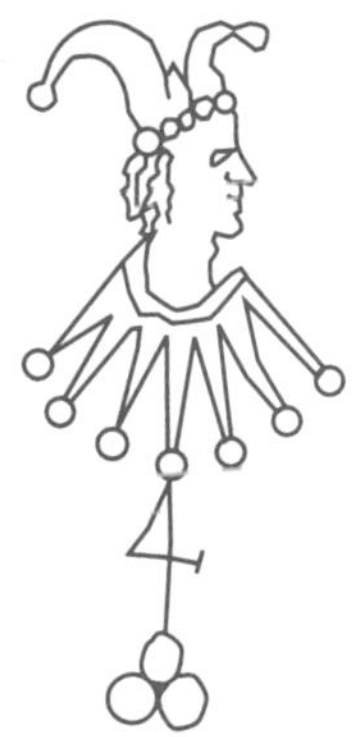

5.9 The watermark of William Rittenhouse, the first American papermaker, and the fool's cap that gave foolscap writing paper its name. Some watermarks are quite complex; most are very simple.

5.10 The dandy roll of a paper machine in the mill of James River Fine Papers at St Andrews.

The characteristics of paper and board

By altering the furnish, and making adjustments to the papermaking machinery, mills are able to produce papers exhibiting very different characteristics. Which kind of paper you choose for a particular job will be determined mostly by the printing process. Offset litho presses require papers that are hard sized, whereas gravure presses need fast ink penetration, and hence "slack" sized paper. If you are dealing with high-quality halftones, you will need a smooth coated paper to do them justice. Economics, too, play a part. Newspapers are cheap and ephemeral, so mechanical woodpulp is a cost-effective choice. Legal documents have to last, so a good-quality rag paper is appropriate.

Paper is specified by its characteristics, and the main ones are weight, bulk, opacity, color, and finish. In the USA, the weight (also called basis weight, poundage, or substance) is measured in pounds per ream of paper cut to its basic size. A **ream** is 500 sheets. The basic size is 25 × 38in for book papers, 24 × 36in for newsprint, and 20 × 26in for cover boards. To avoid misunderstandings, a 60lb book paper is written 25 × 38 – 60 (500). In the rest of the world, the weight is measured in grams per square meter (g/m^2, gsm, or grammage). To convert lbs to g/m^2, multiply by 1·5 (the exact factor is 1·48), and to convert g/m^2 to lbs, multiply by ⅔ (or, more exactly, by 0·6757).

Another common measurement is the **M weight**, which is the weight of 1000 sheets. To convert poundage to M weight, just double the poundage figure.

The **bulk**, or **caliper**, of the paper is its thickness. Rough papers tend to be thicker than smooth papers of the same weight. Thickness is measured by a bulking number – the number of sheets to the inch, under test conditions. The ppi (pages per inch) is twice the bulking number (because there are two pages to the sheet). Another way to describe bulk is to measure four sheets of paper with an instrument called a **micrometer**. This "four-sheet caliper" is expressed in thousandths of an inch, which are referred to as **mils** or points. In continental Europe and the UK, thickness is measured in micrometers and bulk in cm^3/g.

Opacity is one characteristic not complicated by the metric system. It is the property of a paper affecting the **show-through** of printing from the other side of the sheet. Opacity is obviously influenced by both weight and bulk – the heavier and thicker a paper is, the more fibers there are blocking the passage of light. But it is also a function of the fillers added to the paper.

Visual opacity – the opacity of the unprinted sheet – is measured using an instrument called an **opacimeter**, and is expressed as a percentage. A sheet with 100 percent opacity is completely lightproof. A general idea of visual opacity can be gained by using a printed opacity gauge, placed under the sheet (Fig. 5.11).

Printed opacity depends partly on how absorbent the paper is (the more absorbent, the more **strike-through** of ink), and on the paper's ink **holdout** (its capacity to keep ink on the surface). This is a difficult parameter to measure, and the subjective terms high, medium, or low strike-through are used.

5.11 The opacity of paper is now measured using electronic instruments, but until recently the only measure was a subjective one, obtained by placing a printed opacity gauge like this below the sheet and assessing the amount showing through.

The color of a paper is determined by dyes added during the papermaking process, or by coatings added afterward. Color can be affected by the raw materials used. Recycled papers are always grayer than those made from virgin pulp, but this and the speckled appearance can be used as design elements in their own right. Paper also comes in several grades of whiteness, produced by adding **optical brighteners** and other chemicals. The color of paper stock always affects the color of the ink printed on it, determining the lightest highlight in any halftone. You cannot have a highlight that is whiter than the paper, nor a shadow deeper than the color of the ink.

The finish of a paper is a description of its surface. Its texture first takes shape on the wire and under the dandy roll. As previously mentioned, wove and laid papers receive their characteristic texture here. Uncoated papers receive their smoothness in the calender stack. Coated papers are more likely to be calendered or super-calendered off the machine. Distinctive finishes such as ripple and stucco are created by embossing the paper.

For book papers, the roughest finish is called **antique**. This is an uncoated paper with high bulk. A smoother, pressed version is **eggshell**. **Machine finish (MF) paper** has been calendered and is smoother and less bulky than eggshell. **Machine glazed (MG) paper** has been dried against a highly polished cylinder and has one glossy side with the other remaining relatively rough. It is an example of **duplex stock** – paper with a different finish or color on either side.

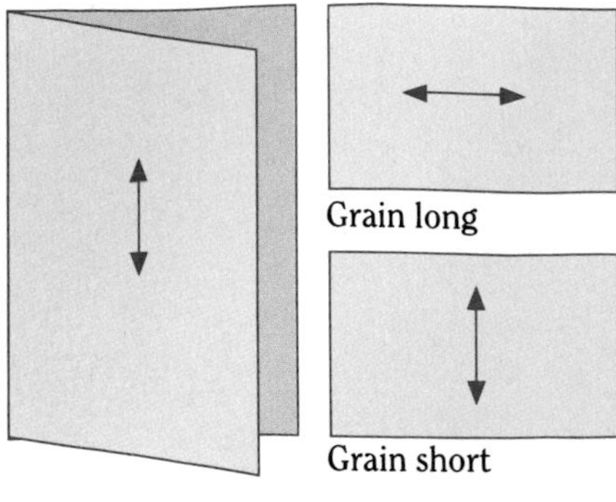

5.12 All machine-made paper has grain, caused by the orientation of the drying fibers. It is important to know the direction of grain, so that it can run parallel to any folds in your publication.

Coating covers the paper fibers with clay. Super-calendering coated paper gives it a highly glossy appearance. Coating produces a paper with excellent ink holdout, which is ideal for color reproduction. Thus coated papers are often called art papers.

The coating can be applied by rollers on the machine (film coating, or machine coating), or by rollers or blades off the machine (conversion coating). Conversion coated papers generally have a thicker coating and are of a higher quality. Blade coating produces a **matte** (dull) surface. Gloss is produced by calendering and super-calendering papers after they have been coated. The highest possible gloss is called **cast coated**: the wet coated web is dried against a highly polished chromium drum. **Chromo paper** is polished on one side only.

Other important characteristics include strength and wet strength, dimensional stability (the ability to stay the same size), rigidity, and **picking** resistance (a binder is used in coatings to prevent fibers from lifting on the press).

And bear in mind that all machine-made papers have grain. Paper folds more easily with than **against the grain**, and ideally books should be designed so that the printed sheets have the grain parallel to the binding (Fig. 5.12).

Stock can be ordered grain long, with the grain running lengthwise, or grain short, with the grain running across the width of the sheet. Grain-long paper stretches less, so gives better color registration with web offset. Grain-short paper is better for fast print runs, because it bends easily around the press rollers and speeds up the printing process.

You can determine the direction of the grain by tearing a piece of paper – it will tear straighter along the grain than against it. Here are two other methods: run one edge of the sheet between the thumb and finger, through the fingernails. If it crinkles into a wavy pattern, that's the edge across the grain (Fig. 5.13). Or mark a swatch and dampen it. It will curl in the direction of the grain. On paper specifications, machine direction is indicated by the symbol (m). Thus 25 × 38(m) is grain long, and 25(m) × 38 is grain short.

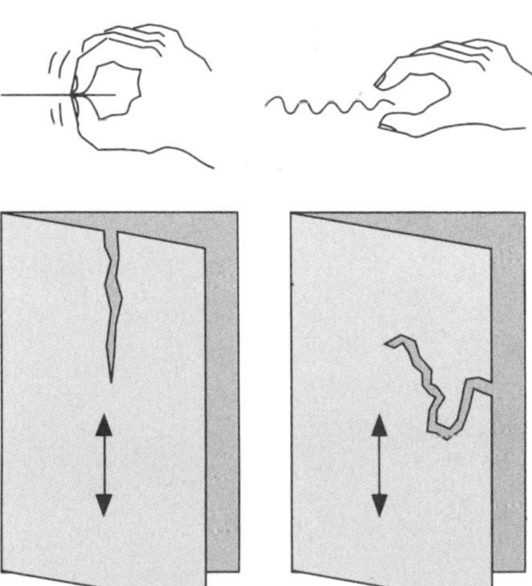

5.13 You can test for grain either by tearing a sheet of paper – it will tear more cleanly in the direction of the grain – or by running an edge between your finger and thumb – if it crinkles, then that's the edge across the grain.

ZANDERS
ikono
Entente Cordiale
CHATEAU BRETEUIL
YOUR VENUE FOR THE DAY
ELEFANTENHAUT
MENU
Tuesday 20th June 1989
Arlequin de Saumon Frais aux Petits Legumes – Sauce Cressonniere
Côte d'Agneau en Habit Doré
Cèpes & Pleurottes – Jus d'Agneau à l'Estragon
Mini Bavarois de Courgettes
Fromages Affinés
Tabatières
Petits Pains Empereur
Vacherin Framboise avec Fruits & Coulis de Framboises
Café Fin Moka

5.14 Every designer should aim to collect "designer packs" of paper samples at every opportunity. Try, too, to collect printed samples.

Choosing the right paper stock

There is ever a rich but bewildering range of papers available, and you should begin to collect samples, along with technical specifications on the characteristics described above. You can buy paper direct from the mill, or from a paper merchant. Paper merchants stock a wider variety of papers, obtained from many mills, both at home and abroad. Some merchants specialize in particular kinds of paper. Most mills and merchants will supply you with a designer's pack of samples (Fig. 5.14). Collect printed samples of paper, too, and always choose a paper in consultation with the person who is going to have to print on it.

As mentioned earlier, for some jobs the printing process itself will narrow down your choice – you would never dream of putting blotting paper through a litho press, for example. Price, too, will be a limiting factor. Handmade paper must be reserved for the most prestigious jobs. And it is possible to over-specify paper. There is little point, for example, in specifying a high-gloss stock if it is to be laminated or varnished later.

Sheet-fed offset litho machines require papers with good surface strength and dimensional stability; web offset paper must also have a low moisture content. Surface finish is not such an issue, as modern offset presses can make a good impression on a wide range of surfaces. Offset ink is tacky, however, and the paper should be well sized to prevent "picking" – the pulling out of surface fibers.

The prerequisites for letterpress printing are smoothness, absorbency, opacity, and compressibility. Paper has to be smooth enough to accept a uniform transfer of ink, and strong enough to take the pressure of the sharp edges of metal type without tearing.

The most important characteristic for gravure is smoothness. However, the paper must not contain any abrasive material on its surface – as matte coated stock does. It must also be absorbent enough to draw the ink out from the cells below the smooth surface of the cylinder.

And the silkscreen process demands that papers be not too absorbent.

The trick is to find the stock that matches the brief for the job – a paper just opaque enough to prevent strike-through, but not too heavy (remember the mailing bill), and with a finish appropriate to the design content. Antique may be fine for type and line illustrations, but for good halftone reproduction you will need a coated stock. Glossy is best for color reproduction, but its shine can interfere with readability in the type sections.

Glossy art paper can sometimes feel thinner than the same weight of matte-coated stock, so you may need to increase the weight when going for glossy. Increasing the weight of the stock on some jobs – on a small print run of small-scale booklets, for example – can be a relatively inexpensive way of improving the overall quality of the print.

It is also important to think hard about what other rigors your paper will have to withstand. There may be a reply coupon on your booklet. If so, is it possible to write on the stock in ballpoint or felt-tip pen without it skipping or smudging? And will that exquisite set of corporate stationery accept additional text from a photocopier or laser printer? A print job may leave your studio looking good, but it also has to perform well in real-life conditions.

Odd-shaped booklets and posters can seem like a good idea at the time. But they can be wasteful on paper, so find out the sizes of stock that the printer can handle, and have a sheet in front of you when you are calculating the size and shape of your layout (Fig. 5.15). Remember, however, that if the sheet is too large, this can affect the quality of color reproduction. And instead of requesting a paper by brand name, try asking printers what they have available – you may get a good deal. But beware – if you need reruns in the future, you may not be able to obtain that stock again.

Paper can represent a large proportion of the cost of any printed job, but, in the words of British typographer Ruari McLean, "can be a relatively inexpensive luxury, when luxuries – so often illegal, immoral, or fattening – are also harder and harder to obtain." Paper can give pleasure, and should always be chosen with a great deal of care.

US STANDARD PAPER SIZES

Grade classification	Basis size* in	Basis size* mm	Weights, lb/ream	Design applications
Bond	17 × 22	432 × 559	13, 16, 20, 24, 28, 32, 36, 40	Letterheads, newsletters
Book	25 × 38	635 × 965	30, 40, 45, 50, 55, 60, 65, 70, 75, 80, 90, 100, 120	Books, catalogs, calendars, annual reports, brochures, magazines
Text	25 × 38	635 × 965	90, 100, 120, 140, 160, 180	Posters, self-mailers, announcements
Cover	20 × 26	508 × 660	25, 35, 40, 50, 55, 60, 65, 80, 90, 100	Business cards, annual report covers, greeting cards

*Basis size: the standard size in a particular grade that determines basis weight

US BOOK SIZES

Name	in	mm	Name	in	mm
Medium 32mo	3 × 4¾	76 × 121	Medium 12mo	5⅛ × 7⅔	130 × 195
Medium 24mo	3⅝ × 5½	92 × 140	Demy 8vo	5½ × 8	140 × 203
Medium 18mo	4 × 6⅔	102 × 169	Small 4to	7 × 8½	178 × 216
Cap 8vo	7 × 7¼	178 × 184	Broad 4to	7 × 8½	178 × 216
12mo	4½ × 7½	114 × 191	(up to 13 × 10)(330 × 254)		
Medium 16mo	4½ × 6¾	114 × 171	Medium 8vo	6 × 9½	152 × 241
Crown 8vo	5 × 7½	127 × 191	Royal 8vo	6½ × 10	165 × 254
Post 8vo	5½ × 7½	140 × 191	Super Royal 8vo	7 × 10½	178 × 267
			Imperial 8vo	8¼ × 11½	210 × 292

Note that American and European usage is to express the width dimension of the book first. In the UK and Far East, depth is shown first.
Sizes quoted are not absolute and may vary slightly.

TRIMMED PAGE SIZES FROM STANDARD US SHEETS

Trimmed page size in (mm)	Number of pages	Number from sheet	Standard paper size in	Standard paper size mm
3½ × 6¼ (89 × 159)	4	24	28 × 44	711 × 1118
	8	12	28 × 44	711 × 1118
	12	8	28 × 44	711 × 1118
	16	6	28 × 44	711 × 1118
	24	4	28 × 44	711 × 1118
4 × 9 (102 × 229)	4	12	25 × 38	635 × 965
	8	12	38 × 50	965 × 1270
	12	4	25 × 38	635 × 965
	16	6	38 × 50	965 × 1270
	24	2	25 × 38	635 × 965
4½ × 6 (114 × 152)	4	16	25 × 38	635 × 965
	8	8	25 × 38	635 × 965
	16	4	25 × 38	635 × 965
	32	2	25 × 38	635 × 965
5¼ × 7⅝ (133 × 194)	4	16	32 × 44	813 × 1118
	8	8	32 × 44	813 × 1118
	16	4	32 × 44	813 × 1118
	32	2	32 × 44	813 × 1118
6 × 9 (152 × 229)	4	8	25 × 38	635 × 965
	8	4	25 × 38	635 × 965
	16	2	25 × 38	635 × 965
	32	2	38 × 50	965 × 1270
Oblong 7 × 5½ (178 × 140)	4	8	23 × 29	584 × 737
	8	4	23 × 29	584 × 737
	16	2	23 × 29	584 × 737
8½ × 11 (216 × 279)	4	4	23 × 35	584 × 889
	8	2	23 × 35	584 × 889
	16	2	35 × 45	889 × 1143
9 × 12 (229 × 305)	4	4	25 × 38	635 × 965
	8	2	25 × 38	635 × 965
	16	2	38 × 50	965 × 1270

US STANDARD ENVELOPE SIZES

Commercial/official Window

Number	Size, in
6	3⅜ × 6
6¼	3½ × 6
6¾	3⅝ × 6½
7	3¾ × 6¾
7¾	3⅞ × 7½
Data Card	3½ × 7⅝
8⅝	3⅝ × 8⅝
9	3⅞ × 8⅞
10	4⅛ × 9½
10½	4½ × 9½
11	4½ × 10⅜
12	4¾ × 11
14	5 × 11½

Booklet

Number	Size, in
2½	4½ × 5⅞
3	4¾ × 6½
4¼	5 × 7½
4½	5½ × 7½
5	5½ × 8½
6	5¾ × 8⅞
6½	6 × 9
6¾	6½ × 9½
7	6¼ × 9⅝
7¼	7 × 10
7½	7½ × 10½
8	8 × 11⅛
9	8¾ × 11½
9½	9 × 12
10	9½ × 12⅝
13	10 × 13

Catalog

Number	Size, in
1	6 × 9
1¾	6½ × 9½
2	6½ × 10
3	7 × 10
6	7½ × 10½
7	8 × 11
8	8¼ × 11¼
9½	8½ × 10½
9¾	8¾ × 11¼
10½	9 × 12
12½	9½ × 12½
13½	10 × 13
14¼	11¼ × 14¼
14½	11½ × 14½

Announcement

Number	Size, in
A–2	4⅜ × 5⅝
A–6	4¾ × 6½
A–7	5¼ × 7¼
A–8	5½ × 8⅛
A–10	6¼ × 9⅝
Slim	3⅞ × 8⅞

INTERNATIONAL "A" SIZES OF PAPER

Size	mm	approx. in
4A0	1682 × 2378	66¼ × 93⅜
2A0	1189 × 1682	46¾ × 66¼
A0*	841 × 1189	33⅛ × 46¾
A1	594 × 841	23⅜ × 33⅛
A2	420 × 594	16½ × 23⅜
A3	297 × 420	11¾ × 16½
A4	210 × 297	8¼ × 11¾
A5	148 × 210	5⅞ × 8¼
A6	105 × 148	4⅛ × 5⅞
A7	74 × 105	2⅞ × 4⅛
A8	52 × 74	2 × 2⅞
A9	37 × 52	1½ × 2
A10	26 × 37	1 × 1½

*Nominal size: in the A series, this equals one square meter

All A series sizes mentioned here are trimmed. "A" sizes can be cut from two stock sizes – R, for trims, and SR, for extra trims or bleeds. A listing of R and SR metric sizes and inch equivalents is below.

Size	mm	approx. in
RA0	860 × 1220	33⅞ × 48⅛
RA1	610 × 860	24⅛ × 33⅞
RA2	430 × 610	17 × 24⅛
SRA0	900 × 1280	35½ × 50⅜
SRA1	640 × 900	25¼ × 35½
SRA2	450 × 640	17⅞ × 25¼

ISO "B" AND "C" SIZES OF PAPER

Size	mm	approx. in
B0	1000 × 1414	39⅜ × 55⅝
B1	707 × 1000	27⅞ × 39⅜
B2	500 × 707	19⅝ × 27⅞
B3	353 × 500	12⅞ × 19⅝
B4	250 × 353	9⅞ × 12⅞
B5	176 × 250	7 × 9⅞
B6	125 × 176	5 × 7
B7	88 × 125	3½ × 5
B8	62 × 88	2½ × 3½
B9	44 × 62	1¾ × 2½
B10	31 × 44	1¼ × 1¾
C0	917 × 1297	36⅛ × 51
C1	648 × 917	25½ × 36⅛
C2	458 × 648	18 × 25½
C3	324 × 458	12¾ × 18
C4	229 × 324	9 × 12¾
C5	162 × 229	6⅜ × 9
C6	114 × 162	4½ × 6⅜
C7	81 × 114	3¼ × 4½
C8	57 × 81	2¼ × 3¼

ISO ENVELOPE STANDARDS

Sheets from the A series can be inserted in the C series envelope, flat or folded. For example, a C5 envelope will accommodate an A5 sheet flat, or an A4 folded once. ISO envelope sizes are all taken from B or C size sheets.

Envelope	mm	approx. in
C3	324 × 458	12¾ × 18
B4	250 × 353	9⅞ × 12⅞
C4	229 × 324	9 × 12¾
B5	176 × 250	7 × 9⅞
C5	162 × 229	6⅜ × 9
B6/C4	125 × 324	5 × 12¾
B6	125 × 176	5 × 7
C6	114 × 162	4½ × 6⅜
DL	110 × 220	4¼ × 8¾
C7/6	81 × 162	3¼ × 6⅜
C7	81 × 114	3¼ × 4½

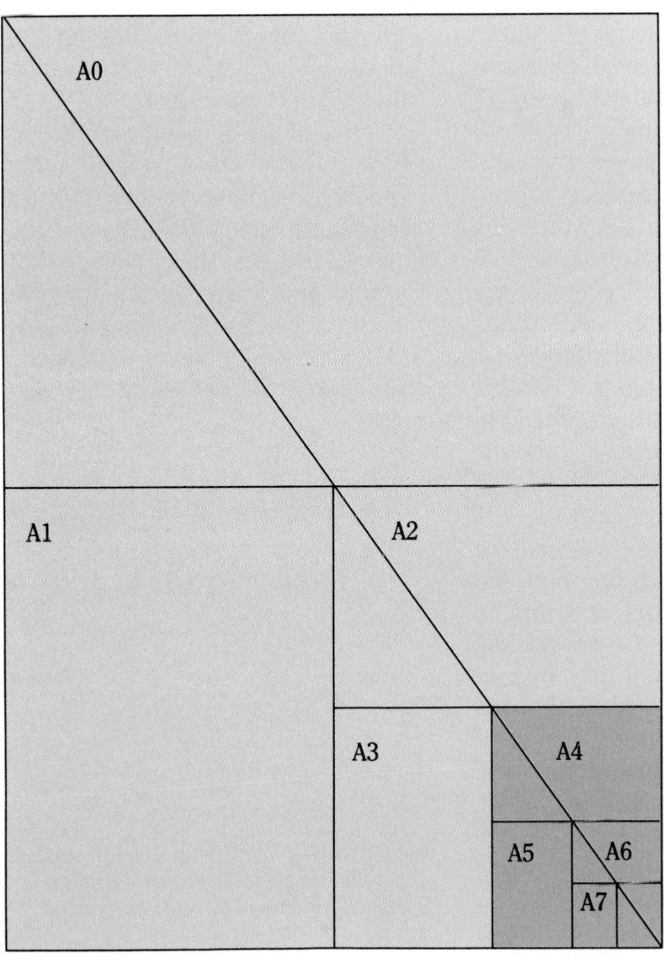

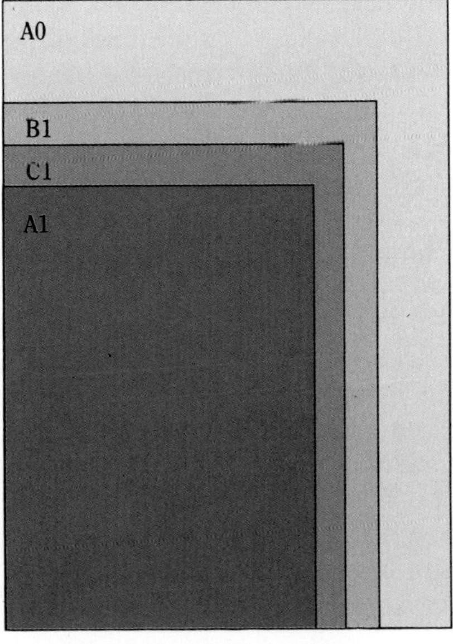

5.15 Paper sizes.

Part 2: inks

Printing inks are very different from the inks used for drawing and writing. They are generally thick and sticky – more the consistency of paint (Fig. 5.16).

The various printing processes make very different demands of the characteristics of the ink: its formulation, viscosity (degree of runniness), tackiness, and rate of drying. Of course, a printer running an offset litho machine will buy ink specially formulated for offset litho. What a designer has to know, however, is that not all offset litho inks are the same, nor do they act in the same way. Even the standard process colors can vary subtly from manufacturer to manufacturer, and from different countries of origin. Until the discovery of phthalocyanine blue in the 1950s, process colors could be very variable indeed.

Formulation

So what are printers' inks made of? All inks are made from three basic constituents: pigments and dyes, a vehicle (or binding substance), and some additives. The **pigments and dyes** give an ink its color. Like the pigments in paint, they come from a wide range of natural and synthetic sources, some organic and some inorganic. Pigments are usually dry and powdery, and have to be ground finely. Dyes are liquid and have to be "coated" (attached to solid particles) before they can be mixed with the other ingredients. Black ink is made from carbon-black, manufactured by burning mineral oil in a restricted air supply.

Colored pigments come from so many different sources and have such individual characteristics that there has to be a great deal of adjustment to the vehicle and additives in order to make them behave with any kind of consistency. Different colored inks behave differently on the press, and dry at different rates. And because of the scarcity of certain pigments, there are variations in price between different colors. Metallic inks, in particular, are expensive. The choice of inks has been made simpler, however, by the adoption of the four process colors for full-color work, and by Pantone's standardization of 11 basic colors, from which over 1000 flat colors can be mixed to formula (see p. 82).

The **vehicle** is the carrier that binds the dry, powdery pigment together. It can be an oil, a natural resin, or an alkyd (a synthetic resin). The type of vehicle is determined by the process. Litho and letterpress inks are oil-based. Screenprint, gravure, and flexographic inks are resin-based and are thinned with a highly volatile solvent, such as alcohol. Non-tainting formulations have to be specified for food packaging.

Very few printing inks are water-based, though a water-based ink would be welcomed by those caring about the environment. Litho could never use a water-based ink, because the process is based on the fact that oil and water do not mix. But water-based inks have been used, for example, for printing candy wrappers by flexography and gravure.

As well as the pigment and vehicle, printing inks contain various additives – mainly driers, but also a selection of anti-oxidants (added to stop the ink from drying in the machine), fillers, and other agents that give the ink particular properties such as scuff-resistance. Printers sometimes mix in further additives to meet the requirements of a specific job.

Different driers are used depending on the process, the material the job is being printed on, and the intended end use. They are metallic salts or compounds of cobalt and manganese, and speed the rate of drying chemically. Paradoxically, too much drier can slow down the rate of drying. And too much drier on the litho press will mix with the watery fountain solution and cause pigment particles to be deposited on the non-image portions of the plate.

Most inks dry by a process called oxidation. The drying oil of the vehicle absorbs oxygen from the air, causing cross-polymerization (linking) within its molecular structure. This makes the ink gel, and then harden. Quick-drying inks and varnishes are "cured" by exposure to ultraviolet light, producing a hard and scuff-resistant film.

The quality of the paper has a marked effect on the ink's drying time. The vehicle soaks quickly into newsprint, leaving the pigment on the surface. That is why ink from most newspapers leaves your fingers (and clothes) dirty. But vegetable oils are now being used to replace the mineral oils, for improved rub resistance, as well as better brightness and sharper dots.

For the higher-quality coated stock used for magazines printed by web offset, the ink is dried in high-temperature ovens and then chilled. The sheets are folded straight away, so the ink has to be dried quickly. Naturally, it has to be able to cope with this rough treatment, and a special solvent-based formulation called **heat-set ink** is used.

Other additives include extenders, which increase the coverage of the pigment and improve ink transfer from press to paper; distillates, which improve the flow characteristics of the ink; and waxes, which improve the slip and scuff resistance of inks used in packaging. Inks with added wax cannot subsequently be varnished.

5.16 Printing inks are traditionally mixed on a slab using a palette knife – a messy job usually reserved for the apprentice printer.

Viscosity and tackiness

The most important characteristic of an ink is its **viscosity** – how runny it is. This property is measured using an instrument called an **inkometer**, or tackoscope.

Litho inks have to be relatively viscous, with high **tack** (stickiness). They must also have a high concentration of pigment. The nature of the process demands the thinnest possible ink film of the strongest possible color. The amount of ink arriving at the paper during the offset litho process is half that of the more direct processes of letterpress and gravure. Litho inks are relatively transparent: yellow printed over blue will produce a recognizable green. They also have to perform well while being almost constantly "contaminated" with the water that coats the litho plate.

Letterpress inks are similar to litho inks, but contain a smaller proportion of pigments. They generally have a higher viscosity, but lower tack. Because there is no water used in the process, the chemistry of letterpress ink can be far less complex.

Inks for gravure and flexography are much more fluid than litho and letterpress inks. Gravure inks are thinned down with additional solvent before printing begins, and deposit a similar amount of pigment onto paper as letterpress. Flexographic ink is the thinnest of all, and has to be formulated not to attack the rubber rollers used in the process.

Silkscreen inks are semi-liquid with good flow characteristics. They have to get through the holes of the screen, but not be so fluid as to spread into the non-image areas. These inks, too, have to be thinned before printing to arrive at the correct viscosity.

Specifying inks

Some inks react unpredictably with other finishes. Colored inks for wet-on-wet printing on a multicolor press, for example, must be "tack graded" to arrive at an ink film of full density. Some colors will **mottle**, or change shade, when varnished. Purples and reflex blue are particularly susceptible. Colors print differently on different substrates: inks on art paper will appear stronger and brighter than on recycled paper (Fig. **5.17**), and different again on plastic.

Colors appear different under different lighting conditions. Printers view colors under standard lighting conditions, an area surrounded by neutral gray and illuminated by a light source with a color temperature of 5000 Kelvin. If you are designing packaging destined for supermarkets, for example, standard conditions will give a false reading. Supermarkets use different colored lighting to seduce people into buying more things, and to make food look more succulent. The colors in the packaging must compensate for these effects – it is essential to view your designs under the lighting conditions for which they are being designed.

Lightfast inks should be specified if the job is to be exposed to sunlight. Magenta and yellow tend to fade faster than black and cyan (look at the covers of paperbacks in the windows of secondhand bookstores). Inks prone to fading are called **fugitive** inks. Silkscreen inks are more lightfast than the others.

Fluorescent and **metallic inks** often need to be underprinted to achieve a satisfactory result, just as black is often underprinted with a percentage of cyan to increase its density. Fluorescent dyes can be added to the process colors to improve the quality of reproduction of illustrations, particularly vibrant watercolors. "Metallic integrated process printing" is a term coined by Pantone to describe a method for adding percentages of gold and silver inks to the process colors. This results in an expensive six-color process, that is printed in the sequence silver, yellow, gold, followed by the remaining process colors. Since normal photography cannot record a metallic finish, the designer or repro house has to estimate the amounts to use, based on charts supplied by Pantone. (Gold and silver can also be applied by blocking and hot-foil stamping; see p. 159.)

Other specialty inks include the magnetic inks used on bank checks and business forms, microencapsulated or "scratch and sniff" inks that add a fragrance to printed work (but be aware of an allergic reaction by some innocent end user), invisible ink for children's books and fraud-resistant lottery tickets, and moisture-resistant inks for packaging applications. Varnishes are a kind of colorless ink used to add gloss to halftones, particularly in prestigious publications such as annual reports. They are also used to add ultraviolet protection to color work that will be exposed to sunlight. If you intend to **spot varnish** photographs or illustrations, you may need to provide artwork or keylines on the mechanical to indicate the areas to be covered. Be sure to discuss any special requirements in the design brief with your printer, and together you will be able to find the correct ink for the application.

5.17 Recycled papers are more absorbent and less white than conventional stock, and printing on them can result in colors lacking in brilliance and saturation – hence the need for different ink formulations, which may themselves be helping to destroy the environment. Calculating the ecological cost of a print job is a complex process. (Cartoon by Phil Dobson.)

Part 3: selecting your supplier

You may not be able to look over the shoulder of your printer, as your design is being printed. But you can make sure that you have chosen the right supplier for the job, and that the printer is in no doubt as to your requirements. There are three main considerations: quality, cost, and the schedule. If you are running to tight deadlines, you may have to pay more. Similarly, quality means more care, and that too can cost money. This is not to say that you cannot produce beautiful printing on a small budget – there are plenty of examples of imaginative design that have used cost constraints to great advantage.

You can play your part, by submitting clean, uncomplicated mechanicals and clear, unambiguous instructions, and by avoiding any superfluous processes that are going to add labor costs to your bill – unless you decide that a special shape or finish is absolutely necessary.

How do you select the supplier appropriate to the job in hand? First, clearly you should not think of asking a small jobbing printer to undertake a complicated color job for a prestigious client. Nor should you ask a fine-art printer to bid for a short-run black-and-white newsletter. There are horses for courses. Second, do not be afraid to ask around for personal recommendations from colleagues. Look for the name of the printer on the examples of printing jobs you have collected. If their credit line is not there, ask their client. Then obtain some competitive bids.

For small jobs, find printers somewhere nearby. If they consistently do good work, stick with them, and build up a friendly relationship. Ask them to bid for jobs, but don't make it too formal a process. They may be able to help you out of a jam one day.

For large-scale jobs, provide each prospective supplier with a clear specification of the job in writing, outlining the size, print run, and finish you want. Insist that their prices are to a format that you specify, so that you can compare like with like. Tell them that if they do not follow the rules, their bid will not even be considered. Listen to them, however, and give as much information as they need to make a sensible bid – you may end up working with them, after all. Listen to any suggestions they may have to reduce costs, and adapt your specification if you can. Ask what possible economies can be made, by adjusting the schedule, the imposition scheme, or the paper stock. Visit the print works if possible, to familiarize yourself with the company's equipment and its capabilities. Examine samples of work that have been done on stock similar to your job.

Indicate whether you or the prospective printer will supply color separations and film, and list the finishing operations you will require. Ask if the printer has these facilities in-house or will have to send out to sub-contractors. If the latter is the case, you may do better to negotiate finishing separately. Likewise, ascertain whose responsibility it will be to buy in the paper stock.

Show a detailed dummy to each company, and take no chances that they may misinterpret any aspect of the job. Decide also if you need a simple bottom-line figure for the whole job, or whether you need a breakdown into ink, paper, platemaking, proofing, prepress, printing, mailing, and shipping.

When you have all the bids, make a decision, and inform everyone who has quoted. You may wish to negotiate a better price, but do not try to act the bigshot by playing one supplier off against another – you may wish to use several of them at a later date. But you may want to promise bigger jobs in future, conditional on this crucial one.

You must now draw up a contract. If the deal is done on the nod or handshake, the terms of a job in the USA will automatically revert to the Printing Trade Customs, originally drawn up in 1922 by the United Typothetae of America, and amended in 1986 by the Graphic Arts Council of North America, Inc. (see p. 201). In the UK it will be governed by the Standard Conditions of Contract for Printers, published by the British Printing Industries Federation; there are other more specialist documents such as the Customs of the Trade for the Manufacture of Books (see p. 200). Other countries have similar codes of conduct. It is as well to be familiar with them – ignorance is no defense.

The Printing Trade Customs formally set out the business relationship between the printer and the client. They state, for example, that quotations not accepted within 60 days are subject to review; that negatives, positives, flats, plates, and other items, when supplied by the printer, remain the printer's exclusive property unless otherwise agreed in writing; that a "reasonable variation" in color between color proofs and the completed job shall constitute acceptable delivery; and that "overruns and underruns not to exceed ten percent on quantities ordered, or the percentage agreed on, shall constitute acceptable delivery."

Any contract made between you and your printer will have legal standing, but if any of the terms contained in the Printing Trade Customs are to be adapted, they must be spelt out precisely, in writing. An underrun of ten percent, for example, on a print run of 10,000 is a perfectly legal shortfall of 1000 copies! You may want to prohibit a shortfall and instead risk a 20 percent overrun.

Make a realistic schedule that includes each stage in the process – design and mark-up of copy, typesetting, paste-up, prepress, make-ready (setting up the press), printing, and finishing – and let everyone concerned have a copy for comment. Anticipate any delays in ordering paper, vacations (use a calendar with weekends and holidays clearly marked), and shipping. Check proofs meticulously, bearing in mind that any error you miss will be multiplied hundreds or thousands of times. Things may go wrong, but careful planning and communication should eliminate too many surprises.

Part 4: printing processes

The various printing technologies have already been mentioned many times. Paper, ink, and printing process are all interdependent, and a choice of any one of them cannot be made in isolation. Once the decision to choose a particular printing process has been made, there is very little that a designer needs to or can do. If the mechanical is perfect, and the scans are good, then a good printer will produce a good result. There are things that can go wrong, however, and a little knowledge of how the printing processes work will go a long way in helping you to choose the right supplier and thus avoid any problems.

Printing processes can be categorized into one of four main types: relief, intaglio, planographic, and stencil (Fig. 5.18). Letterpress is a form of **relief printing** invented by the ancient Chinese. Dating back to about AD 730, it is by far the oldest of the printing technologies. Flexography is another form of relief printing, which had to await recent advances in materials technology. In relief printing, the printed **impression** is made by a raised surface coated with ink and pressed against the paper, or other substrate.

Intaglio printing uses a plate with incised lines or grooves. Ink is applied, and then wiped from the surface. An impression is made when the substrate is pressed against the surface of the plate, drawing the ink out from the recesses. Gravure is a kind of intaglio process. The **planographic printing** process, of which lithography is the only example, is perhaps the most mysterious, as everything happens on the surface of the plate. It works simply because oil and water do not mix. **Stencil printing**, or screenprinting, is, like relief printing, an ancient technique; earlier Oriental stencils were held together by meshes of human hair.

Offset lithography is by far the most common form of printing nowadays. There will be some designers who in the course of their careers use nothing else. It is rare these days for anyone to print by letterpress, but its historical significance is great. Unless you work in packaging design, it is unlikely that you will ever come across flexography or screenprinting. And unless you design mail-order catalogs or glossy magazines, you may never have to work with gravure. But you never can tell!

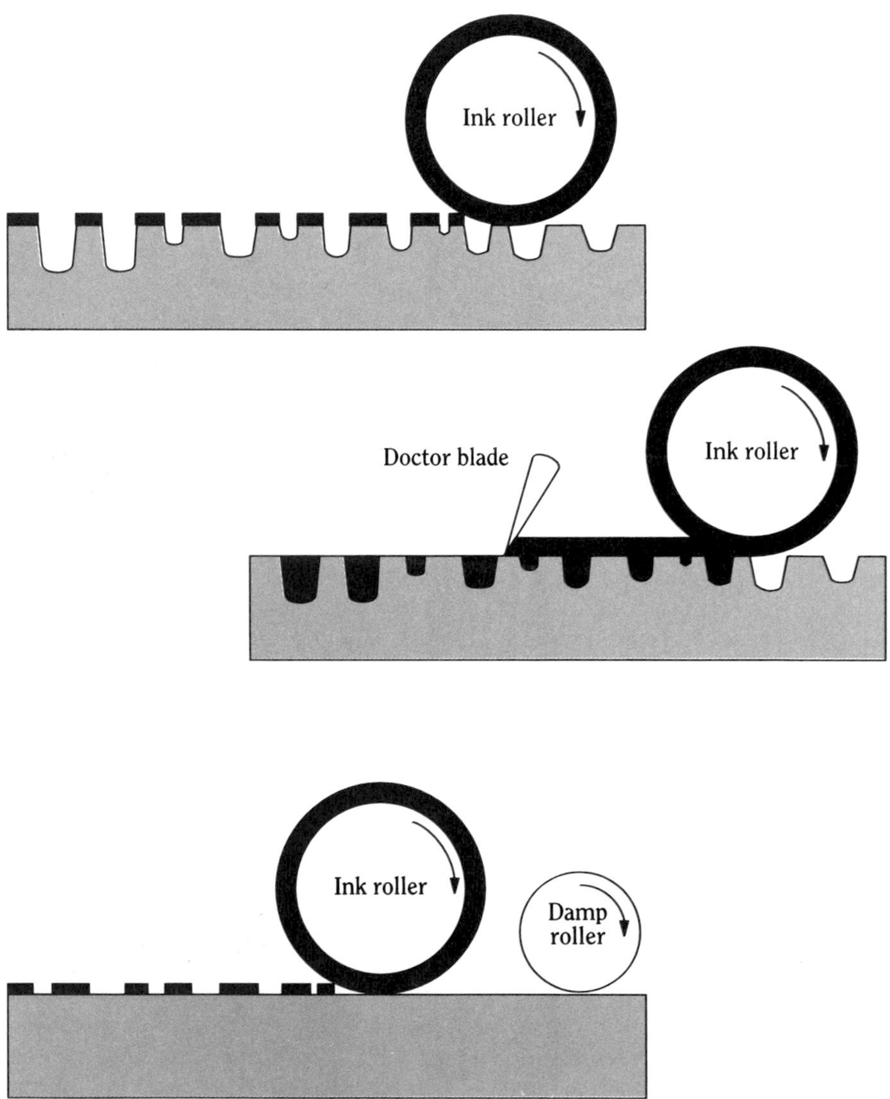

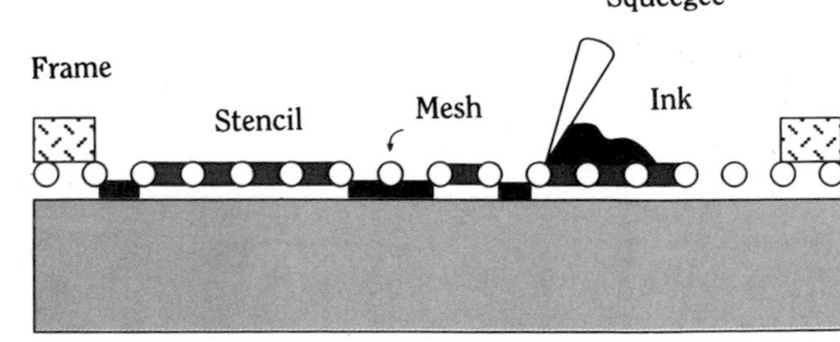

5.18 There are four main printing methods. Relief has ink sitting on the raised surface of the plate or type. Intaglio has ink in the grooves and recesses, while lithography is a planographic process with the ink on the surface, sticking only to the dry areas of the plate. And screenprinting forces the ink through a mask supported by a mesh.

Offset lithography

In Prague (now in Czechoslovakia) in around 1798, Alois Senefelder was experimenting with Solnhofen limestone to find a cheaper alternative to engraving images on copper. His experiments with etching in relief were a failure, but he did notice that he could print just as well without the relief. That discovery, along with the invention of photography in the mid-19th century, changed the course of printing history. It rendered letterpress virtually obsolete, and made **offset lithography** the predominant print technology of the 20th century.

The word **lithography** means "writing on stone." Senefelder discovered that if a design is drawn on a limestone surface using a greasy crayon, and then the surface is "etched" with a solution of gum arabic, water, and a few drops of nitric acid, the area that has been drawn on will become permanently receptive to grease. The undrawn area desensitized by the gum solution will be permanently resistant to grease. If the stone is later dampened and greasy ink is applied from a roller, the ink will stick to the design but not to the rest of the surface. Impressions can then be taken which are exact replicas of the original design.

Over the years, the same properties were discovered in more manageable zinc and aluminum plates. Then the **offset process** was developed to overcome the limitations of these metal plates. It involved taking an impression not directly from the plate but from an intermediate **blanket**. The offset process has several clear advantages. Metal plates are easily damaged, and offsetting the image onto rubber protects them from damage. The resilience of the rubber blanket enables impressions to be made on even quite rough papers, and other substrates such as tinplate. Furthermore, the design on the original stone had to be drawn as a mirror image of the finished design for it to print correctly. But because the image is first offset – printed to the blanket – and then onto the paper, the design for offset litho can be positive and "right reading."

Lithography would have become much more popular a lot sooner if it had not been for the fact that typesetting was a problem. It was possible to transfer type set by letterpress onto the litho plate using paper with the ink still wet. But it wasn't until the invention of photography that type could be put onto a litho plate with any kind of quality control.

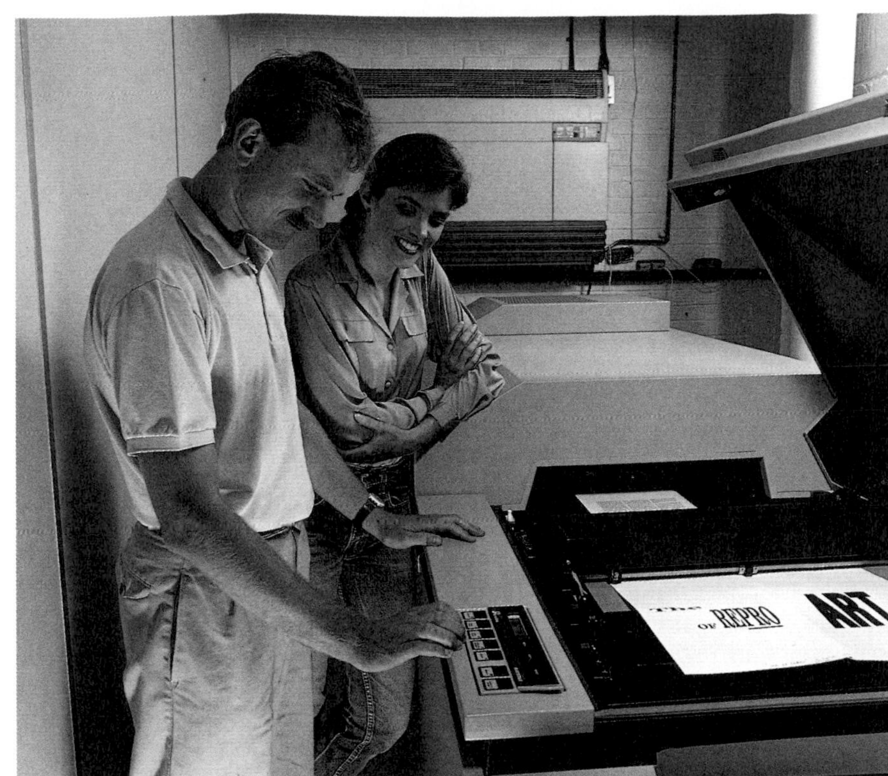

5.19 Plates for offset lithography are made in a printing down frame. The film or flat is put emulsion down, in direct contact with the plate, which is then developed either chemically or using a xerographic process.

Platemaking is the process by which the design is transferred onto a printing **plate** from the artwork or mechanical, either photographically or electrostatically, by a process resembling photocopying (Fig. 5.19). Offset litho plates have to be thin and flexible enough to wrap around a cylinder. Small plates are supplied pre-sensitized with a light-sensitive diazo compound or photopolymer, and are made from metal, plastic, or paper. Paper and plastic are used for short runs, up to 1000 copies. Because they stretch and distort on the press, they are only suitable for single-color work. They are exposed under a process camera, "developed" electrostatically, and "fixed" by heat. Alternatively, the plates are placed in direct contact with the artwork and the image is transferred using a photographic process similar to the production of PMTs (see p. 76).

Metal plates are made from aluminum with a granular surface, which gives the plate water-carrying properties, and provides anchorage to the image. Litho plates for larger machines and some smaller conventional metal plates can be exposed from either negative or positive film. As we have seen in Chapter 4, stripping and film make-up for black-and-white work is generally done using negative film. It follows that negative-working plates will be used for single-color work. Negative-working plates are less expensive than positive-working ones and are used in print runs of up to 100,000 copies. Most multicolor work, however, makes use of flats assembled from positive film, because it is easier to keep the separations in register. In this case, positive-working plates are used.

The exposure or **burn** is made by ultraviolet light in a printing-down frame which holds the plate in direct vacuum contact with the flat. On exposure, the diazo or photopolymer resin coating of a **negative-working plate** radiated by the ultraviolet light undergoes a chemical reaction to become ink-attracting. This then forms the image on the plate that will print. The rest of the coating, unexposed to the ultraviolet light, is washed off during subsequent processing. Finally, a gum arabic solution is applied to the surface to make the non-image areas water-attracting and ink-rejecting.

When **positive-working plates** are exposed in the frame, it is the sensitized photopolymer coating radiated by the ultraviolet light that is made unstable on exposure, and it is this portion that is removed during processing. The unexposed areas are the ones that will print. Again, the plate is gummed to make the non-image areas unattractive to ink. Since the image can be further destabilized by light, positive-working plates have a shorter life than negative-working ones. Some plates can be baked to "fix" and harden the image. Deletions can be made to a positive-working plate, by using a special eraser or brush-applied fluid. This can be useful for printing run-ons of a poster, for example, with dates or venues deleted.

All plates are subject to wear. After around 500,000 copies (or sometimes much lower numbers) have been printed, both the image and the surface grain start to break up. Multi-metal plates with surfaces of hard-wearing chromium are specially designed for long print runs of between 800,000 and a million.

Plates can also be made directly from a dtp or prepress system. Du Pont-Howson's Silverlith plate cuts out the film stage by exposing the aluminum plate inside the drum of an imagesetter, such as Purup's 7100, by the action of a blue argon-ion laser. The Silverlith plate is sensitive to blue light, with similar characteristics to film. It can be used for color separations, and to overlay scanned halftones onto a plate already exposed to a PostScript page layout.

The press manufacturer Heidelberg has gone one step further, with plates being made while they are actually in position on the press. At the time of writing, computer-to-press imaging is only available on the A3 size GTO SRA3 press. The litho plates are expensive, and limited to runs of 5000. Developed by Presstek, they have a polyester base overlaid with layers of aluminum and silicon. They are mounted on the press cylinders. The layouts from a dtp system drive a Linotype-Hell raster image processor, which in turn controls the electron beam that burns off the aluminum and silicon. There is one such electro-erosion unit on each of the four-color printing heads. Ink adheres to the polyester, and is repelled by the silicon, and so no water is necessary in the process.

THE LITHO PRESS

Offset litho presses range from the small-scale **sheetfed** machines found in jobbing printers all over the world (Fig. 5.21), to the huge presses used to print magazines and newspapers onto continuous webs, or rolls, of paper. The basic principles of the process are always the same (Fig. 5.20). A litho machine comprises: a **plate cylinder** onto which the plate is securely clamped; a resilient rubber-coated cylinder, called the **blanket cylinder**; an **impression cylinder**; a system of inking rollers called the **ink pyramid**; and a **plate-damping unit**. The litho plate is dampened, and then inked. Next, the inked image is transferred (offset) to the blanket. The paper moves between the blanket and the impression cylinders, which are "packed" to ensure complete contact, and the image in ink is transferred from the blanket onto the paper stock.

A single-color sheetfed machine prints single sheets in one color at a time. A mechanism called a feeder pushes each sheet in turn between the blanket and the impression cylinder. Sheets are lifted one by one by vacuum suckers, and are then sent through the machine by blasts of air and conveyor belts. High-speed presses use a **stream feeder**, which presents sheets to the rollers overlapping slightly. Detectors cut-out the printing unit if a sheet is defective or if two sheets are picked up together.

The front and side lays are adjustable stops which position the sheet before it enters the machine. The grippers – sets of metal fingers on the impression cylinder – grab the sheet and pull it through. A gripper allowance of ½ inch (15mm) must be made when estimating the printed area of a sheet. After it has been printed, it is released, and the delivery mechanism stacks it with the others, **jogging** them constantly to neaten the pile. To stop the wet image from **offsetting** onto the next sheet in the pile, anti-**setoff** spray is applied as the sheet falls onto the pile, separating it from its neighbors by a layer of fine particles.

Meanwhile, inside the machine, the damping system deposits a fine layer of moisture onto the plate's surface before it passes under the inking rollers. One or two cloth-covered rollers, supplied by a **fountain** roller, are used to regulate the amount of dampening. Alcohol can be used for up to 20 percent of the solution, to lower the surface tension and lessen the moisture uptake of the paper. Damp paper stretches, and anything that reduces this effect will improve the quality of the printing, especially in close-register color work.

Ink is introduced to the roller pyramid from a reservoir via an adjustable metal blade. Ink flow can be controlled by a computer taking densitometer readings from the printed sheets. This can also record ink settings that can be re-used if the job is to be reprinted. It is possible, though very messy and unpredictable, to print two colors from a single plate on a single-color offset press by using one color at one end of the fountain, another at the other end – the colors will blend in the middle. This is called **split fountain** printing.

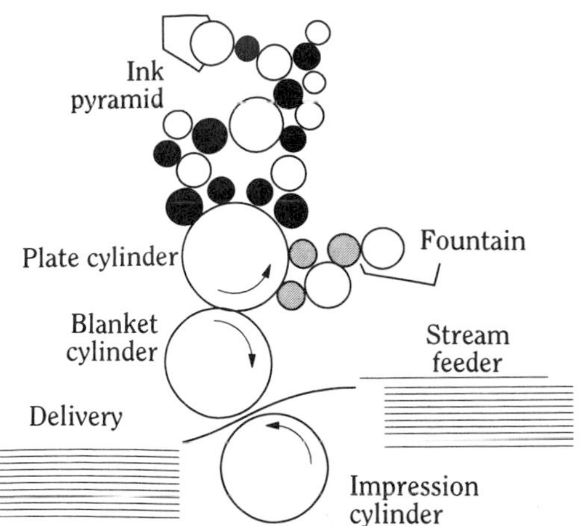

5.20 The layout of a small sheet-fed offset litho machine. The plate is first dampened by the fountain, then inked by the ink pyramid. The image is transferred to the rubber blanket cylinder and onto the paper, which is pressed between the blanket and the impression cylinder.

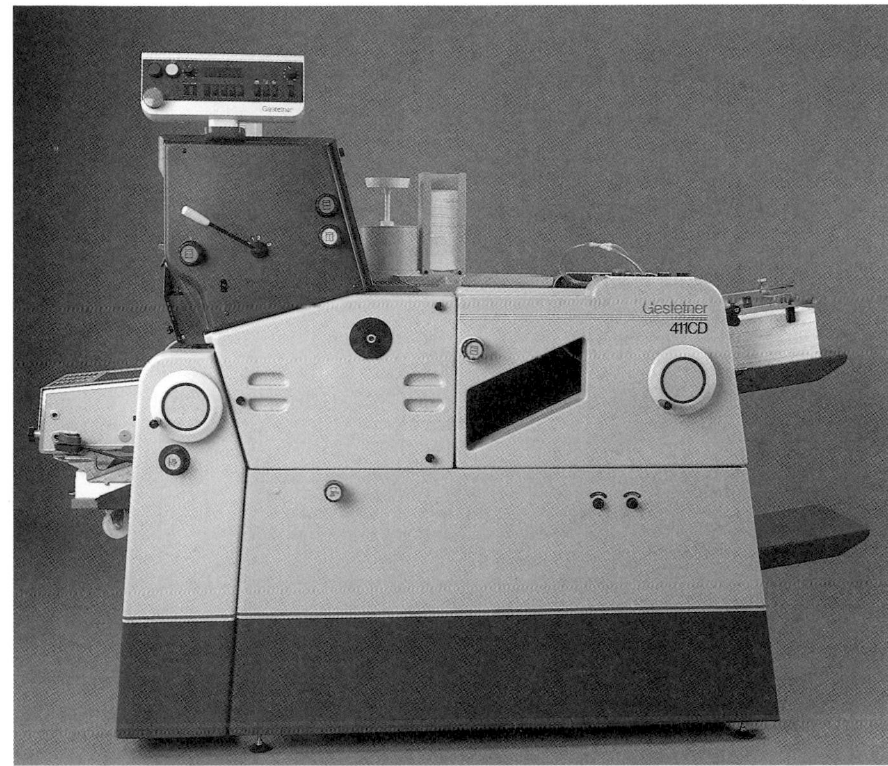

5.21 The Gestetner 411CD – a typical small offset litho machine.

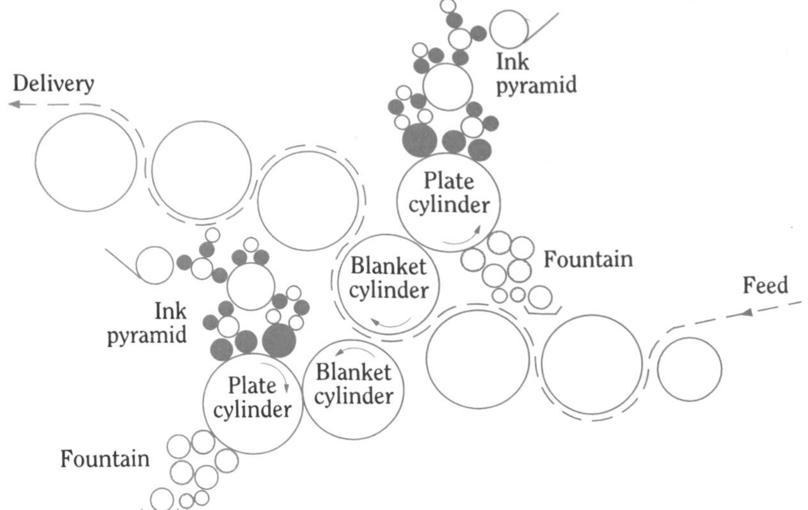

5.22 A perfecting press can print both sides of the sheet in one pass. Here there is no impression cylinder – the two blanket cylinders press against one another.

A **perfecting press** (Fig. 5.22) is a printing press that can print both sides of the sheet in one pass. One type of perfector is a **blanket-to-blanket press**, which has the two blanket cylinders printing at the same time, so that an impression cylinder is unnecessary.

Multicolor work can be printed in many different ways. An **in-line** machine has several single units arranged to print one color after another. Stock is conveyed to the next unit by grippers on transfer cylinders. A **converter** machine (Fig. 5.23) has a drum mechanism that can reroute the paper so that it can print either two colors together on one side of a sheet or (when converted) one color on each side of the sheet. A four-unit converter can print four colors on one side, or two each on both sides.

Web-fed machines (Fig. 5.24) print from a continuous roll of paper stock, which is printed and then folded and cut into sheets in a single pass. All web-fed machines print both sides of the sheet, and in web-offset, blanket-to-blanket designs are common. The length of the final sheet is determined by the circumference of the cutting cylinder. This cut-off length determines the press printing size you choose for a job. A single-width press with a width of 34 inches (850mm) and a cut-off length of 24 inches (600mm), produces eight 8¼ × 11¹¹⁄₁₆in (A4) pages to view, or 16 pages perfected (printed both sides) to a section.

A multiple-unit web-offset machine can have several web reels in

5.23 Using a converter configuration, you can either print both sides of a sheet in one pass, or one side in two colors.

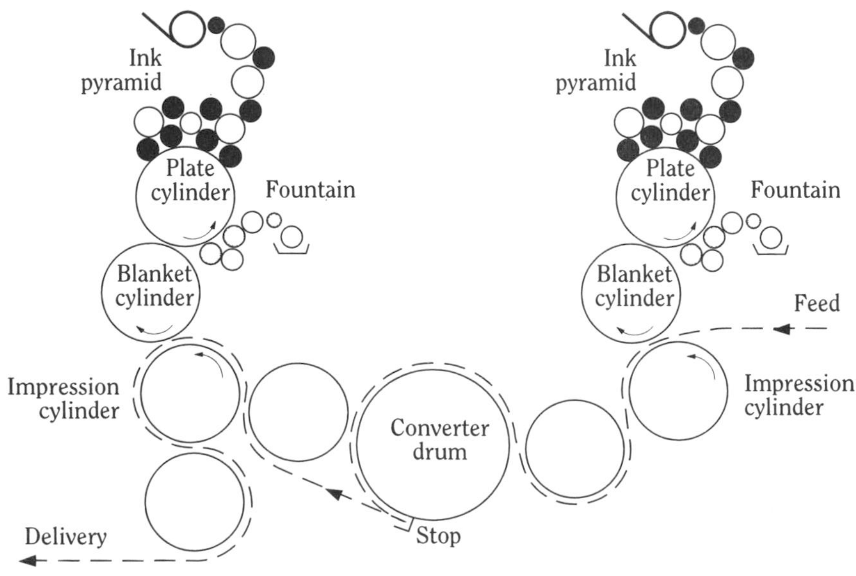

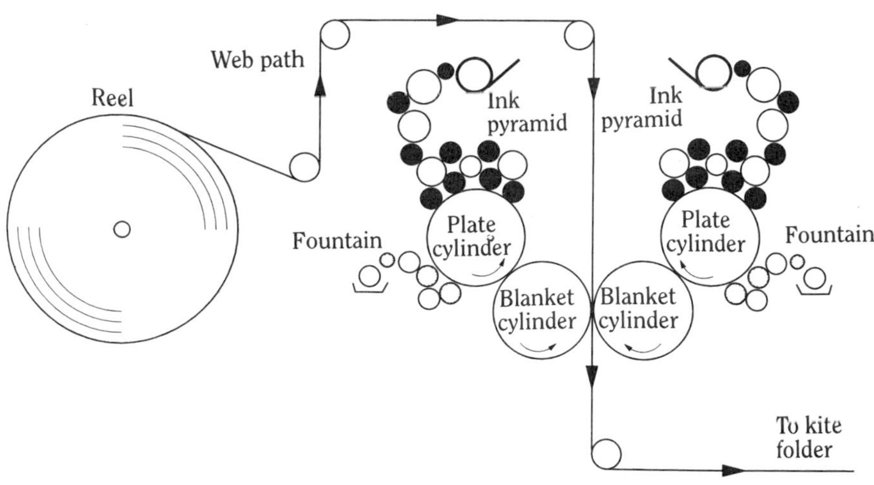

5.24 In this web offset configuration, the web is printed on both sides in one pass. A typical web press consists of several units like this, one after the other.

5.25 After printing and drying, the web is folded down the middle on a kite folder – as here at Headley Bros in Ashford, England.

operation. A five-unit web-offset machine with one reel in operation has the capacity to print four process colors plus one Pantone color, or one 16-page full-color section and one black-and-white 16-page section at the same time. A six-unit press, using only one or two printing units for each of two or three reels, can produce printings of flat color and black in many different permutations. On newspapers, for example, one cylinder might be reserved for printing late "stop press" items.

Web tension in the press is controlled by a dancer roller, which can apply a brake to the reel. When the reel runs out, the press is stopped and a new one is connected. On larger presses, this can be done automatically by a "flying paster," which attaches the end of the old reel to the beginning of the new one, then accelerates the new reel up to press speed, all while the press is running.

After printing, the web is dried in a series of gas-fired ovens, then chilled (however, newspapers often use **cold-set ink**, which does not require this treatment). To avoid smudging, it is vital that the ink is dry before the web passes over a former, or kite, which makes the first fold in the direction of motion. This is the part of the press always shown in old films, where it looks as though the web is disappearing into a slit (Fig. 5.25). The paper is then cut into sections, and folded again down to the correct page size. Magazines are trimmed with a three-knife trimmer. Newspapers are usually left untrimmed. For books, the web is slit into ribbons, which are passed over polished turner bars on cushions of air, for better alignment during trimming.

Web machines are used for long print runs, typically over 20,000 copies, on jobs with tight deadlines. With web, all the colors can be printed, both sides, on one pass, with folding done in-line. However, registration is often not as accurate as on sheetfed presses. Trim sizes are restricted as well; non-standard sizes and finishes are better handled by sheetfed machines.

Gravure

The biggest rival to the huge web-offset presses is **gravure**. This is an intaglio process that is used to print everything from the highest quality postage stamps and banknotes, through glossy magazines and mail-order catalogs, down to rough-and-ready wallpapers and gift wrapping paper.

Although related to earlier intaglio methods of printing, such as etching and copper engraving, gravure is a relatively recent process, invented in the middle of the 19th century by photographer Fox Talbot, as a means of reproducing **continuous tone** (see p. 22).

Present-day gravure machines are huge high-speed **rotary presses** that print from a web of paper. (Gravure is sometimes also called **rotogravure**.) The engraved cylinder is partially immersed in a bath of thin, solvent-based ink (Fig. **5.26**). Its surface is flooded with ink, and as it revolves it is wiped clean with a flexible steel blade called a doctor blade, leaving ink only in the image areas. A web of paper is pressed against the surface of the engraved cylinder by a rubber-covered impression cylinder, and the ink is transferred to the paper. The web passes to a folder and then a drier, similar to those found on web-offset machines.

The important point about gravure is that it prints continuous tones by means of cells – containers of ink cut into the surface of the cylinder (Fig. 5.27). Larger-diameter or deeper cells hold more ink, and thus deposit a thicker layer of ink, and hence make a darker printed image. This produces continuous-tone images that are almost screenless, as the ink from neighboring cells merges during printing. A drawback is that type is also printed this way, so it is less sharp than that produced by offset litho.

In the original process, cells were of equal size but different depths. This arrangement has been superseded either by cells of both varying depth and size, or by cells of constant depth but varying size. The latter method is used mainly for textiles and packaging design.

Preparing artwork for gravure is exactly the same as for offset litho (see Chapter 4), except that the typesetting is scanned as well as the tone. The complete artwork for the job is scanned in one pass. This is converted into signals that control a diamond engraving stylus which cuts into the surface of a blank copper cylinder, producing the pattern of cells (Fig. 5.28). After engraving, the cylinder can be chromium-plated for extra durability. Cylinders coated with polymer resin can be cut directly by laser. These may prove to be cheaper in the long run, as the resin can be replaced and cut again.

Because of the considerable expense involved in engraving the cylinders, gravure is reserved for jobs such as women's magazines with very high print runs – typically 250,000 copies or more – or for jobs demanding the highest quality of halftone reproduction.

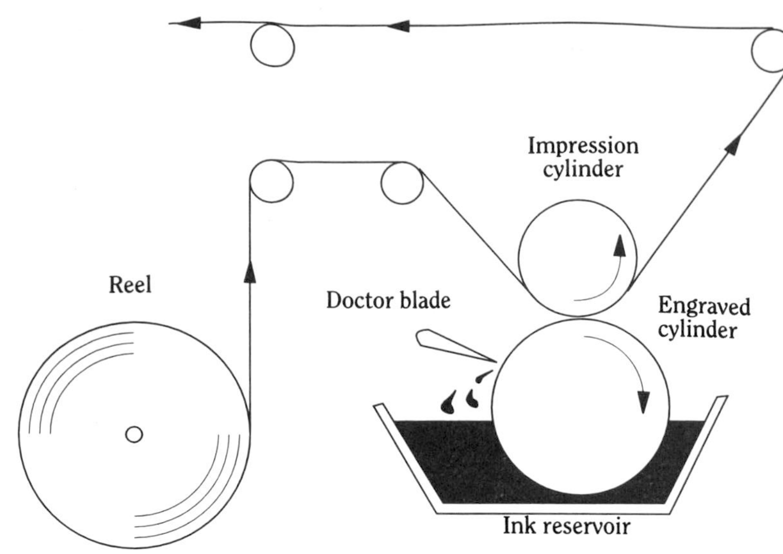

5.26 A gravure press is invariably web-fed. The engraved gravure cylinder is inked and then its surface is wiped clean by a doctor blade. The paper is printed as a result of pressure between the plate cylinder and the impression cylinder.

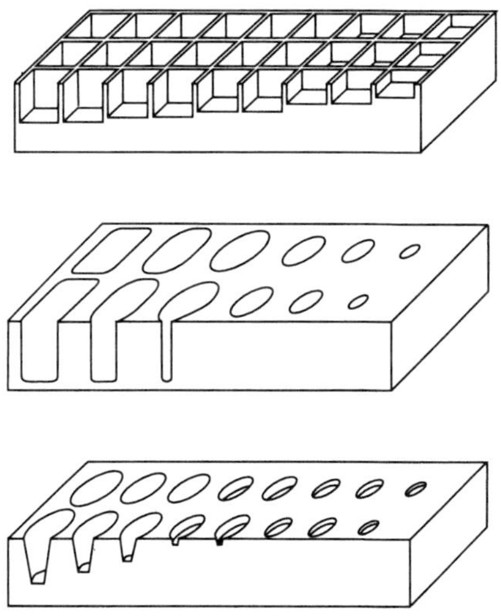

5.27 Coventional gravure cells have equal area but differing depth – the deeper the cell, the darker the impression (top). Other kinds of cell include those with variable area and equal depth, used mainly for packaging (center), and – for the highest quality work – those with variable area and variable depth (bottom).

5.28 Cylinders at the press of R. R. Donnelley in Chicago. Engraving gravure cylinders is very expensive, and thus the process is only economical for long runs.

Letterpress

Until the 1960s, **letterpress** was the most popular form of printing. Now it is virtually obsolete, except for small limited-edition presses producing fine editions of books. The hot-metal typesetting side of the process survives, but mostly only to produce repro proofs that are then incorporated into mechanicals and printed by offset litho. Conversely, photoset mechanicals can be used to produce plates that print on letterpress machines. But increasingly, large letterpress machines are being converted to flexography (see below), in which the heritage of letterpress lingers on.

Letterpress is a relief process, invented by the Chinese. It was adapted to western use by Gutenberg, and perfected in the late 19th century, with the introduction of iron steam-powered presses. The beautifully crafted Stanhope, Columbian, and Albion presses from the golden age of letterpress, with their ornamental cast-iron eagles and fanciful beasts, have long been relegated to science museums and the entrance halls of modern printers (Fig. 5.29). But like steam locomotives, some have been lovingly restored by enthusiasts and put to use. They create that three-dimensional tactile quality of impression that litho and gravure cannot achieve.

There are three types of letterpress machine: flatbed, platen, and rotary. The **flatbed** is the oldest, being derived from wine and textile presses (Fig. 5.30). The forme containing the locked-up wrong-reading type and blocks is placed horizontally on the bed of the press. Paper is placed over it, and a screw is turned or a lever pulled to apply pressure. The cylinder flatbed is a press that has the forme and paper on a bed that is inked and then moved under a heavy impression cylinder. The cylinder is lifted to allow the bed to return to its starting position.

The **platen** principle has the forme positioned vertically, with the platen – a heavy metal plate – swinging forward and upward with the paper (Fig. 5.31). It makes an impression as it snaps shut, like a clamshell, vertical and parallel with the forme. Platen presses can still be seen in operation, printing business cards.

A rotary press cannot print directly from the forme. A curved copy of the forme, called a stereotype, must first be cast. A *papier-mâché* mold, called a flong, is taken from the forme, and is used to make a one-piece metal, rubber, or plastic plate. It is then fixed around the cylinder. Rotary presses can be sheetfed or web-fed. During the changeover of newspapers from letterpress to offset litho, a process called photopolymer direct relief was used to make plastic or nylon plates for letterpress from photoset mechanicals. Flexography (see below) uses a similar process.

Letterset is a process whereby the image is first offset onto a rubber blanket, as in offset litho. It is used for printing on metal and plastic cartons and cans.

5.29 Most old iron letterpress machines, such as this Columbian, have been relegated to the foyers of large corporations, or gardens, as mere ornamental features. Thankfully, some are being restored and put back to work.

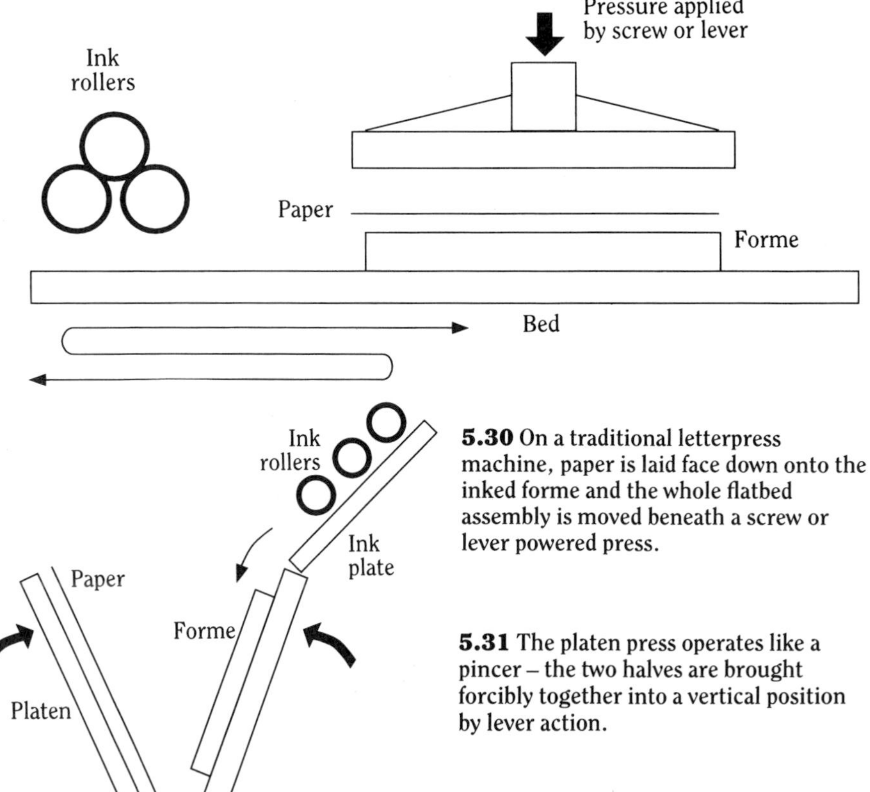

5.30 On a traditional letterpress machine, paper is laid face down onto the inked forme and the whole flatbed assembly is moved beneath a screw or lever powered press.

5.31 The platen press operates like a pincer – the two halves are brought forcibly together into a vertical position by lever action.

Flexography

Flexography is a relief process, a form of letterpress, which prints using flexible rubber or photopolymer plates (Fig. 5.32). The process was first demonstrated in 1890 by Bibby, Baron & Sons of Liverpool, UK, as a means of printing on non-absorbent packaging materials. It was further developed in the 1920s to make use of **aniline dyes**, derived from coal tar, and had various names. The term flexography was coined in 1952 as a result of a competition sponsored by the packaging industry. It was thought that any name containing the words "coal tar" had connotations that would not be acceptable by the general public in the context of packaging for foodstuffs.

Flexography presses are rotary web-fed machines, similar in layout to gravure machines (Fig. 5.33). Like gravure, flexo generally uses thin inks, usually solvent-based. Water-based inks containing fluorescent dyes can also be printed using flexography. It is an economical process only for very large print runs, typically measured in millions of copies.

Artwork is prepared exactly as for offset litho. The plates are produced in the same way as the stereotypes for letterpress, and are flexible enough to be attached to the printing cylinder using adhesive. Corrections can be patched into existing plates. The plates do distort in use, and some image spread should be expected and catered for in the design. Halftones and small type should be avoided, and so should any areas of reversed-out type, which could fill in.

Because of the plates' squashiness, flexo is used for food packaging applications that require flexibility – printing on plastic bags and other non-absorbent stock, such as cellophane and metal foil, and corrugated surfaces (Fig. 5.34).

The process competes with gravure for printing magazines and paperback books on cheap newsprint. The plates do have a tendency to "plug up" with fibers from rougher stocks, however.

5.32 Many flexography machines are converted rotary letterpress machines.

5.34 Flexography is used for unglamorous applications, such as cardboard boxes (above), and for difficult packaging materials such as waxed paper and plastic, as the examples below designed by Stan Noble of designers Towers Noble show. Stan Noble often makes extensive use of a Quantel Paintbox in arriving at the concepts for his designs.

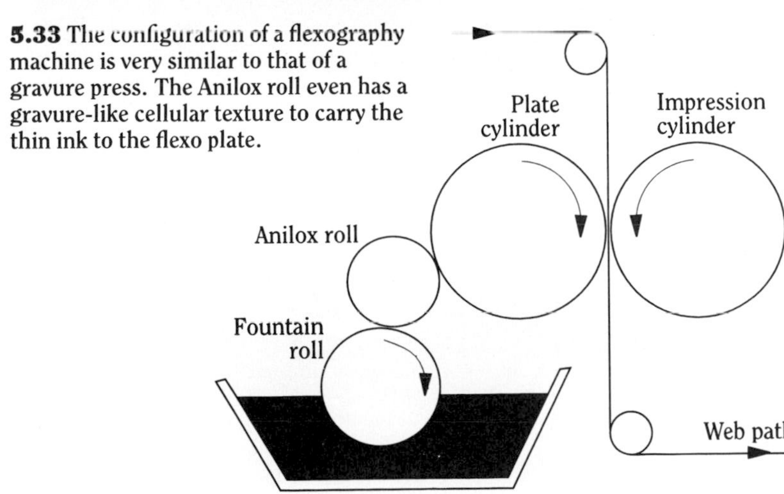

5.33 The configuration of a flexography machine is very similar to that of a gravure press. The Anilox roll even has a gravure-like cellular texture to carry the thin ink to the flexo plate.

Screenprinting

At the other end of the spectrum, the **silkscreen** process, or **screenprinting**, is used for only relatively short print runs of up to 15,000 copies. The name derives from its craft origins when a screen of silk material was used to support the stencil bearing the image through which ink was squeezed (Fig. 5.35). Today, the screen is made from synthetic gauzes or metal meshes.

Despite its almost exclusive associations with poster design and the prints of Andy Warhol, screenprinting is an extremely versatile process. It is a simple and direct method of delivering ink, and can thus be used to print on any kind of substrate, even on curved and uneven surfaces. It can produce thick and opaque deposits of ink, in brilliant saturated colors, and with high chemical and abrasion resistance. Applications for screen printing range from printed circuit-boards in electronics, through bottles and cartons, to T-shirts, point-of-display advertising, compact discs, and logos on the sides of vehicles.

The screen has two functions: to support the stencil, and to regulate the ink. The screen itself is supported in a wooden or metal frame, evenly tensioned using air-powered or mechanical devices. Most screens are made from polyester. This is a precision woven mesh for close register work, with high stability and low sensitivity to variations in temperature and humidity. Other screen materials include polyamide, which has good wear resistance and elasticity. It is used for printing three-dimensional objects. Stainless steel screens have the highest dimensional stability, plus chemical and physical resistance. They are used for ceramic decoration and printed circuit-boards.

The mesh has two main characteristics: the count and the grade. The **mesh count** is the number of threads per inch. The lower the count, the less support there will be for detail, and the heavier the deposit of ink. The **mesh grade** relates to thread thickness, which influences the weight of the ink film. There are four grades: S, M, T, and HD. S is the

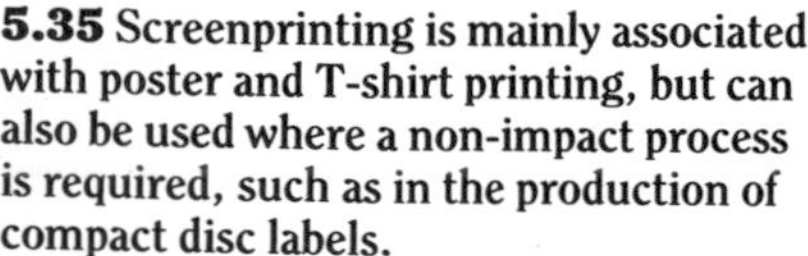

5.35 Screenprinting is mainly associated with poster and T-shirt printing, but can also be used where a non-impact process is required, such as in the production of compact disc labels.

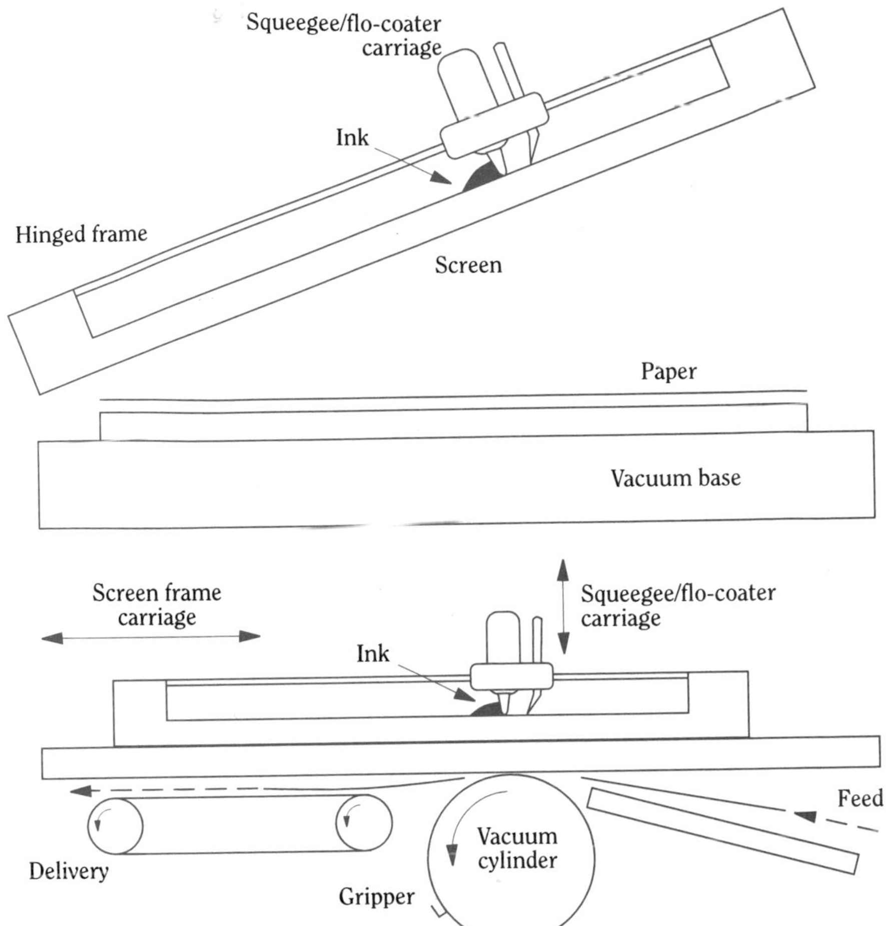

5.36 Most screenprinting is very labor-intensive, using a hand-operated bench configuration – literally pulling the squeegee across the surface of the screen. The process can be automated on a rotary machine – the squeegee and flo-coater remain in the same position while the screen moves. Paper is pulled by a gripper between the screen and a vacuum cylinder.

thinnest, giving a 50 to 70 percent open area; HD is the heaviest, giving a 20 to 35 percent open area. One chooses a count and grade depending on the application, ink, and halftone screen being used.

Stencils can be cut by hand from water- or solvent-soluble laminate film, and are either ironed onto the screen using heat or mounted using a solvent. A pen plotter equipped with a cutting knife can be used by the designer to cut out "line" stencils direct from a dtp system. The unwanted areas are "weeded out" and discarded (don't forget enclosed areas like the bowls of letters such as b).

More complex stencils are made photomechanically. Artwork is prepared as for offset litho, and a film positive is made at the repro house. One method uses presensitized gelatin film exposed to ultraviolet light in contact with the positive. This is then hardened in hydrogen peroxide, and the sticky stencil is mounted to the underside of the frame. When it is dry, the polyester base is peeled off and discarded.

A more direct method uses a screen coated on both sides (more thickly on the underside) with a light-sensitive polymer emulsion. After exposure to ultraviolet light in contact with positive film, the image areas are washed away with water. This leaves a stencil that completely encapsulates the screen mesh.

Presses for screenprinting range from simple bench-mounted configurations operated by hand (using a rubber squeegee to force ink through the mesh) to fully automatic rotary machines (Fig. 5.36). On bench presses, a metal blade called a flo-coater, which is mounted behind the squeegee, returns the ink to its pre-printing position. The angle, pressure, and speed of both the squeegee and the flo-coater can be adjusted. Once set, the machine will produce consistent results throughout the print run. Fast cylinder-bed presses have the squeegee and flo-coater stationary. The stock, supported on a vacuum bed, moves in unison with the screen.

Screenprinting is a direct non-impact process producing thick, bright colors, but it is not recommended for close registration work, nor for smaller sizes of type. Halftones pose problems because of possible moiré effects caused by the gauze of the mesh interfering with the screen. Moiré can be minimized, however, by using a stencil production system with good dot formation; by angling the mesh between four and nine degrees to the axis of the frame; or by using a "grained" or textured screen rather than a pattern of dots.

Collotype

Collotype, or photogelatin, was and is still the only process that can print continuous tone without screening (Fig. 5.37). It is used for limited-edition art prints of exceptional quality. It is a slow process capable of only small print runs.

To produce a collotype, a right-reading unscreened negative is first made from the original. This is contact printed to an aluminum plate coated with light-sensitive gelatin. The gelatin hardens in proportion to the amount of light falling on it: highlights remain soft, darker areas are harder. The plate is prepared for printing by flooding it with a solution of water containing glycerine – the soft areas absorb more than the harder ones. Ink is then applied. It adheres to the hardened areas, and progressively less in the softer parts. An impression is made, producing a continuous tone image with a mottled grain.

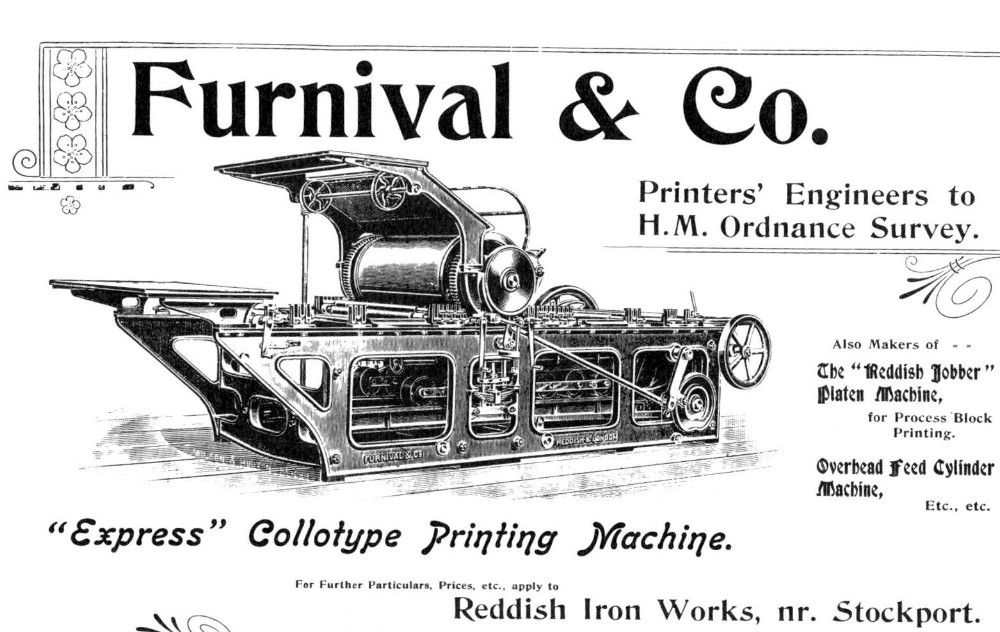

5.37 Collotype is the only process that can print a full tonal range without screening. It is relatively rare, and examples are impossible to show in a book that has been printed by offset litho (see also Fig. **1.9**).

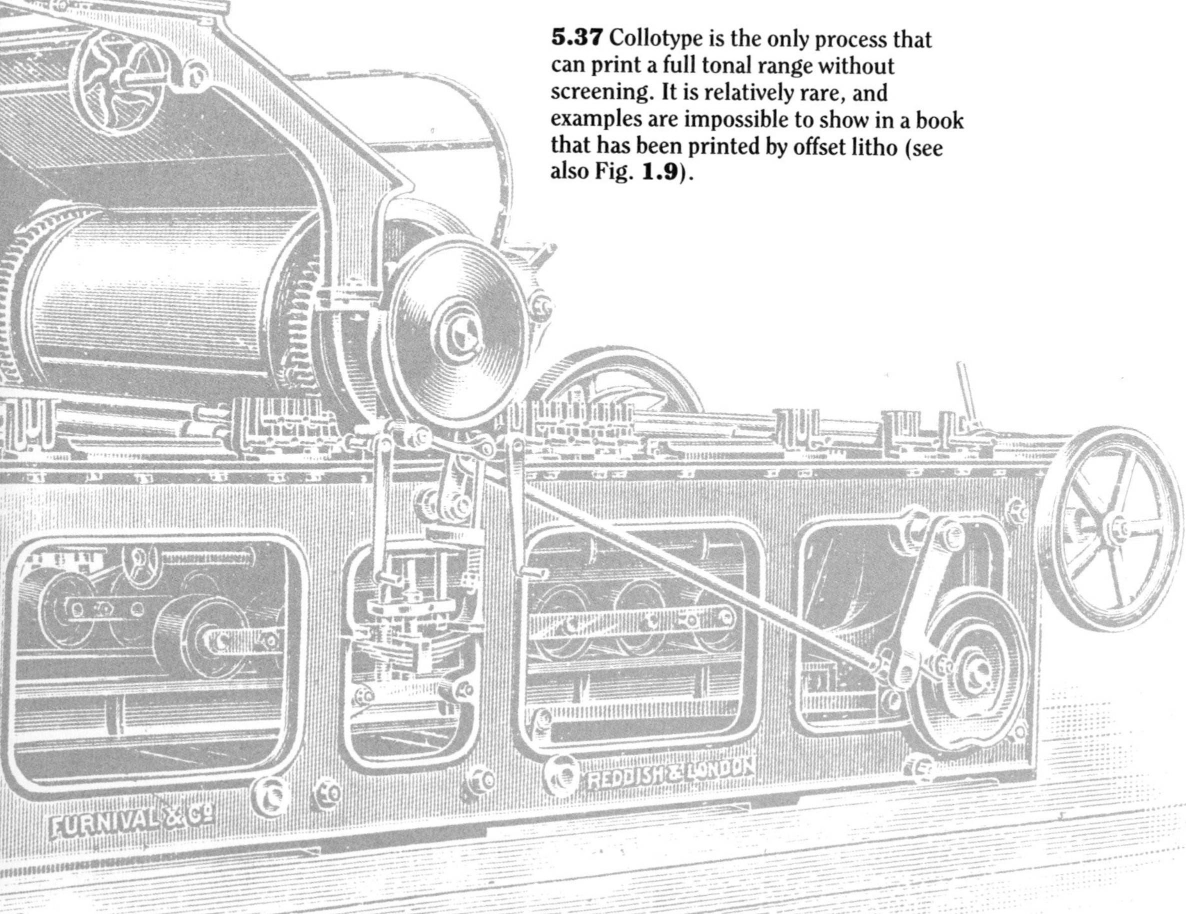

Xerography

Xerography, or photocopying, promises to replace small-scale offset litho in the near future. A photocopier can print direct from artwork or a mechanical, enlarging and reducing instantly. For small print runs, photocopying is cheaper than offset litho, with all its set-up costs. The results are dense and black, and photocopiers can now print on a wide range of paper stock.

Machines such as the Canon Color Laser Copier can produce full-color work direct from artwork, or from a disc from a dtp system (Fig. 5.38). They can scan halftones too. The cost per sheet is relatively expensive, but falling all the time.

Xerography was invented in 1938 by Chester Carlson, and developed by the Xerox Corporation. Artwork is placed face down on a glass plate, and is illuminated by a fluorescent light which travels the length of the image. The reflected image is directed through lenses onto an electrostatically charged drum. This charge leaks away where light from the image falls on the drum. A resin-based powder, called toner, is attracted to the image areas. This pattern of toner is transferred to a sheet of paper, where it is fixed by heat (Fig. 5.39).

Laser copiers work like combined scanners and imagesetters by scanning the image digitally, and using a laser to write the image onto the electrostatic drum.

5.38 The ubiquitous photocopier – this is a Canon CLC 500 laser copier – is the print technology of the future. Already you can print direct from a mechanical or a dtp disc, and the quality and cost per sheet will soon be on a par with offset litho.

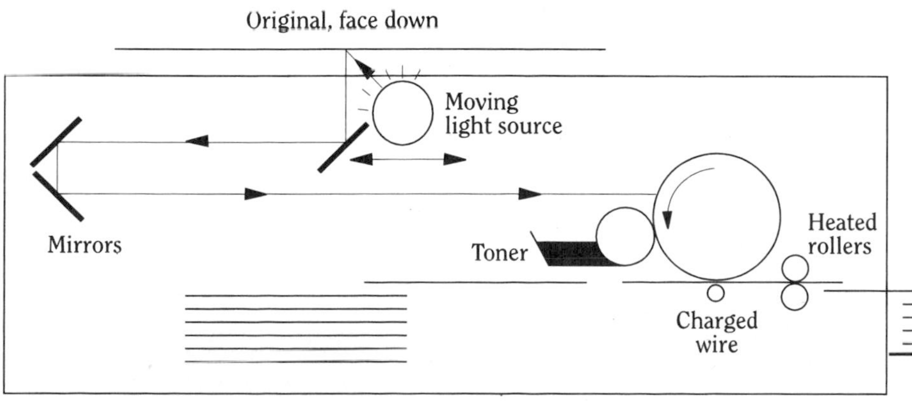

5.39 Inside a photocopier, a light source scans the artwork and this image is transferred via mirrors onto an electrostatically charged drum. Toner adheres to the image, and is transferred to the paper and fixed by heat. In a laser copier, all this is done digitally, just like a combination laser scanner and laser printer.

CREATIVE PHOTOCOPYING

The photocopier can be more than just a means of duplicating precious proofs, or enlarging and reducing "for position only" prints. It is also a creative medium in its own right.

Helen J. Holroyd uses a standard mono photocopier to produce her colorful collages (Fig. 5.40). She starts with a black-on-white ink drawing and copies it several times using different colored toner, and on different colored papers. The copies are then cut up in different ways and combined with parts of the drawing in other colors to form the collage. It is possible to produce several prints from one set of photocopies.

Another technique is to copy the drawing onto acetate and color in the back of the photocopy – a process akin to the coloring of cells in animation. The result can range from a subtle stained-glass effect to a vivid cartoon style illustration, depending on the type and texture of paint employed.

Paul Nunneley uses the quite considerable capabilities of the Canon Color Laser Copier to recolor, distort, and manipulate original transparencies (Fig. 5.41). The Canon CLC is a combination scanner, copier, and printer. It can copy from either flat artwork or transparencies, and enlarge or reduce the whole image or a portion of it from 50 to 400 percent. For larger sizes, it will "tile," for example, a series of 16 A3 copies to make an A1 poster. It can also combine two originals into one copy, color black-and-white originals, and convert a color on the original to any other (Fig. 5.42). The shape of the original can be changed too – stretched or condensed.

Nunneley uses a combination of all these techniques in making his illustrations. He will also interrupt the scanner, alter the focus, and change the image from positive to negative to achieve the effects shown here. It is even possible to create images with no originals, using colors and masks generated by the copier itself.

5.40 *Margot* by Helen J. Holroyd, created by photocopying an ink drawing onto colored paper using different colored toners and collaging the resulting prints.

5.41 A Canon-created "still" from a storyboard for an animated film entitled *Apathy Rex* being made by Paul Nunneley in conjunction with brother Mark.

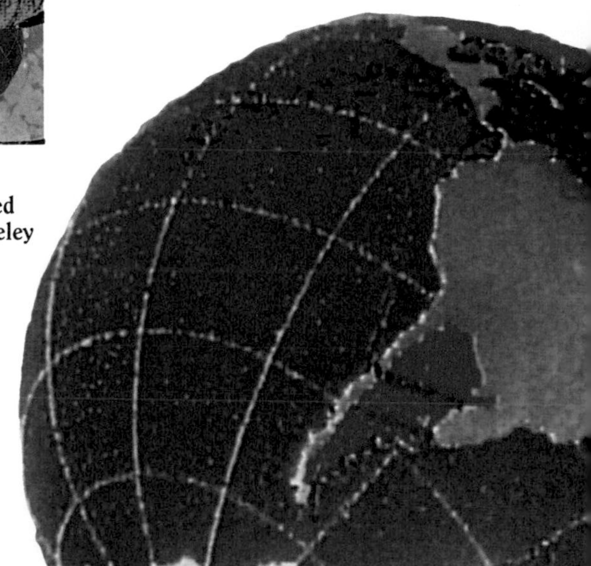

5.42 From the original transparency shown here, Paul Nunneley made these prints by adjusting the colors, contrast, and shape on a Canon CLC 500.

Printing processes: the pros and cons

OFFSET LITHO

Advantages Extremely flexible and cost-effective for most jobs, wide range of presses from jobbing sheetfed machines to large web-fed presses, short set-up time, positive-working or negative-working, prints effectively on wide range of stock.

Disadvantages Needs more attention than gravure for consistency over long print runs, ink translucent and prone to more problems than in the other processes.

GRAVURE

Advantages High-quality high-speed continuous-tone reproduction and rich blacks, prints well on cheaper stock, very economical for long print runs, fast process after make-ready.

Disadvantages Type is screened, solvent-based inks, only viable for large print runs, expensive to set up, corrections require new cylinder, proofing expensive.

FLEXOGRAPHY

Advantages Fast make-ready, prints well on non-absorbent stock, possibility of using water-based ink, prints well on cheap paper stock.

Disadvantages Image spread, poor halftones, usually have to use solvent-based ink, expensive to set up.

SCREENPRINTING

Advantages Non-impact process, versatile, prints on any kind of substrate and on curved or uneven surfaces, can be used to produce thick and opaque deposits of ink, in brilliant saturated colors, and with high chemical and abrasion resistance.

Disadvantages Small print runs, not recommended for halftones because of possible moiré effects, close registration and four-color work difficult, cannot print smaller sizes of type.

LETTERPRESS

Advantages Quality of impression, wide range of original typeface designs (hand-set repro proofs can be taken for printing by offset litho).

Disadvantages Inflexible for design, expensive now that big presses have largely been taken out of service.

COLLOTYPE

Advantages High-quality screenless continuous-tone reproduction.

Disadvantages Slow, very expensive, short print runs only.

XEROGRAPHY

Advantages Inexpensive for short print runs, no set-up costs, no film or plates, no ink, can print direct from dtp.

Disadvantages Cannot print large sheets, color reproduction often poor and almost always variable, restricted paper stock.

Things that can go wrong

The printed publication can only be as good as your original artwork or mechanical. And that's why, if there's something wrong with the printed result, you should always check your artwork before you start blaming the printer. Of course, some jobs may *look* better, printed in color on beautiful paper, but they can never actually *be* better than the original. A printer may work miracles, but every time your copy goes through a process it loses quality. That's why you should aim to get from artwork to plate with as few intermediate stages as possible.

If the typesetting you have produced is thin because the toner in the laser printer needs changing, then the printer can beef it up, but you will lose definition. The printer can't put back what was never there in the first place. Corrections to the mechanical can be a problem, too, introducing type of a different density, and cut lines where corrections have been pasted in. Okay, so your artwork is perfect. The type is crisp and black, all the hairline serifs are visible, and the halftones have a screen appropriate to the paper stock. What else can go wrong?

There are all kinds of problems associated with the paper, the ink, and the press, and how they interact with each other. Some of these have been mentioned earlier, but for the sake of completeness, they will be listed here in alphabetical order.

Backing is a lightening of color that occurs if ink removed from the fountain roller is not replaced by the flow of new ink.

Catch-up occurs in offset litho when insufficient water on the plate causes non-image areas to print (Fig. 5.43).

Chalking, or powdering, happens mainly with matte coated stock and is caused when the vehicle from the ink is absorbed, leaving only pigment on the surface. It becomes apparent when dry ink starts to rub off the image or smudge, and unfortunately is only noticed after the job is finished. In emergencies, the original plate can be used to overprint a layer of transparent size to try to bind the ink to the paper.

Color variation during a run is caused by altering ink-to-water balance, or by stopping the press.

Crawling is an imperfection in the surface of the ink, occurring when thick ink overprints wet ink.

Crocking is smudging or transfer of dry ink onto printed sheets.

Crystallization is a result of careless overprinting. If the ink of the first printing dries too hard before overprinting is done, it can repel the second color.

Damper marks are patterns over the print caused by worn damper covers or too much pressure.

Dot gain shows when halftone shadows fill in or if the print looks too dark, and is caused by bad film-to-plate contact, over-exposure of the plate, over-absorbent paper, or over-inking. However, it will always occur to some degree, so an allowance should be made at the proofing stage.

Doubling – two dots where there should be only one – is caused when wet ink is picked up by the blanket on a subsequent printing. If it is off register, it prints as a ghost dot nearby.

Emulsification is what happens when water gets into the litho ink. Most litho inks are designed to accept some emulsification, but too much results in a wishy washy appearance.

Flocculation produces a surface like orange peel, and is an ink defect. It occurs when the pigment is not properly dispersed in the vehicle.

Ghosting is the word for faint areas, usually in solid blocks of color, caused by some parts of the image taking more than their fair share of ink, leaving other areas deficient. Some ghosting problems can be foreseen, and imposition schemes can be changed to prevent them. On small-format jobs, try to distribute solid areas evenly. Ghosting is also the term used to describe the dull image on the reverse side of a sheet caused by a printed image that has affected the drying and trapping of ink applied to the other side.

Halation appears in halftones as a halo-like light around a dark area, and is a prepress problem that should be picked up before plates are made.

Hickies are dark spots surrounded by uninked halos, or just plain white specks, that appear at random (Fig. 5.44). They are caused by dust, paper fibers, or foreign bodies from the ink that have found their way onto the blanket. A solution is to run uninked paper through the press, and then wash the blanket.

5.43 Catch-up.

5.44 Hickies.

Linting is a problem created by paper fibers that get onto the blanket, plate, or rollers of a press.

Low spot is a loss of image caused by an indentation on the blanket, often because plate and blanket are insufficiently packed.

Moiré patterns are unwanted "basket-weave" effects. They occur when the screen angles on multicolor work have not been set correctly, or sometimes when there is regular patterning on an image, or when a halftone has been rescreened.

Mottle is an uneven, blotchy application of ink, caused by a mismatch between ink and paper stock, or too much dampening water on the blanket.

Offset see setoff.

Paper curl can be caused by too much dampening water, or can happen because the stock has not acclimatized to the relative humidity of the press room. Wavy edges appear if the stack of paper has a lower moisture level than the surroundings. Tight edges are caused by a higher moisture level in the stack. See also tail-end hook.

Picking is a lifting of the paper's surface most noticeable in solid areas, caused by ink that is too tacky, a press running too fast, or a paper surface with too low a "picking resistance."

Piling is caused by a build-up of ink on the press rollers, or by particles from uncoated stock which adhere to the blanket and break up the image on the following sheets.

Registration problems are caused by poor stripping at the flat stage (check the proofs) or by paper stretching on the press (Fig. 5.46).

Scuffing is a problem in packaging design, where print is likely to receive rough handling. Choose a scuff-proof ink or try a coat of varnish.

Scumming is when ink starts to appear on the non-image parts of the plate (Fig. 5.45). It can be caused by a badly done deletion, or more likely it's time for the plate to be replaced.

Setoff, or offset, occurs when the wet image on a sheet of paper prints onto the paper above or below it in the pile, or later rubs off in a bound book (Fig. 5.45). Anti-setoff spray should separate each sheet by a fine layer of particles.

Show-through is when you can see right through a sheet of paper to the printing on the other side. Choose a more opaque stock next time.

Skewing is a problem that occurs during printing if the paper, blanket, and cylinder are not in proper contact.

Slurring is when halftones start to fill in, and is caused by too much ink, or slippage from smooth paper. There is a portion of the color bar on the proof specifically for indicating slurring.

Snowflaking in solid areas is a problem caused by water droplets in the litho ink. In gravure it can happen because inadequate pressure prevents the paper from taking the ink from one or more cells.

Spreading is an enlarging of the image caused by too much ink, or too much pressure between blanket and plate.

Sticking, or blocking, occurs when there is so much setoff that the sheets stick together.

Strike-through is like show-through, only worse – it is when the ink penetrates the whole thickness of the sheet. Change stock, or use a different ink formulation.

Tail-end hook – when solid areas near the back edge of a sheet make it curl down – is caused by paper adhering to the blanket too tightly as it is pulled off by the delivery grippers, and it happens if the ink is too tacky.

Tinting happens when pigment finds its way into the fountain, discoloring the background.

Tracking, or stripping, is when several colored images are printed in a row and inking becomes uneven as a result.

5.45 Scumming and setoff.

5.46 Misregistration.

Part 5: finishing

All the processes that convert the printed sheets into folded and bound publications are collectively known as **finishing** operations. These can also include print-related operations such as die-stamping, thermography, varnishing, and laminating.

Die-stamping is a process for producing a three-dimensional low relief effect on paper or cover board (Fig. 5.47). It works as a kind of heavy-handed letterpress, with the additional assistance of a hollowed out recess on the other side. The hollowed out recess is in fact the die; the stamping part, the counter-die. The die is placed face upward beneath the paper. It is made in steel from artwork, either etched photographically like a process block, or engraved by a computer-controlled machine tool.

Die-stamping can be used **blind**, to produce the subtle effect found on letterheads, or inked. Or the die can be used with metal foil, to make the bold impression that is so popular on the covers of blockbuster paperback books. **Die-cutting** uses sharp steel rules in a wooden die to cut shapes from paper.

A cheaper way to obtain a low relief is by means of **thermography**. A freshly printed image is dusted with transparent thermography powder. This sticks to the ink and, when heated, swells into the third dimension. High-gloss and matte finishes are available. It is worth knowing, however, that sheets printed using thermography can later be a problem when put through laser printers, as the thermographic printing can melt.

Embossing is a process similar to die-stamping, and also gives the stock an area of texture. The lettering on the spine of a hardback book is formed by **blocking** in gold or silver leaf using a brass, or die. This time, the die is in relief and the effect is below the surface of the substrate.

Hot-foil stamping, or leaf stamping, transfers a foil coating from a carrier roll of polyester, by means of a heated die. The coating can be metallic, matte, pearl, or even a **hologram** (Fig. 5.48).

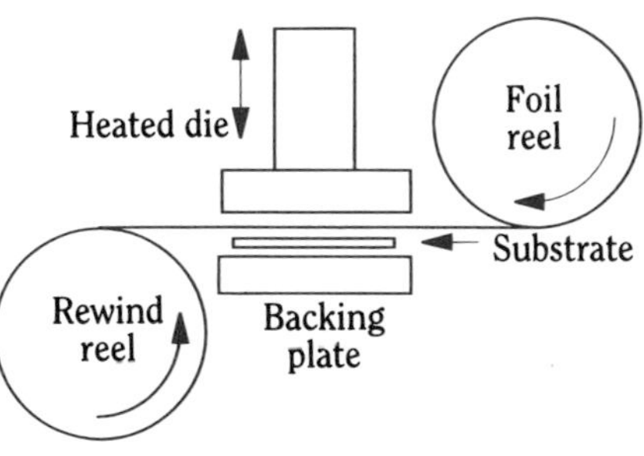

5.47 Die-stamping is used to add glamor to the kind of blockbuster paperback book you see on station magazine booths. They can be stamped blind, giving a subtle three-dimensional effect, or inked, or foil blocked in gold, silver, or other metallic colors.

5.48 In hot-foil blocking, the foil passes from a roll and is stamped onto the substrate by the action of heat.

Spot varnishing of halftones to add gloss and intensity has already been mentioned in the discussion of inks (see p. 138). Overall **varnishing**, as a finishing operation, is carried out by running printed sheets through rollers. Machine varnish (**lacquer**) can be applied using a conventional litho machine, but the sheen it produces is barely noticeable. High-gloss or liquid lamination is a nitrocellulose coating requiring a special machine. Ultraviolet varnish, which dries on exposure to ultraviolet light, also produces high gloss and scuff-resistance. Two layers of varnish, printed wet-on-wet, give a very smooth glossy finish.

Lamination adds strength as well as gloss. Film lamination is glued to the stock as it goes through a heated roller under high pressure. It is applied from a roll onto overlapping sheets, leaving the gripper edge and the sides free for any other processing. But laminated sheets must be left for two days for the adhesive to dry completely, before operations such as guillotining or embossing can be performed with confidence. Ultraviolet lamination cures more quickly.

Ink that is to be varnished or laminated should be quick drying, with little residual solvent, and absolutely no wax additives. Too much anti-setoff spray can have an adverse effect on either process. Metallic inks are a problem, and should be left alone. They have their own sheen, after all.

Folding and binding

After these print-related finishes have been applied, the stock can be folded (Fig. 5.49). There are three types of folding machine. **Buckle folders** (Fig. 5.50) are the most commonplace. The sheet enters a pre-set distance and is stopped and buckled back at the fold line by two inward-revolving rollers. These nip the flat sheet, then fold it and carry it forward to the next "plate," where the process is repeated. **Knife folders** (Fig. 5.51) are used in bookwork. Here a blunt knife is used to nip the sheet between two rollers. They are very precise, but slower than buckle folders. **Combination folders** give the best of both worlds.

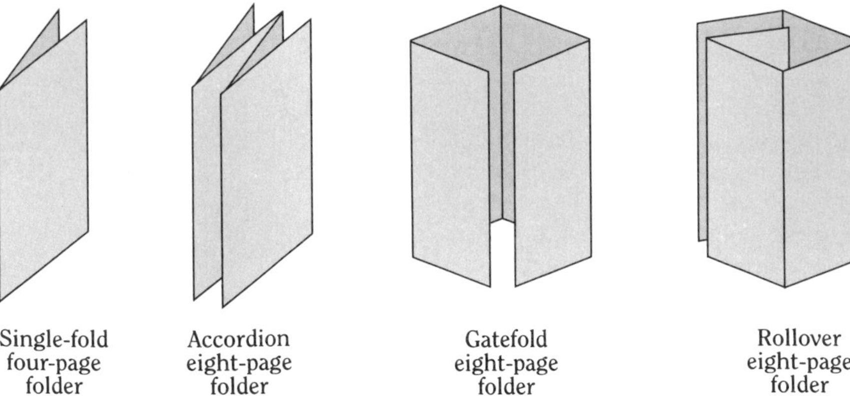

5.49 There are many different ways to fold a folder. Here are some examples – but remember to make economical use of your printed sheet before you specify an exotic fold.

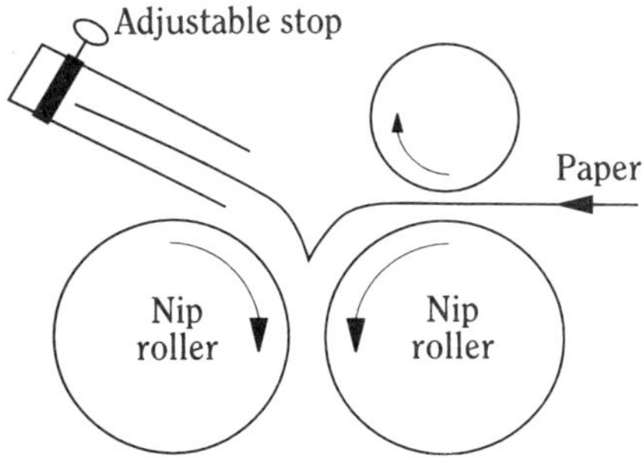

5.50 In a buckle folder, the sheet is brought to rest by an adjustable stop before being forced between a pair of nip rollers.

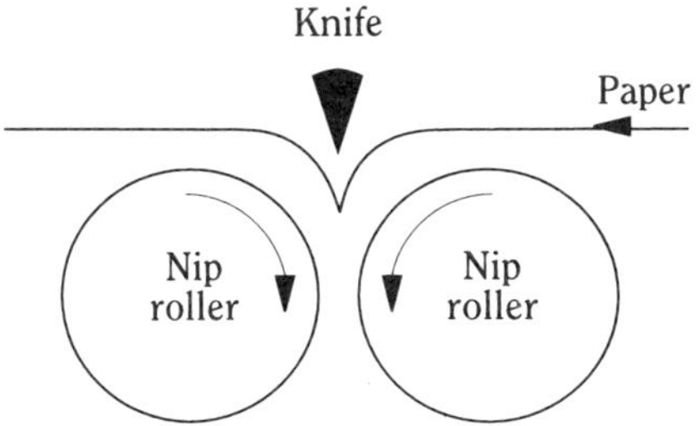

5.51 A knife folder is used for more exacting work – a knife-like device pushes the sheet between two nip rollers, producing a much sharper fold.

Single-sheet jobs then go straight to the guillotine for trimming. Multi-page jobs first have to be united with the other pages, **gathered** on conveyor belts, bundled flat, and collated (put in order). For books, the sections are gathered one next to the other. Printed marks on the spines of sections, called backstep marks, indicate the correct sequence visually. Letters or numbers printed on the signatures are a double check.

Loose **inserts** are single sheets of paper or even sometimes booklets, that are added, generally by hand, to a magazine. They fall out when the magazine is shaken.

Tipping-in is adding a single page to a publication, either by pasting down the inside edge, or by wrapping a short strip around the fold. This is a labor-intensive process, and thus very expensive. Illustrations that were printed intaglio, or on art paper, used to be tipped in to books. **Tipping-on** is pasting a smaller illustration, an errata slip, or a reply coupon onto a page.

Perforation can be done on the printing press, by means of a perforating strip attached to the impression cylinder (eventually ruining the blanket), or on a special finishing machine.

Magazines and booklets are bound in one of two ways: by saddle-stitching or perfect binding. **Saddle-stitching** (Fig. 5.52) is a fancy way of saying stapling, though the wire staples used in saddle-stitching are longer and rounder than office staples. Saddle-stitching gets its name from the inverted V saddle onto which the sections are placed. Sections are opened out and placed one inside another, inserting larger sections inside smaller ones, and with the cover on top. This is the least expensive form of **binding**, but can only be used with publications of up to around 128 pages, depending on the paper stock. On thicker publications, take note of paper creep – pages near the center will be narrower after trimming than those near the covers (see p. 106). Specify stainless steel wires so that they don't rust.

Side-stabbing (Fig. 5.53) inserts the wires from front to back, near the

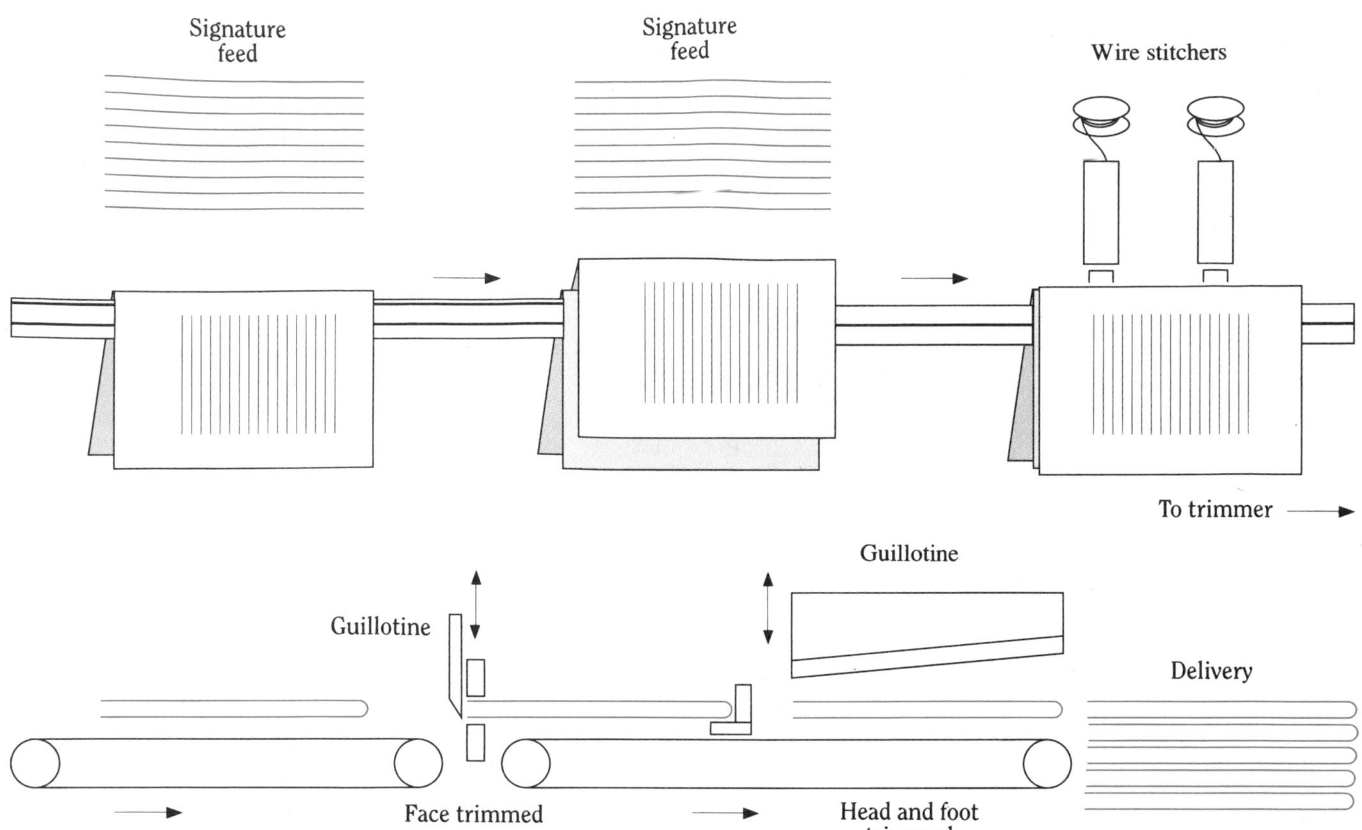

5.52 In saddle-stitching, the folded and collated signatures move along a conveyor on saddles the shape of inverted Vs. Wire staples are then inserted along the fold of the spine.

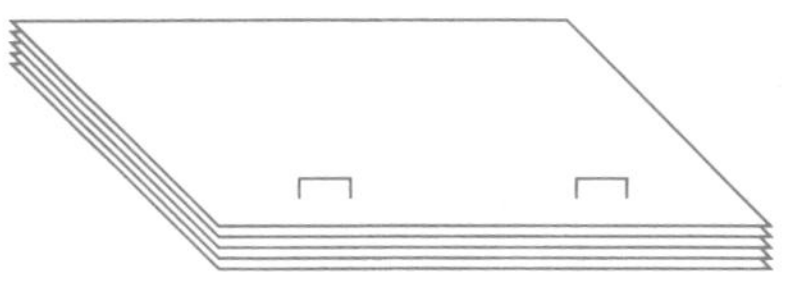

5.53 In side-stabbing, the wire staples are inserted through the front of the signature, along the back edge close to the spine.

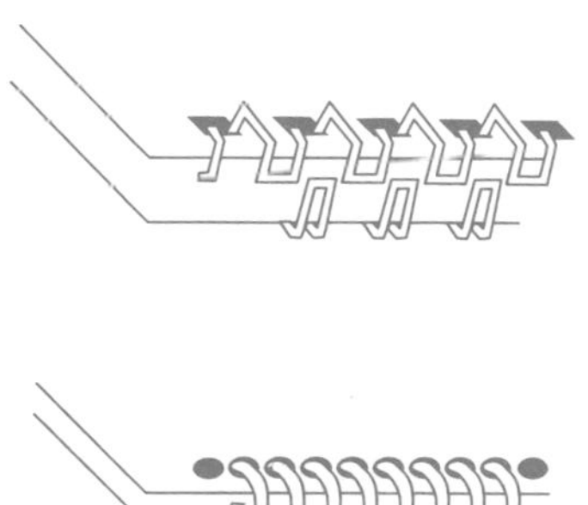

5.54 Spiral binding is used for calendars, manuals, and cookery books – wherever the publication has to fold perfectly flat. Wire-O gives a neater finish.

spine, disguised by the creased **hinges** of the covers.

Calendars, cookbooks, and technical manuals are usually **spiral-bound** (Fig. 5.54) so as to lie flat. The sheets are punched with a line of round or slotted holes near the **spine**. Wire is then coiled through the holes and crimped. **Wire comb**, or Wire-O, bindings and **plastic comb** bindings give a more finished look.

Perfect binding (Fig. 5.55), unsewn binding, or cut-back binding, can be far from perfect unless a good glue is used. For this process, the sections are gathered and collated as before, and presented to the machine spine down. The edge is notched, or milled off and roughened, and adhesive is applied. The covers are folded, scored, and wrapped around the pages. The adhesive is then cured by heat, and the pages are trimmed. Perfect-bound magazines have a flat spine, onto which a title, date, and a résumé of the contents can be printed. But the process is slower and more expensive than saddle stitching, and double-page spreads can be a problem with copy disappearing into the gutter. Fold the magazine back and it falls apart! Mass-market paperback books are often printed two-up, head to head, and only cut apart after perfect binding.

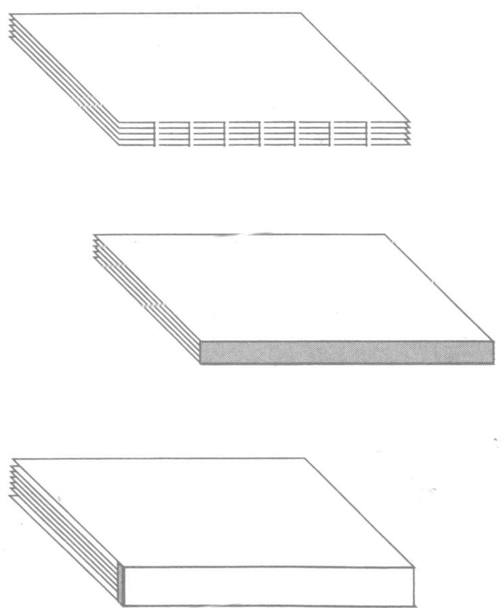

5.55 In perfect binding, the signatures are collated, then the spines are cut off, roughened, and spread with glue to attach the covers.

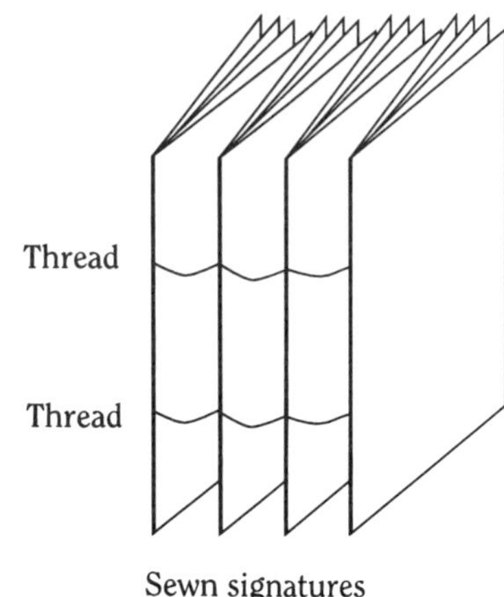

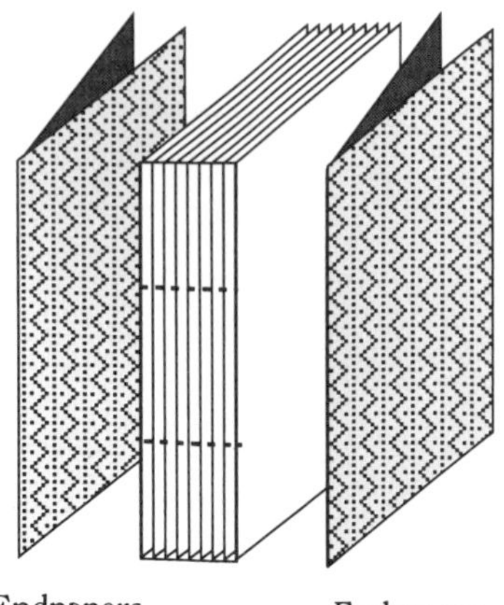

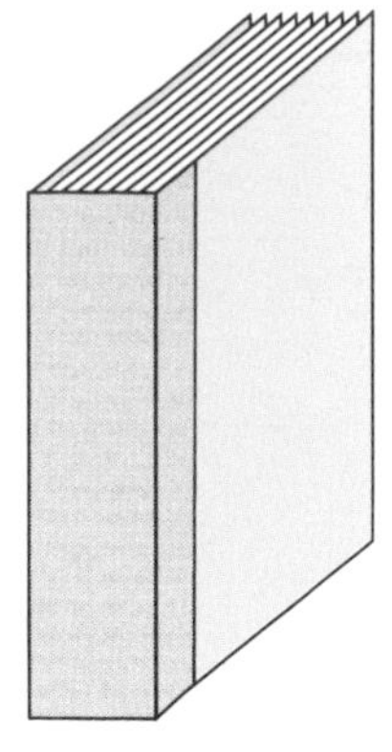

5.56 Case-bound books consist of a book-block, a hard cover and endpapers that are assembled at the final stage of binding.

Hardback books are sometimes perfect bound, but the sections can instead be sewn though the spine with thread – this is called **section sewing**. They are then gathered together into a book-block. **Thread-sealing** combines features of perfect binding and section sewing (but no thread runs between sections).

Side-sewing is a method used for children's books, in which the thread goes front to back, as in side-stabbing. This produces a stronger binding than section sewing, with the disadvantage that the book will not fold flat.

A case-bound, or hardback, book (Fig. 5.56) has a hard case made apart from the pages. The book-block and cover are assembled, along with tipped-on endpapers, at the final stage of binding. Endpapers are usually of heavier stock than the text pages, and are sometimes decorated. **Rounding and backing (R & B)** is a combined operation that puts a rounded shape into the spine of the book-block, and a joint below the shoulder (Fig. 5.57). Some books are rounded; others are left with flat spines. Linings are glued to the spine; **headbands** and **tailbands** – and perhaps a bookmark – are added; and the endpapers are glued to the insides of the cases. Book jackets can be wrapped around the cased book by hand or by machine.

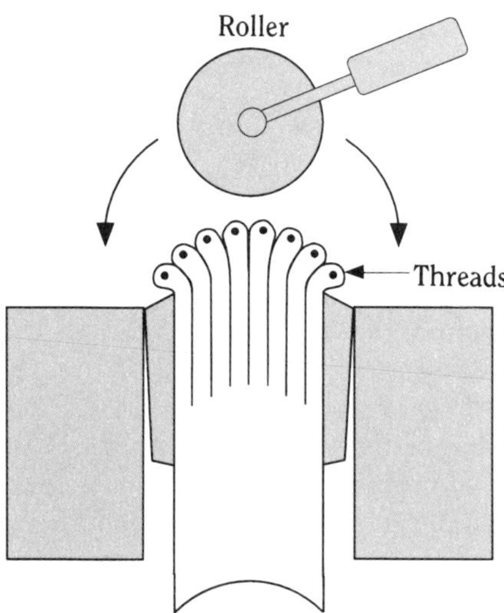

5.57 The thread used to sew the book block makes it thicker at the spine. Rounding keeps the book in good shape; backing produces a neat shoulder.

Cases are made from heavy board, with the grain parallel to the spine to prevent warping. The material used to make the case of a hardback book look attractive is known as the covering. It can be of non-woven material, such as embossed paper, fiberfelts, or plastic-coated fiber, or a form of starch-filled cloth or **buckram**. A **quarter bound** book (Fig. 5.58) has the spine and an adjacent strip of the cover bound in an expensive material, maybe leather, with the rest of the sides in something cheaper. A **half binding** has, in addition, triangles at the corners in the expensive material. Leather, embellished with gold blocking and tooled decorations, is reserved for expensive limited-edition books.

After binding and counting, the job is parcelled up in waterproof packaging or shrink-wrapping, is boxed, correctly labeled, put onto pallets, and shipped to its destination – and your job is done.

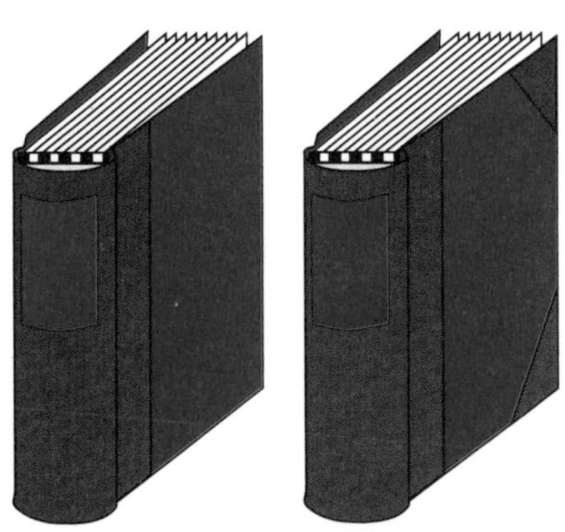

5.58 A quarter bound book and a half bound book with its additional triangles at the corners.

Summary

On press is that part of the production process over which the graphic designer has the least amount of hands-on control. What the designer does possess, however, is the power of *selection*. An appropriate choice of paper, ink, and printer should ensure a predictable outcome, given that the designer's input is as near perfect as can be, and bearing in mind the merits and limitations of the various printing processes.

Paper, ink, and printing process are all interlinked. The size of the print run and the budget for the job are also important considerations. Offset litho and letterpress demand thick and sticky inks; conversely, the inks for gravure and flexography need to be thin and runny. Consequently, gravure and flexo are able to print at high speed onto relatively poor stock – and flexo can print onto the most difficult surfaces, such as cellophane and waxy board. But there is a trade-off. Flexo and gravure cylinders are expensive to produce, and so the process is only viable for large print runs.

Most designers will spend most of their careers working with offset lithography, which is perhaps the most economical and versatile process of all. But there will perhaps come a time when you need to produce a design for a plastic carrier bag, for example, and have to evaluate the relative advantages and constraints of flexography and screen-printing, and modify the design appropriately. Or there may come a time when you wish to produce a high-quality invitation card on hand-made paper using letterpress. With the information outlined in this chapter, you will be confident of making the right choice.

So, too, with finishing. The expected end use of a printed product and the budget are key factors in the choice of perfect binding, say, over wire stitching, or varnishing over lamination. Only experience will teach you to make the correct choices every time, but, forearmed with the knowledge contained in this chapter, you will at least be aware of all the options open to you.

File
ayer: 100
Rasters
Pixels

6. Computers

Until only a few years ago, graphic designers could send corrected galleys, a rough layout, and marked-up illustrations along to the typesetter or repro shop and expect the rest of the job to be completed by others. As they waited for ozalid and color proofs, many were blissfully unaware of the revolution taking place in print production. And the printers and compositors were happy to keep things that way.

But slowly at first, and quickening all the time, that revolution has begun to invade the designer's studio. Of course, the advances can be ignored, but it will be the designers who embrace the opportunity with enthusiasm who will succeed in tomorrow's competitive markets.

The computer brings control and flexibility to the designer's desktop. It won't do the designing for you, of course. A computer is merely a tool, to be put to work as and when necessary, alongside the pencil and layout pad. It is an extremely powerful tool, nevertheless, and it is waiting to be used.

All of the equipment described in this chapter will be found in many designers' studios before very long, and it is important to know its role in the design process, how it works, what it is currently capable of, what its limitations are, and what trade-offs you will be expected to make. Thus forearmed, you will be able to take on the suppliers' salespeople, and make sound buying decisions that will ensure a successful implementation.

Finally, the health and safety aspects of a computer installation are discussed, so as to safeguard the well-being of the most valuable component of the production system – the graphic designer.

Simply having a computer does not make you into a better designer. If you need any evidence, take a look at the advertisements in any dtp magazine, especially for dealers and bureaux. Those people have offices bristling with computers, use all the software daily, and possess just about every font you could imagine. And still their ads look terrible.

They have fallen for the vendors' sales pitch: that with a computer, some dtp software, and a selection of fonts, you don't need a designer – *anyone* can be a designer. It's not true.

But a good designer, armed with a computer, can do wondrous things. The main advantage is almost *total control* of your design, from initial concept to finished product. There is a down side to this, though. If it is control you want, you'll have to take responsibility for all your design decisions – you won't be able to blame the typesetter, for instance, if you don't get the setting you thought you specified. And you'll have to learn something about computers.

WHAT EQUIPMENT DO YOU NEED TO GET STARTED?

- a computer: an Apple Macintosh, IBM PC, or IBM compatible, such as a Compaq
- a keyboard
- a high-definition monitor, preferably of large format (19in/483mm or more)
- a mouse (and mouse pad) or other pointing device, such as a rolling ball or digitizer
- a dot matrix or bubblejet black-and-white printer
- applications software, such as Quark XPress or Aldus PageMaker

AND OPTIONALLY:

- a PostScript-compatible laser printer
- an inkjet, thermal transfer, or dye sublimation color printer
- a desktop or handheld scanner
- a modem
- more applications software, such as FreeHand, Illustrator, PhotoShop, or Digital Darkroom

Part 1: hardware and software

First, some basic definitions. The stuff you can see and touch – the computer and all the ancillary equipment, the peripherals – is the **hardware**. **Software** is the unseen factor of a system which supplements the brainpower and experience of the designer and makes the hardware come alive. It arrives on **floppy discs**, like the music on a CD, and is copied onto the computer's own **hard disc** (The original floppy disc is kept in a safe place, in case anything should go wrong with the hard disc.)

The word **system** is used a lot. It is a catch-all term, and usually means "everything" – the hardware and software together, as in a desktop publishing (dtp) system. The software that looks after the internal workings of the computer is called the operating system. And an item of software can be referred to as a program, a package, or again, a system.

Most people recognize a computer from the name it has on the front: it may be an IBM PC, a Compaq (Fig. 6.1), or an Apple Macintosh (Fig. 6.2). These are all called **personal computers.** A personal computer is a self-contained system that sits on the desktop, that you do not have to share with anyone else, and that is powerful enough to do the job you have in mind.

6.1 This Compaq DeskPro 386/25e is an IBM PC-compatible desktop computer. It has an Intel 80386 processor with a clock speed of 25Hz.

6.2 At the top end of the Apple Macintosh range are the Quadras, based around Motorola 68040 processor chips. This is the Quadra Model 300, shown with a 21 inch color display.

The next grade up is a computer called a **workstation**, from a supplier such as Sun or Silicon Graphics (Fig. 6.3). These, too, are self-contained systems, but can be linked together into networks (see p. 189). They are much more powerful than personal computers, but they take up more space and are more expensive.

The old-fashioned kind of computer that has several "dumb" terminals sharing a set of large metal boxes located in an air-conditioned room is called a **minicomputer**. The largest computers of all are called **mainframes**, and handle the payrolls for multinational companies. The average graphic designer will probably never see a minicomputer or a mainframe.

Although the abbreviation PC stands for personal computer, it refers to a specific class of personal computer, namely the IBM PC and compatible computers from suppliers such as Compaq. The Apple Macintosh is a personal computer, but not a PC. It operates in a fundamentally different way to the IBM PC and compatibles. Programs designed for the PC will not work on a Macintosh, and vice versa, although *versions* of a program such as PageMaker are available for both kinds of computer and will operate in similar ways.

There are two other classes of computer that deserve more than a footnote. First, there are the "games" machines, Commodore's Amiga and Atari's ST, which are capable of quite sophisticated dtp. And second, the laptops, palmtops, organizers, pocketbooks, and notepads that come collectively under the category of "portable." The **NeXT cube** (Fig. **6.4**), developed by ex-Apple boss Steve Jobs, is also worthy of a mention. Not only is it a good-looking machine, but it has the Apple pedigree and extra functionality (such as Display PostScript, which uses the imagesetter outlines to draw the screen representations of type) that designers do not yet realize they need.

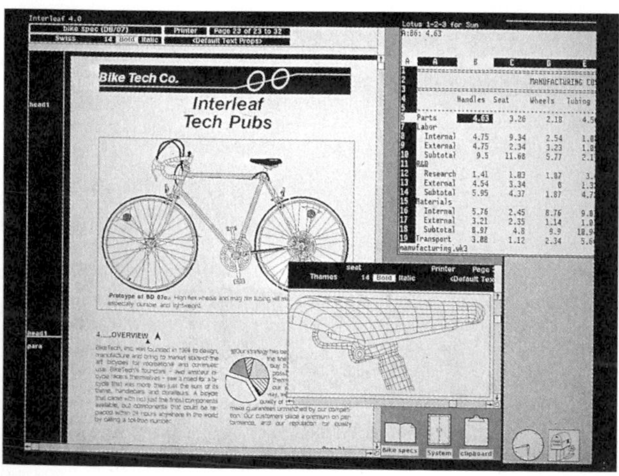

6.3 A Sun SparcStation is categorized as a workstation, and the processor box usually sits under the desk. It is based around a RISC (reduced instruction set computer) chipset.

6.4 (right) The NeXT cube, with its extra functions, is finding a niche for itself in graphic design studios.

Software

There are many levels of software inside the computer which are mainly invisible to the user. At the lowest level, you need a program built into the machine that loads (or boots, as in "pull yourself up by the bootstraps") all the other programs.

At the next level is the **operating system.** This looks after the computer's internal workings, particularly the operation of the hard disc memory. It is often specific to the make of computer: PCs use MS-DOS. The Macintosh's operating system is just a number, such as System 6.0.7 or System 7. Workstations mostly use a version of AT&T's Unix, such as Xenix or A/UX (the names of the variants usually have an x in them somewhere). The operating system comes with the computer when you buy it, and upgrades can be bought on floppy discs and installed on the hard disc. You usually see evidence of the operating system at work only when you switch the computer on. It checks that everything is in working order, then awaits your instructions. If anything is wrong, it will put an error message on the screen and you will have to refer to the manual and take remedial action.

The most visible level of software is the **application,** which you buy on floppy discs, along with an operating manual. Applications software converts the general-purpose computer, that cannot do anything, into the kind of system the user wants. It can be one of a number of things: a spreadsheet, a dtp package, paint software, or a computer game. Software suppliers each have their own methods of numbering versions. It is important to know which version you have, to ensure compatibility, for example, between your program and the one at the **service bureau.** Some of the more expensive applications come with a device called a dongle that has to be connected between, say, the keyboard and the computer. This prevents you from copying the software to a friend. New versions of software packages are being released all the time – some are really significant improvements on the previous release, some are merely "fixes" that correct bugs.

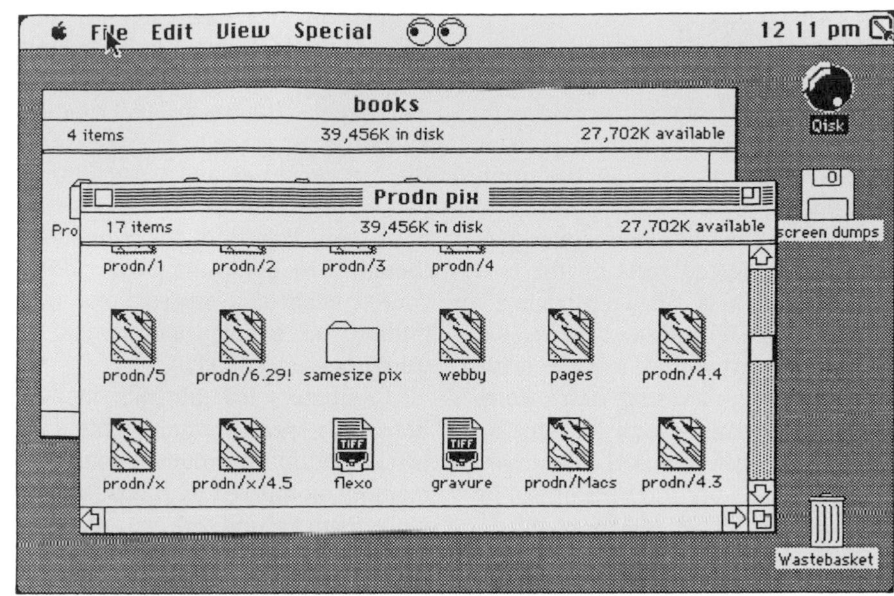

6.5 This screen shot from the author's Mac shows its **WIMP** (windows, icons, mouse, and pull-down menus) GUI. Documents – drawings or text – are represented in the window by icons and are selected by pointing and clicking the mouse-controlled cursor. Software commands are chosen from pull-down menus, which can also be selected by moving the mouse pointing device.

A **bug** is an error in the program, hidden away in the depths of the computer code – a mistake made by the programmer. The term was coined in the late 1950s by computer pioneer Grace Hopper, who found a real insect interfering with the working of her computer.

All programs have bugs, just as all computers do inexplicable things now and then. Thus there is all the more reason to save your current job to the hard disc as frequently as possible, rather than leave it in the short-term memory. A few but by no means all programs do this automatically. It is a good idea also to back up (copy) anything important onto floppy discs at the end of every session. Then put the floppy discs in a safe place.

A **virus** is worse than a bug – it is a self-replicating piece of mischief, introduced surreptitiously into your computer by malicious computer addicts called "hackers."

Software is written in a programming language. The computer's own language is called **machine code,** which is expressed in hexadecimal numbers (numbers in base 16). It is gibberish to all but the most hardened hacker. Computers "think" in binary code (using the numbers in base 2: 0 or 1, on or off), but this is too cumbersome for humans to get to grips with. Binary, however, is conveniently convertible to hexadecimal. One step up from machine code is **assembler,** which substitutes short mnemonics such as MPY for multiply, one-for-one, for the hexadecimal numbers. Easiest to use are the so-called high-level languages such as **Basic** (beginners all-purpose symbolic instruction code) and **C.** These use English words, arranged using simple grammar, which is later "compiled" or "interpreted" into machine code. Even higher-level languages are sometimes available so that users can customize (adapt) the applications software to their own preferred ways of working.

But today it is completely unnecessary to learn a programming language. The operating system of the Macintosh, for example, contains an "intuitive" GUI (graphical user interface; Fig. **6.5**) that simplifies communication between the human and the computer. Commands are chosen from lists called **menus,** and most things can be done by **tools.** A pen tool, for example, allows you to draw lines on the screen. The user selects them by pointing at small pictures called **icons,** using a device such as a "mouse" (more of which later).

The processor

The "brain" of a computer is usually housed in a featureless box, perhaps with a floppy disc slot in the front, and with the odd light flashing to show that the hard disc is working. The display screen rests on the box. The latest style is called a pizza box – it is the shape of a takeaway pizza box.

At the heart of the computer is the **cpu (central processing unit)**, comprising a microprocessor silicon chip or set of chips (chipset). The main manufacturers are Intel (identified by the numbers 80286, 80386, 80486 ... 80X86), who supply the chips for the PC and compatibles, and Motorola (identified by the numbers 68000, 68020, 68030 ... 680X0), who supply the chips for the Apple Macintosh.

Most workstation vendors have followed IBM and for speed of operation have opted for the simpler RISC (reduced instruction set computer) architecture for their chips. Sun's version is called SPARC (scalable processor architecture).

Raw speed in computer terms is measured in **MIPS (millions of instructions per second)**. A DEC Vax minicomputer from the 1970s is the touchstone, rated at 1 MIPS; a Compaq Deskpro 486/33L runs at 20 MIPS; Sun workstations at 3–28·5 MIPS; a Silicon Graphics 4D/35 graphics workstation at 33 MIPS.

Instructions are sychronized by an internal clock, and the **clock speed** is another measurement of potential speed of processing. Clock speed is measured in MHz (megahertz, or millions of cycles per second). For example, a Macintosh Classic is built around a 68000 cpu chip running at 8MHz; a Mac IIfx has a 68030 running at 40MHz. At every tick of the clock, the cpu processes an instruction, or part of one. These are not the instructions you key into the computer, though. The computer breaks down your complicated instructions into millions of simple ones, which it calculates very quickly.

Computers for graphics applications have special requirements. Pictures take up enormous amounts of memory, compared with text, and to move them around, the cpus on these systems require some help. They are therefore augmented with various speed-increasing subsystems – such as floating-point co-processors to handle the repetitive math involved in manipulating images. They also need printed circuit-boards (pcbs), or cards, to control the color graphics on the screen. On bigger systems with "intelligent" displays, these functions are handled by the device itself. DMA (direct memory access) can be used to expedite the movement of data from the disc straight to the screen, bypassing the cpu.

All this, however, is pure speed and, like the top figure on an automobile's speedometer, is an abstract quantity. Some computers may be able to redraw the screen after a tricky manipulation more quickly than others. But how quickly a designer actually completes a given job ultimately depends both on the efficacy of the software and on the proficiency of the operator.

Memory: rom and ram

Computers have two sorts of chip-based memory. **Rom (read-only memory)** chips have instructions manufactured into them, and they cannot be altered. These instructions remain on the chip even when the computer is switched off. Rom chips contain some of the computer's operating system, and give a computer its "personality." Their contents are a secret. Apple will not disclose the code on its rom chips, and that is why you cannot buy a Macintosh-compatible computer. (There are some Mac-compatible portables around, but for them to work you first have to remove the rom chips from an existing Macintosh.)

Local memory, containing the immediate job in hand, is in the form of **ram (random access memory)** chips which are wiped clean each time the computer is switched off (Fig. **6.6**). This, of course, includes any form of power failure, however fleeting. The amount of ram a computer has available is measured in **bytes**, each equal to 8 **bits** (bit is short for binary digit). A kbyte, k, or kilobyte is not a thousand bytes as you may have expected, but 1024 bytes, which is equal to 2^{10} (2 to the power of 10, or $2 \times 2 \times 2 \times 2 \times 2 \times 2 \times 2 \times 2 \times 2 \times 2$). A megabyte, written 1 Mbyte, is more than a million bytes. A gigabyte, or Gbyte, is more than 1000 Mbytes.

The reason for the strange number 1024 is as follows. Computers count in binary numbers, 0s and 1s. (Hexadecimal, referred to earlier, is easily converted to binary and is more convenient for computer scientists to deal with.) Thus, to a computer, "round numbers" are always powers of 2 (such as 4, 8, 16, 32, 64, 128, 256, 512, and 1024), and that is why you will often see these numbers associated with computers.

ASCII (American Standard Code for Information Interchange), the worldwide format for encoding alphanumeric text, allocates a single byte per character. This chapter contains over 64·5 kbytes of information. The hard disc on my computer is capable of containing 70 Mbytes, and that is quite modest by graphic design standards.

Saved data is stored in a hard (Winchester) disc drive. This can hold 20 or more Mbytes. It is advisable to back-up important data to floppy discs, which can hold around 800 kbyte chunks of information, or onto streamer tape drives, which use cartridges similar to audio cassettes.

Removable hard discs can be added to your system. They are useful for overflow, archiving, and for transporting large files to an imagesetting bureau. For memory intensive operations, you can buy WORM (write once read many) optical drives that store many Gbytes of data. A device containing several optical disc drives is called a jukebox. CD-rom drives are compact disc players for computers which hold large amounts of bought-in data, such as fonts and clip art.

Data travels round the computer on "buses," which are like clumps of wires. There are two main buses: the memory bus and the data bus. A 32-bit computer has a data bus 32 bits wide, i.e. 32 bits of data can travel around the computer and be processed at the same time. The "width" of the bus determines how much data can be processed at each tick of the clock, and how much ram memory can be managed.

A typical home micro from the early 1980s had an 8-bit processor and a 16-bit memory bus. It could thus address only 2^{16} permutations of 0s and 1s, which equals 64k possible memory locations in ram. A 32-bit processor can handle several Mbytes. Some computers also have "cache memory." This is a portion of ram that holds the most recently used data from the hard disc ready for further action, thus increasing the apparent speed of access to the user.

FRAME BUFFERS

A **frame buffer** is a short-term memory store between the processor and the screen. If you want to display images and representations of "real" typefaces up on your computer screen, you will need one. (A traditional typesetter's computer could only display simple alphanumeric characters in ASCII format – they looked nothing like the type being set.)

The frame buffer contains the current image in the form of a bitmap of pixels (picture elements; see below). It comprises several layers or planes, with one bit (a 1 or a 0) stored for each pixel on each plane. The number of planes, and hence the number of bits allocated to each pixel, determines how many colors or "grayscale" shades the displayed pixel can be (see also p. 173).

A mono screen, without grayscales, has 1 bit per pixel. An 8-plane system can handle 2^8 (256) different colors or grayscales. A 24-plane system can display a staggering 16·8 million, a number considered sufficient to produce realistic looking images. A 32-bit system has 24-bits allocated to color, the rest for other things – in the Macintosh's 32-bit Quickdraw, for example, the extra 8 bits are called the "alpha channel" and are available for animation effects.

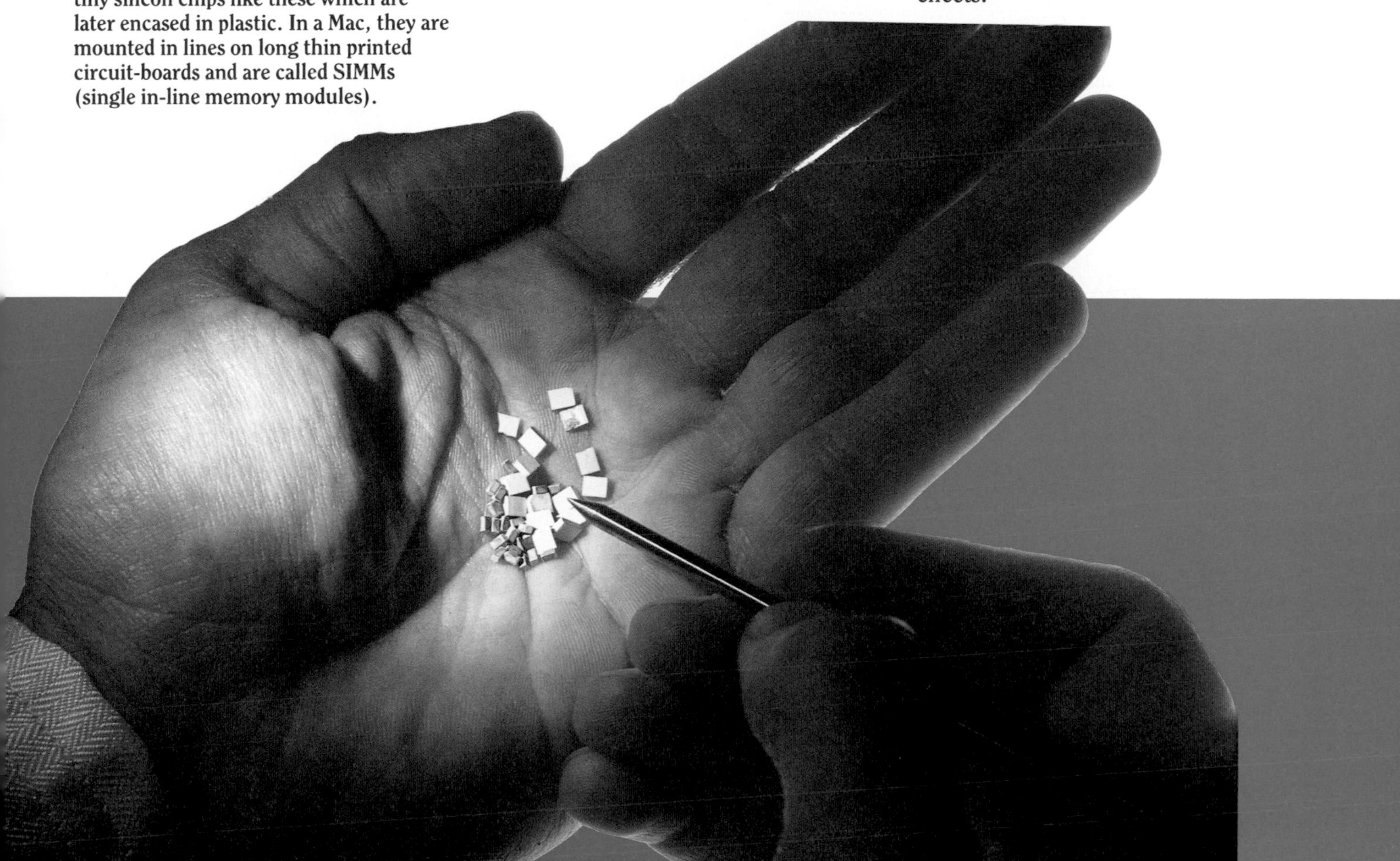

6.6 Ram memory comes in the form of tiny silicon chips like these which are later encased in plastic. In a Mac, they are mounted in lines on long thin printed circuit-boards and are called SIMMs (single in-line memory modules).

Displays

The computer's display is the window through which we view whatever is being designed, and through which we interact with the software. It is important to remember, however, that the image on the screen is more often than not a crude representation of the page that exists inside the computer's memory. Printed output will always be crisper, in the correct typeface, and with the letterspacing you have specified in the software. The output quality is dependent on the output device – whether it be a low-resolution laser printer or a high-resolution imagesetter – not on the quality of the screen.

The majority of computer displays are based on the cathode ray tube (CRT), the tube that takes up most of the space in a television set. What make the CRT work are substances called phosphors: electrically active materials that luminesce when bombarded by electrons.

Computer and television screens are called raster displays, from the Latin *rastrum*, or rake (Fig. 6.7). The electron gun at the back of the CRT scans the whole screen in horizontal lines, top to bottom, usually 60 times a second (60Hz). On a non-interlaced display, every line is scanned each cycle. In a television set, alternate lines are scanned each cycle, resulting in two "fields" per cycle. This is known as an interlaced display. Most computer companies make screens that are non-interlaced, because they flicker less than interlaced screens.

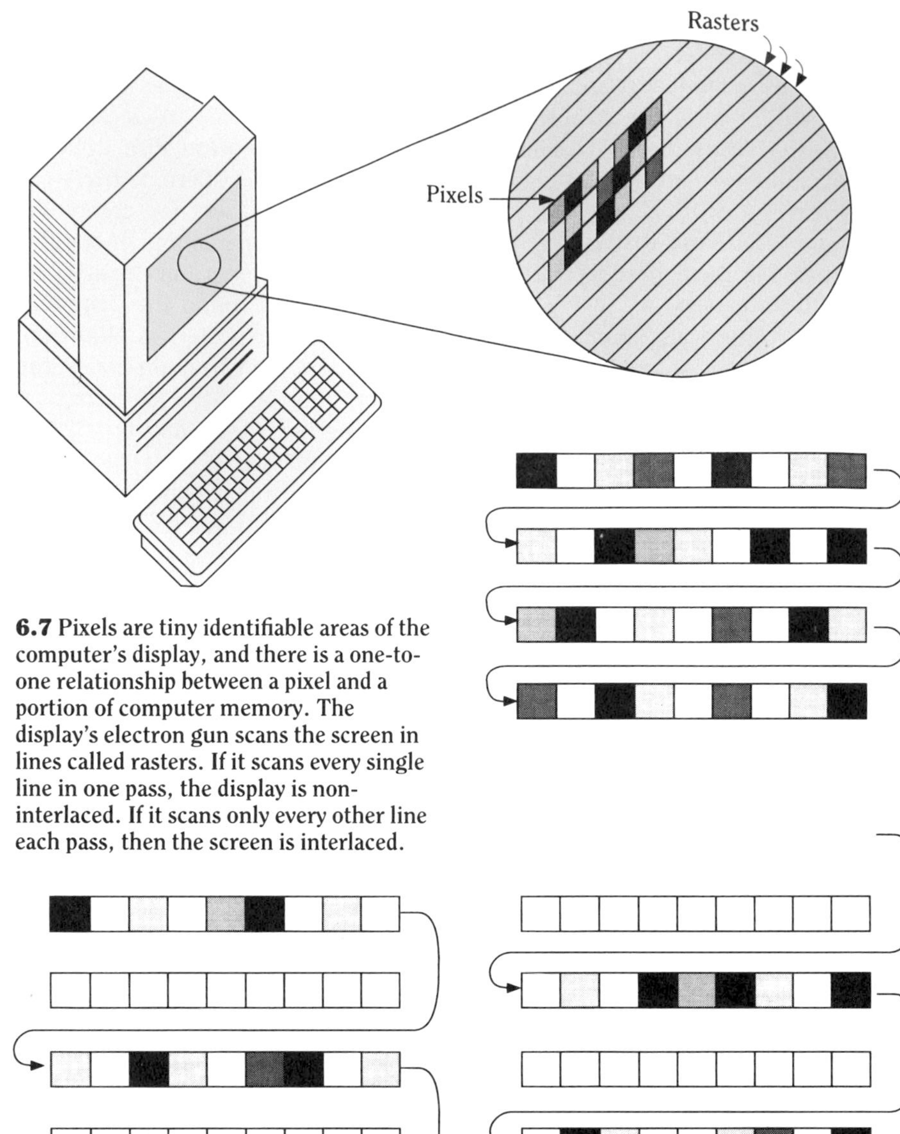

6.7 Pixels are tiny identifiable areas of the computer's display, and there is a one-to-one relationship between a pixel and a portion of computer memory. The display's electron gun scans the screen in lines called rasters. If it scans every single line in one pass, the display is non-interlaced. If it scans only every other line each pass, then the screen is interlaced.

Each scan line is chopped into chunks called pixels (picture elements). Pixels are the screen equivalent of dots (see Chapter 3), and as we have discussed earlier, each pixel on the screen is described by one or more bits in the frame buffer. The resolution (fineness) of a raster display is measured by the number of pixels horizontally by the number of scan lines vertically. The resolution of an IBM PS/2 in **VGA (video graphics array)** mode for a Mac IIci is 640 × 480. For higher resolutions – 1280 × 1024, for example – you will need a plug-in graphics card (printed circuit-board) and a special high-resolution screen (see below).

Other technologies, such as the liquid crystal displays found in portable computers, are smaller, slower, and of lower quality than CRTs. Liquid-crystal shutters controlling cathode-ray tubes are being used in oscilloscopes, and the technology has also been utilized in prototype "electronic drawing boards" and large-screen preview displays. They control a laser as it writes onto a translucent drawing-board-sized combined digitizer/screen.

Meanwhile, vendors use optical illusions such as **anti-aliasing** (Fig. 6.8) to improve the perceived resolution of their screens. Anti-aliasing smooths out the staircase effect seen on diagonal lines near the horizontal. It does so by coloring the pixels around the diagonals that actually

6.8 Anti-aliasing is a way of fooling the eye into thinking your screen has a higher resolution than it actually has. Low-res screens produce jagged edges, especially on diagonals. Shading the pixels near the edges with a mixture of the foreground and background colors results in a fuzziness that looks smooth at a distance.

define the line or edge in subtle shades of the current foreground and background colors.

Both the Mac and PC come with their own regular screens – the Mac IIci comes with a 13 inch (330mm) screen as standard. If you are doing lots of dtp work you will need a larger-format display: either 17 inch (432mm), 19 inch (483mm), or 21 inch (533mm). And if you are viewing scans of photographs or continuous-tone illustrations, you will not be satisfied with a simple 1-bit **monochrome** screen. You will need a **grayscale monitor**. This is, so to speak, a kind of halfway between a black-and-white screen and a color screen, giving you a large screen area plus tone definition. Grayscale monitors such as the Eizo Flexscan, Hitachi SilverMac, and the SuperMac Platinum mostly have switchable resolutions from 640 × 480 through to 1152 × 870. You will also be able to choose the "depth" of the bit planes: from 1-bit (just black or white) to 8-bit, or 256 shades of gray. TPDs (two-page displays) from Radius, Apple, and SuperMac give you just that – a 21 inch (533mm) screen almost the size of an 8½ × 11in (216mm × 279mm) double-page spread (Fig. 6.9). And the Radius Pivot is a screen that can be tilted between formats, from portrait to landscape (Fig. 6.10).

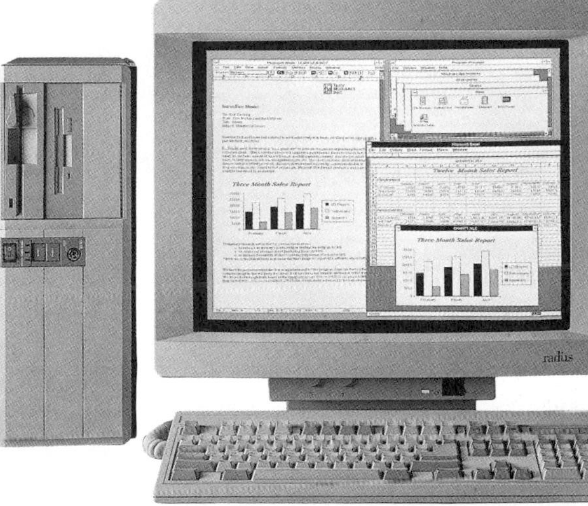

6.9 With a TPD (two-page display), like this one from Radius, you can work on a double-page spread without having to zoom and pan all the time.

6.10 A tilting screen – this one is a Radius Full Page Pivot – can turn from a landscape to portrait, depending on the orientation of the job.

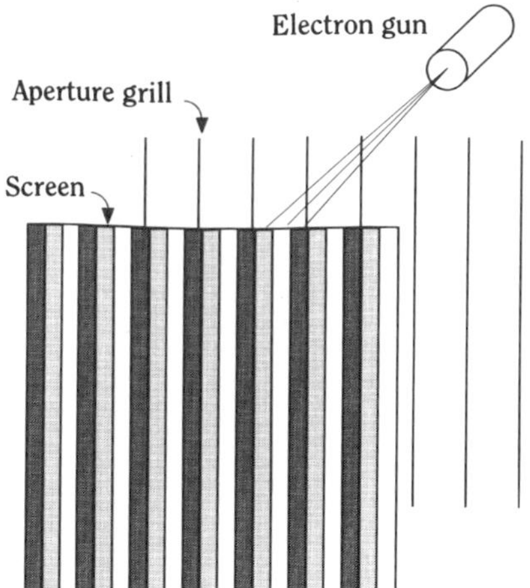

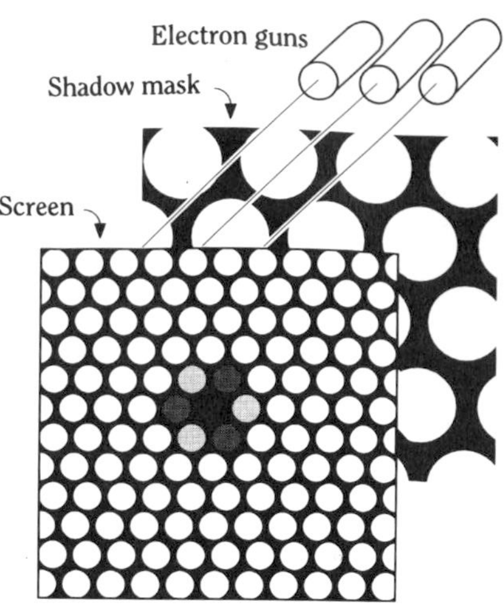

6.11 (above) Displays are built around two distinct technologies: those based on Sony's Trinitron with their vertical lines, and the more conventional shadowmask screens mainly manufactured by Hitachi.

6.12 (left) Displays must be calibrated regularly if their color reproduction is to remain faithful. A Radius color calibrator makes sure that Pantone colors on the screen bear a good resemblance to printed colors.

Color display systems come in two parts: the color screen itself, and the graphics card that drives it. The monitor's tube comes from one of two major manufacturers: Hitachi and Sony. The traditional tubes, which are mainly manufactured by Hitachi, have three electron guns, one each for the red, green, and blue dots on the screen (Fig. **6.11**). On their way to the screen, the beams are synchronized by a shadowmask – a metal mask with precisely placed holes through which the beams pass. A Sony Trinitron tube uses a single gun, and the shadowmask is a grid of fine vertical slots. A Trinitron tube is flatter and has a sharper, brighter picture, but it is heavier than regular screens and gives noticeable vertical lines of color.

The graphics card contains the frame buffer, and is either 8-bit, for 256 displayable colors, or 24-bit, for 16·7 million colors. An 8-bit card stores information about which colors are being used (the current palette) in a color look-up table. This is like an array of pigeon holes. Each contains the "address" of four numbers: an index number, plus values for the red, green, and blue output levels that add together to display your chosen color. With 24-bit color, you have direct access to all 16·7 million colors, not just a selection of 256, and there is no need for the intermediate indexing. Each color – red, green, blue – is allocated an 8-bit value, to drive the red, green, and blue electron guns in the tube.

The color coming from a color monitor, being transmitted light, will never be the same as the color reflected from a printed page (see p. 85), and the color output will change as the phosphors age. To make the colors on the screen as faithful as possible, you must **color calibrate** your screen regularly. There are two ways of doing this. Both use an optical sensor to take readings directly from colors on the screen (Fig. **6.12**). Software then compares them with Pantone colors and recalibrates for color "temperature" appropriate to the application and local lighting conditions. The Radius software then makes adjustments to the color look-up tables. The Barco method adjusts the processor on the graphics card. It is also possible to adjust the "gamma correction" to improve the detail on scanned images.

Input devices

The input device is the means by which the designer tells the machine and the software what to do. The particular method used for human/computer interaction is called the computer's graphical user interface (GUI). Originally, you would have had to type commands using the computer's keyboard. Apple Macintosh then introduced the "point and click" approach, and all the Mac's applications now make use of a mouse pointing device to "pull down" menus (lists of options), select icons (pictures that represent tools and documents), and open and close windows (active areas of the screen). This form of GUI is gradually migrating to other systems. Microsoft's Windows 3 for PCs and X-Windows for workstations are other examples.

Computer graphics users have long abandoned exclusive use of the keyboard that always comes with the computer, in favor of other methods for manipulating on-screen cursors and entering shape descriptions. However, keyboard-entered shortcut commands remain popular with experienced so-called "power" users, who find mouse operations slow compared with typing "command-P" to print, for example.

There are many alternatives to the mouse, however. There are rolling balls, joysticks, thumbwheels, and digitizing tablets – which come with a pen-like stylus or a mouse-like puck with buttons depending on the user's preference.

The **digitizing tablet** (Fig. 6.13) performs a dual role: it can be used to point and pick software commands from a menu, or to make pictures. Most, like the Summagraphics Bitpad, are electromagnetic devices containing a grid of fine wires embedded into the work surface. Others use sonic techniques to detect the position of the stylus or puck.

6.13 Digitizers are essential for precision drawing and tracing. Wacom's digitizing tablets are cordless, and are available with either a puck or a stylus.

6.14 (above) Most computers come with a standard mouse pointing device, but you don't have to stick with it. Logitech makes cordless mice, and mice for children.

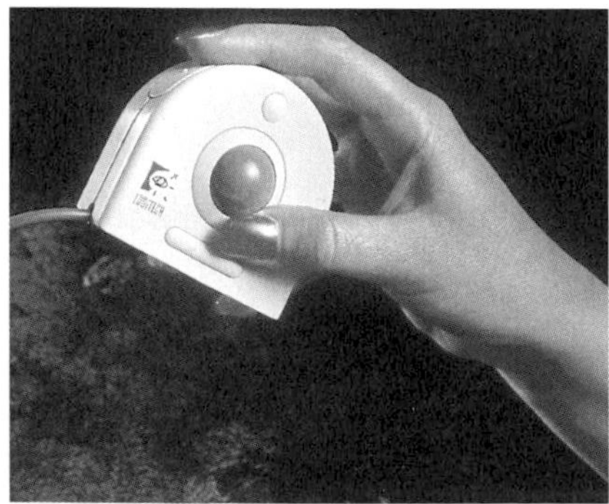

6.15 The Logitech TrackMan portable – a rolling ball is a much more sensitive controller than a mouse.

A digitizer with a cordless pressure-sensitive stylus, from a supplier such as Wacom, can be used with some draw and paint programs to create images more intuitively than with a mouse and keyboard.

The mechanical **mouse** (Fig. 6.14) suffers from friction or the lack of it (use a special mouse pad rather than the slippery surface of the desk). And, as it works in relative coordinates rather than absolute ones, it gets lost in space. It is fine for menu picking, but little use for drawing. Turn the mouse upside down, however, and you have the **rolling ball** (Fig. 6.15) – a device that has been used in air-traffic control for decades. These are much more sensitive to touch than joysticks. They are less prone to breakage, don't trap dirt, and have a small "footprint."

Scanners

Desktop scanners (Fig. 6.16) allow the designer to input already existing images into the system – commissioned photographs, stills from videos, or images plagiarized from magazines. A **frame grabber** is another input device – a small television camera mounted above a well lit baseboard – which can be used not only to input pictures, but also for silhouettes of small three-dimensional objects.

Scanned data, whether it comes from a television camera, a video stills camera, or a laser scanner, is in its raw form a bitmapped image (see p. 70). A bitmap is good enough for a paint system to get to grips with. However, a drawing package will need some conversion, and the scanned image is best used as a background layer, to be traced over. Halftones can be input directly, in a format called TIFF (tagged image file format).

The most popular scanners for the studio are the single-color flatbed desktops, which look similar to photocopiers. The early models worked like photocopiers, with a moving scan head containing a fluorescent tube slowly moving from end to end of the original, recording a 300 dpi (dots per inch) bitmap 1-bit deep (i.e. only black or white). More recent models use CCDs (charge-coupled devices) to recognize and store images 8-bits deep at up to 900 dpi. Scanned grayscale images can be retouched using a package such as PhotoShop or ColorStudio. Import them to a dtp package such as Quark XPress or Aldus PageMaker, and convert them to screened halftones later in the process.

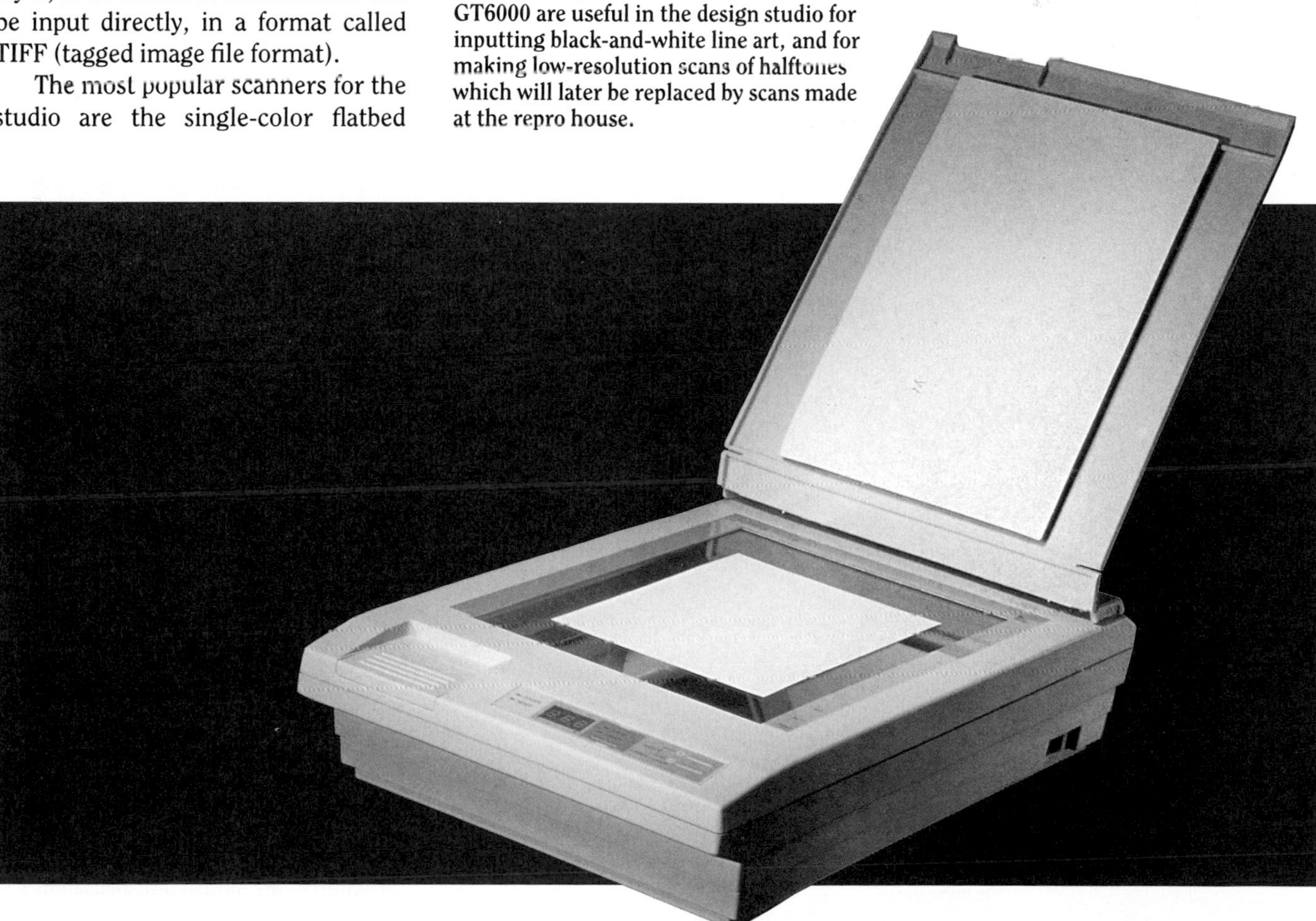

6.16 Desktop scanners like this Epson GT6000 are useful in the design studio for inputting black-and-white line art, and for making low-resolution scans of halftones which will later be replaced by scans made at the repro house.

A rule of thumb says you should scan at a resolution that is twice the screen you plan to use for printing, if the image is to be reproduced at same size. So a scanner with a resolution of 300 dpi will just about be able to produce a halftone at same size with a screen of 150 lines. Although this will be good enough for newspaper or newsletter reproduction, for other jobs a scanned image should be used for position only, and replaced with a professionally screened image at the film stage. And if that is all you will be needing a scanner for, then there are some inexpensive hand-held scanners available, such as Logitech's ScanMan (Fig. **6.17**), that will do the job. The 4 inch (102mm) width can be overcome by reducing the artwork first, using a PMT machine or photocopier.

Desktop color scanners produce a quality far below that of the drum scanners found at repro shops. They work like mono scanners by scanning the image three times, using red, green, and blue lamps. At best, a desktop scanner can capture 24-bits per pixel, compared with the 48-bits a drum scanner can "see." In practise, the scanner can usually resolve no more than 6-bits per color. There are other issues to consider, as well. A 24-bit image takes up a great deal of memory: anything between 4 and 8 Mbytes when it is first scanned. Subsequent processing increases the size of the file. Quark XPress, for example, will convert the TIFF file into five EPS (Encapsulated PostScript) files: a master preview plus data for each of the cyan, magenta, yellow, and key (black) separations. Thus a 7 Mbyte TIFF file can grow to occupy over 20 Mbytes. Multiply that by the number of color pictures in your publication, and you can begin to understand the magnitude of the problem.

The time it takes to convert a PostScript file to a raster file to drive the imagesetter in the RIP (see p. 118) can work out to be extremely expensive for color, negating any advantages you may have gained by bringing color scanning in-house. And finally, desktop color scanners are not very good at scanning small-format transparencies. You have to purchase a high-resolution scanner designed especially for slides, such as the 4000 dpi Nikon LS3500. But beware – a scan of a 35mm slide can take up as much as 55 Mbytes! Nevertheless, both hardware and data compression software are ever improving and "desktop repro" will soon be a reality.

6.17 Handheld scanners are affordable, and despite their size limitations – most have a maximum width of 4 inches (102mm) – are almost indispensable. This is the Logitech ScanMan Model 32.

Output devices: lasers and imagesetters

A graphic designer will be most likely to output to a nearby laser printer for proofing, and send a disc to a service bureau for imagesetting on bromide paper or film.

Laser printers (Fig. **6.19**) work on a similar principle to laser photocopiers. In a photocopier, the light reflected from the white areas of an image causes a rotating drum charged with static electricity to lose its charge, so the toner doesn't stick. In a laser printer, however, there is no "original," so the laser draws a negative image onto the drum, removing charge from the white areas.

Laser printers, such as Apple's LaserWriter family and Hewlett-Packard's LaserJet, are small-format and print in black-and-white only. The resolution is rarely greater than 300 dpi, which is adequate for proofing and producing artwork for low-grade publications such as newsletters (especially if the copy is output larger than the finished size, and then reduced down on a photocopier or PMT machine).

Versatec has a large-format (A0, approximately 33 × 47in or 841 × 1189mm) laser plotter which has a resolution of 400 dpi and produces an A0-size plot in 70 seconds regardless of the amount of detail. Color, too, is on the way – via an interface with Canon's Color Laser Copier 500. It will be possible to take a floppy disc into your local high street copy shop and come away with full-color prints.

An imagesetter (Fig. **6.18**) is a high-resolution laser printer; the best known are the Linotronic family. The ubiquitous Linotronic 300 has been upgraded to the 330. This has the capacity to produce halftone screens to 150 lines at seven selectable resolutions (but see below) the top one being 3386 dpi. The top of the range is the model 630. Color imagesetters include Scitex's Dolev-PS (Fig. **6.20**).

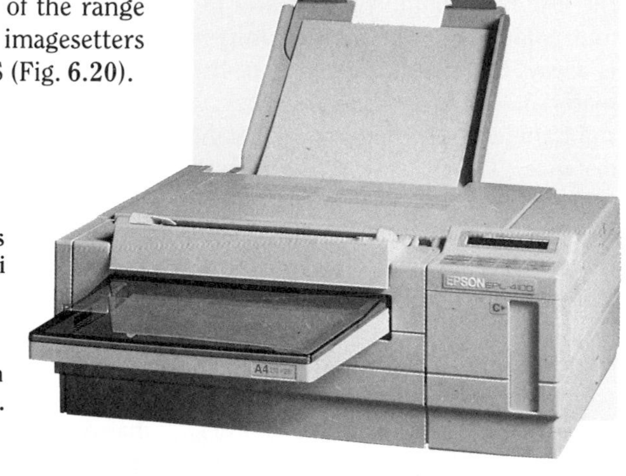

6.19 Laser printers like this Epson EPL4100 give 300 dpi black-and-white output on plain paper, which can be good enough quality to use as camera copy for jobs such as newsletters and pricelists.

6.18 (above) For high-resolution bromide prints and film, you will have to send your discs to a service bureau where they will be output on something like this Linotronic 330 imagesetter.

6.20 High-end color imagesetters such as this Scitex Dolev-PS are used to produce high-quality film separations.

There are two types of imagesetter: flatbeds and drum (Fig. 6.21). Most Linotronics are flatbeds; the Linotronic 630 and imagesetters from Scangraphic, Agfa, Scitex, and Purup are drum-based. Both types have similar optical systems comprising a helium-neon laser, some focusing and collimating (straightening out) optics, one or more mirrors to deflect the beam, a modulator for switching the beam on and off, and a gray-step filter wheel for adjusting the beam's intensity. The difference lies in the exposure unit.

Scangraphic argues that the drum layout shortens the route of the laser, leading to higher precision. The film or paper remains motionless during the exposure, simplifying register for four-color work. The rotating mirror is always the same distance from the material, and the beam is always at right angles to the material. Constant distance, travel, and angle ensure uniform density of exposure and sharp dots. In other models, the laser's route is further simplified by using a laser diode mounted inside the drum.

In a flatbed imagesetter, the paper or film is moved forward, one scan line at a time, by stepper motors. Flatbed imagesetters have to use complex optical systems to ensure that the beam reaching the film or paper is uniform in strength. Imperfections in all the extra optics can lead to slurring, and loss of brightness and contrast. This results in weaker (less sharp) dots.

The resolution of an imagesetter is measured in dpi, and these should not be confused with halftone dots, which are measured in lpi (lines per inch). A halftone dot is a cluster of many imagesetter dots, which we'll call spots here. An average imagesetter might deliver a resolution of 847 dpi, i.e. 847 distinct spots can be laid along a line one inch long with their edges just touching. At the top end of the scale, both the Purup 2026 and the Agfa SelectSet 5000 use an argon-ion laser generating a resolution of 2540 dpi.

The size of a laser's spot cannot easily be altered, and so halftone dots are built up by overlapping the spots (Fig. 6.22). The **addressability** of an

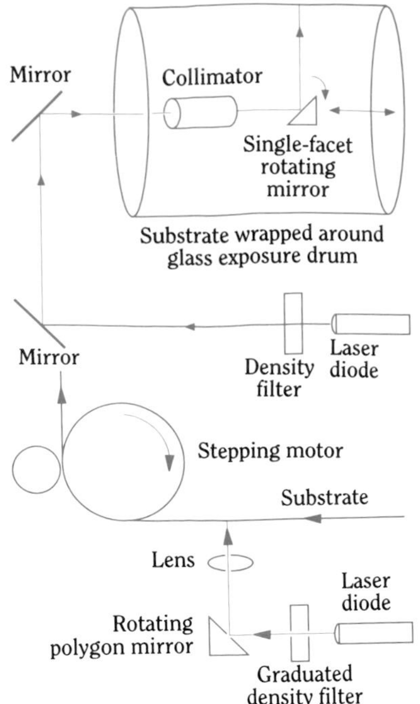

6.21 Flatbed and drum imagesetter configurations. Each has its particular pros and cons, but the drum-based ones seem to offer the better and more consistent quality of output.

imagesetter is the accuracy with which the centers of the spots can be placed in proximity with each other. Thus an addressability of 2540 dpi means that the centers of two spots can be positioned $\frac{1}{2540}$ inch apart. So, when we talk about resolution, we are more correctly talking about addressability. The Linotronic 330 has a resolution of 1270 dpi, but an addressability of between 635 and 3386 dpi.

We are told that the higher the resolution (but read addressability), the better the print quality. But this is not always the case. A ScanText 2051, for example, is capable of addressing 3251 dpi, but there comes a point where there is so much overlapping of spots that any difference in quality is marginal. Similar results could be obtained using a lower setting of, say, 1693 dpi.

To print documents containing PostScript files (see p. 68) – such as typesetting or an image from a program such as FreeHand or Illustrator – an imagesetter has to operate with a device called a RIP (raster image processor, discussed on p. 118), usually housed in a separate box. A RIP is a computer in its own right, containing a microprocessor chip probably more powerful than the one in your computer, such as Motorola's 68040. "Ripping" color halftones is a time-consuming business: pages can take hours to convert, first into PostScript, and then into the raster bitmap an imagesetter can read.

Much of the delay takes place inside the designer's Mac, as the computer begins the process of converting the design into a PostScript description. A way to get round this is to send only the text, rules, and non-scanned graphics to the RIP, along with instructions describing the size, cropping, and position on the page of the scanned pictures (the high-resolution files). There is a parallel here with the procedure used by the Scitex Visionary system (described on p. 118), a process also know as **APR (automatic picture replacement)**.

The picture commands, tagged onto the PostScript file, are part of a standard known as the open prepress interface (OPI), originally proposed by Aldus. A page description can thus be transferred from a Mac to a faster, more powerful Unix-based workstation at the typesetters, and thence to the RIP. A designer's Mac is thus liberated to do what it does best – page design and layout.

6.22 Resolution and addressability are two different, but related, parameters of an imagesetter. Resolution is the number of dots edge to edge in a line measuring an inch; addressability is a measure of how close, center to center, those dots can be placed next to one another.

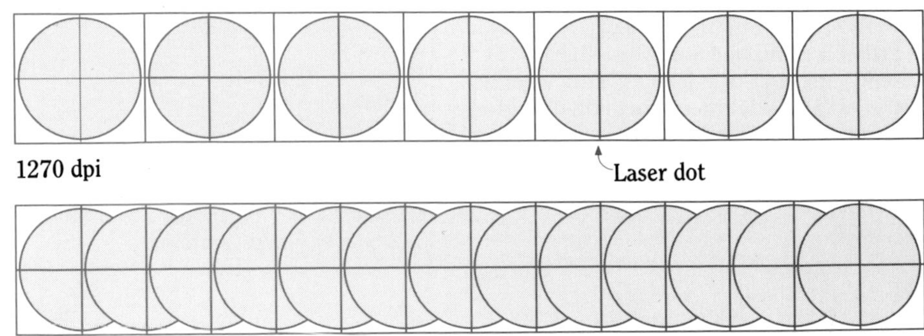

HARDCOPY: OTHER TECHNOLOGIES

There are many other forms of output, especially for color, and one or more of the machines described here will be found in the designer's studio before long. If the quality of output is not important or if a quick-look plot is needed, a dot-matrix printer (Fig. 6.23) like Apple's ImageWriter LQ may be good enough. They are cheap and can double-up with your word processor. With a cyan, magenta, yellow, and black ribbon, 14 colors can be created. The resolution is coarse, equivalent to around 72 dpi, and color fill can be messy (Fig. 6.24).

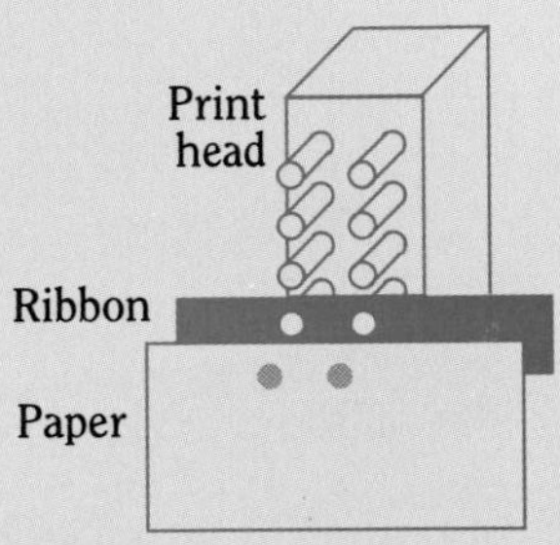

6.23 Dot-matrix printers make use of straightforward mechanical technology – metal pins banging through an inked ribbon. They are cheap and reliable, but the quality of output is poor.

He found out a new thing — namely, that to promise not to do a thing is the surest way in the world to make a body want to go and do that very thing.

He found out a new thing — namely, that to promise not to do a thing is the surest way in the world to make a body want to go and do that very thing.

He found out a new thing — namely, that to promise not to do a thing is the surest way in the world to make a body want to go and do that very thing.

6.24 Here we compare the output quality of a 72 dpi Apple ImageWriter dot-matrix printer in "best" mode with a new ribbon, a 300 dpi Hewlett-Packard DeskWriter bubblejet printer in "best" mode, and a 300 dpi Apple LaserWriter laser printer.

Inkjet plotters (Fig. 6.25) spray jets of microscopic electrically charged droplets of ink onto a moving roll of paper. These jets of ink are deflected by electromagnets – just like the electron beam in a television tube – to build up the image. **Bubblejet plotters** (Fig. 6.26) have an array of thin nozzles in the print head, each of which is full of ink, held there by surface tension. A small heating element causes a bubble to form which forces the ink out of the nozzle and onto the page (Fig. 6.27).

Another variation is the **thermojet plotter**, which sprays melted plastic onto the paper.

Apple's StyleWriter is a low-cost single-color bubblejet plotter which prints at 360 dpi – more dots per inch than a laser plotter maybe, but bigger and rougher dots! Hewlett-Packard's DeskWriter is faster and sturdier. Color inkjets, such as CalComp's Colormaster Plus and Linotype's Color 30 can print A3-size (approximately 12 × 17in, or 297 × 420mm) prints with bleed at 300 dpi.

6.25 Inkjet plotters, like this Tektronix Phaser III, work by shooting minute drops of ink at the paper. The Phaser is described as a phase-change inkjet: solid sticks of ink are melted in the printhead, squirted at the paper, then cold fused.

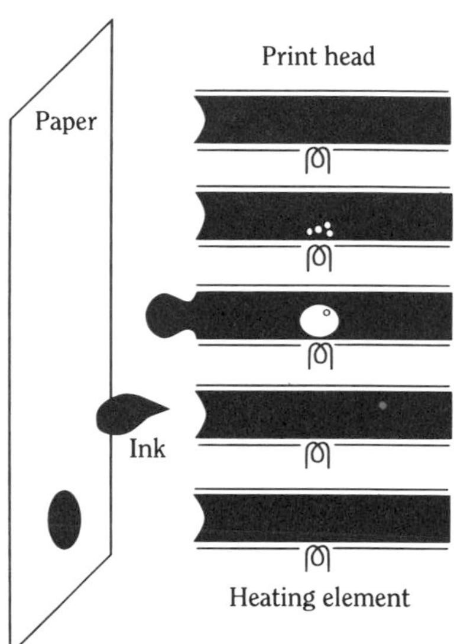

6.27 In bubblejet plotters, such as Apple's StyleWriter, a heating element causes bubbles to form in the print head, thus forcing drops of ink to fly onto the paper.

6.26 Inkjet and bubblejet printers produce bright, saturated colors, yet though they are often rated above laser printers in terms of resolution, the dots are bigger and more prone to smudging.

Thermal-transfer plotters (Fig. 6.28) use an inked-roll cartridge sandwiched between the mechanism and the drawing. It acts like carbon paper, "ironing" the image onto clay-coated paper. The three process colors (and sometimes black) are applied, one at a time, by melting dots of wax onto the paper or acetate at a resolution of 300 dpi (Fig. 6.29). Printers such as the QMS ColorScript and the Tektronix Phaser II are also used for color proofing. The machines are cleaner and dryer than inkjets, but consumables are more expensive. Thermal-transfer machines produce solid, bright colors, but tend to print blues and greens darker than inkjets. **Direct thermal printers**, such as the Océ G9800 series, "burn" a 406 dpi monochrome image into specially coated paper using thermal heads.

6.28 (below) A technical drawing of the Tektronix Phaser II thermal-transfer plotter, produced on Adobe Illustrator by Bob Harrington. The plotter produces PostScript output to A4 size. The Océ G5242 PS (right) works to A3 size, with bleed.

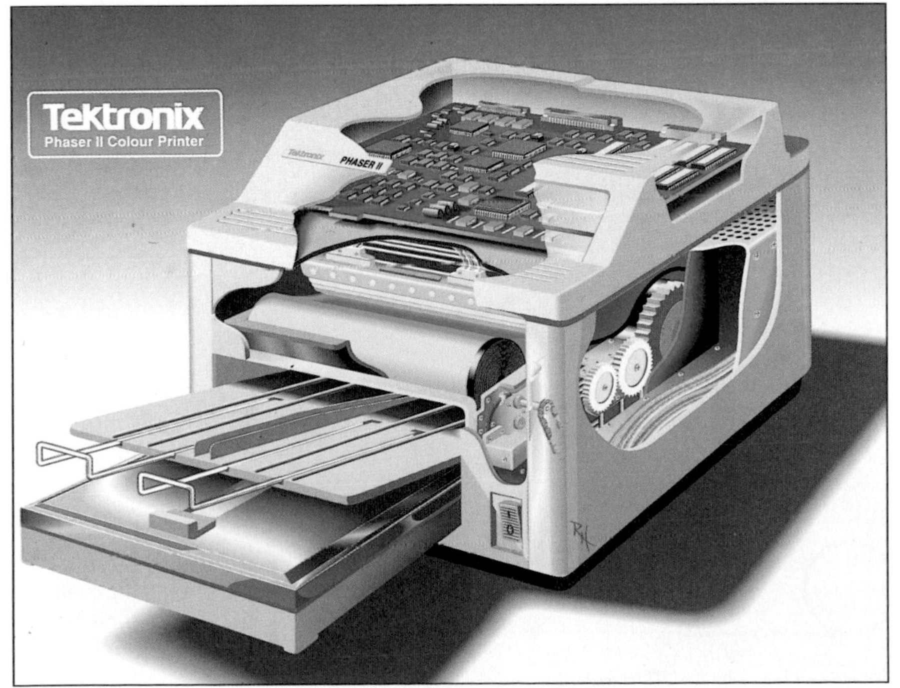

Roll of transfer material
Take-up reel
Heating element
Wax
Paper path
Roller

6.29 In the thermal-transfer process, rolls of transfer paper containing colored wax are "ironed" onto smooth paper by hundreds of individually controlled heating elements.

Thermal-transfer and inkjet printers produce all their colors by a process called **dithering** (Figs **6.30** and **6.31**), which is analogous to halftone screening. Pixels of cyan, magenta, and yellow (and sometimes black) are interspersed in regular patterns. Some printers use a fixed pattern of dithering, which results in a distinct step between colors. Others can make use of different patterns, leading to smoother gradations.

Laser, thermal-transfer, and inkjet printers are available with or without a PostScript driver, the PostScript versions being more expensive. It is possible to produce acceptable results without PostScript by using Adobe Type Manager or TrueType fonts (or PostScript fonts converted to TrueType using a program such as FontMonger). For most graphic designers committed to PostScript, and who need fast and consistent output, a PostScript-compatible printer will be essential.

Perhaps the best contender yet for color hardcopy is dye sublimation (Fig. 6.32). Machines from Mitsubishi and Hitachi mix the ink on the treated paper, without dots or dithering. So 16·7 million possible colours and 256 grayscales are smoothly blended together into a photographic quality image almost good enough to go as artwork straight to the printers.

Sublimation is the phenomenon whereby certain substances go directly from a solid to a gaseous form, without the usual intermediate liquid stage. The thermal head on a dye-sublimation printer varies the temperature so that the amount of dye emitted is continuously controlled.

At present, both the machines and the media for dye sublimation are very expensive. With the creation of a market for home video stills cameras, dye sublimation will become much less expensive. It is possible to envisage high street film processing shops providing a dye-sublimation service.

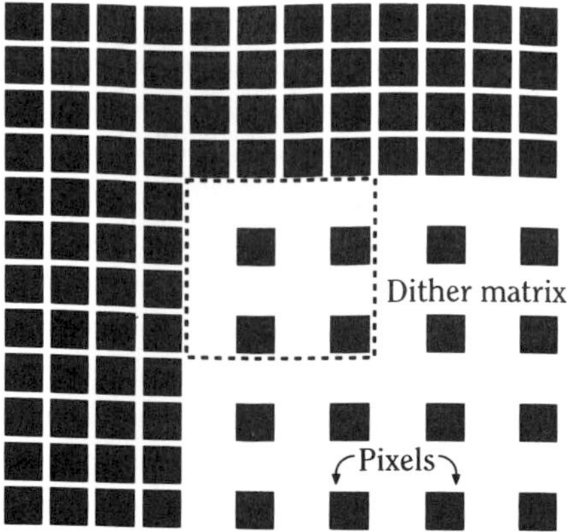

6.30 Most output technologies can produce only one size of dot in just one intensity. This is fine for line work and flat color, but for smooth blends between colors, they have to resort to a trick called dithering, which introduces deliberate randomness into a dot pattern.

6.31 (below) Simple 1-bit dithering can be seen in this close-up – a laser plot of a chair produced by Kanwal Sharma of Lewis Sharma Design, a studio in Bristol, England, specializing in design for disabled people.

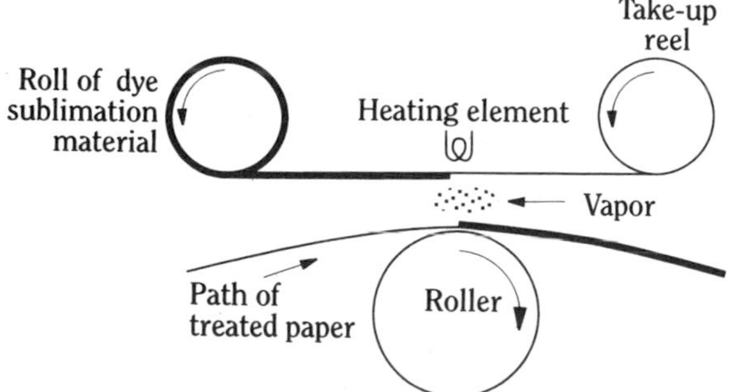

6.32 Dye-sublimation printers can produce an almost photographic quality of output, without dots or dithering, by melting and merging the inks right on the surface of the paper.

Designers will sometimes want to take a 35mm or larger format transparency off the system. A **film recorder** (Fig. 6.33), from a company such as Matrix or Hitachi, captures the image on a small flat CRT tube built into the device, making three consecutive exposures through red, green, and blue filters. The Solitaire 16 from Management Graphics, Inc. can produce 35mm, 70mm, 5 × 4in, and 10 × 8in transparencies from Mac output at a staggering 16,000 lines resolution. They claim 68 billion texture-free solid colors. Using the Solitaire 8xp RIP, a 4000 line image in 35mm format has an exposure time of 27 seconds, and an 8000 line image can be produced in 50 seconds.

A **pen plotter** will have limited use in most graphic design studios. An exception is where the graphic designer does a lot of packaging design work. The pen plotter will be used to draw out fold and cut lines for the flat-pattern development of the carton or box being designed.

A pen plotter, with a cutting knife replacing the pen or pencil, can also be used to prepare flat-color masks for silkscreen printing (see p. 150), and for cutting out vinyl letters for large-scale displays and signs (Fig. 6.34).

There are two main types of pen plotter. Desktop plotters have the pen moving in all directions on a stationary piece of paper, held in place horizontally by a suction pump. Larger drum plotters have the pen moving in one direction and the paper in the other. These use abrasive pinch rollers to grip the edges of the paper, eliminating the necessity for sprocketted paper or film.

Roland's CAMM-1 is a desktop plotter modified for cutting vinyl and Rubylith film (see p. 108). Large format flatbed and drum production plotter/cutters are made by Zund, Wild, Aristo, and Kongsberg. Laser cutters are used for acrylics.

Plotter and cutters are vector devices, moving from point to point as on a graph, and the code that drives them conforms to a standard called HP-GL (Hewlett-Packard graphics language). PostScript is a vector format too, even though most computer devices encountered by the graphic designer work on the raster principle. PostScript to HP-GL conversion is necessary to drive a plotter directly from a PostScript package.

6.33 Film recorders are used to produce photographic transparencies direct from computer disc. They work by exposing the film three times – once for each of the primary colors – using small flat cathode-ray tubes.

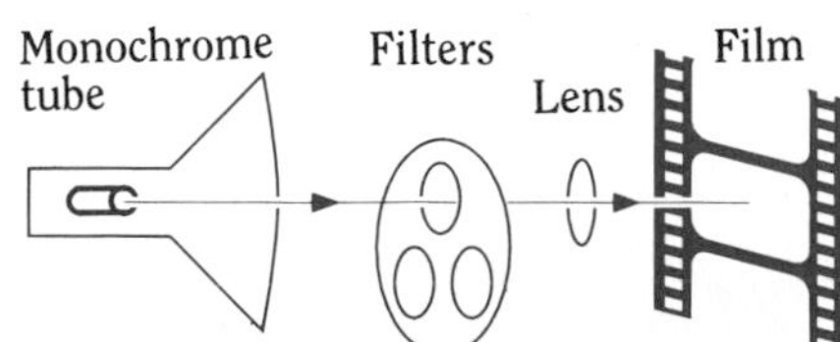

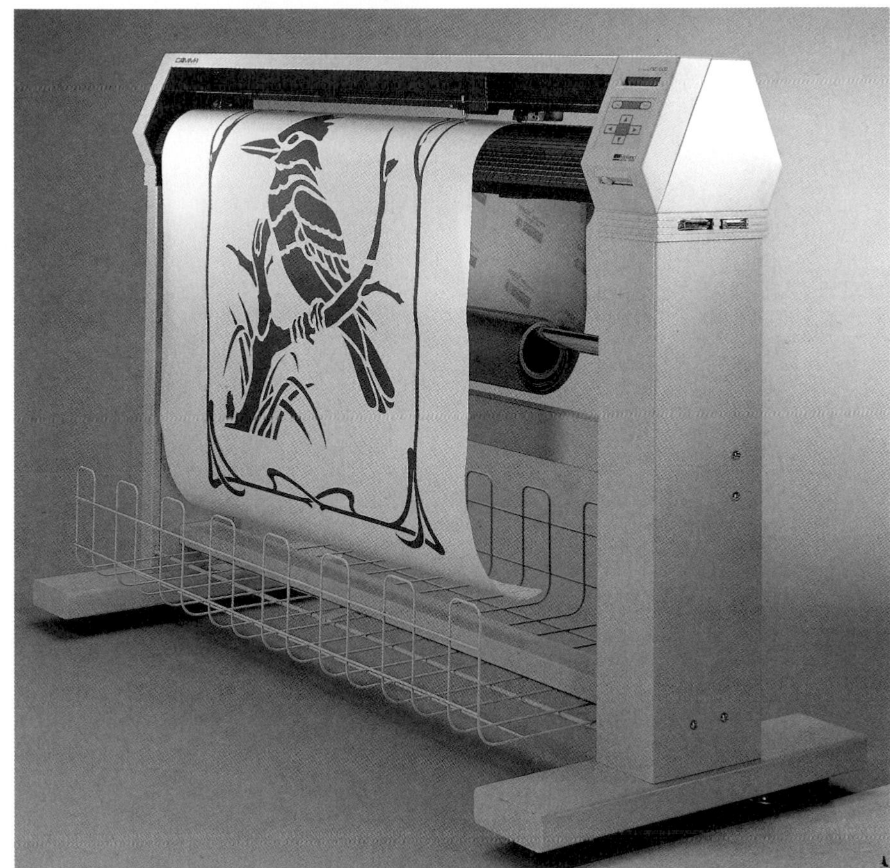

6.34 Pen plotters are rarely used by graphic designers. An exception is when they are equipped with a cutting knife in place of the pen, like this Roland CAMM-1, and are used to produce masks for screenprinting or to cut vinyl letters for large signs.

Part 2: designing for the small screen

Most graphic designers work almost exclusively with print. Increasingly, however, there will be a demand for people who can design for the small screen – either for television, or for the important area of "interaction design" – designing the graphics for products that employ a screen-based method of operation.

6.35 State-of-the-art computer graphics from London-based production house Digital Pictures. Alec Knox animated this 30-second title sequence, from a design by Andrew Sides of Baxter Hobbins Sides, for the current affairs program *This Week*. Seven colored globes – representing continents and days of the week – shatter and align to produce the final title frame.

The processes are much simpler than designing for print. For television and film work, designers used to produce lettering on boards, which were then placed in front of the camera. Nowadays, everything is created on a computer system and output direct to video, or, in the case of sports and current affairs programs, broadcast live (Fig. 6.35).

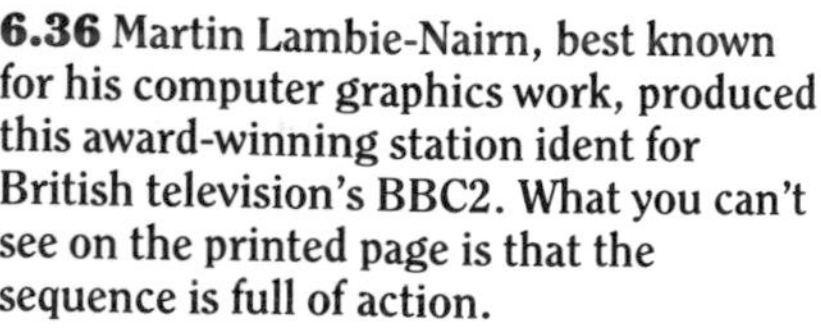

6.36 Martin Lambie-Nairn, best known for his computer graphics work, produced this award-winning station ident for British television's BBC2. What you can't see on the printed page is that the sequence is full of action.

Design for television adds the time dimension to graphic design – the words and letters can move! Everyone is now familiar with the clichés of flying chrome-plated logos, and the dreaded green grid of the late seventies has long been pensioned off. But TV graphics still tend to overuse drop shadows and graduated tints, just because they are easy to do. You don't need to use sophisticated solid modeling with photorealistic rendering techniques such as ray tracing to achieve a memorable effect, as the award-winning idents for British TV's BBC2 by Martin Lambie-Nairn prove (Fig. 6.36).

Another area opening up to graphic designers is that of interactive database design (Figs 6.37–6.39), for use in art galleries and museums, or for distribution on CD-rom. Collectively known as hypermedia, and created using computer programs such as HyperCard or Macromind Director, these "stacks" mimic conventional books. The difference is that the "reader" can flip around at will, usually by pointing to a highlighted word in the text, or by choosing a new topic from a menu. The problem for the designer – apart from organizing the stack so as not to frustrate the reader by too many dead ends – is one of legibility. The amount of text on any one page must be kept to a minimum (although it is possible to scroll a large amount of text within a window) because low-resolution text on a screen is tiring to read. The graphics must also be carefully laid out to avoid unwanted effects such as "pixel beards" where a letter or graphic interacts unfavorably with a background tint.

6.37 A "page" from an electronic encyclopedia for Cable & Wireless, designed by Rory Matthews of Brighton-based Cognitive Applications. The system uses a 19 inch touchscreen, and also makes use of sound, animation, and full motion video clips.

6.38 Gary Stewart of the Royal College of Art, London, has used Macromind Director to create this interactive computer-based tutorial for dtp users with no previous typographic training.

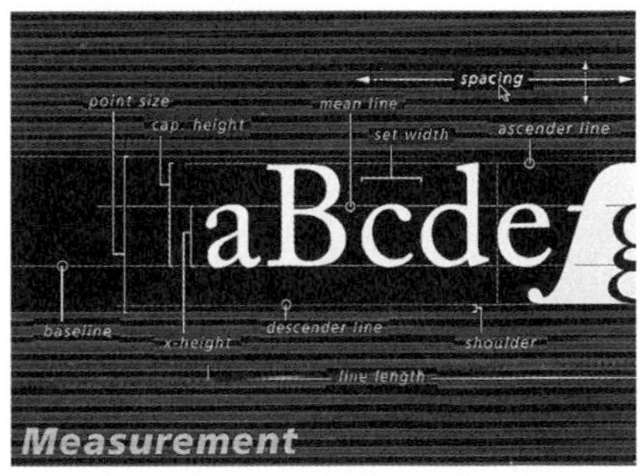

6.39 West-coast designers IDEO are at the forefront of interaction design, which aims to use graphic design to help users make sense of unfamiliar products. These screen icon designs are based on Claris's software packaging identity. To achieve the watercolor effect, Bruce Browne used a manual anti-aliasing technique – adding lighter tones to soften the jagged edges caused by the pixels on the screen.

Part 3: choosing a system

Turnkey systems

A **turnkey system** is a complete package of hardware and software dedicated to a particular task. You turn the (imaginary) key, and off you drive. The system may be assembled from standard pieces of equipment, bought in from well known manufacturers and "badge engineered" (i.e. the turnkey vendor's logo is stuck on the front). Or perhaps the vendor will have modified it somewhat. The software that does the job is usually only available from the turnkey vendor. (If it is subsequently sold separately from the turnkey system, it is said to be unbundled.)

The attraction to the user is that everything needed for a working system is purchased from one source, with a single maintenance contract and one technical support person to call if things go wrong. The disadvantages are that the system cannot usually be used for other tasks – to run the studio administration, for example. And you are "locked in" to one supplier for any future updates of the hardware and software. The trend today is toward "open systems" with standardized GUIs, and the ability for programs to be able to pass information between each other. This may not be possible with a turnkey. It may have a quirky interface, and once you have learnt to use it, that knowledge will apply to that system only.

Nevertheless, there are still several turnkey systems around, aimed at highly specialized applications. There are systems targeted at packaging designers, with their need to design in three dimensions and then produce flat-pattern developments of cartons, for example. Another group of turnkeys is aimed at screenprinters and signwriters, who need to cut letters and masks out of vinyl and Rubylith.

Turnkey systems are usually much more expensive than an equivalent system assembled from component parts selected by you. The vendors have been guilty of trading on people's fear of computers by stressing that their menus, for example, make use of the terms and language peculiar to that trade. But these days, much more flexible systems can be assembled quite painlessly from standard PCs or Macs, plus any make of plotter or cutter and inexpensive, off-the-shelf software.

Selecting, upgrading, and networking the system

Selecting and cost-justifying a system is a very personal business. Read the computer magazines, visit trade shows, and talk to other users doing similar work to that of your studio. Methodologies exist that use spreadsheet programs to enable you to quantify the benefits of introducing a computer system into your studio. These may be understandable to an accountant or bank manager and be instrumental in securing you a loan to make the purchase. But of course they cannot predict the future. Ultimately, the success of an installation is down to you. You will have to understand what the system is capable of doing, and how it can save you time and materials, while producing a quality product.

Once a successful installation has been established, however, expansion happens rapidly. This can take two forms: expansion of hardware – adding more systems, more memory, more output devices – and expansion into new application areas. On the Macintosh particularly, programs

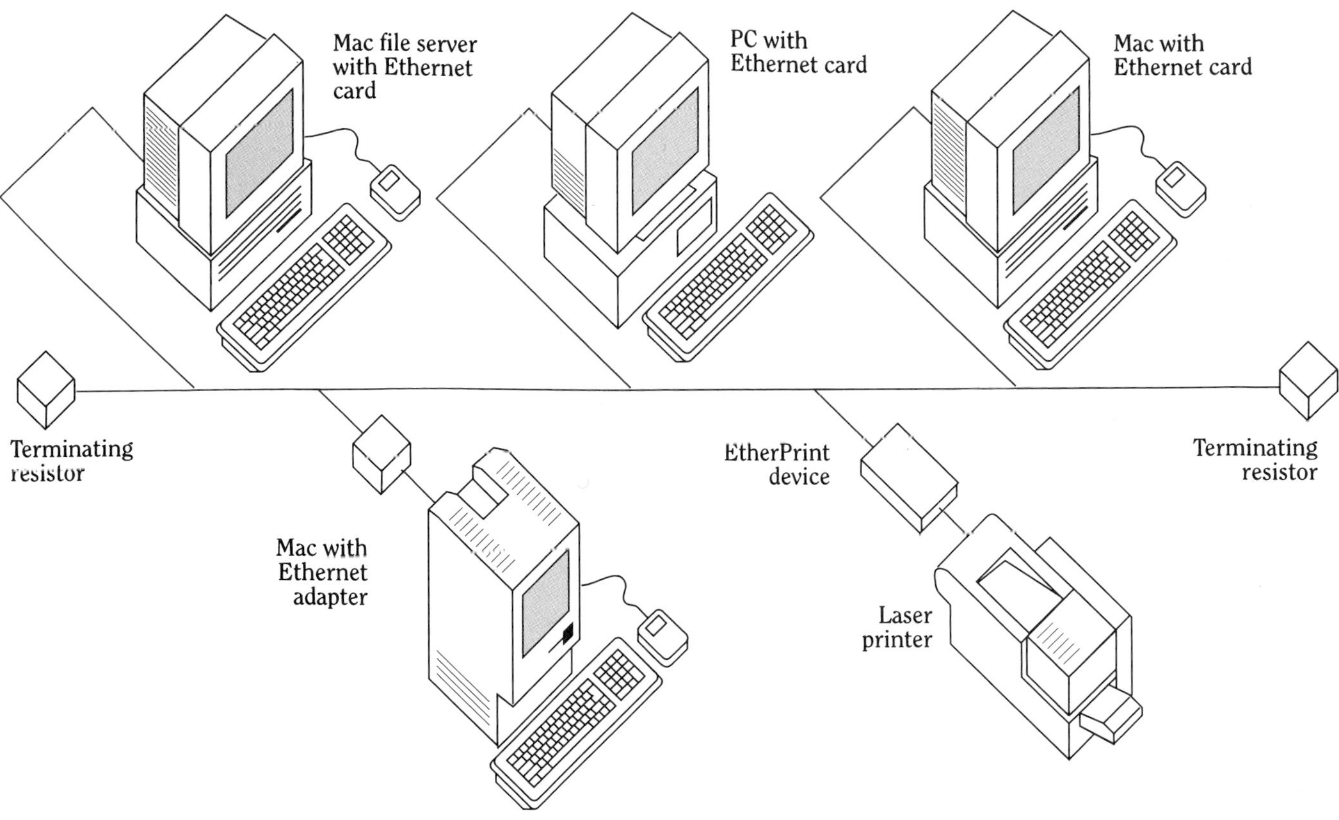

6.40 Networking means that you can link computers together to send electronic mail or to share resources, such as a laser printer. You can also work with others on large projects.

have a common look and feel, which reduces the culture shock when you encounter new software. With the enormous number of "desk accessories" available, it is difficult to resist becoming addicted to every latest application that comes along.

As soon as you have more than one system, they can be networked together (Fig. 6.40). There are three main reasons for **networking:** (1) to exchange files and messages with nearby members of your team using Email (electronic mail); (2) to share expensive resources such as laser printers and disc drives; and (3) to work jointly with others in your studio on a large-scale project – in a workgroup.

Networking has a language all of its own, and acronyms like ISO/OSI and TCP/IP abound. All you need to know is that the most famous LAN (local-area network) is called Ethernet. It operates via a single length of coaxial cable or twisted-pair telephone cable, and was developed by Xerox, DEC, and Intel and introduced in 1980. Other kinds of LAN include IBM's token ring system.

Workstations were designed from the outset to be networked, so there should be no problem there. On the Macintosh, networking is fairly straightforward, having been made much simpler by the introduction of System 7. For Email, one system is designated Email server – the place where messages are stored and forwarded – and the others are called clients. Full networking is achieved when a "file server" is set up. Any computer in the network can act as a server. (In larger networks the file server is a dedicated computer with a large disc drive, but with no screen.) This provides shared storage for programs (though it is faster to keep your own local copy), files, or fonts that everyone on the network can access. It is the responsibility of the applications software to say who has read-only access, and who has the authority to make changes to the master files.

Ethernet is faster, but is also more expensive to implement. It is possible to mix PCs and Macs on the same network. Sitka's TOPS (there is no official explanation of the acronym, except that it may have started life as "transparent operating system") was developed by Sun, and is the oldest of the mixed environment networks.

A **modem** (the word is short for modulator/demodulator) is a device that allows you to send files down the telephone to the systems of your clients and typesetters. It is also possible to send and receive faxes direct from your hard disc (no paper is needed), using plug-in cards.

Networking, though complicated, is not really difficult. It does, however, ultimately take you into a new league of computer management. While your studio may not want or be able to afford a systems manager, someone will have to take responsibility for the smooth operation of the system: developing filing systems, watching out for viruses, maintaining the shared resources, and so on.

Health and safety

As computers become commonplace, so must health and safety issues be taken seriously. It is rare indeed, for example, to find ergonomically adjustable desks and chairs in large organizations, so what chance does the smaller design studio have? But they cost little compared with the total investment in hardware and software, and can prevent lower-back damage to the most valuable component of the system – the designer. If that is not an incentive, then it should be noted that many of the recommendations are or will become legal requirements (Fig. 6.41).

Desks should be as thin as possible and adjustable for height; chairs should have five castors and give good lumbar (lower-back) support. When you sit on your chair, upper and lower legs should be at right angles and feet comfortably on the floor. A footrest may have to be provided, if desk height is not adjustable, subject to sufficient leg clearance. The display screen should, ideally, be tiltable to an optimum 38 degrees below the horizontal. The angle between your upper and lower arm, when typing, should be 90 degrees.

There is a body of knowledge existing on such hazards as WRULD (work-related upper-limb disorders) and RSI (repetitive strain injury) – a disorder of the hands and wrists causing numbness, swelling, tingling, and ultimately complete seizure. Keyboard operators have already suffered severe damage, and employers have already been sued for large sums, so do not wait until it is too late. Educate everyone to take frequent "thinking" breaks away from the system. A break of 15 minutes in every 75 minutes of continuous computer use is recommended.

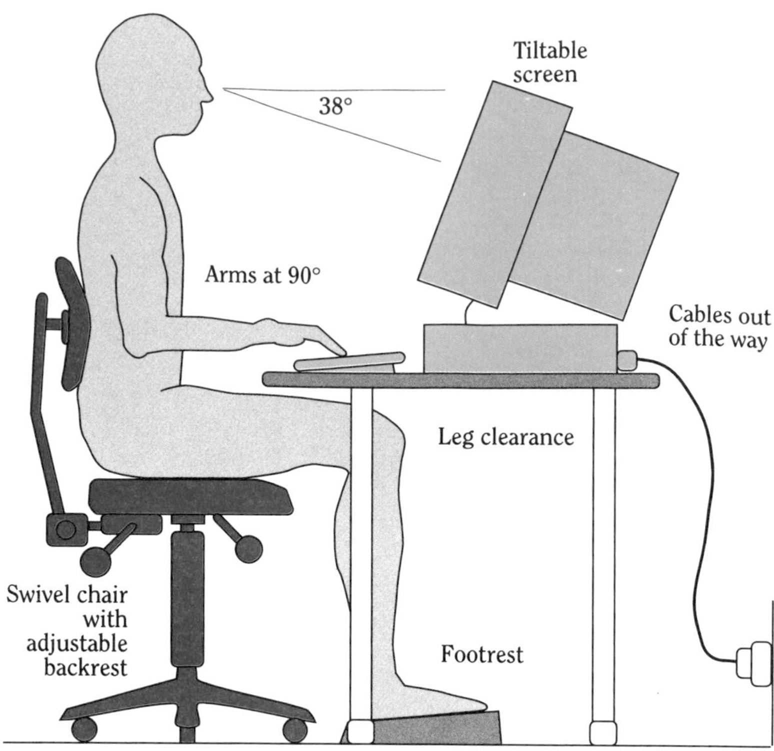

6.41 If you are to be working at the computer for long periods, it is vitally important to have the correct ergonomic conditions to reduce the possibility of computer-related health problems such as repetitive strain injury, backache, and eyestrain.

Lighting should be diffuse and indirect. Fluorescent lights should have diffuser shades and should run parallel to the user's line of vision. Avoid glare and reflections, and color schemes that are excessively bright or dark. No user should have to face a window, and vertical blinds should be fitted, to be closed on sunny days. Regular eye tests are recommended. Because of the possibility of radiation, pregnant women should have the right to keep away from computers during pregnancy, without loss of pay, status, or career prospects.

The health risk from static build-up and electromagnetic radiation from computers is an issue still hotly debated. Emissions from the front of a computer, i.e. through the screen, are in fact lower than from the sides or back. The computer screen should be at arm's length from your body – anyone sitting closer than 28 inches (711mm) from the front is at some risk. Nobody should sit closer than 36 inches (914mm) from the sides or back of a computer screen. Anti-glare screens do not help to cut down harmful radiation, unless they specifically say that they do. Radiation from mono and grayscale screens is lower than from color ones, and larger screens do not seem to emit any more radiation than smaller ones.

Photocopiers and laser printers should be placed where the air is changed at least once an hour, at least 3¼ yards (3m) away from the nearest person, and preferably in a separate, well-ventilated room to disperse the fumes produced by the toner. Noisy printers should also be fitted with hoods and be kept well away from the workers.

Finally, stress and anxiety can be reduced through appropriate and thorough training. This can be as simple as sitting down with the software manual for an hour or two each week to practice shortcuts, or spending time looking over the shoulder of the "resident guru" at work. Or it can involve taking time off from your paying projects regularly, to attend more formal training courses.

Summary

Computers are here to stay. You may not be able to purchase your own yet. But you probably have access to a system at school or college, or in the design studio where you are working. Your typesetter almost certainly has a system, and may be in the process of converting up from a dedicated typesetting system to a more general-purpose dtp system. When you see what it can do, you'll want one too!

Of course, there will be designers and typographers who are reluctant to take the plunge, and there will always be a place for those who can conceptualize designs using just a pencil and paper. But they will miss out on the flexibility and control that a computer system can offer.

However, there is no such thing as a free lunch. There is a price to be paid for working on computer. The machinery will never be a panacea. It will never do the design work for you – in fact, it will probably make you work harder! You will have to do things that maybe before you left for the typesetter or printer to sort out. If you choose to go the computer route, the entire print production process will become your concern ... and your responsibility. The benefits are enormous, not only in cost savings, increased creativity, and improved quality, but also in job satisfaction and personal fulfillment.

Investing in dtp is no longer a risky venture. It is a mature technology and there is a huge body of experience within the graphics design industry for you to draw upon.

Glossary

ACCORDION FOLD or **CONCERTINA FOLD** A folding method in which two or more parallel folds are made in opposite directions

ACETATE A clear film used as an overlay on a MECHANICAL, for the production of separations for flat color, for example, or for KEYLINES

ACHROMATIC STABILIZATION See GRAY COMPONENT REPLACEMENT

ADDITIVE COLORS The primaries of transmitted light: red, green, and blue-violet

ADDRESSABILITY A measure of how close the centers of the dots that make up type or drawings can be placed next to each other on an output device such as a laser printer; see also RESOLUTION

AGAINST THE GRAIN Folding or feeding paper stock at right angles to the orientation of the fibers

AGFAPROOF A proprietary prepress color proofing system

ALIGNMENT Placing type or images so that they line up either horizontally or vertically

ALPHANUMERIC CHARACTER SET A complete set of letters, numbers, and associated punctuation marks; see also **FONT**

ANILINE DYE Synthetic dye used in flexographic ink

ANTI-ALIASING An optical trick to make hard jagged edges on low-resolution computer screens and color output look smoother

ANTIQUE PAPER A book paper with a rough finish

APPLICATION Computer software that does a particular task, such as desktop publishing

APR (AUTOMATIC PICTURE REPLACEMENT) This uses a low-resolution halftone in a dtp layout, which will be replaced at the repro house by a high-resolution scanned image

ASCENDER The part of a lower-case letter such as k or d that extends above the body of type

ASCII (AMERICAN STANDARD CODE FOR INFORMATION INTERCHANGE) A text-only format of 256 codes used to represent an alphanumeric character set with no additional information about its size, font, or spacing

ASSEMBLER A low-level computer programming language that uses mnemonics, such as MPY for multiply

ASSEMBLY Collecting and arranging design elements on film to create the FLAT used for platemaking

AUTHOR'S CORRECTIONS Corrections that are made to a galley proof by the author or editor, which may contain new material or changes of mind that will have to be paid for

AUTO-REVERSING FILM Film that can be used to copy negative-working film to negative-working film without the need for an intermediate positive

BACK EDGE The margin closest to the spine

BACKING A problem of lightening of color in printing that occurs when ink removed from the fountain roller is not replaced by the flow of fresh ink

BACKSTEP MARK Black mark printed on a SIGNATURE that shows where the final fold will be. After collation, the marks should fall in a stepped sequence

BACK UP Printing on the other side of the sheet; in computer terminology, to copy important work onto FLOPPY DISCS or streamer tape

BAD BREAK In justified setting, hyphenation of a word that looks wrong

BARYTA Smooth paper used for letterpress repro proofs

BASELINE The imaginary horizontal line on which letters sit

BASIC (BEGINNERS ALL-PURPOSE SYMBOLIC INSTRUCTION CODE) A high-level computer programming language which uses English words and phrases

BASTARD SIZE Any non-standard size, especially of paper

BINDING Fixing together folded signatures into multipage publications, using glue, thread, or metal wires. Also the cover and backing of a book

BIT The primary unit in computers – a binary digit (a 1 or a 0)

BITMAP A picture or letter made from a pattern of dots or PIXELS on a RASTER device such as a computer display or laser printer

BLANKET The intermediate rubber roller on an offset litho press that transfers the image from the plate to the paper

BLANKET CYLINDER The cylinder on an offset litho press to which the blanket is attached

BLANKET-TO-BLANKET PRESS An offset litho press that can print both sides of a sheet in one pass – the sheet passes between two blanket cylinders and there is no need for an impression cylinder

BLEED Part of the image that extends beyond the trim marks of a page

BLIND A method of die-stamping or embossing in three-dimensional low relief without foil or ink

BLOCKING Producing the lettering on the spine of a hardback book, usually in gold or silver leaf, by means of a die; see also STICKING

BLUE AND RED KEYS A method for ensuring the close registration of color separations using a key image in blue or red as a guide

BLUEPRINT or **BLUE** A dyeline proof for checking the position of design elements and stripped-in halftones before the plate is made, also called OZALID

BODY TYPE Type below 14 point, used for the main body of text, as opposed to DISPLAY type

BROMIDE Smooth high-contrast photographic paper used for PMTs

BROWNLINE or **BROWNPRINT** A proof made from a lithographic negative similar to a BLUEPRINT but producing a brown image

BUBBLEJET PLOTTER A form of inkjet printer in which a heating element causes bubbles to eject the ink

BUCKLE FOLDER A folding machine that uses an adjustable stop to buckle the sheet, which is then forced between two nip rollers

BUCKRAM A heavy coarse-thread binding cloth

BUG A mistake in a computer program which makes unpredictable things happen

BULK See CALIPER

BURN Exposure of a litho plate

BURNISHING Rubbing down pressure-sensitive lettering such as Letraset

BYTE Eight bits, corresponding to one ASCII character

C A structured computer programming language

CALENDERING Smoothing and compressing paper as it travels through the paper machine

CALIPER The thickness of paper, also called bulk

CAMERA-READY COPY or **MECHANICAL** A complete and finished layout of type and images ready to be photographed by a process camera

CAST COATED Paper with a high-gloss finish

CASTING OFF Calculating how much space the text in a manuscript will occupy when set in type

CATCH-UP Printing on non-image areas, caused by insufficient water

CHALKING Pigments smudging or rubbing off, caused by improper curing of paper which results in too rapid an absorption of the binding vehicle in ink

CHASE In letterpress, the rectangular metal frame holding type and blocks; when locked up, it is called a FORME

CHROMO PAPER A type of paper polished on one side only

CLIP ART Copyright-free illustrations, available as conventional artwork and in formats that can be used directly in dtp-produced publications

CLOCK SPEED The length of the processing cycle in a computer, measured in MHz

CMYK Cyan, magenta, yellow, and key (black). This is the system used to describe and separate colors for printing. Other systems include RGB (red, green, blue) for transmitted color, as on computer screens, and HLS (hue, luminance, saturation), a more theoretical description. The PANTONE MATCHING SYSTEM matches colors by mixing 11 basic colors

COATING Adding a layer of china clay to a paper to increase its smoothness

COLD-METAL SETTING or **STRIKE-ON** Typesetting produced directly onto paper using a typewriter or rub-down lettering

COLD-SET INK Solid ink that is melted and used with a hot press, solidifying when it contacts the paper

COLLATING or **GATHERING** Bringing pages and signatures together for binding

COLLOTYPE Printing process using a plate coated with gelatin – the only process to reproduce continuous-tone images without screening

COLOR BAR A printer's check appearing on color proofs to show up any faults in color registration, print density, dot gain, and slurring

COLOR CALIBRATE To adjust the output values of a computer screen to correspond more faithfully to true colors

COLOR CAST An unfaithful color on a color picture, often found on a subject photographed against a strongly colored background

COLOR DISPLAY SYSTEM The color computer display screen itself, and the graphics card that drives it

COLOR-KEY A 3M proprietary dry proofing system using plastic laminates

COLOR SEPARATIONS A set of films for the cyan, magenta, yellow, and black components of a full-color image.

COMBINATION FOLDER A folding machine that uses both the knife and buckle methods in combination

COMPOSING STICK A device used in hand setting for assembling a line of type

COMPOSITOR The person who sets type

CONTINUOUS TONE or **CONTONE** Artwork or photography containing shades of gray, as opposed to LINE COPY

CONVERTER An offset litho press that can be converted to print either two colors on one side of a sheet or one color on both sides in one pass

COPY The raw material of the graphic designer: the text, type, artwork, and mechanicals

COPY FITTING Marking up type so that it fits a given space in a layout

COPY PREPARATION Adding the instructions to text that define how it is to be set; MARKING UP is the manual method of copy preparation

CPU (CENTRAL PROCESSING UNIT) The "brains" of a computer, usually a chip or chipset

CRAWLING An imperfection in the surface of ink, occurring when thick ink overprints wet ink

CROCKING Smudging or transfer of dry ink onto printed sheets

CROMACHECK Proprietary off-press proofing system from Du Pont which uses plastic laminates

CROMALIN Proprietary off-press proofing system from Du Pont which uses dry toners and light-sensitive sheets

CROP MARKS Lines to indicate which portions of a photograph or illustration are surplus to requirements

CROPPING Choosing not to use portions of a photograph and marking an overlay on the original to indicate which portions of the image are to be printed

CROSS-HEADINGS Display type used to interest the reader and break up gray areas of body type

CRYSTALLIZATION When the ink of the first printing dries too hard before overprinting, it can repel the second ink and also produce poor TRAPPING

CURE Acclimatize paper to the temperature and humidity of the press room

CUT-OUT Remove irregular areas of a photograph to make a subject stand out

CYAN Process blue – really more a turquoise

DAMPER MARKS Patterns over the print caused by worn damper covers or too much pressure

DECKLE The natural wavy edge to paper; also the frame used to make handmade paper

DENSITOMETER An instrument used to measure the density of printed color

DESCENDER The part of a lower-case letter such as p or g that extends below the baseline

DESKTOP SCANNER A device for converting line and halftone copy into a digital form readable by a dtp program

DIAZO A proof made by direct contact with film positives; see also BLUEPRINT and BROWNLINE

DIDOT POINT A unit of measurement used in continental Europe equivalent to 0·0148 inch (0·376mm), 7 percent larger than the American point

DIE-CUTTING Using sharp steel rules in a wooden die to cut shapes from paper

DIE-STAMPING Producing a three-dimensional low relief effect on paper or cover board using a metal die and counter-die

DIFFUSION TRANSFER A semi-automatic process for making enlargements or reductions of line or halftone copy. A negative is produced in the process camera and transferred to a receiver sheet to create the **BROMIDE** positive; see also PMT and VELOX

DIGITIZING TABLET A device used for computer drawing and painting using a puck or stylus on a flat sensitized plate

DIMENSIONAL STABILITY The desirable property of paper that prevents it from stretching and distorting during processing or printing due to changes in humidity or dampness

DINGBAT A symbol or ornament such as ☜ or ❀ that is treated as a character in a font

DIRECT THERMAL PRINTER An output device that burns an image into special paper

DISPLAY TYPE Type above 14 point set for headlines or other display purposes; some fancy display faces are available in capitals only

DITHERING A crude computer method of screening. Thermal transfer and inkjet printers produce their colors by interspersing pixels of cyan, magenta, and yellow (and sometimes black) in regular patterns, grouped together in either two-by-two or four-by-four matrixes

DOCUMENT In computer language, any job you are working on is called a document, whether it is a drawing, a piece of text, or a page layout

DOT-FOR-DOT A method of screening already screened halftones to prevent moiré patterns

DOT GAIN or **DOT SPREAD** As individual dots begin to join in darker areas of a halftone there can be an apparent jump in what should be a continuous tone

DOT-MATRIX PRINTER An output device that uses pins striking a ribbon to transfer ink to the paper

DOUBLING Two printed dots where there should only be one. It is caused by wet ink picked up by the blanket on a subsequent printing. If it is off register, it prints as a ghost dot nearby

DPI Dots per inch, a measure of the resolution or addressability of a raster device such as a laser printer

DRAWDOWN A smear of ink from a smooth blade used to check the quality of an ink on a particular paper stock

DRAW PROGRAMS or **OBJECT-ORIENTED PROGRAM.** A computer program that stores images in terms of the lines and curves used to create them; see also PAINT PROGRAM

DROP CAP A large initial letter dropping into the lines below and signaling the beginning of the text

DROP-OUT Complete removal of the dots in highlight areas of a halftone

DRY PROOF A color proof made without ink, such as a Cromalin

DTP Desktop publishing – electronic page make-up

DUMMY A "concept model" of a publication, usually a miniature folded version, showing the position of pages; also a book without printing made up to the correct number of pages in a particular paper stock for the purpose of weighing, designing the dust jacket, and generally seeing how the finished product will look

DUOTONE A high-quality halftone with a full tonal range made from two printings, either black and one other color, or black twice

DUPLEX STOCK Paper that has different finishes or colors on either side

DYELINE See DIAZO

DYE-SUBLIMATION PRINTS Color proofs produced by mixing vaporized dyes on the surface of the paper

EARMARKS Distinguishing features of a typeface used for identification, named after the ear of a lower-case g

EGGSHELL PAPER A smooth pressed type of book paper

EM The width of a letter M, or a square em-quad space, which is different for each typeface, unlike a PICA EM, which is ⅙ inch

EMBOSSING A finishing process producing an image in low relief

EMULSIFICATION What happens when water gets into the litho ink. Most litho inks are designed to accept some emulsification, but too much results in a wishy washy appearance

EMULSION SIDE The duller side of film, which can be scratched

EN The width of a letter N, half an em

EPS Encapsulated PostScript, a format for transferring drawings created in Illustrator and FreeHand, for example, into dtp programs

FACE See TYPEFACE

FAMILY A set of fonts related to a basic roman typeface, which may include italic and bold plus a whole spectrum of different "weights"

FEATHERING Ink spreading from the edges of type, caused by poor quality ink or paper

FILLERS Additives in papermaking that improve the properties of the stock, for example increasing bulk and preventing FEATHERING

FILLING IN When halftone dots or the bowls of letters such as a or b fill solid with ink

FILM High-contrast photographic film used to transfer the image to the plate; can be positive (the image looks the same as the mechanical) or negative (the white areas show black and vice versa)

FILM RECORDER Output device for making transparencies from an image created in the computer

FINAL Film containing all the pages and design elements assembled ready to make the plate

FINISHED ARTIST Person who makes a neat camera-ready mechanical from a designer's rough layout

FINISHING All the processes that convert printed sheets into folded and bound publications

FLAT All the film assembled by the stripper to make a 16- or 32-page plate

FLATBED A press that prints from flat plates rather than the curved ones required by ROTARY PRESSES

FLAT COLOR, MATCH COLOR, or **SPOT COLOR** A single printing of a Pantone color, printed solid or as tints, in register with the black

FLATPLAN A diagram showing the position of pages in a publication along with a brief description of their content, used mainly to identify full-color and flat-color sections

FLAT-TINT HALFTONE A black halftone printed over a tint of color, faking a DUOTONE

FLEXOGRAPHY (FLEXO) A form of relief printing, using fast drying inks and rubber or plastic plates on a rotary letterpress

FLOCCULATION An ink defect that produces a surface like orange peel, caused by pigment that is not properly dispersed in the VEHICLE

FLOPPED Laterally inverted – normally applied to halftones that have been stripped into film wrongly

FLOPPY DISC Magnetic medium for storing and archiving digital information and for carrying computer documents around, from the studio to the service bureau, for example

FLONG See MAT

FOLIO Page number, or a single sheet of a manuscript

FONT A complete set *in one size* of all the letters of the alphabet, with associated ligatures (joined letters), numerals, punctuation marks, and any other signs and symbols

FONT MASTERS A set of type designs in one or more sizes that are scaled (enlarged or reduced) to create all the intermediate sizes

FONT METRICS The information about horizontal spacing built into a typeface by its designer

FOOT The bottom margin of a page

FORE EDGE The margin of a page furthest away from the spine

FORME A locked-up chase in letterpress; also another name for a FLAT

FOUNTAIN The ink reservoir in letterpress, or the container for the solution that dampens the rollers of an offset litho press

FOUR-COLOR PROCESS Full-color printing in which colors are approximated by various percentages of the process colors: cyan, magenta, yellow, and black. A full-color image is separated by filters into four different films – one for each of the four process colors – and four plates are used for the printing

FRAME BUFFER Computer memory that holds the current image on the screen

FRAME GRABBER An input device that uses a television camera to capture a picture or three-dimensional object, or a video frame; it converts it into digital form readable by a computer program

FUGITIVE Inks that fade when exposed to light

FURNISH The liquid pulp that is converted into paper

GALLEY A typesetting proof for checking the setting before the type is made up into pages; they are generally long and thin

GANGING UP Grouping together several transparencies to be scanned together; also printing a group of different jobs on the same sheet of paper using a single plate

GATHERING See COLLATING

GHOSTING Printing fault of a repeated image appearing next to the correct image, caused by faulty imposition; also a dull image on the other side of the sheet – this happens when the printed image affects the drying and trapping of wet ink on the reverse

GOLDENROD Orange or yellow opaque masking paper used to make up a final

GOLDEN SECTION An aesthetically pleasing proportion with many examples in nature; the ratio is 34:21 or 8·1:5

GRAIN The orientation of fibers in paper, which lie in the direction of flow in a papermaking machine. Grain long means the grain is in the direction of the sheet's length. Grain short means the grain is in the direction of the sheet's width

GRAVURE or **PHOTOGRAVURE** An INTAGLIO PRINTING process in which the image is etched into the surface of a cylinder. The deeper the ink, the darker the tone

GRAY COMPONENT REPLACEMENT or **ACHROMATIC STABILIZATION** Removing percentages of cyan, magenta, and yellow that cancel each other out to produce neutral grays, and replacing them with a tint of black

GRAYSCALE MONITOR A computer screen that displays shades of gray, as well as black and white

GREEKING Gray lines that indicate the presence of type on a dtp screen; also the nonsense setting (usually Latin!) used by designers to show the position of type on a rough layout or dummy

GRID The underlying structure for a page layout as prescribed by the designer and usually preprinted onto layout sheets or boards

GRIPPER EDGE The edge of a sheet held by metal fingers in the press – a term used in imposition. The gripper margin is the allowance that avoids any damage by the grippers to the printed image

GUI (GRAPHICAL USER INTERFACE) What you see on the screen when you want to communicate with the program, the most famous of which is the WIMP interface of the Apple Macintosh, derived mostly from the Smalltalk project at Xerox's PARC. Other "standards" include Windows 3 for the PC and X-Windows for workstations

GUTTER The combined margin of a book or folder on each side of the spine; the margin on one side of the spine is called the BACK EDGE. The term gutter is also used for any vertical space, such as that between two columns

HAIRLINE RULE A rule thinner than ½ point

HALATION or **HALO EFFECT** When ink builds up around letters or dots, leaving the center lighter

HALF BINDING The spine, adjacent strips of the cover, and the triangles at the corners are bound in one material, maybe leather, and the rest of the book in a less expensive material

HALFTONE A continuous-tone image converted to line by turning it into a pattern of dots, either electronically, by laser, or by photographing it through a screen

HARDCOPY Something from a dtp system

that you can hold in your hand – usually a paper proof

HARD DISC Permanent magnetic memory, usually within the computer

HARDWARE The parts of a computer system that you can see and touch

HEAD The margin at the top of a page

HEADBAND A decorative feature added to a case-bound book at the top of the spine

HEAT-SET INK Web ink that is dried quickly by heat then chilled

HICKIES Imperfections in litho printing caused by any dry hard particles on the cylinder or blanket, also called fisheyes, bull's eyes, donuts, and Newton's rings

HINGE The crease in a book cover near the spine

HINTING In dtp, a method for changing the shapes of characters – especially those of small sizes – so that they look better on low-resolution printers

HLS (HUE, LUMINANCE, SATURATION) A method for specifying color; see CMYK

HOLDOUT The paper property that makes it resist the absorption of ink

HOLOGRAM A three-dimensional image created by laser photography, reproduced by hot-foil stamping or embossing onto reflective backed mylar

HOT-FOIL STAMPING Transferring a foil coating from a carrier roll of polyester to paper or cover board by means of a heated die

HOT-METAL SETTING Casting molten lead into molds to produce type for letterpress printing

HOUSE STYLE Standards of consistency concerning spelling and use of English (or any other language) as laid down by a particular publisher, or to be used within a particular publication

HUE The rainbow parameter of a color that distinguishes red, for example, from blue

HYPHENATION The division of words, usually between syllables, pairs of consonants or pairs of vowels

ICON A small picture on a computer screen representing an application, tool, or document

IMAGESETTER A high-resolution output device, producing typesetting or whole pages on bromide paper or film

IMPOSING TABLE In letterpress, the place where galleys are assembled

IMPOSITION The layout of pages such that after printing, folding, collating, and trimming, they will all end up in the correct order and the right way up

IMPRESSION The process of transferring ink from the plate to the paper during printing

IMPRESSION CYLINDER In an offset litho press, the cylinder that presses the paper against the blanket cylinder

INKJET PLOTTER An output device that creates an image by spraying tiny drops of ink onto paper; see also BUBBLEJET PLOTTER

INKJET PRINTS Color proofs produced digitally by an inkjet plotter

INKOMETER or **TACKOSCOPE** An instrument for measuring the tackiness of ink

INK PYRAMID In an offset litho press, the system of rollers that conveys ink to the plate

IN-LINE An in-line press has several single units arranged to print one color after another; in-line also describes a process, such as folding or gluing, that happens straight after the printing, in the same pass

INSERT Any printed material that is included between signatures or in the middle of a signature during binding. Material wrapped around a signature is called a "wrap". A loose insert is not attached to the "parent" publication and will fall out when it is shaken

INTAGLIO PRINTING A method in which the ink is contained in grooves below the surface of the plate and transferred to dampened paper by pressure

JOGGING Vibrating paper stock before trimming to bring all the edges into alignment

JUSTIFIED Type set with edges that are aligned both left and right. Justified setting requires hyphenation and variable spacing between words

KERNING Adjusting the spacing between pairs of letters, such as T and A, to improve the aesthetic appearance; see also TRACKING

KEY Black in four-color printing; see CMYK

KEYLINE The marks on a mechanical's overlay that indicate the position of tints, halftones, and bleeds. A keyline artist is a person who assembles the finished mechanical

KNIFE FOLDER A folding machine that uses a knife to force the sheet between two nip rollers

k–p DISTANCE The distance from the top of a letter k to the bottom of a letter p

LACQUER See VARNISHING

LAID A paper texture created on the Fourdrinier wire; it has a characteristic lined appearance

LAMINATION Coating paper or cover board with a clear film to add strength and gloss

LANDSCAPE The orientation of a page when the width is greater than the height

LASER PRINTER An output device in which black toner is attracted to an image on a drum that has been electrostatically charged by the action of a laser; the image is transferred to paper and fixed by heat

LAYDOWN SEQUENCE The sequence colors are printed – usually yellow, magenta, cyan, and finally black

LAY EDGE The left side of the sheet as it passes through the press

LEADING or **INTERLINE SPACING** The space between lines of type; in letterpress these were strips of lead

LEAVE EDGE The edge of a sheet opposite the GRIPPER EDGE

LETTERPRESS A RELIEF PRINTING process, in which ink is transferred from the raised surface of metal or wooden type directly onto paper

LETTERSET An indirect letterpress printing process, in which the image is first transferred to a blanket, and then onto the paper

LIGATURE Two or more letters, such as fi and ffl, joined together into one character

LINE Artwork in black (or any other single color) and white only, with no intermediate tones of gray, which will print without first being screened

LINE AND TONE COMBINATION A two-stage process combining the line and tone components of an illustration such as a pen and wash drawing

LINEN TESTER See LOUPE

LINES Measurement of a halftone screen, short for lines per inch; the higher the lines, the finer the screen

LINOTYPE A typesetting machine for letterpress in which a whole line of type (line o' type), or slug, is cast in one operation

LINTERS In papermaking, the fibers left on the cotton seed once the longer fibers for yarn-making have been removed

LINTING A printing problem caused by paper fibers that get onto the blanket, plate, or rollers of a press

LITERALS In proofreading, the spelling mistakes and transposition of letters caused by typing errors

LITHOGRAPHY A PLANOGRAPHIC PRINTING process in which greasy ink is transferred from the surface of a dampened plate or stone directly onto paper. OFFSET LITHOGRAPHY, usually shortened to offset litho, prints first onto a rubber or plastic blanket, and then onto the paper

LOUPE Designer's magnifying glass, also called a linen tester or eyeglass; used for checking color transparencies and halftones

LOW SPOT Loss of image caused by an indentation in the blanket

LUMINANCE See VALUE

MACHINE CODE The lowest level of computer language – lists of hexadecimal numbers

MACHINE FINISH (MF) Paper that has been calendered and is smoother and less bulky than EGGSHELL PAPER

MACHINE GLAZED (MG) Paper that has been dried against a highly polished cylinder and has one glossy side while the other remains relatively rough

MAGENTA The process color red; really more a purple

MAINFRAME A very large computer; not often seen in print production

MAKE-READY Setting up the press ready to print

MAKE-UP Assemble, position, and paste type and graphic elements to produce a mechanical or flat

MANUSCRIPT The original copy for typesetting, shortened to Ms

MARGINS The areas of white between the

text and the edges of the page

MARK UP Write instructions on text to define how it is to be set

MASK A shape cut out of opaque material such as Rubylith or Goldenrod to shield film from exposure to light

MASTER PROOF A clean and neat proof onto which the corrections and comments of all interested parties are collated

MAT or **FLONG** In letterpress, a *papier-mâché* mold taken from the FORME and used to make a STEREOTYPE; an abbreviation for MATRIX

MATCH COLOR See FLAT COLOR

MATCHPRINT A proprietary prepress proofing system from 3M

MATRIX A metal mold used to cast metal type; also any array or pattern of pixels, as in DITHERING; see also MAT

MATTE Dull finish, the opposite of glossy

MEASURE The width of a line of type – usually the column width, specified in pica ems

MECHANICAL Camera-ready artwork on boards, or all the line artwork for a page layout with the halftones marked "for position only," also called CAMERA-READY COPY. Mechanical separations are sets of overlays in register containing the artwork for flat color

MECHANICAL TINTS Patterns of dots simulating shades of gray or flat color added by the process blockmaker (Ben Day tints) or printer according to the designer's instructions

MENU In computing, a list of options or commands from which you are invited to choose

MESH COUNT A measure of the fineness of the mesh in the screens used in screenprinting – the number of threads per inch

MESH GRADE Thread thickness in the screens used in screenprinting

METALLIC INKS Inks that contain metal dust and produce a sheen when printed

MICROMETER An instrument for measuring very small distances; also one thousandth of a meter

MIL One thousandth of an inch

MINICOMPUTER A very large computer requiring an air-conditioned room of its own; minicomputers are smaller than mainframes but bigger than microcomputers or personal computers

MIPS (MILLIONS OF INSTRUCTIONS PER SECOND) Measure of the raw speed of a computer

MODEM A device that enables digital information to be sent down the telephone, short for modulator/demodulator

MOIRÉ Unwanted "basket-weave" effects caused by superimposed regular patterns, such as halftone dots. Screens must be set at angles that minimize moiré

MOLD-MADE PAPER Paper made by a semi-automatic process to resemble handmade paper

MONO, MONOCHROME Black-and-white, or the various tones of one color

MONOTYPE A letterpress typesetting machine that casts individual metal letters in a two-stage process

MOTTLE An uneven IMPRESSION caused by too much dampening water or the wrong choice of paper and ink

MOUSE In computing, a small pointing device used to control a cursor on the screen

M WEIGHT The weight of paper as measured per thousand sheets

NEGATIVE-WORKING PLATE Offset litho plate prepared by exposure to negative film

NETWORKING Linking computers together so that they can communicate with each other and share output devices such as laser printers

NEWSPRINT Inexpensive, rough, absorbent paper used for printing newspapers and magazines

NeXT CUBE A computer based on a 68040 chip, designed by Steve Jobs

OFFSET Abbreviation for offset lithography; also the same as setoff – when ink transfers from one printed sheet to the back of another

OFFSET LITHOGRAPHY or **OFFSET LITHO** A PLANOGRAPHIC PRINTING process in which greasy ink is transferred from the surface of a dampened plate first onto a rubber or plastic blanket, and then onto the paper

OFFSET PROCESS See OFFSET LITHOGRAPHY

ONE-UP Printing a single job on one plate. Quality is better controlled, but it is usually more economical to print two-up, i.e. two different jobs, or the same job in tandem, on one plate

OPACIMETER An instrument for measuring the opacity of paper

OPACITY The property of a paper affecting the show-through of printing from the other side of the sheet

OPERATING SYSTEM Behind-the-scenes computer software that takes care of the internal workings of the computer

OPI Open prepress interface, originally proposed by Aldus, which enables files from different programs to be used together

OPTICAL BRIGHTENERS Additives to paper that increase its brightness by glowing under the influence of ultraviolet light

ORIENTED POLYPROPYLENE (OPP) LAMINATION The standard book-jacket lamination film

ORPHANS A single word or a few words, usually less than a third the measure of the setting, forming a line of their own at the end of a paragraph; see also WIDOW

ORTHOCHROMATIC Film sensitive to the blue end of the spectrum used for line work – red records as black, and marks in light-blue pencil are invisible; see also PANCHROMATIC

OUT OF REGISTER The blurred effect that occurs when film separations or plates are misaligned

OVERLAY A sheet of acetate or trace over a photograph or in registration with a mechanical containing artwork for flat color, keylines, or instructions to the printer

OVERMATTER Setting or images that are excess to requirements, to be used in the next issue of a magazine, for example

OVERPRINT Color, usually black, printed over flat color

OVERRUNS or **RUN-ONS** Sheets printed beyond the quantity specified, to compensate for spoilage or for the client's own use

OZALID See BLUEPRINT and BROWNLINE

PAGEMAKER A page-layout program from Aldus

PAGE PROOF A proof showing type arranged on a page, along with folios, running headlines, captions, and sometimes the position of illustrations

PAGINATION The sequence of pages in a book or folder

PAINT PROGRAM or **PAINT SYSTEM** A computer program that stores the image on the screen as a bitmap; see also DRAW PROGRAM

PANCHROMATIC Film that records all colors equally, as opposed to ORTHOCHROMATIC, which does not "see" the blue end of the spectrum

PANTONE MATCHING SYSTEM (PMS) A widely used proprietary system for specifying flat color in percentages of 11 standard colors; coordinating papers and markers corresponding to Pantone colors can also be purchased

PAPER CREEP ALLOWANCE Allowing for the thickness of paper at the spine of a thick saddle-stitched publication by shifting the margins on the mechanical so that the margins remain consistent after the sheets are trimmed

PAPER CURL Wavy edges caused by the stack of paper having a lower moisture level than the surroundings, or tight edges caused by the stack having a higher moisture level

PASTE UP To cut and assemble typesetting, line art, and halftones onto board using gum or wax to produce a mechanical

PEN PLOTTER A point-to-point output device used mainly for engineering drawings; if equipped with a knife in place of the pen it can be used to cut stencils for screenprinting or vinyl letters for signs

PERFECT BINDING Binding trimmed single sheets of paper with glue to produce a book or magazine with a flat spine

PERFECTING PRESS A press that prints both sides of the sheet at the same time

PERFORATION Producing the tear-along lines on coupons or stamps, for example, by piercing with sharp metal strips

PERSONAL COMPUTER A stand-alone desktop computer; a PC is an IBM Personal Computer or a software-compatible system from a vendor such as Compaq

PHOTOGRAVURE See GRAVURE

PHOTOTYPESETTING or **PHOTOSETTING** A process in which type is set onto bromide paper or film by exposure of light through a matrix containing tiny negatives of the letters, or directly by the action of a laser beam

PICA or **PICA EM** A unit for measuring type equal to ⅙ inch, or 12 points; on a typewriter, the normal pitch of ten characters per inch

PI CHARACTERS Greek and mathematical signs, used with but not typically part of a font

PICKING Removal of some of the surface of paper during printing

PIGMENTS AND DYES Components of printing inks that give it color

PILING Sticking or caking of ink pigment on the blanket or plate

PIN REGISTER Accurate positioning system for color separations – both films and plates – with punched holes and corresponding pins

PITCH On typewriters, the number of characters per inch

PIXEL Pixel is short for picture element and refers to the dot on a computer display. The resolution (sharpness) of a raster display is measured by the number of pixels horizontally by the number of scan lines vertically, e.g. 1280 × 1024

PLANOGRAPHIC PRINTING Any process using a plate on which both the printing and non printing areas are on the same surface, for example, lithography

PLASTIC COMB A type of ring binding found on reports and manuals

PLATE A metal or plastic sheet with a photosensitive face onto which an image is chemically etched, either changing the characteristics of the surface as in LITHOGRAPHY, or cutting below the surface as in RELIEF or INTAGLIO PRINTING

PLATE CYLINDER In an offset litho press, the cylinder to which the plate is attached

PLATE-DAMPENING UNIT In offset litho, the system of rollers that dampens the plate before inking; see also FOUNTAIN

PLATEN A small letterpress that acts like a clamshell, bringing a flat plate and the paper together in an opening and closing motion, as opposed to a ROTARY PRESS

PMT Photomechanical transfer, a DIFFUSION TRANSFER process for enlarging or reducing line art; also called a BROMIDE

POINT A unit for measuring type equal to approximately 1⁄72 inch (exactly 1⁄72 inch in dtp), abbreviated pt; also a measure of paper bulk equivalent to one thousandth of an inch (a MIL)

PORTRAIT The orientation of a page when the height is greater than the width

POSITIVE-WORKING PLATE An offset litho plate prepared by exposure to positive film

POSTSCRIPT An outline description language for type developed by Adobe and licenced to suppliers such as Linotype, Monotype, Agfa, and AM Varityper. Type 1 PostScript fonts contain hinting and encryption; see also EPS and TRUETYPE

PREPRESS PROOF A proof taken directly from the film separations, to check that the color will print correctly

PRESS PROOF A proof taken from the plates that will be used to print the finished job, and on the specified paper stock, usually on a special proofing press

PRINTING-DOWN FRAME In offset litho, a device for holding the film and plate in contact during exposure to ultraviolet light

PRINT RUN The number of copies to be produced in one printing, also called the press run

PROCESS CAMERA A camera designed to enlarge or reduce artwork and mechanicals and to produce film positives and negatives

PROCESS COLORS The four colors – cyan (process blue), magenta (process red), yellow, and key (black) – used to approximate full-color artwork

PROGRESSIVES A set of proofs showing the four color separations printed in various combinations; also called Hollywoods or progs

PROOF Hardcopy that allows you to check the accuracy of setting, the position of design elements on a page, or the fidelity of color after separation

PROOFING PRESS A small press used to produce proofs

PROPORTIONAL SCALE See REPRODUCTION CALCULATOR

QUAD A square space in typesetting used as a unit of measurement, such as an em quad or en quad

QUARTER BINDING The spine and adjacent strips of the cover are bound in one material, maybe leather, and the rest of the sides in a less expensive material

RAM (RANDOM ACCESS MEMORY) Quick-access temporary memory in a computer containing the job in hand, in the form of chips

RANGED LEFT/RIGHT Ranged left is a method of setting type in which the type is aligned on the left-hand side and ragged on the right. Ranged right is ragged on the left and aligned on the right

RASTER A horizontal scan line on a computer screen or output device

REAM 500 sheets of paper

RECTO The front of a sheet of paper, or the right-hand page of a publication, opposite of VERSO

REFLECTED LIGHT Colors from an object or flat artwork, as opposed to TRANSMITTED LIGHT from a light source or transparency

REFLECTION COPY Any original art viewed by light reflecting from its surface, as opposed to TRANSMISSION COPY such as a 35mm slide

REGISTER or **REGISTRATION** Correct positioning of one color separation in relation to the others during printing. A register mark is a symbol used on copy and film to ensure accurate registration

RELIEF PRINTING A printing process, such as LETTERPRESS and FLEXOGRAPHY, in which ink lies on the raised surface of the plate but not in the grooves and is transferred to the paper by pressure

REPRODUCTION CALCULATOR or **PROPORTIONAL SCALE** A slide-rule type instrument for estimating the size of an illustration after reduction or enlargement

REPRODUCTION PROOF or **REPRO PROOF** A crisp proof on art paper of letterpress setting to be used on a mechanical

RESIST A substance used on plates for preventing the non-printing areas from etching

RESOLUTION A measure of the fineness and quality of an output device, usually measured in dots per inch (dpi) – the number of dots that can be placed end to end in a line an inch long; see also ADDRESSABILITY

RETOUCHING Modifying or correcting photographic images either manually with dye and airbrush, or electronically to a scanned image using a program such as PhotoShop or ColorStudio

REVERSED OUT When type is set in white against a black or flat color background

RGB (RED, GREEN, BLUE) A system for specifying color on a computer screen; see also CMYK

RIGHT-READING EMULSION DOWN (RRED) Film used for offset litho platemaking in which the image appears the correct way round when the film is viewed from the shiny (non-emulsion) side, also called wrong-reading emulsion up (WREU)

RIGHT-READING EMULSION UP (RREU) Film used for direct forms of platemaking, such as letterpress and flexography, in which the image appears the correct way round when the film is viewed from the dull emulsion side, also called wrong reading emulsion down (WRED)

RIP Raster image processor – a device that converts a PostScript file into a bitmap

RIVERS Unwanted space running vertically and diagonally in chunks of (mainly justified) type – to be avoided

ROLLING BALL A pointing device that controls the position of a cursor on the computer screen

ROM (READ ONLY MEMORY) Permanent unalterable computer memory in the form of chips

ROMAN Normal type, as opposed to italic or bold, abbreviated rom; also a kind of type with serifs, such as Times New Roman

ROTARY PRESS A press that uses a cylinder as its printing surface, as opposed to a FLATBED or PLATEN press

ROTOGRAVURE See GRAVURE

ROUNDING AND BACKING (R & B) Putting a rounded shape into the spine of a book-block, and a joint below the shoulder

RUBYLITH A red transparent masking material

RUNAROUND Type set around a photograph or other design element, deviating from the normal measure
RUNNING HEADS Headlines that appear in the same (or a symmetrical) position on every page of a publication except where chapter titles occur or if illustrations outside the grid area displace them
SADDLE STITCHING A binding method using wire staples along the fold of the publication
SANS SERIF Type without SERIFS
SATURATION or **INTENSITY** A measure of the color's position in the range from neutral gray to fully saturated, or bright, color
SCALING Enlarging or reducing – usually applied to an image – and calculating the percentage of enlargement or reduction so as to anticipate the space it will occupy on a layout
SCANNER An electronic device used to convert transparencies into halftone separations
SCATTER PROOFS Proofs with several illustrations printed randomly together on one sheet, not in their correct positions on the page
SCREEN A piece of glass or plastic used to convert continuous-tone copy into a halftone; also the number of dots, expressed in lines per inch
SCREENPRINTING A printing process using a stencil supported on a mesh or screen; ink is forced through the open mesh but is prevented from reaching the non-image areas of the paper by the stencil
SCUFFING A problem in packaging design, where print is more likely to receive rough handling; scuffproof ink, lamination, or a coat of varnish is the solution
SCUMMING A printing problem caused when the plate accepts ink where it shouldn't
SECTION SEWING A binding method in which signatures are sewn through the spine with thread before being casebound
SELF COVER A cover printed on the same paper stock as the rest of the publication, using the same plate as pages from the inside
SEPARATION Film in register relating to one of the four process colors; also artwork or film in register relating to flat color
SERIES A complete range of sizes in the same typeface
SERIF The mark that terminates the ends of the letters in some typefaces
SERVICE BUREAU A place where you can rent expensive equipment by the hour, or have laser prints, bromides, and film output from an imagesetter from your floppy disc at a price per sheet
SET The width of a letter
SETOFF or **OFFSET** This occurs when the wet image on a sheet of paper prints onto the paper above or below it in the pile. Anti-setoff spray can be used to separate each sheet from the next by a fine layer of particles
SET SOLID Type set without leading, for example 10/10pt
SET-UP TIME The time it takes to make-ready and set up the press to run your job
SHEETFED A press taking single sheets of paper
SHEETWISE A form of imposition using one plate to print the front of a sheet, and another to print the back
SHINGLING See PAPER CREEP ALLOWANCE
SHOW-THROUGH or **STRIKE-THROUGH** Being able to see through a sheet of paper to the printed impression on the other side
SIDE BEARINGS The space allocated on either side of a letter by its designer to stop adjacent letters from touching and to achieve an aesthetically pleasing appearance when words are set
SIDE STABBING A form of binding in which wire staples are inserted near the spine from front to back
SIGNATURE Several pages for a book, printed from the same plate and arranged so that they can be folded and trimmed to make a section, usually of 16 pages. A BACKSTEP MARK on the spine shows how several signatures are to be arranged so they bind in the correct sequence
SILKSCREEN See SCREENPRINTING
SIZE In papermaking, substances added to the furnish to make the paper less absorbent, which can also be coated or sprayed onto the web at a later stage of the process at the size press; sizing can also be used to mean SCALING
SKEWING A printing problem that occurs when paper, blanket, and cylinder are not in proper contact
SLUG A line of letterpress type from a LINOTYPE machine, or a piece of metal used for word spacing
SLURRING Distortion of the image, with dots appearing elongated or smeared, caused by too much ink or slippage of stock
SLURRY In papermaking, fibers with lots of water
SNOWFLAKING In offset litho, a problem of water droplets in the litho ink that spoil solid areas; in gravure the effect is caused by inadequate pressure which prevents the paper from taking the ink from one or more cells
SOFTWARE The list of thousands of instructions that turn a general-purpose computer into a machine for a particular purpose, such as desktop publishing
SORTS In letterpress, individual pieces of metal type
SPINE The bound edge of a book or magazine, where the fold is
SPIRAL-BOUND A method of binding used for calendars, cookery books, and manuals, using a wire spiral inserted through holes in the pages
SPLIT FOUNTAIN Printing two colors on an offset press by using one color at one end of the fountain and another at the other end – the colors blend in the middle
SPOILAGE Wasted printed sheets that are discarded
SPOT COLOR See FLAT COLOR
SPOT VARNISH Applying patches of varnish, often to halftones
SPREADING An enlarging of the image caused by too much ink, or too much pressure between blanket and plate
STANDARD LIGHTING CONDITIONS A light source with a color temperature of 5000 Kelvin
STANDARD VIEWING CONDITIONS An area to view color proofs, surrounded by neutral gray and illuminated by STANDARD LIGHTING CONDITIONS
STARVATION GHOSTING An unwelcome effect that results in uneven printing, and is due to some extent to the placement of dense black elements in certain positions on the plate
STENCIL PRINTING A printing process, such as **SCREENPRINTING**, using a stencil supported on a mesh or screen; ink is forced through the open mesh but is prevented from reaching the non-image areas of the paper by the stencil
STEP-AND-REPEAT A method for copying film, so that two or more of the same job can be printed from one plate
STEREOTYPE or **STEREO** A letterpress plate made by casting lead in a *papier-mâché* mold (a MAT or flong) taken from the FORME. It can be flat for flatbed presses or curved for rotary machines
STET A proofreading mark meaning reinstate, or "let it stand," i.e. print what was there originally
STICKING or **BLOCKING** So much SETOFF that the sheets stick together
STREAM FEEDER A mechanism on high-speed sheetfed presses that presents sheets to the rollers overlapping slightly
STRIKE-ON SETTING See COLD-METAL SETTING
STRIKE-THROUGH See SHOW-THROUGH
STRIPPING IN Inserting halftones on film into the film made from a mechanical. A stripper is a person who assembles film into the final
STYLE SHEET A document that sets out the specifications for a publication or series of publications, listing such things as the typeface, size, leading of body text, headlines, and captions
SUBSTRATE Any sheet material to be printed – paper, board, plastic, or another substance. Also the carrier material in film, for example, onto which a layer of emulsion is deposited
SUPER-CALENDERING Smoothing paper by pressing it between highly polished cylinders, done off the machine
SURPRINT Superimposing type onto a tint of the same color – they share the same film and are printed together
SWATCH BOOK A book of tear-off color samples; the most commonly used come from Pantone

SYSTEM A catch-all term meaning all the computer equipment you need to make things work (as in "the system's down"); also the operating system (as in System 7); or a set of software tools (as in a dtp system)

TACK The adhesive property of an ink

TAILBAND A decorative feature added to a casebound book at the bottom of the spine

TAIL-END HOOK When solid areas near the back edge of a sheet make it curl down, caused by paper that adheres to the blanket too tightly as it is pulled off by the delivery grippers because the ink is too tacky

THERMAL-TRANSFER PLOTTER An output device that prints by "ironing" colored wax onto paper by the action of heat

THERMAL-TRANSFER PRINTS Color proofs produced by melting colored waxes onto paper

THERMOGRAPHY Creating a raised impression by using a heat-treated resinous powder

THERMOJET PLOTTER A form of inkjet printer which sprays melted plastic onto the paper, also known as a phase-change inkjet

THREAD-SEALING A combination of some of the features of perfect binding and section sewing, but no thread runs between sections

TIFF Tagged Image File Format, a protocol for dealing with scanned photographs in dtp programs

TINT Shades of a flat color created by patterns of dots similar to halftones, specified as a percentage of the solid color

TINTING A printing problem of pigment finding its way into the fountain, discoloring the background

TIP IN A page-size insert glued to the edge of a SIGNATURE

TIP ON A small insert glued to the surface of a page, such as a coupon

TOOL A facility in a computer program that makes something happen – a circle tool, for example allows you to draw circles in different ways; tools are usually represented by ICONS

TRACKING Adjusting the spacing between all letters, as opposed to KERNING, which only adjusts the space between pairs of letters; also, when several colored images are printed in a row and inking becomes uneven as a result

TRANSPARENCY A color slide, usually either 35mm, 5in by 4in, or 10in by 8in, so-called TRANSMISSION COPY

TRANSMISSION COPY Copy, such as transparencies and film positives, viewed by TRANSMITTED LIGHT

TRANSMITTED LIGHT Colors from a light source or a transparency, as opposed to REFLECTED LIGHT from a print or flat artwork

TRAP A small nick in the design of letters to allow for ink spread, especially around junctions

TRAPPING Creating an overlap between areas of flat color to compensate for any misregistration – usually the lighter color overlaps the darker; also any area of color overlapping another

TRIM AND CENTER MARKS Indications of where paper sheets are to be trimmed and folded; they mark out the finished page area

TRUETYPE An outline description format from Apple and Microsoft which rivals POSTSCRIPT

TURNKEY SYSTEM A packaged and integrated assembly of hardware, software, and support. Turnkey suppliers buy in equipment from third parties and repackage or "badge engineer" the components, perhaps adding some proprietary go-faster boards as well as their own software, before passing on the thoroughly tested value-added system to the end user

TWO-UP See ONE-UP

TYPEFACE The design of a font

TYPE SPECIFICATION A list of all the typefaces, sizes, and leading to be used for body type, headlines, captions, and so on, in a publication or series of publications; see also STYLE SHEET

UNDERCOLOR ADDITION (UCA) Adding a tint of process color to add density to a black

UNDERCOLOR REMOVAL (UCR) Reducing the amount of color in areas of shadows, to save ink and improve trapping

UNITS Letters of different widths in a typeface are allocated different numbers of units in accordance with a scheme that is devised by the typographer and the type foundry and dependent on the output process being used

VALUE OR LUMINANCE The parameter of color describing the lightness or darkness, changed by adding black or white to a particular hue

VARNISHING Coating areas of a page with a colorless varnish or lacquer to improve gloss on halftones, for example

VEHICLE The component of a printing ink that carries and binds the pigment

VELOX A halftone on BROMIDE paper that can be pasted onto a mechanical and used for undemanding printing

VERSO The back of a sheet of paper, or the left-hand page of a publication, opposite of RECTO

VGA (VIDEO GRAPHICS ARRAY) Developed by IBM for the PS/2 computer. Its standard resolution is 640 × 480 pixels, extendible to 1024 × 768, and it can display 256 colors from a palette of 256k

VIGNETTE A halftone that fades to nothing around the edges

VIRUS A pernicious and self-replicating piece of mischief that can cause havoc in a computer, introduced on floppy discs of dubious origin

VISCOSITY The amount of flow and tack in an ink

WATERMARK A symbol or mark manufactured into paper which can be seen when the sheet is held to the light

WEB A continuous roll of paper used on web-fed presses, cut into sheets after printing

WET-ON-WET One color is still wet as another is printed

WIDOW A single word or part of a word from the end of a paragraph left at the top of a new column or page; see also ORPHANS

WIMP Windows, icons, mouse, and pull-down menus (or windows, icons, menus, and pointing device), the original Mac GUI with which the user tells the computer what to do by pointing and clicking at icons (little pictures) and menu items (lists of available options) on the screen using a mouse or other pointing device

WINDOW A transparent hole in a negative awaiting a halftone to be stripped in; also an active and independent area of a computer screen

WIRE COMB A form of spiral binding used for reports, cookery books, and manuals

WOODFREE Chemical woodpulp for papermaking

WOODPULP Wood that has been debarked and separated into fibers for papermaking, either by grinding (mechanical woodpulp) or by cooking in chemicals (chemical or woodfree woodpulp)

WORK-AND-TUMBLE An imposition scheme in which both sides of a job can be printed, in two passes, by a single plate: one side is printed, then the sheet is turned head-over-heels so that the gripper edge changes ends

WORK-AND-TURN An imposition scheme in which both sides of a job can be printed, in two passes, by a single plate: one side is printed, then the sheet is turned sideways so that the gripper edge remains the same

WORKSTATION A type of networkable computer, more powerful than a personal computer, made by vendors such as Sun and Silicon Graphics

WOVE A paper texture introduced on the Fourdrinier wire; it has a characteristic woven appearance (or sometimes no detectable texture); see also LAID

WRONG-READING EMULSION DOWN (WRED) See RIGHT-READING EMULSION UP (RREU)

WRONG-READING EMULSION UP (WREU) See RIGHT-READING EMULSION DOWN (RRED)

X-HEIGHT The height of a letter x in a particular typeface – a typographic measurement that ignores the height of the ascenders and descenders

XEROGRAPHY A copying process using black toner attracted to an image on an electrostatically charged drum; the toner is transferred to paper and fixed by heat

XPRESS A page-layout program from Quark

Customs of the Trade for the Manufacture of Books

Prepress, platemaking, printing, and binding

(a) Litho plates made by the printer are the property of the printer and may be destroyed after completion of printing (unless otherwise agreed with the publisher).

(b) Both film and photoset material used for litho platemaking become the property of the publisher when payment has been made in full. Film is usually held without storage charge for two years after invoice. Before making a storage charge for film, the printer should offer the publisher an opportunity to make his own storage arrangement. A charge to recover removal costs may be made for any film transferred, but it will be the printer's responsibility to check that the film is complete before despatch. All charges should be agreed with the publisher before implementation.

(c) Some film is produced by plate projection systems and cannot be processed without separate coded instructions, either on disc or in the form of magnetic cards. Where such instructions are individual to the work in question, rather than forming part of a more general database, these are also considered to be the publisher's property.

(d) Where offset printing is ordered separately from composition, the printer's responsibility is limited to reproducing the image supplied to him. However, any technical or other defect noticed by the printer in the material thus supplied should be brought to the publisher's attention as soon as possible.

(e) Estimates usually provide that materials, when supplied by the customer, including artwork, reproduction copy, tapes, film, plates, paper and binding materials shall be suitable for their purpose. Provided the publisher has been given adequate forewarning of cost, the printer or binder may charge for any additional work (such as retouching, film spotting, excess blanket-washing, paper conditioning, handling pre-printed covers) incurred when materials are found during production to be inconsistent with the standards on which the estimates were based. Where it is not practical for such warning to be given, the publisher should be informed without delay and remedial costs passed on.

(f) Final intermediates used in the production of work for a publisher should not be destroyed or erased without the written agreement of the publisher, but the publisher should not expect the printer to store items indefinitely. The publisher is entitled to remove any such material on payment of appropriate handling charges.

(g) It is normally assumed that publisher's property (e.g. artwork, photographs, the property of third parties supplied by the publisher etc.) is held and worked on by the printer/binder at the publisher's risk. The printer/binder should, however, exercise great care in handling and storing such property and if it is damaged before the production process is completed, the question of restitution should be the subject of negotiation between the parties. Camera ready copy, artwork, photographs etc. are normally returned to the publisher upon completion of manufature unless otherwise agreed and should not be destroyed without the written agreement of the publisher.

(h) To avoid the possibility of subsequent disagreement, printing and binding orders should always be comprehensive, specifying precisely the materials the printer/binder is to use, and include the delivery date required and agreed price where appropriate.

(i) If a manufacturer folds more sheets than are covered by the publisher's initial instructions, he does so at his own risk. However, it is open to him to negotiate with the publisher to recover his folding costs if the sheets are then sold or bound.

(j) In the case of multi-volume sets, where individual volumes are not available separately, the manufacturer should charge for the production of complete sets only. Any surplus copies of individual volumes should be referred to the publisher for mutual agreement as to disposal.

(k) A storage charge may be proposed by the binder for any sheets, covers, bound stock and other material belonging to the publisher and kept on his behalf. A schedule of such items should be made to the publisher before any storage charge is made, and an opportunity given to the publisher to give disposal instruction.

(l) Incidental imperfections. It is the responsibility of the printer or binder to make good incidental imperfections or, should this be impractical or unduly costly, he may opt to offer the publisher financial compensation as an alternative, on the basis of a fully annotated title page. This is intended to reflect the full printing and binding cost of the book and is customarily set as 25 percent of the published price; it is, however, accepted that it is open to the manufacturer to negotiate alternative arrangements with publishers of mass market paperbacks or specialised academic works with an extended stockholding life or where it is felt exceptional considerations apply.

(m) Edition imperfections. It is recognised that when substantial numbers of an edition are delivered in a faulty condition, and the fault lies with the supplier, the precise remedy must be a matter for individual negotiation between publisher and printer or binder.

(n) It is the responsibility of the supplier despatching goods to ensure that accurate documentation is sent with them with a copy to the publisher.

(o) Covers. If the printer/binder has a specific manner in which he wants covers printed on a sheet, he should make it clear at the outset. Where covers are supplied to the binder it is the publisher's responsibility to ensure that imposition is correct. This might include the number of copies on a sheet, margins between covers for two-up binding etc.

Ownership, insurance, and liability

(a) Ownership of the work will normally pass to the publisher at the moment of payment in full, but a different arrangement may be mutually agreed between publisher and manufacturer.

(b) The publisher and the typesetter/printer/binder is each normally responsible for the insurance of his own property, including property in transit. The publisher's responsibility for the insurance of work done is from the earlier of: (1.) work delivered to the publisher, or to his nominated delivery address; (2.) payment in full by the publisher. In this way the publisher insures the work from the moment when he has an insurable interest in it. The publisher is responsible for the insurance of material stored at his request in whatever form. The typesetter is responsible in the case of a failure or loss of work in progress and should insure against such a likelihood. The value for insurance purposes should cover the cost of replacement of tapes and discs to the same stage as when they were lost or damaged. The publisher should insure for any consequential loss as a result of loss or damage. The typesetter will not be responsible for any consequential loss.

(c) For insurance purposes the publisher's property on the supplier's premises includes all materials supplied by the publisher such as manuscripts, tapes and discs, artwork, photographs, transparencies, camera-ready copy, film, paper and, where a trade binder is used, printed sheets and printed covers that have been paid for by the publisher.

(d) The typesetter/printer/binder is entitled not to proceed with any work which, in his opinion, is or may be of an illegal or libellous nature, or an infringement of third party rights.

Materials

(a) Storage. As part of his service the printer holds publisher's white paper free of charge for 60 days pending instructions to print. If he is required to hold it for a

longer period he may implement a storage charge, unless it is agreed that special circumstances exist, such as stock papers which are delivered and used in regular quantities.
(b) Advice Procedure. Paper supplied by the publisher should be advised to the printer before delivery and the advice note should specify the publisher and the title for which it is intended. On receipt of the paper, the printer should send the publisher an out-turn sheet quoting full details of the delivery and, if necessary, a report. Sheets and other goods provided by, or on behalf of, the publisher are not normally counted or checked when received, but the supplier should advise the publisher of any apparent shortages or damage as soon as discovered.
(c) Paper supplied on reel. Before ordering, the publisher should ask the printer to specify the type of reel centre required, maximum diameter of reel and type of splice, and any other special requirements. The publisher should instruct the paper supplier to ensure that the end wrapping is flat, any joins are clearly marked, that a specification giving full details of each consignment, including the actual metre length per reel, is sent when the reels are delivered, and that delivery dates are arranged with the printer. The printer's spoilage is calculated on a length basis not on a weight basis. Reels are not checked when supplied, but the printer should advise the publisher of any shortage or damage as soon as possible.
(d) Spoilage allowances. Where the publisher supplies the paper, the printer must specify in his estimate the quantity and sheet or reel size of paper required including an allowance for printing and binding spoilage. It must be emphasised that this allowance should always be mutually agreed beforehand, particularly in the case of recycled or thin papers where higher than normal allowances may be required. Any use of material in excess of the specified quantity should be notified to the publisher and the cost borne by the printer, unless it is an agreed paper fault or change to the specification.
(e) Binding. If the binding is to be done in quantities smaller than the print run, it is the publisher's responsibility to allow for the extra binder's spoilage required, if necessary by increasing the print order. Each individual binding order will necessitate a spoilage allowance. For the first and last sections the publisher may need to allow the binder more spoilage than for the rest of the book.

General
A Outwork Certain elements of the work may have to be sub-contracted because the supplier is not equipped to execute them. Where a supplier needs to sub-contract work which he would normally do, he should consult his customer, where practical, before doing so. During the period of outwork the supplier retains sole responsibility for any costs incurred, the quality of the work, the production of the quantity of copies, and completion of the work by the date previously agreed; and for insurance in accordance with Section 3. A separate invoice must not be submitted, unless agreed in advance with the Publisher.

B Schedules and delays (a) A production schedule, where timing is critical, should be submitted and agreed in writing, based on a realistic assessment of the circumstances at the time. Any delay on either side should be notified to the other parties concerned as soon as it is foreseen, and the remainder of the schedule re-negotiated. If the manufacturer has reserved machinery time for a particular order at the customer's request and the order is postponed, then the customer and manufacturer should make every effort to find other suitable work to fill the reserved time. If neither party can find such suitable work, it is open to the manufacturer to seek to negotiate appropriate compensation.
(b) A broken promise of delivery by an agreed date does not constitute a breach of contract if it is caused by force majeure (as generally recognised in the printing industry) nor, if caused in any other way, does it involve a penalty unless: (1.) a penalty for any delay in completion has been agreed; and (2.) the customer has not himself defaulted on any dates in the agreed schedule for the work.

C Cancellation Orders can only be cancelled on terms that compensate the supplier for any costs incurred for any material purchased or services performed, unless the publisher can demonstrate that the supplier is responsible for the grounds of cancellation.

D Terms of payment Terms of payment, including any special arrangements such as stage payments and the charging of interest on overdue amounts etc., should be agreed between supplier and customer before the order is placed. In the absence of such prior agreement, payment will be in 30 days. The following are examples of current practice:
(a) Typesetting is customarily invoiced on completion of the contracted process. However, where a single supplier is responsible for composition and machining, the invoice may be rendered for the two processes if agreed in advance.
(b) Interim payments may, in certain circumstances, be negotiated for composition, machining or binding.
(c) It is normal practice to allow a plus or minus tolerance of 5 percent on the ordered quantity of books. If all books are bound in the first instance the invoiced quantity printed should be the same as the invoiced quantity bound when produced by the same supplier. If shortages occur, the publisher reserves the right to invoice the printer or binder for the excess use of materials (if supplied by the publisher) relative to that shortfall. It is a matter for negotiation between manufacturer and publisher as to how variations from these tolerances are dealt with.
If it is important that the publisher receives the exact number of copies ordered or not less than the exact number, this should be made clear when the quotation is sought and clearly stated on the order. This usually occurs with short run printing.
(d) Except where covered by prior agreement, an invoice for composition may be rendered 60 days after completion of any proofing stage, where the proofs have not been returned to the supplier for further work to be done.
(e) Where materials are supplied by the printer, the charge for such materials shall be invoiced as part of the printing or binding as appropriate. Paper may only be invoiced in advance by the printer by prior agreement.
(f) The existence of an unresolved query on the invoices does not release the publisher from his obligation to pay the parts of the invoice not under query.
(g) VAT will be charged where appropriate whether or not it has been included in the estimate.

(Extracts)

Printing trade customs

1. **Quotation** A quotation not accepted within 60 days is subject to review. All prices are based on material costs at the time of quotation.

2. **Orders** Orders regularly placed, verbal or written, cannot be cancelled except upon terms that will compensate printer against loss incurred in reliance of that order.

3. **Experimental work** Experimental or preliminary work performed at the customer's request will be charged for at current rates and may not be used until the printer has been reimbursed in full for the amount of the charges billed.

4. Creative work Creative work, such as sketches, copy, dummies and all preparatory work developed and furnished by the printer, will remain his exclusive property and no use of the same shall be made, nor any ideas obtained therefrom be used, except upon compensation to be determined by the printer, and not expressly identified as included in the selling price.

5. Condition of copy Upon receipt of original copy or manuscript, should it be evident that the condition of the copy differs from that which had been originally described and consequently quoted, the original quotation shall be rendered void and a new quotation issued.

6. Preparatory materials Working mechanical art, type, negatives, positives, flats, plates and other items when supplied by the printer, shall remain his exclusive property unless otherwise agreed in writing.

7. Alterations Alterations represent work performed in addition to the original specifications. Such additional work shall be charged at current rates and be supported with documentation upon request.

8. Prepress proofs Prepress proofs shall be submitted with original copy. Corrections are to be made on "master set," returned "OK" or "OK with corrections," and signed by customer. If revised proofs are desired, request must be made when proofs are returned. Printer cannot be held responsible for errors under any or all of the following conditions: if the work is printed per customer's OK; if changes are communicated verbally; if customer has not ordered proofs; if the customer has failed to return proofs with indication of changes; or if the customer has instructed printer to proceed without submission of proofs.

9. Press proofs Unless specifically provided in printer's quotation, press proofs will be charged for at current rates. An inspection sheet of any form can be submitted for customer approval, at no charge, provided customer is available at the press during the time of make-ready. Lost press time due to customer delay, or customer changes and corrections, will be charged at current rates.

10. Color proofing Because of differences in equipment, processing, proofing substrates, paper, inks, pigments and other conditions between color proofing and production pressroom operations, a reasonable variation in color between color proofs and the completed job shall constitute acceptable delivery.

11. Overruns and underruns Overruns or underruns not to exceed ten percent on quantities ordered, or the percentage agreed upon, shall constitute acceptable delivery. Printer will bill for actual quantity delivered within this tolerance. If customer requires guaranteed exact quantities, the percentage tolerance must be doubled.

12. Customer's property The printer will maintain fire, extended coverage, vandalism, malicious mischief and sprinkler leakage insurance on all property belonging to the customer, while such property is in the printer's possession; printer's liability for such property shall not exceed the amount recoverable from such insurance. Customer's property of extraordinary value shall be insured through mutual agreement.

13. Delivery Unless otherwise specified, the price quoted is for single shipment, without storage, F.O.B. local customer's place of business or F.O.B. printer's platform for out-of-town customers. Proposals are based on continuous and uninterrupted delivery of complete order, unless specifications distinctly state otherwise. Charges related to delivery from customer to printer, or from customer's supplier to printer, are not included in any quotations unless specified. Special priority pickup or delivery service will be provided at current rates upon customer's request. Materials delivered from customer or his suppliers are verified with delivery ticket as to cartons, packages or items shown only. The accuracy of quantities indicated on such tickets cannot be verified and printer cannot accept liability for shortage based on supplier's tickets. Title for finished work shall pass to the customer upon delivery to carrier at shipping point or upon mailing of invoices for finished work, whichever occurs first.

14. Production schedules Production schedules will be established and adhered to by customer and printer, provided that neither shall incur any liability or penalty for delays due to state of war, riot, civil disorder, fire, labor trouble, strikes, accidents, energy failure, equipment breakdown, delays of suppliers or carriers, action of government or civil authority and acts of God or other causes beyond the control of customer or printer. Where production schedules are not adhered to by the customer, final delivery date(s) will be subject to renegotiation.

15. Customer-furnished materials Paper stocks, inks, camera copy, film, color separations and other customer-furnished material shall be manufactured, packed and delivered to printer's specifications. Additional costs due to delays or impaired production caused by specification deficiencies shall be charged to customers.

16. Terms Payment shall be whatever was set forth in the quotation or invoice unless otherwise provided in writing. Claims for defects, damages or shortages must be made by the customer in writing within a period of 15 days after delivery of all or any part of the order. Failure to make such a claim within the stated period shall constitute irrevocable acceptance and an admission that they fully comply with terms, conditions and specifications.

17. Liability Printer's liability shall be limited to stated selling price of any defective goods, and shall in no event include special or consequential damages, including profits (or profits lost). As security for payment of any sum due or to become due under terms of any agreement, printer shall have the right, if necessary, to retain possession of and shall have a lien on all customer property in printer's possession, including work in progress and finished work. The extension of credit or the acceptance or guarantee of payment shall not affect such security interest and lien.

18. Indemnification The customer shall indemnify and hold harmless the printer from any and all loss, cost, expense and damages (including court costs and reasonable attorney fees) on account of any and all manner of claims, demands, actions and proceedings that may be instituted against the printer on grounds alleging that the said printing violates any copyrights or any proprietary right of any person, or that it contains any matter that is libelous or obscene or scandalous, or invades any person's right to privacy or other personal rights, except to the extent that the printer contributed to the matter. The customer agrees, at the customer's own expense, to promptly defend and continue the defense of any such claim, demand, action or proceeding that may be brought against the printer, provided that the printer shall promptly notify the customer with respect thereto, and provided further that the printer shall give to the customer such reasonable time as the exigencies of the situation may permit in which to undertake and continue the defense thereof.

Further reading

Nancy Aldrich-Ruenzel and **John Fennell (eds)**. *Designer's Guide to Typography*. Oxford: Phaidon, 1991. A collection compiled from articles first published in *Step-by-Step Graphics* magazine, including contributions from Neville Brody and April Greiman.

Nancy Aldrich-Ruenzel (ed). *Designer's Guide to Print Production*. New York: Watson-Guptill, 1990. Another collection compiled from articles first published in *Step-by-Step Graphics* magazine.

Fernand Baudin. *How Typography Works (and Why it is Important)*. London: Lund Humphries, 1989. An idiosyncratic handwritten text based on a series of blackboard lectures by the Belgian graphic designer.

D. E. Bisset et al. *The Printing Ink Manual*. London: Northwood, 1961 (and subsequent editions). Everything you need to know about ink.

Alison Black. *Typefaces for Desktop Publishing: a User Guide*. London: ADT Press, 1990. A cold look at what to expect in the way of type quality from a dtp system.

Rob Carter. *American Typography Today*. New York: Van Nostrand Reinhold, 1989. A guide to the work of contemporary American typographers, with a chronology of other important typographers.

David Collier. *Collier's Rules for Desktop Design and Typography*. Wokingham, England: Addison-Wesley, 1991. A lively and graphic look at dtp design by a former partner of DeCode design.

James Craig. *Production for the Graphic Designer*. New York: Watson-Guptill, 1976 (revised edition 1990). An updated version of Craig's definitive work.

James Craig and **William Bevington**. *Working with Graphic Designers*. New York: Watson-Guptill, 1989. Graphic design explained to lay people.

Terence Dalley (ed). *The Complete Guide to Illustration and Design*. London: Phaidon, 1980. Well illustrated guide to the practise of illustration and graphic design.

April Greiman. *Hybrid Imagery*. London: ADT Press, 1990. Lots of computerized trickery from the doyenne of the West Coast avant garde.

Steven Heller and **Anne Fink**. *Low Budget High-Quality Design*. New York: Watson-Guptill, 1990. Lots of tips on how to produce effective graphics on a low budget.

Dard Hunter. *Papermaking: the History and Technique of an Ancient Craft*. New York: Dover, 1943. An authoritative history of papermaking.

Terry Jeavons and **Michael Beaumont**. *An Introduction to Typography*. London: Quintet/The Apple Press, 1990. A colorful illustrated book on all kinds of type.

Ruari McLean. *The Thames and Hudson Manual of Typography*. London: Thames and Hudson, 1980. An authoritative history of typography from an eminent typographer and designer.

Philip B. Meggs. *History of Graphic Design*. New York: Van Nostrand Reinhold, 1983. A definitive and well illustrated history of graphic design through the ages.

John Miles. *Design for Desktop Publishing*. London: Gordon Fraser, 1987. Straightforward guide to the fundamentals of layout, for non-designers, from a partner of Banks and Miles.

John Peacock et al. *The Print and Production Manual*. London: Blueprint, 1990 (5th edition). Dry but exhaustive manual for printers.

Christopher Perfect and **Gordon Rookledge**. *Rookledge's International Typefinder*. London: Sarema Press, 1990. A useful encyclopedia of typefaces along with their identifying earmarks, recently revised by Phil Baines.

Erik Spiekermann. *Rhyme & Reason: a Typographic Novel*. Berlin: H. Berthold AG, 1987. A beautifully made treatise on typography in the style of *Tristram Shandy*.

Other sources of information

It is not possible to list here the names and addresses of all the suppliers and manufacturers of graphic design products worldwide. To begin collecting type specimens, paper samples, and other reference materials, the first port of call should always be your local friendly graphic design or art supplies store, where you should be able to obtain samples of most products. Second, take the industry magazines (a list is given here) and look out for advertisements offering samples on receipt of a cut-out coupon.

Magazines and journals

USA

Art Direction, Trade Publications Inc., NY

Communication Arts, 410 Sherman Avenue, Palo Alto, CA 94303

Design Quarterly, Walker Art Center, Vineland Place, Minneapolis, MN 55403

Desktop Communications, 48 East 43rd Street, NY 10017

Emigré, 48 Shattuck Square, 175 Berkeley, CA 94704–1140

Graphic Design USA, Kaye Publications, 120 E 56th Street, NY 10022

Graphis, 141 Lexington Avenue, NY 10016

How, 1507 Dana Avenue, Cincinnati, OH 45207

MacWorld, 501 Second Avenue, San Francisco, CA 94107

Print, 104 5th Avenue, NY 10011

Publish! 501 Second Avenue, San Francisco, CA 94107

Seybold Report on Desktop Publishing, 428 East Baltimore Pike, PO Box 644, Media, PA 19063

Step-by-Step Graphics, 6000 North Forest Park Drive, Peoria, IL 61614–3592

U & lc, 216 East 45th Street, NY 10017

UK

Baseline, Esselte Letraset, St George's House, 195–203 Waterloo Road, London SE1 8XJ

Creative Review, 50 Poland Street, London W1V 4AX

Desktop Publishing Today, Blair House, 184–186 High Street, Tonbridge, Kent TN9 1BQ

DTP, 14 Rathbone Place, London W1P 1DE

Eye, 26 Cramer Street, London W1M 3HE

Graphics World, Datateam House, Tovil Hill, Maidstone, Kent ME15 6QS

MacWorld (UK edition), IDG Communications, 99 Grays Inn Road, London WC1X 8UT

MacUser, 14 Rathbone Place, London W1P 1DE

Xyz-Direction, Haymarket Trade and Leisure Publications Ltd, 38–42 Hampton Road, Teddington, Middlesex TW11 0JE

Useful abbreviations and acronyms

APR automatic picture replacement
ASCII American Standard Code for Information Interchange
A/UX a workstation operating system, a version of Unix
A/W artwork
C a high-level computer language
CCD charge-coupled device
cm ^{3}/g cubic centimeters per gram
CMYK cyan, magenta, yellow, key (black)
cpu the central processing unit at the heart of a computer
CRC camera-ready copy
CRT cathode ray tube
DMA direct memory access
dpi dots per inch
DPS double-page spread
dtp desktop publishing
EPS Encapsulated PostScript
Gbyte gigabyte
g/m ^{2} grams per square meter
gsm grams per square meter
GUI graphical user interface
HD grade of mesh for screenprinting with 20–35% open area
HLS hue, luminance, saturation
HP hot pressed, a handmade paper finish
HP-GL Hewlett-Packard graphics language
Hz Hertz, or cycles per second
IBC inside back cover
IBM PC a make of personal computer
IFC inside front cover
ISO/OSI a computer networking acronym
k kilobyte, 1024 bytes (kbyte is more common usage)
kbyte kilobyte, 1024 bytes
LAN local-area network
l.c. lower case
lpi lines per inch
M grade of mesh for screenprinting
(m) machine direction in paper
Mbyte megabyte
MF machine finish paper
MG machine glazed paper
MHz megahertz, or millions of cycles per second
MIPS millions of instructions per second
Ms manuscript
MS-DOS PC's operating system
NOT not hot pressed, a handmade paper finish
OBC outside back cover
OFC outside front cover
OPI open prepress interface
OPP oriented polypropylene lamination
PC personal computer
pcb printed circuit-board
PMS Pantone Matching System
PMT photomechanical transfer
ppi pages per inch
pt point, a measurement of type size
ram random access memory – short-term computer memory
R & B rounding and backing
RC resin-coated
RGB red, green, blue
RIP raster image processor
RISC reduced instruction set computer
rom read-only memory – permanent computer memory
RRED right-reading emulsion down
RREU right-reading emulsion up
RSI repetitive strain injury
S grade of mesh for screenprinting with 50–70% open area
SIMM single in-line memory module
SPARC scalable processor architecture
S/S same size
stet reinstate deleted material
T grade of mesh for screenprinting
TCP/IP computer networking acronym
TIFF tagged image file format
TDP two-page display
u.c. upper case
UCA undercolor addition
UCR undercolor removal
UV ultraviolet
VGA video graphics array
WIMP windows, icons, mouse, and pull-down menus
WOB white on black
WORM write once read many – computer optical drives
WRED wrong-reading emulsion down
WREU wrong-reading emulsion up
WRULD work-related upper-limb disorders
WYSIWYG what you see is what you get

Acknowledgements

Calmann & King Ltd and the author wish to thank the institutions and individuals who have kindly provided photographic material or artwork for use in this book:

Art Directors Photo Library, London: 2.42, 3.3, 4.18, 5.5, 5.6 (John Frye), 5.19, 5.25, 5.29 (Archie Miles), 6.9, 6.10, 6.12; The Bridgeman Art Library, London: 2.2A, 2.2B; Paul Brierley, Harlow, Essex: 3.16, 6.13; Nick Day, Brighton: 1.7, 1.11, and all chapter openers; DC Comics, Inc., New York: 3.30; Du Pont UK Ltd: 4.22; Toni Emchovitz, Brighton: 0.1, 0.9; Mary Evans Picture Library, London: 2.8, 2.34; David Foenander, Milton Keynes: 0.2, 0.3, 0.4, 0.5, 0.6, 0.7, 0.10, 0.11, 1.12, 3.21, 5.47; Foghorn Studio, Brighton: 5.40; Fontworks UK, London: 2.39, 2.52, 2.53; Sonia Halliday, Weston Turville, Buckinghamshire: 5.1; The Kobal Collection, London: 3.9; Lambie-Nairn & Company, London and the BBC, London: 6.36; Lefevre Gallery, London: 3.19; Linotype-Hell Ltd: 6.19; The Mansell Collection, London: 1.1, 1.6, 2.3A, 2.4, 3.1; Helen Melhuish, London: 2.49; The Metropolitan Museum of Art, New York: 3.15; New York Convention & Visitors Bureau: 3.10; O'Brien Associates, London: 6.18; Alan Pipes, Brighton: 2.7, 2.13, 2.14, 2.15, 2.16, 2.17, 2.19, 2.23, 2.29, 2.48, 3.5, 3.17, 3.18, 4.1, 4.2, 4.3, 4.4, 4.7, 4.8, 4.10, 4.11, 4.12, 4.13, 4.14, 4.16, 4.19, 4.20, 4.24, 4.25, 4.26, 4.27, 4.30, 5.3, 5.4, 5.7, 5.9, 5.11, 5.12, 5.13, 5.15, 5.18, 5.20, 5.22, 5.23, 5.25, 5.26, 5.27, 5.30, 5.31, 5.33, 5.36, 5.39, 5.48, 5.49, 5.50, 5.51, 5.52, 5.53, 5.54, 5.55, 5.56, 5.57, 5.58, 6.5, 6.7, 6.11, 6.21, 6.22, 6.26, 6.29, 6.30, 6.32, 6.33, 6.40, 6.41; Ann Ronan Picture Library, Taunton, Somerset: 1.3, 1.4, 1.5, 1.8, 1.9, 2.5; Science Photo Library, London: 5.2; Spy Corporation, New York: 4.6B; Toppan Pte Ltd, Singapore: 0.8, 0.12, 0.13, 0.14, 0.15, 0.16, 0.17; Roger Viollet, Paris: 3.8; David Wood, Brighton: 3.25; Zefa Picture Library, London: 2.40, 2.41 (J. Pfaff), 2.43, 2.44 (J. Pfaff), 3.22 (J. Pfaff), 5.14, 5.32, 6.5.

Literature extracts in Chapter 2 taken from *Little Women* by Louisa M. Alcott and *The Adventures of Huckleberry Finn* by Mark Twain; extract on page 181 taken from *The Adventures of Tom Sawyer* by Mark Twain; *Customs of the Trade for the Manufacture of Books* © The Publishers Association and The British Printing Industries Federation, 1992, extracts reprinted by kind permission.

Index